THE ROAD TO THE WHITE HOUSE, 2000

The Politics of Presidential Elections

Postelection Edition

THE ROAD TO THE WHITE HOUSE, 2000

The Politics of Presidential Elections

Postelection Edition

Stephen J. Wayne

Georgetown University

Bedford/St. Martin's
Boston ◆ New York

For Bedford/St. Martin's

Sponsoring Editor for Political Science: Marilea Polk Fried
Senior Editor, Publishing Services: Douglas Bell
Production Supervisor: Dennis J. Conroy
Project Management: Publisher's Studio/Stratford Publishing Services, Inc.
Text Design: Stratford Publishing Services, Inc.
Photo Research: Deborah Goodsite
Cover Design: Donna Lee Dennison
Cover Images: Balloons at Republican Convention (detail), CORBIS/Philip Gould. Democratic National Convention (detail), CORBIS/Wally McNamee. Press interviewing candidate (detail), CORBIS/Robert Maass. Campaign buttons (front and back cover) courtesy of Political Americana; photography by Martin Paul, Ltd.
Interior Display Buttons: Private collection. Photography by Preston Lyon.
Composition: Stratford Publishing Services, Inc.
Printing and Binding: Haddon Craftsman, an RR Donnelley & Sons Company

President: Charles H. Christensen
Editorial Director: Joan E. Feinberg
Director of Editing, Design, and Production: Marcia Cohen
Manager, Publishing Services: Emily Berleth

Library of Congress Control Number: 00-110341

Manufactured in the United States of America.

5 4 3 2 1 0
f e d c b a

For information, write: Bedford/St. Martin's, 75 Arlington Street,
Boston, MA 02116   (617-399-4000)

ISBN: 0-312-39304-0   (paperback)
       0-312-23993-9   (hardcover)

Acknowledgments

To my mother, Muriel Wayne,
and to the memory of my grandmother, Hattie Marks,
and my father, Arthur G. Wayne.

PREFACE

We have just ended another presidential election cycle, the one that bridged two centuries. As have the others that preceded it, it was a lengthy, grueling campaign, one that contained much strident rhetoric, many promises, claims, and criticisms, and a great deal of political imagery. Was it worth it?

Your answer will probably depend on how satisfied you were with the process and the results. But the fact remains that it was the fifty-fourth time that the American electorate has chosen its president in a peaceful manner and, with the possible exception of the Civil War, where those who lose abide by the results. This is what democracy is all about: popular choice and majority rule.

Hopefully, many of you followed the last election fairly closely. It was probably easier to follow than to understand. You may have read about it in newspapers, viewed campaign events on television, heard about it on the radio, or accessed the candidates' Web sites; you may have even seen one of them in person. But what you observed was only a portion of the whole election — a subjective one at that. Candidates, their advisers, media representatives, and other groups have certain perspectives that they wish to convey to influence our vote.

There is more, however, to presidential elections than meets the eye. Campaign planners work hard to design a strategy to maximize their vote. They understand the intricacies of the process. They know how the system works, who are its beneficiaries, and where they should concentrate their campaign resources. They understand the requirements of finance legislation — how to comply with it, get around it, and take advantage of it. They appreciate the psychological and social motivations of voters and have a feel for which appeals are likely to be most effective most of the time. They are aware of party rules and the ways to build a winning coalition during the nomination period. They can sense the rhythm of conventions and know when events should be scheduled and how various interests can be placated and orchestrated. They know how to organize and plan a general election campaign and how best to present their candidate to the voters in the media. They can usually predict what will happen in the election and interpret the results so as to enhance their political position and governing potential. They may not need to read this book.

On the other hand, people who want to get behind the scenes of presidential campaigns, who want to know why particular strategies are being adopted, why certain tactics are being utilized, whether these strategies and tactics are likely to achieve the desired results, how the candidates deal with the mass media, why the election turns out the way it does, and what implications the vote has for the new president's ability to govern, should benefit from the information contained in this book.

The Road to the White House, 2000: The Politics of Presidential Elections — Postelection Edition is a straightforward "nuts-and-bolts" discussion of how the system is designed and works. It is primarily concerned with facts, not opinions; with practice, not theory; with implications, not speculations. It summarizes the state of the art and science of presidential electoral politics.

The book is organized into four main parts. The first discusses the arena in which presidential elections occur. Its three chapters examine the electoral system, campaign finance, and the political environment. Chapter 1 provides a historical overview of nominations as well as elections; Chapters 2 and 3 examine recent developments. Highlighted are the financial and political considerations that candidates need to consider as they plan and structure their presidential campaigns.

Parts II and III are structured sequentially. They describe distinct yet related stages of the presidential campaign: the race for convention delegates during the competitive phase of primaries and caucuses; the interregnum that follows when one candidate for a party's nomination gains dominance and obtains a majority of the delegates; and the nominating convention itself which makes the designation official and serves as a springboard for the presidential campaign. Chapter 4 examines reforms in the delegate selection process and their impact on candidates, parties, and voters. In the light of these selection rules, the chapter then describes strategies for seeking a party's presidential nomination and illustrates those strategies with examples from recent campaigns. Chapter 5 carries this discussion from the end of the contested phase of the nominating process, usually several months before the party conventions are scheduled to meet, to the anointing, policy-setting, and public relations roles of contemporary political conventions. In Chapter 6, the organization, strategy, and tactics of presidential campaigns are assessed, again with examples from recent campaigns. Chapter 7 examines media politics, focusing on how the news media cover the campaign, how the candidates try to affect that coverage, how they circumvent some of it, and how all of this influences the electorate on election day.

The fourth part of the book looks at the election and beyond by exploring the implications for the government and for the political system. Chapter 8 discusses and evaluates the presidential vote by asking such questions as: What does it mean? Do the voters provide a mandate for the new president? How does the election affect the president's ability to govern? Chapter 9 considers problems in the electoral system and possible reforms. It examines some of the major difficulties that have affected the political system from party rules to finance issues to media coverage and to the vote itself in the Electoral College. This chapter also looks at proposals advanced for improving the electoral system: how it can be made more equitable; how it can be made more responsive to popular choice; and how that choice can be conveyed more effectively to elected and appointed officials.

These issues are not easy to resolve. Members of Congress, academicians, journalists, and other students of the American political system have been debating them for some time, and that debate is likely to continue. Without information on how the system works, we cannot intelligently participate in it or improve on it. In the case of presidential politics, ignorance is definitely not bliss nor is the norm always or usually the ideal.

The road to the White House is long and arduous. In fact, it has become more difficult to travel than in the past. Yet, surprisingly, given all the criticism, there continue to be many travelers. Evaluating their journey is essential to rendering an intelligent judgment on election day. However, more is at stake than simply choosing the occupant of the Oval Office. The system itself is on trial in every presidential election. That is why it is so important to understand and appreciate the intricacies of the process. Only an informed citizenry can determine whether the nation is being well served by the way we go about choosing our president.

Few books are written alone, and this one was no exception. For the 2000 edition, I was fortunate to have two excellent research assistants, Dr. Fengyan Shi and Ms. Keiko Ono, a Ph.D. candidate at Georgetown, to help me collect and analyze data from recent elections, review and synthesize the new literature, and aid me in numerous other ways in revising the manuscript.

I would also like to express my thanks to the political scientists who have reviewed various editions of this book: John Bruce, University of Mississippi; Richard L. Cole, University of Texas at Arlington; Anthony Corrado Jr., Colby College; Stephen C. Craig, University of Florida at Gainesville; James W. Davis, Washington University; Gordon Friedman, Southwest Missouri State University; Jay S. Goodman, Wheaton College; Anne Griffin, the Cooper Union; Marjorie Randon Hershey, Indiana University; Hugh L. LeBlanc, George Washington University; Kuo-Wei Lee, Pan-American University; Robert T. Nakamura, State University of New York at Albany; Richard G. Niemi, University of Rochester; Diana Owen, Georgetown University; Charles Prysby, the University of North Carolina at Greensboro; Michael Robinson, formerly of Georgetown University; Lester Seligman, University of Illinois; Earl Shaw, Northern Arizona University; John W. Sloan, University of Houston; Priscilla Southwell, University of Oregon at Eugene; William H. Steward, University of Alabama; Edward J. Weissman, Washington College; and Clyde Wilcox, Georgetown University.

I also wish to acknowledge with gratitude and thanks the many people at Bedford/St. Martin's, especially Marilea Polk Fried, sponsoring editor for political science, Doug Bell, senior editor, and others who have contributed in numerous ways to the editing, production, and marketing of this book.

Finally, everyone makes personal sacrifices in writing a book. My wife, Cheryl Beil, and my sons, Jared and Jeremy, were no exceptions, allowing me to take leave to my Vermont hideout in the summers of 1999 and 2000 to do my writing without interruption. As always, they gave me lots of encouragement. Jared, especially, helped me keep my political views in check with his own, different perspective. I wish to thank my family for being accommodating and especially understanding.

Stephen J. Wayne
Georgetown University

CONTENTS

About the Author

Stephen J. Wayne (Ph.D., Columbia University) is a professor of government at Georgetown University. Besides being a veteran instructor of American government, he has been a Washington insider specializing in presidential politics for over thirty years. He has authored numerous articles and authored or coauthored several books about American government and the presidency, including *The Politics of American Government,* Third Edition, *The Legislative Presidency, Presidential Leadership: Politics and Policy Making,* Fifth Edition (with George C. Edwards III), and his latest book, *Is This Any Way to Run a Democratic Election?* Invited frequently to testify before Congress and the political parties and to lecture to senior federal and corporate executives, Professor Wayne also has shaped public opinion about the presidency and electoral politics as a commentator for radio, television, and newspapers.

PROLOGUE: THE ELECTION THAT WOULDN'T END

The 2000 election was unusual in several respects. It was the most expensive on record. It was one of the longest, having begun in 1998. The campaign was highly concentrated, even more so than in previous elections. Techniques of modern polling and focus groups were used to determine where, when, and how resources could be most effectively spent.

The election was also highly competitive, encouraging the news media to commission daily polls to discern how voters were reacting to the candidates' appeals and inclining to vote. Prior to the election, the polls, by and large, revealed a divided electorate and a contest too close to call. And the polls were right. When the results of the election were tabulated, they showed that out of over 104 million cast, less than 350,000 votes separated the major party candidates.

But an American presidential election is not decided by the popular vote. It is decided in the Electoral College, a voting system which the Framers of the U.S. Constitution preferred to a direct election. They preferred it for several reasons: They did not want candidates making blatant public appeals for votes; they did not have much faith in the judgment of the masses or in the integrity of the states to conduct a fair election and tabulate an accurate vote; and they wanted to ensure the executive's independence and the selection of the most qualified candidate as president, not necessarily the most popular.

By design, the Electoral College consisted of electors, to be designated in any manner the state legislatures decided and equal in the number to the senators and representatives of that state. The electors, who could not hold another federal government position, would meet on a specified day to choose the president and vice president. Each elector could cast two votes. The person who received the most votes, provided it was a majority, would be elected president and the person with the second most votes, vice president. In the event the Electoral College vote was not decisive, the House of Representatives, voting by state, would determine the president from among the five top candidates.[1] The Senate was given the authority to select the vice president if the electoral vote did not do so.

The House has elected a president only twice — Jefferson in 1800 and Adams in 1824. The Senate has chosen the vice president once — in 1836. There was, however, one other disputed election in which the Congress was involved, that of 1876. Amid charges of fraud, ballot tampering, and voter intimidation, two different slates of electors were certified from three southern states; in addition, there was another dispute over an elector from Oregon. The controversy over who were the legitimate electors presented Congress, divided by partisanship, with a difficult problem.

To try to resolve the matter fairly, Congress appointed a fifteen-person commission consisting of seven Democrats, seven Republicans, and one independent, Supreme Court Justice David Davis. However, before the commission could meet, Justice Davis was appointed to the U.S. Senate by the Illinois legislature. His replacement on the commission, Supreme Court Justice Joseph Bradley, an independent Republican, sided with his fellow partisans on all the contested electors, thereby giving Republican Rutherford B. Hayes a one-vote Electoral College victory over his Democratic opponent, Samuel J. Tilden. Although Tilden had won the popular vote, Congress accepted the commission's recommendations. It was alleged that southern Democrats did so in exchange for Hayes's promise to withdraw federal troops from the South.

Before 2000, the only other election in which the popular vote winner did not receive an Electoral College majority occurred in 1888. In that election, Benjamin Harrison beat Grover Cleveland by narrowly winning several large states, even though Cleveland received about 90,000 more popular votes than Harrison.

In the twentieth century, the Electoral College did not reverse the popular vote in any election. In fact, in most of them, it expanded the plurality vote winner's margin of victory, thereby enlarging the president's mandate for governing and limiting any voting disputes to the states in which they occurred. One such dispute arose in 1960, an election in which John F. Kennedy's popular vote margin over Richard Nixon was only 100,000 out of more than 68 million votes cast. Republicans charged fraud and illegal voting in Illinois and Texas. Although the allegations appeared to have some merit, Nixon chose not to contest the election. Texas was controlled by the Democrats, and Nixon's chances of winning were slim; without Texas, Illinois would not change the outcome in the Electoral College. Kennedy still would have had a majority.

There were other close races in which a relatively few votes in key states could have made a difference. George Wallace's third-party candidacy in 1968 had the potential of denying one of the major party candidates an Electoral College majority, but it did not do so. Eight years later, Jimmy Carter defeated Gerald Ford by less than 2 percent of the popular vote. A change of less than 8,000 votes in two states — Ohio and Hawaii — would have given Ford an Electoral College majority. But here again, Ford decided not to challenge the results in these states.

Close elections combined with strong third-party movements provide the Electoral College with its greatest challenge. In the 2000 election, the first condition was present and, for a time, it appeared that the second one might be as well. With partisanship driving the vote and dividing the electorate, even a relatively small impact by a third-party candidate such as Ralph Nader of the Green Party could have affected the popular vote in several key states. This potential encouraged the Gore campaign to target Nader voters in close states, with some success.

In the end Nader received less than 3 percent of the overall vote, and no more than 10 percent in any single state.

Contributing to the closeness of the 2000 election was the concentration of the campaign in five of the eight large states. The Democrats' success in winning four of these states along with New York and California ensured a sizable vote for Al Gore. But with the exception of the Northeast and Pacific Coast regions, the remainder of the country tilted toward Governor George W. Bush with the outcome in Florida in doubt. Not only did the Florida situation create a potential discrepancy between the popular and electoral vote, but until it was decided, neither candidate had an Electoral College majority.

Thus, the presidential campaign continued into a postelection phase. The contest proceeded simultaneously within three arenas: legal, political, and institutional. The objectives of the participants were threefold: (1) to win the Florida vote; (2) to enhance the stature of their candidate in the eyes of the public; and (3) to position that candidate as favorably as possible to take over the reins of government and govern effectively.

The postelection campaign was expensive, costing millions of dollars and forcing both sides to go back to their major donors for more money. Bush set a limit of $5,000 for additional contributions to his legal fund, but Gore did not.[2] The Democrats consulted more than one hundred lawyers and collected thousands of affidavits from citizens who claimed confusion, harassment, or other illegalities when trying to vote. Both parties assembled thousands of partisans and bused them throughout Florida to the county election offices and courts in which the challenges were made. Although most of the demonstrations in which these partisans were engaged were for public consumption, one was so raucous and threatening that Democrats claimed it actually coerced the Miami-Dade election board into rejecting a hand count of all disputed ballots in the county after initially approving a sample count.

THE LEGAL CHALLENGES

Although there were myriad legal issues in the Florida election, four stood out: ballot confusion, ballot validation, ballot tabulation, and the official certification of the results.

The confusion stemmed from a "butterfly ballot" used in Palm Beach County where many retirees live. Designed by a Democratic campaign official, the ballot was intended to help senior citizens read the names of the candidates more clearly by using larger type. To fit all the names on a single punch card, however, two columns had to be used with the punch holes for voting, or "chads," as they are called, between them. (For a facsimile of the ballot see the figure on page xxii.)

Although Democrats Al Gore and Joe Lieberman were listed second on the left-hand column, their chad was positioned third, after the chad of the candidates on the right-hand column, Pat Buchanan and Ezola Foster of the Reform Party. Some voters, who claimed that they intended to vote for the Democratic candidates, punched out the second rather than the third chad which registered as a vote for Buchanan. Others, in confusion, pushed out both the second and third chads,

THE PALM BEACH BALLOT

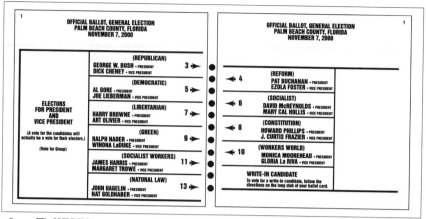

Source: TheWPBFChannel.com, December 14, 2000.

thereby invalidating their vote because they had, in effect, voted twice for president. However, there was no confusion over the place to vote for Bush and Cheney. It was the first chad on the ballot.

The actual vote tabulation in this county provided some evidence of the confusion. The Buchanan vote was larger in Palm Beach than in any other Florida county.[3] Moreover, Palm Beach had a larger percentage of ballots in which no presidential vote was recorded than all but two of the sixty-seven counties in the state. Aggrieved Democrats in the county immediately filed a lawsuit to contest the election and demand a new vote. A Florida state court, however, rejected their request, effectively terminating the revote option.

A second issue concerned ballots that were not properly included in the machine count. Many counties in Florida still use the punch-card system of voting in which chads, a small perforated box on the card, must be removed with a specially designed instrument. The holes in the card are then tabulated by a machine. However, if a chad is not completely removed, the vote may not be counted. The Gore campaign alleged that thousands of presidential votes in three Democratic counties — Miami-Dade, Broward, and Palm Beach — were not counted because part or all of a chad was still attached to the ballot. In other words, voters had not completely punched through the card. Democrats appealed to country officials for a hand count of these ballots.

One county, Palm Beach, began such a count; another, Miami-Dade, initiated a sample count to see whether a hand count was merited; the third, Broward, initially chose not to do so. Gore's representatives put pressure on the reluctant counties to proceed with a count of these untabulated ballots while Bush's attorneys went to federal court to stop it, arguing that a selective hand count in some counties was unfair to people in other counties.

Before the court had rendered a judgment, however, Florida's secretary of state, a Republican appointee, certified the original county vote as the official one to which only absentee ballots, postmarked no later than election day and received by the counties within one week of the election, could be added. The secretary of state's certification prompted Gore's legal team to go to state court to force the secretary to accept hand-counted votes and an amended vote total submitted after the certification. A Florida circuit court ruled that the secretary had discretion to accept or reject additional vote counts submitted by counties as long as she did not exercise that discretion arbitrarily. The secretary then asked the counties to justify why they wished to amend their original submission with an additional hand count of some votes. When they did so, however, she rejected their arguments, thereby forcing Gore's attorneys to take the entire matter to the Florida Supreme Court.

In an extraordinary session, televised across the country, lawyers for both sides debated the hand count and vote deadline issues within the context state and federal law and the U.S. Constitution. The Gore side claimed that the only way to ensure a "full, fair, and accurate" vote that represented the will of the Florida electorate would be to count the disputed ballots by hand. But Bush contended that such a hand count was blatantly unfair to those who had acted in accordance with the rules and procedures of the state. Moreover, Bush's lawyers argued that to extend the deadline for certified results would in effect change the Florida election law which required countries to report their vote one week after the election. To change the law, they claimed, would violate a 1887 federal statute which requires states to choose their electors by laws that are enacted prior to election day.

The Florida Supreme Court, consisting of eight judges all but one of whom were appointed by Democratic governors, sided with Gore and proceeded to give the counties an additional six days to submit a revised vote that included hand-counted ballots. Bush's lawyers appealed the Florida Supreme Court's decision to the U.S. Supreme Court.

What followed was a frantic hand count in two counties while a third, Miami-Dade, decided not to go ahead with one, in part because officials believed that they could not do so within the time frame established by the court. At the time of the court-imposed deadline, only one country, Broward, had submitted a recount that moved Gore to within 537 votes of Bush. Palm Beach County was unable to get its votes in by the 5:00 PM deadline. The county submitted its revised tabulation several hours later, too late to be included in the revised state vote count.

Still trailing his Republican opponent, Gore went back to state court to seek a court order forcing an immediate hand count in Miami-Dade, but a Florida appeals court refused to do so as did the state Supreme Court. These refusals prompted Gore to return to state court to ask for a court order to count the disputed ballots in Miami-Dade and include the revised vote totals from Palm Beach that had been completed after the deadline.

Meanwhile Democrats in two other Florida counties filed suit to exclude all absentee ballots from these counties on the grounds that Republicans had been given an opportunity to add required voter registration numbers, omitted erroneously by a glitch in the software program that printed the request forms, to the forms to obtain absentee ballots while Democrats were not given a chance to do so. Had these 15,000 absentee ballots been excluded, Bush would have lost his lead in the Florida vote count. But they were not. The judges ruled that even though Florida election officials had exercised poor judgment in permitting Republicans to add registration numbers to the request form, that judgment did not adversely affect the vote that was cast. People who voted by absentee ballot did so in the manner in which they desired and thus their votes should be counted.

On Monday, December 4, nearly a month after the presidential election, the U.S. Supreme Court vacated the Florida Supreme Court's verdict that had extended the deadline for hand-counted ballots on the grounds that their legal basis for this decision was unclear. They remanded the case back to the Florida Supreme Court for clarification and judgment.

Later in the day, a Florida state court judge dismissed Gore's claims for an additional hand count of thousands of ballots from Palm Beach and Miami-Dade Counties that had registered no presidential preference as well as the hand-counted ballots that had been submitted after the court-imposed deadline. In doing so, the judge held that Gore's attorneys had not provided statistical evidence to demonstrate the *probability*, not a mere *possibility*, that the results of the Florida election would be different had if a hand count were to occur and be included in the vote totals. The judge also refused to overturn the certification of Florida's electoral vote for Bush. In a last-ditch effort to salvage a Florida victory, Gore appealed this state court judgment to the Florida Supreme Court.

Thus, the state Supreme Court was faced with two issues: One concerned its decision and the legal basis on which it was predicated for extending the state certification deadline for those counties that chose to submit an amended vote based on disputed hand-counted ballots; the other was Gore's appeal to overturn the state court decision that additional hand counts and time to certify results were not merited because the burden of proving that these counts would change the result had not been met.

In a 4-to-3 decision, the court again sided with Gore. It ordered immediate recounts of the ballots that had not been included in the machine tabulation in *all* Florida counties, not just Palm Beach and Miami-Dade. It also accepted the Palm Beach County hand count that had been submitted after its deadline and additional Miami-Dade ballots that had been hand counted in a sample precinct. The court's decision extended the controversy and kept the Florida vote in doubt. Bush's lawyers immediately appealed the decision to the U.S. Supreme Court.

Meanwhile the Florida legislature, controlled by the Republicans, convened in a special session to name the state's electors in the event that the Florida vote was still tied up in litigation at the time the electors had to be designated in order to cast their electoral votes. The session presented the real possibility that Congress might have to choose among competing slates of Florida electors.

The final legal maneuvering ended in the U.S. Supreme Court which had accepted Bush's appeal of the Florida Supreme Court decision to start an immediate hand count of disputed ballots. The U.S. Supreme Court enjoined the count of the disputed ballots, which was already under way, pending its hearing of the case and issuing a judgment on the matter. On December 11, 2000, one day before Florida was supposed to designate its electors, the Court heard oral arguments in the matter. Its decision followed the next evening.

The Supreme Court reversed the Florida Supreme Court's judgment on the grounds that the latter's decision did not specify minimal procedural requirements for recounting that would be necessary to ensure that all voters in the state were treated fairly and equally. In order words, the U.S. Supreme Court objected to the discretion which Florida counties exercised under that state's Supreme Court ruling that they consider the intent of the voter when looking at punch cards in which a presidential vote was not tabulated in the machine count.

A majority of the U.S. Supreme Court went on to conclude that there was not sufficient time to establish such a standard because the Florida Supreme Court recognized the state legislature's intention to abide by the federal law's "safe harbor rule" which requires that any controversy or contest over the designation of the electors be settled by December 12. The U.S. Supreme Court issued its decision at 10:00 PM on December 12. Four justices dissented from the finding that time had run out on the Florida Supreme Court. Two of the dissenters felt that the December 18 deadline, the day on which the electors are required to cast their votes, was sufficient time for the Florida Supreme Court to try to fashion a procedural process that met the test of constitutionality. The two other dissenters felt that the Florida Supreme Court had acted properly, that the vote count was legal, and that it should not have been halted by the U.S. Supreme Court.

Gore was naturally disappointed with the Supreme Court's decision but had no viable options. All of his legal remedies had been exhausted. On December 13, 2000, he conceded the election. Bush had won Florida by less than 1,000 votes out of over 6 million that were cast. Florida's twenty-five electoral votes gave him a bare majority of Electoral College. Bush won 271 electoral votes compared to Gore's 267, despite the fact that Gore led in the popular vote by over 300,000.

THE POLITICAL CAMPAIGN

During the period in which attorneys for the candidates were engaged in their legal battle, their spokespeople were engaged in a public relations campaign for the hearts and minds of the American people. James Baker III, former White House chief of staff and treasury secretary for President Reagan and secretary of state for President Bush, was designated as the principal spokesman for the Bush campaign. Baker contended that the Florida vote had been properly tabulated, retabulated, and retabulated again, including the absentee ballots and the hand counts of one county. The voters had decided, he argued, and Bush had won each count. Other campaign officials, notably Karen Hughes, the head of communications, and Ari Fleischer, press spokesman, reinforced the "it's over; he won" theme. Implicitly, they also created the impression that the only way that Bush could lose the election was if the Democrats "stole" it from him in Florida.

At the outset of the controversy, Bush had received some flack from Democrats for saying that he would begin transition planning. He was accused of trying to preempt the Florida results. For the most part, however, Bush stayed out of the public eye, maintaining the appearance of "business as usual" as Texas governor. He did, however, reply to Gore's public statements, displaying confidence that he would win and reiterating the campaign's position that the Florida election had been lawfully conducted and the state's votes properly counted.

Although Gore had won the popular vote in the country as a whole and was leading in the Electoral College, he was put on the defensive by virtue of his initial concession in the early morning hours following the election, Bush's lead in the first count and recount in Florida, and the burden of getting the courts to order extended deadlines and new vote counts. In his public relations campaign, Gore urged patience, defended the principle that every vote should be counted, and disputed the notion that the country was mired in a constitutional crisis. On the contrary, he noted that the electors did not have to be determined until December 12 and did not vote until December 18. During this period, he reiterated his determination to contest the election in Florida as long as he had legal avenues to do so.

Former Clinton Secretary of State Warren Christopher served as the Gore campaign's official spokesman while chief attorney, David Boise, addressed the legal issues in court and to the news media. Vice President Gore and his running mate, Joseph Lieberman, made several public statements that articulated the campaign's after-the-election-theme — in a democracy, every vote counts only if every vote is counted. It was this principle that mattered, they said, more so than who won.

Both candidates' public relations efforts seem to have their desired effect. For Bush, his campaign successfully reinforced the impression that he was ahead and would be the likely winner. It also diverted attention from the results of the popular vote in which he trailed the vice president. For Gore, the public relations campaign bought him time, legitimized his challenge, and maintained partisan support for his candidacy. Most Americans subscribed to the principle that counting all the votes was necessary and proper. Neither did Americans feel that the system was in crisis.

As the controversy dragged on in the Florida courts, however, there was increasing impatience for the impasse to end and a winner to be decided. Whereas a majority of people had indicated on November 19 that they were willing to wait at least a little while longer for a final resolution of the matter, by early December that percentage had declined to one-third. In contrast, 63 percent of the population believed the situation had gone on too long and wanted it to end.[4] As the public's patience wore thin, Gore's favorable image began to decline and the perception that Bush would win increased. The table at right sums up public opinion over the course of the controversy.

One of the reasons for the public's impatience was the media frenzy that surrounded the controversy. In the first week following the election, the television evening news shows devoted 183 stories to the Florida vote, more than to the Clinton-Lewinsky scandal during its first week and more than to Princess Diana and John F. Kennedy, Jr. in the first week of news coverage after their tragic deaths.[5] Not only was the issue given extensive coverage on the news, it was also given considerable live coverage. The oral arguments before the Florida Supreme Court were televised as were the arguments before the state circuit court; the arguments before the U.S. Supreme Court were heard on radio immediately after the Court's session. The Florida verdicts were broadcast as were several short public announcements by Gore and Bush. Even the movement of the ballots from

PUBLIC OPINION ON THE FLORIDA VOTE CONTROVERSY

Question	Percentage	
Approve of the Candidates' Handling of the Situation	**Bush**	**Gore**
November 11–12	53%	52%
November 19	55	49
November 26–27	54	42
December 2–4	57	39
Favorable Opinion of Each of the Candidates	**Bush**	**Gore**
November 13–15	53%	53%
December 2–4	56	46
Gore Should Concede Now		
November 19	46%	
November 26–27	56	
December 2–4	58	
December 10	53	

Source: Gallup Poll, "Public Opinion on Key Issues in the Florida Recount Situation," December 2000, <http://www.gallup.com/poll/releases/pr001206c.asp>.

Miami-Dade and Palm Beach Counties were televised by a camera crew in a helicopter that hovered over the trucks transporting the ballots to Tallahassee.

And the public did pay attention. A national survey taken for the Joan Shorenstein Center at Harvard University in early December found that most Americans said they were paying reasonably close attention to developments in Florida. However, the survey also revealed that levels of interest were declining over the course of the controversy, as were levels of satisfaction in the electoral process. In fact, two out of three people found the situation "depressing."[6]

INSTITUTIONAL CONSEQUENCES: THE TRANSITION AND BEYOND

Transition planning was delayed but not halted by the controversy. During the course of the presidential campaign, aides for both candidates had been quietly collecting information. At the end of November, Bush formally designated his running mate, Dick Cheney, as head of his transition team. Gore choose Roy Neel, a former chief of staff for the vice president and later deputy White House chief, to oversee his transition planning. Although the Democratic transition was put on hold during the legal challenges, the Republican transition was not. In fact, a temporary office was opened near Cheney's home in Fairfax, Virginia, because the General Services Administration, which controlled the official transition offices for the incoming administration, refused to allocate them until a winner became clear.

The Clinton administration also did not begin the official transition until the Florida vote controversy was decided. However, Clinton did authorize national security briefings for Bush and his designated aides. As vice president, Gore already had access to these briefings. To speed up the process, the administration also offered to begin FBI background checks on both candidates' nominees for Cabinet positions.

Clinton designated White House Chief of Staff John Podesta as his primary transition representative. Departments and agencies were asked to draft transition documents that included budget matters, pending issues, and reauthorizations that would be necessary, as well as information on the political positions within the agency and civil service personnel.

In addition, a variety of think tanks and academic institutions had transition projects under way. The American Enterprise Institute, the Brookings Institution, the Heritage Foundation, and the Rand Corporation had all been working on aspects of transition planning — from the appointment process to White House staffing to fostering better legislative relations — and to the domestic and foreign policy issues that the new administration would have to address. These projects as well as scholarly studies on past transitions were also given to the designated representatives. There was no shortage of information or willingness to share it.

Even though transition planning was occurring behind the scenes, the election controversy was still cause for concern. Usually, presidents-elect can count on the country rallying behind its new leader for a short period of time. Also, presidents-elect generally enjoy less criticism by the press and the opposition party during their so called "honeymoon period," which can last as long as their first one hundred days in office. Usually, presidents-elect can claim a popular mandate by virtue of the majority or at least plurality of the electorate who voted for them. And usually the party of the president-elect gains seats in Congress, putting it in a better position to help its newly elected president. None of these factors were evident in 2000, however.

Partisanship was alive and well. Although there was the ritual call for bipartisan support for the new president-elect after the controversy was decided, although the public had signaled its willingness to accept the candidate who won the Electoral College vote, although most elected officials said that they would work together for the country's interests, there was also a residue of partisan animosities, barely below the surface, that threatened to erupt at any moment and undermine the unifying attempts of the new president.

The absence of a popular vote majority, the fragile Republican congressional majority, and the way in which the Florida election results were finally determined by a bitterly divided Supreme Court did little to mollify the partisan passions evident during the Clinton impeachment, the 2000 election campaign, and the vote controversy that followed. Nor could the new president take solace in the experience of his non-plurality predecessors — John Quincy Adams, Rutherford B. Hayes, and Benjamin Harrison. Each encountered stiff political opposition during his term in office. Each served only one term. Each was defeated for reelection. Clearly, the new president faced a tough road ahead, one that promised to be equally, if not more, difficult than the road to the White House.

NOTES

1. The Twelfth Amendment to the Constitution, ratified in 1804, reduced that number to three and required the electors to cast separate votes for the president and vice president.
2 John M. Broder, "Loyal Contributors Keep Both Candidates in Cash," *New York Times,* November 22, 2000, A19.
3. There were also more Reform Party registrants in that county and it was an area in which Buchanan campaigned. However, even he was surprised by the size of his vote.
4. Gallup Poll, "Americans Divided on Vote Recount but Majority Say Florida Situation Has Gone on Too Long," December 5, 2000, <http://www.gallup.com/poll/releases/pr001205.asp>.
5. Center for Media and Public Affairs, "Media Feeding Frenzy in Florida," November 22, 2000.
6. Joan Shorenstein Center on the Press, Politics, and Public Policy, Harvard University, "As Election Contest Drags on, Americans' Dissatisfaction Grows," December 7, 2000, <http://www.vanishingvoter.org>.

THE ROAD TO THE WHITE HOUSE, 2000

The Politics of Presidential Elections

Postelection Edition

PART I

THE
ELECTORAL
ARENA

PRESIDENTIAL SELECTION: A HISTORICAL OVERVIEW

1

INTRODUCTION

The road to the White House is circuitous and bumpy. It contains numerous hazards and potential dead ends. Those who choose to traverse it need considerable skill, perseverance, and luck if they are to be successful. They also need substantial amounts of time and money. For most candidates there is no such thing as a free or easy ride to the presidency.

The Framers of the Constitution worked for several months on the presidential selection system, and their plan has since undergone a number of constitutional, statutory, and precedent-setting changes. Modified by the development of parties, the expansion of suffrage, the growth of the media, and the revolution in modern communications technology, the electoral system has become more open and participatory but also more contentious, more complex, and more expensive. It has also "turned off" more people who for a variety of reasons have chosen not to participate.

This chapter is about that system: why it was created; what it was supposed to do; what compromises were incorporated in the original plan; how it operated initially; what changes subsequently affected that operation; whom these changes have benefited; and what effect all of this has had on the parties, the electorate, and American democracy.

In addressing these questions, I have organized the chapter into four sections. The first discusses the creation of the presidential election process. It explores the motives and intentions of the delegates at Philadelphia and describes the procedures for selecting the president within the context of the constitutional and political issues of that day.

The second section examines the development of nominating systems. It explores the three principal methods that have been used — partisan congressional

3

caucuses, brokered national conventions, and state primaries and caucuses. It also describes the political forces that helped to shape them and, in the case of the first two, destroyed them.

The third section discusses presidential elections. It focuses on the most controversial ones: those decided by the House of Representatives (1800 and 1824), those influenced by Congress (1876), and those unreflective of popular choice (1888) or in which a relatively small number of votes could have changed the outcome (1960, 1968, and 1976). In doing so, the section highlights the evolution of the Electoral College.

The final section of the chapter examines the current system. It describes its geographic and demographic biases, whom it benefits, and whom it hurts. The section also discusses the system's major party orientation and its adverse impact on third party candidacies.

THE CREATION OF THE ELECTORAL COLLEGE

Among the many issues facing the delegates at the Constitutional Convention of 1787 in Philadelphia, the selection of the president was one of the toughest. Seven times during the course of the convention the method for choosing the executive was altered.

The Framers' difficulty in designing electoral provisions for the president stemmed from the need to guarantee the institution's independence and, at the same time, create a technically sound, politically effective mechanism that would be consistent with a republican form of government: a government based on consent, a representative government, but not a direct democracy in which everyone had an opportunity to participate in the formulation of public policy. They wanted an electoral system that would choose the most qualified person but not necessarily the most popular. There seemed to be no precise model to follow.

Three methods had been proposed. The Virginia Plan, a series of resolutions designed by James Madison and introduced by Governor Edmund Randolph of Virginia, provided for legislative selection. Eight states chose their governors in this fashion at the time. Having Congress choose the president would be practical and politically expedient. Moreover, members of Congress could have been expected to exercise a considered judgment. Making a reasoned, unemotional choice was important to the delegates at Philadelphia, since many of them did not consider the average citizen capable of doing so.

The difficulty with legislative selection was the threat it posed to the institution of the presidency. How could the executive's independence be preserved if the election of the president hinged on popularity with Congress and reelection on the legislature's appraisal of the president's performance in office? Only if the president were to serve a long term and not be eligible for reelection, it was thought, could the institution's independence be protected so long as Congress was the electoral body. But ineligibility also posed problems, as it provided little incentive for the president to perform well and denied the country the possibility of reelecting a person whose experience and success in office demonstrated qualifications that were superior to others.

Reflecting on these concerns, Gouverneur Morris urged the removal of the ineligibility clause on the grounds that it tended to destroy the great motive to good behavior, the hope of being rewarded by a reappointment.[1] A majority of the states agreed. Once the ineligibility clause was deleted, however, the term of office had to be shortened to prevent what the Framers feared might become unlimited tenure. With a shorter term of office and permanent reeligibility, legislative selection was not nearly as desirable, since it could make the president beholden to the legislature.

Popular election was another alternative, although one that did not generate a great deal of enthusiasm. It was twice rejected in the convention by overwhelming votes. Most of the delegates felt that a direct vote by the people was neither desirable nor feasible.[2] Lacking confidence in the public's ability to choose the best-qualified candidate, many delegates also believed that the size of the country and the poor state of its communications and transportation in the eighteenth century precluded a national campaign and election. The geographic expanse was simply too large to permit proper supervision and control of the election. Sectional distrust and rivalry also contributed to the difficulty of holding a national election.

A third alternative was some type of indirect election in which popular sentiment could be expressed but would not dictate the selection. James Wilson first proposed this idea after he failed to generate support for a direct popular vote. Luther Martin, Gouverneur Morris, and Alexander Hamilton also suggested an indirect popular election through intermediaries. It was not until the debate over legislative selection divided and eventually deadlocked the delegates, however, that election by electors was seriously considered. Proposed initially as a compromise toward the end of the convention, the Electoral College system was accepted by the delegates after a short debate. Viewed as a safe, workable solution to the election dilemma, it was deemed consistent with the constitutional and political features of the new government. Popular election of the electors was not precluded, but neither was it encouraged by the compromise.

According to the proposal, presidential electors were to be chosen by the states in a manner designated by their legislatures. To ensure their independence, the electors could not simultaneously hold a federal government position. The number of electors was to equal the number of senators and representatives from each state. At a designated time the electors would vote and send the results to Congress, where they would be announced to a joint session by the president of the Senate — the vice president. Each elector had two votes since a president and vice president were to be selected separately. The only limitations on voting were that the electors could not cast both their ballots for inhabitants of their own states and they could not designate who they wished to be president and vice president.[3]

Under the initial plan, the person who received a majority of votes cast by the Electoral College was elected president, and the one with the second highest total, vice president. In the event that no one received a majority, the House of Representatives would choose from among the five candidates with the most electoral votes, with each state delegation casting one vote. If two or more individuals were tied for second, then the Senate would select one as vice president. Both of these provisions were subsequently modified by the Twelfth Amendment to the Constitution. (See page 14.)

The electoral system was a dual compromise. Allowing state legislatures to establish the procedures for choosing electors was a concession to the proponents of a federal system; having the House of Representatives decide if there was no Electoral College majority was designed to please those who favored a stronger national government. Designating the number of electors to be equal to a state's congressional delegation gave the larger states an advantage in the initial voting for president; balloting by states in the House if the Electoral College was not decisive benefited the smaller states.

The large-small state compromise was critical to the acceptance of the Electoral College plan. It was argued during the convention debates that in practice the large states would nominate the candidates for president and the small states would exercise the final choice.[4] So great were sectional rivalries and distrust at the time, that the prospect of a majority of the college agreeing on anyone other than George Washington seemed remote.

THE DEVELOPMENT OF NOMINATING SYSTEMS

Although the Constitution prescribed a system for electing a president, it made no reference to the nomination of candidates. Political parties had not emerged prior to the Constitutional Convention. Factions existed, and the Framers of the Constitution were concerned about them, but the development of a party system was not anticipated. Rather, it was assumed that electors, whose interests were not tied to the national government, would make an independent judgment in choosing the best possible person as president.

In the first two elections the system worked as intended. George Washington was the unanimous choice of the electors. There was, however, no consensus on who the vice president should be. The eventual winner, John Adams, benefited from some informal lobbying by prominent individuals prior to the vote.[5]

A more organized effort to agree on candidates for the presidency and vice presidency was undertaken in 1792. Partisan alliances were beginning to develop in Congress. Members of the two principal groups, the Federalists and the Anti-Federalists, met separately to recommend individuals. The Federalists chose Vice President Adams; the Anti-Federalists picked Governor George Clinton of New York.

With political parties evolving during the 1790s, the selection of electors quickly became a partisan contest. In 1792 and 1796, a majority of the state legislatures chose them directly. Thus, the political group that controlled the legislature also controlled the selection of electors. Appointed for their political views, electors were expected to exercise partisan judgment. When in 1796 a Pennsylvania elector did not, he was accused of faithless behavior. Wrote one critic in a Philadelphia newspaper: "What, do I chuse Samuel Miles to determine for me whether John Adams or Thomas Jefferson shall be President? No! I chuse him to act, not to think."[6]

Washington's decision not to serve a third term forced Federalist and Anti-Federalist members of Congress to recommend the candidates in 1796. Meeting separately, party leaders agreed among themselves on the tickets. The Federalists urged their electors to support John Adams and Thomas Pinckney, while the Anti-Federalists (or Democratic-Republicans, as they began to be called) suggested Thomas Jefferson and Aaron Burr.

Since it was not possible to specify presidential and vice presidential choices on the ballot, Federalist electors, primarily from New England, decided to withhold votes from Pinckney (of South Carolina) to make certain that he did not receive the same number as Adams (of Massachusetts). This strategy enabled Jefferson with 68 votes to finish ahead of Pinckney with 59, but behind Adams, who had 71. Four years of partisan differences followed between a president who, though he disclaimed political affiliation, clearly favored the Federalists in appointments, ideology, and policy, and a vice president who was the acknowledged leader of the opposition party.

Beginning in 1800, partisan caucuses, composed of members of Congress, met for the purpose of recommending their party's nominees. The Republicans (as the Democratic-Republicans became known) continued to choose candidates in this manner until 1824; the Federalists did so only until 1808. In the final two presidential elections in which the Federalists ran candidates, 1812 and 1816, top party leaders, meeting in secret, decided on the nominees.[7]

"King Caucus" violated the spirit of the Constitution. It effectively provided for members of Congress to pick the nominees. After the decline of the Federalists, the Democratic-Republican nominees were, in fact, assured of victory — a product of the dominance of the party.

There were competing candidates within the Democratic-Republican caucus, however. In 1808, Madison prevailed over James Monroe and George Clinton. In 1816, Monroe overcame a strong challenge from William Crawford. In both cases, the electors united behind the successful nominee. In 1820, however, they did not. Disparate elements within the party selected their own candidates.

Although the caucus was the principal mode of candidate selection during the first part of the nineteenth century, it was never formally institutionalized. How, by whom, and when meetings were called varied from election to election. So did attendance. A sizable number of representatives chose not to participate at all. Some stayed away on principle; others did so because of the choices they would have to make. In 1816, less than half of the Republican members of Congress were at their party's caucus. In 1820, only 20 percent attended, and the caucus had to adjourn without formally supporting President Monroe and Vice President Daniel D. Tompkins for reelection. In 1824, almost three-fourths of the members boycotted the session.

The 1824 caucus did nominate candidates. But with representatives from only four states constituting two-thirds of those attending, the nominee, William Crawford, failed to receive unified party support. Other candidates were nominated by state legislatures and conventions, and the electoral vote was divided. Since no candidate obtained a majority, the House of Representatives had to make the final decision. John Quincy Adams was selected on the first ballot. He received the votes of thirteen of the twenty-four state delegations.

The caucus was never resumed. In the end it fell victim to the decline of one of the major parties, the decentralization of political power, and Andrew Jackson's stern opposition. The Federalist Party had collapsed as a viable political force. As the Republican Party grew from being the majority to the only party, factions developed within it, the two principal ones being the National Republicans and the Democratic Republicans. In the absence of a strong opposition there was little to hold these factions together. By 1830, they had split into two separate groups, one supporting and one opposing President Jackson.

Political leadership was changing as well. A relatively small group of individuals had dominated national politics for the first three decades following the ratification of the Constitution. Their common experience in the Revolutionary War, the Constitutional Convention, and the early government produced personal contacts, political influence, and public respect that contributed to their ability to agree on candidates and to generate public support for them.[8]

Those who followed them in office had neither the tradition nor the national orientation in which to frame their presidential selection nor the national recognition to build support across the country for their candidates. Most of this new generation of political leaders owed their prominence and political influence to states and regions and their loyalties reflected these bases of support. The growth of party organizations at the state and local level affected the nomination system. In 1820 and 1824, it evolved into a decentralized mode of selection with state legislatures, caucuses, and conventions nominating their own candidates. Support was also mobilized on regional levels.

Whereas the congressional caucus had become unrepresentative, state-based nominations suffered from precisely the opposite problem. They were too sensitive to sectional interests and produced too many candidates. Unifying diverse elements behind a national ticket proved extremely difficult, although Jackson was successful in 1824 and again in 1828. Nonetheless, a system that was more broadly based than the old caucus and could provide a decisive and mobilizing mechanism was needed. National nominating conventions filled the void.

The first such convention was held in 1831 by the Anti-Masons. A small but relatively active third party, it had virtually no congressional representation. Unable to utilize a caucus, the party turned instead to a general meeting, which was held in a saloon in Baltimore, with 116 delegates from thirteen states attending. These delegates decided on the nominees as well as on an address to the people that contained the party's position on the dominant issues of the day.

Three months later a second convention was held in the same saloon by opponents of President Jackson. The National Republicans (or Whigs, as they later became known) also nominated candidates and agreed on a platform critical of the Jackson administration.

The following year the Democratic-Republicans (or Democrats, as they were later called) also met in Baltimore. The impetus for their convention was Jackson's desire to demonstrate popular support for his presidency as well as to ensure the selection of Martin Van Buren as his running mate. In 1836, Jackson resorted to another convention — this time to handpick Van Buren as his successor.

The Whigs did not hold a convention in 1836. Believing that they would have more success in the House of Representatives than with the nation as a whole, they ran three regional candidates, nominated by the states, who competed against Van Buren in their areas of strength. The plan, however, failed to deny Van

Buren an electoral majority. He ended up with 170 votes compared with a total of 124 for the other principal contenders.

Thereafter, the Democrats and their opponents, first the Whigs and then their Republican successors, held nominating conventions to select their candidates. The early conventions were informal and rowdy by contemporary standards, but they also set the precedents for later meetings.

The delegates decided on the procedures for conducting the convention, developed policy statements (addresses to the people), and chose nominees. Rules for apportioning the number of delegates were established before the meetings were held. Generally speaking, states were accorded as many votes as their congressional representation merited, regardless of the number of actual participants. The way in which the delegates were chosen, however, was left up to the states. Local and state conventions, caucuses, or even committees chose the delegates.

Public participation was minimal. Even the party's rank and file had only a small role. It was party leaders who designated the delegates and made the deals. In time it became clear that successful candidates owed their selection to the heads of the powerful state organizations, not to their own political prominence and organizational support. But the price they had to pay, when calculated in terms of patronage and other political payoffs, was often quite high.

Nineteenth-century conventions served a number of purposes. They provided a forum for party leaders, particularly at the state level. They constituted a mechanism by which agreements could be negotiated and support mobilized. By brokering interests, conventions helped unite the disparate elements within a party, thereby converting an organization of state parties into a national coalition for the purpose of conducting a presidential campaign.

Much of the bartering was conducted behind closed doors. Actions on the convention floor often had little to do with the wheeling and dealing that occurred in the smaller "smoke-filled rooms." Since there was little public preconvention activity, many ballots were often necessary to reach the number which was required to win the party's nomination, usually two-thirds of the delegates.

The nominating system buttressed the position of individual state party leaders, but it did so at the expense of rank-and-file participation. The influence of the state leaders depended on their ability to deliver votes, which in turn required that the delegates not exercise independent judgment. To guarantee their loyalty, the bosses controlled their selection.

Demands for reform began to be heard at the beginning of the twentieth century. The Progressive movement, led by Robert La Follette of Wisconsin and Hiram Johnson of California, aimed to break the power of state bosses and their machines through the direct election of convention delegates or, alternatively, through the expression of a popular choice by the electorate.

Florida became the first state to provide its political parties with such an option. In 1904, the Democrats took advantage of it and held a statewide vote for convention delegates. One year later, Wisconsin enacted a law for the direct election of delegates to nominating conventions. Others followed suit. By 1912, fifteen states provided for some type of primary election. Oregon was the first to permit a preference vote for the candidates themselves.

The year 1912 was also the first in which a candidate sought to use primaries as a way to obtain the nomination. With almost 42 percent of the Republican delegates selected in primaries, former President Theodore Roosevelt challenged incumbent William Howard Taft. Roosevelt won nine primaries to Taft's one, yet lost the nomination. (See Table 1–1.) Taft's support among regular party leaders who delivered their delegations and controlled the convention was sufficient to retain the nomination. He received one-third of his support from southern delegations, although the Republican party had won only a small percentage of the southern vote in the previous election.

Partially in reaction to the unrepresentative, "boss-dominated" convention of 1912, additional states adopted primaries. By 1916, more than half of them held a Republican or Democratic contest. Although a majority of the delegates in that year were chosen by some type of primary, many of them were not bound to support specific candidates. As a consequence, the primary vote did not control the outcome of the conventions.

The movement toward popular participation was short-lived, however. Following World War I the number of primaries declined. State party leaders, who saw these elections as a threat to their own influence, argued against them on three grounds: they were expensive; they did not attract many voters; and major candidates tended to avoid them. Moreover, primaries frequently encouraged factionalism, thereby weakening the party's organizational structure.

In response to this criticism the reformers, who supported primaries, could not claim that their principal goal — rank-and-file control over the party's nominees — had been achieved. Public involvement was disappointing. Primaries rarely attracted more than 50 percent of those who voted in the general election, and usually much less. The minority party, in particular, suffered from low turnout for an obvious reason — its candidates stood little chance of winning the general election. In some states rank-and-file influence was further diluted by the participation of independents.

As a consequence of these factors, some states that had enacted new primary laws reverted to their former method of selection. Others made their primaries advisory rather than mandatory. Fewer convention delegates were selected in them. By 1936, only fourteen states held Democratic primaries, and twelve held Republican ones. Less than 40 percent of the delegates to each convention that year were chosen in this manner. For the next twenty years the number of primaries and the percentage of delegates hovered around this level.

Theodore Roosevelt's failure in 1912 and the decline in primaries thereafter made them at best an auxiliary route to the nomination. Although some presidential aspirants became embroiled in primaries, none who depended on them won. In 1920, a spirited contest between three Republicans (General Leonard Wood, Governor Frank Lowden of Illinois, and Senator Hiram Johnson) failed to produce a convention majority for any of these candidates and resulted in party leaders choosing Warren Harding as the standard-bearer. Similarly, in 1952, Senator Estes Kefauver, who chaired the highly publicized and televised Senate hearings on organized crime, entered thirteen of seventeen presidential primaries, won twelve of them, and became the most popular Democratic contender, but failed to win his party's nomination.

The reason Kefauver could not parlay his primary victories into a convention victory was that a majority of the delegates were not selected in this manner. Of those who were, many were chosen separately from the presidential preference vote. Kefauver did not contest these separate delegate elections. As a consequence, he obtained only 50 percent of the delegates in states where he actually won the presidential preference vote. Moreover, the fact that most of his wins occurred against little or no opposition undercut Kefauver's claim to being the most popular and electable Democrat. He had avoided primaries in four states where he feared that he might either lose or do poorly.

Not only were primaries not considered to be an essential road to the nomination, but running in too many of them was interpreted as a sign of weakness, not strength. It indicated a lack of national recognition, a failure to obtain the support of party leaders, or both. For these reasons, leading candidates tended to choose their primaries carefully, and the primaries, in turn, tended to reinforce the position of the leading candidates.

Those who did enter primaries did so mainly to test their popularity rather than to win convention votes. Dwight D. Eisenhower in 1952, John F. Kennedy in 1960, and Richard M. Nixon in 1968 had to demonstrate that being a general, a Catholic, or a once-defeated presidential candidate would not be fatal to their chances. In other words, they needed to prove they could win the general election.

With the possible exception of John Kennedy's victories in West Virginia and Wisconsin, primaries were neither crucial nor decisive for winning the nomination until the 1970s. When there was a provisional consensus within the party, primaries helped confirm it; when there was not, primaries could not produce it.[9] In short, they had little to do with whether the party was unified or divided at the time of the convention.

Primary results tended to be self-fulfilling in the sense that they confirmed the front-runner's status. Between 1936 and 1968, the preconvention leader, the candidate who was ahead in the Gallup Poll before the first primary, won the nomination seventeen out of nineteen times. The only exceptions were Thomas E. Dewey in 1940, who was defeated by Wendell Willkie, and Kefauver in 1952, who lost to Adlai Stevenson. Willkie, however, had become the leader in public opinion by the time the Republican convention met. Even when leading candidates lost a primary, they had time to recoup. Dewey and Stevenson, defeated in early primaries in 1948 and 1956 respectively, went on to reestablish their credibility as front-runners by winning later primaries.

This situation in which the primaries were not the essential route to the nomination changed dramatically after 1968. Largely as a consequence of the tumultuous Democratic convention of that year, in which the party's nominee and platform were allegedly dictated by party "bosses," demands for a larger voice for rank-and-file partisans increased. In reaction to these demands, the Democratic Party began to look into the matter of delegate selection. It enacted a series of reforms designed to ensure broader representation at its convention. To avoid challenges to their delegations, a number of states that had used caucus and convention systems changed to primaries. As Table 1-1 indicates, the number of primaries began to increase as did the percentage of convention delegates chosen from them.

TABLE 1–1 ★

NUMBER OF PRESIDENTIAL PRIMARIES AND PERCENTAGE
OF CONVENTION DELEGATES FROM PRIMARY STATES,
BY PARTY, 1912–2000

	Democratic[†]		Republican	
Year	Number of State Primaries	Percentage of Delegates from Primary States*	Number of State Primaries	Percentage of Delegates from Primary States
1912	12	32.9%	13	41.7%
1916	20	53.5	20	58.9
1920	16	44.6	20	57.8
1924	14	35.5	17	45.3
1928	17	42.2	16	44.9
1932	16	40.0	14	37.7
1936	14	36.5	12	37.5
1940	13	35.8	13	38.8
1944	14	36.7	13	38.7
1948	14	36.3	12	36.0
1952	15	38.7	13	39.0
1956	19	42.7	19	44.8
1960	16	38.3	15	38.6
1964	17	45.7	17	45.6
1968	17	37.5	16	34.3
1972	23	60.5	22	52.7
1976	29*	72.6	28*	67.9
1980	31*	74.7	35*	74.3
1984	26	62.9	30	68.2
1988	34	66.6	35	76.9
1992	39	78.8	38	80.4
1996	34	62.6	43	90.0
2000	40	85.7	43	93.1

* Does not include Vermont, which holds nonbinding presidential preference votes but chooses delegates in state caucuses and conventions.

[†] Includes party leaders and elected officials chosen from primary states.

Sources: 1912–1964, F. Christopher Arterton, "Campaign Organizations Face the Mass Media in the 1976 Presidential Nomination Process" (paper delivered at the Annual Meeting of the American Political Science Association, Washington, D.C., September 1–4, 1977); 1968–1976, Austin Ranney, *Participation in American Presidential Nominations, 1976* (Washington, D.C.: American Enterprise Institute, 1977), table 1, 6. The figures for 1980 were compiled by Austin Ranney from materials distributed by the Democratic National Committee and the Republican National Committee; figures for elections since 1980 were compiled by the author from data supplied by the Democratic and Republican National Committees and the Federal Election Commission.

New finance laws, which provided for government subsidies for preconvention campaigning, and increased media coverage, particularly by television, also added to the incentive to enter primaries. By 1972, primaries had become decisive. In that year, Senator Edmund Muskie, the leading Democratic contender at the beginning of the process, was forced to withdraw after doing poorly in the early contests. In 1976, President Gerald Ford came close to being the first incumbent president since Chester A. Arthur in 1884 to be formally denied his party's nomination because of a primary challenge by Ronald Reagan. In 1980, President Jimmy Carter was also challenged for renomination by Senator Edward Kennedy, as was George Bush by Pat Buchanan in 1992. Bill Clinton was not challenged in 1996, but he had to raise money and wage a major nomination campaign to ensure that a credible candidate would not oppose him.

Since the 1970s, primaries have revolutionized the presidential nomination process. They are used to build popularity rather than simply reflect it. Challengers can no longer hope to succeed without entering them; incumbents can no longer ignore them.

The impact of primaries has been significant, affecting the strategies and tactics of the candidates, the composition and behavior of the convention delegates, and the decision-making process at the national conventions. These nomination contests have shifted power within the parties. They have enlarged the selection zone of potential nominees. They have also made governing more difficult. Each of these developments will be discussed in subsequent chapters.

THE EVOLUTION OF THE GENERAL ELECTION

The general election has changed as well. The Electoral College no longer operates in the manner in which it was designed. It now has a partisan coloration. There is greater public participation, but it is still not direct. Although the system bears a resemblance to its past form, it has become more subject to democratic influences. However, it continues to contain electoral biases.

The electoral system for president and vice president was one of the few innovative features of the Constitution. It had no immediate precedent, although it bore some relationship to the way the state of Maryland selected its senators. In essence, it was invented by the Framers, not synthesized from British and American experience, and it is one aspect of the constitutional system that has rarely worked as intended.

Initially, the method by which the states chose their electors varied. Some provided for direct election in a statewide vote. Others had the legislatures do the choosing. Two states used a combination of popular and legislative selection.

As political parties emerged around the turn of the nineteenth century, state legislatures maneuvered the selection process to benefit the party in power. This maneuvering resulted in the selection of more cohesive groups of electors who shared similar partisan views. Gradually, the trend evolved into a winner-take-all system, with most electors chosen on a statewide basis by popular vote. South Carolina was the last state to move to popular selection, doing so only after the Civil War.

The development of the party system changed the character of the Electoral College. Only in the first two elections, when Washington was the unanimous choice, did the electors exercise a nonpartisan and presumably independent judgment. Within ten years from the time the federal government began to operate, they quickly became the captives of their party and were expected to vote for its candidates. The outcome of the election of 1800 vividly illustrates this new pattern of partisan voting.

The Federalist Party supported President John Adams of Massachusetts and Charles C. Pinckney of South Carolina. The Democratic-Republicans, who had emerged to oppose the Federalists' policies, backed Thomas Jefferson of Virginia and Aaron Burr of New York. The Democratic-Republican candidates won, but, unexpectedly, Jefferson and Burr received the same number of votes. All electors who had cast ballots for Jefferson also cast them for Burr. Since it was not possible in those days to differentiate the candidates for the presidency and vice presidency on the ballot, the results had to be considered a tie, though Jefferson was clearly his party's choice for president. Under the terms of the Constitution, the House of Representatives, voting by state, had to choose the winner.

On February 11, 1801, after the results of the Electoral College vote were announced by the vice president, who happened to be Jefferson, a Federalist-controlled House convened to resolve the dilemma. Since the winners of the 1800 election did not take office until March 4, 1801, a "lame-duck" Congress would have to choose the next president.[10] A majority of Federalists supported Burr, whom they regarded as the more pragmatic politician. Jefferson, on the other hand, was perceived as a dangerous, uncompromising radical by many Federalists. Alexander Hamilton, however, was outspoken in his opposition to Burr, a political rival from New York, whom Hamilton regarded as "the most unfit man in the United States for the office of President."[11]

On the first ballot taken on February 11, Burr received a majority of the total votes, but Jefferson won the support of more state delegations.[12] Eight states voted for Jefferson, six backed Burr, and two were evenly divided. This left Jefferson one short of the needed majority. The House took nineteen ballots on its first day of deliberations, and a total of thirty-six before it finally elected Jefferson. Had Burr promised to be a Federalist president, it is conceivable that he could have won.

The first amendment to reform voting procedures in the Electoral College was enacted by the new Congress, controlled by Jefferson's party, in 1803. It was accepted by three-fourths of the states in 1804. This amendment to the Constitution, the twelfth, provided for separate voting for president and vice president. It also refined the selection procedures in the event that the president or vice president did not receive a majority of the electoral vote. The House of Representatives, still voting by states, was to choose from among the three presidential candidates with the most electoral votes, and the Senate, voting by individuals, was to choose from the top two vice presidential candidates. If the House could not make a decision by March 4, the amendment provided for the new vice president to assume the presidency until such time as the House could render a decision.

The next nondecisive presidential vote did not occur until 1824. That year, four people received electoral votes for president: Andrew Jackson (99 votes), John

Quincy Adams (84), William Crawford (41), and Henry Clay (37). According to the Twelfth Amendment, the House of Representatives had to decide from among the top three, since none had a majority. Eliminated from the contest was Henry Clay, who happened to be Speaker of the House. Clay threw his support to Adams, who won. It was alleged that he did so in exchange for appointment as secretary of state, a charge that Clay vigorously denied. After Adams became president, however, he nominated Clay for secretary of state, a position Clay readily accepted.[13]

Jackson was the winner of the popular vote in 1824. In eighteen of the twenty-four states that chose electors by popular vote that year, he received 192,933 votes compared with 115,696 for Adams, 47,136 for Clay, and 46,979 for Crawford. Adams of Massachusetts, however, had the backing of more state delegations. He enjoyed the support of the six New England states, and with Clay's help, the representatives of six others backed his candidacy. The votes of thirteen states, however, were needed for a majority. New York seemed to be the pivotal state and Stephen Van Rensselaer, a Revolutionary War general, the swing representative. On the morning of the vote, Speaker Clay and Representative Daniel Webster tried to persuade Van Rensselaer to vote for Adams. It was said that they were unsuccessful.[14] When the voting began, Van Rensselaer bowed his head as if in prayer. On the floor he saw a piece of paper with "Adams" written on it. Interpreting this as a sign from the Almighty, he dropped the paper in the box. New York went for Adams by one vote, providing him with the barest majority.[15]

Jackson, outraged at the turn of events, urged the abolition of the Electoral College. His claim of a popular mandate, however, was open to question. The most populous state at the time, New York, did not permit its electorate to participate in the selection of electors. Rather, the New York legislature made the decision. Moreover, in three of the states in which Jackson won the electoral vote but lost in the House of Representatives, he had fewer popular votes than Adams.[16]

Opposition to the system mounted, however, and a gradual democratization of the process occurred. More states began to choose their electors directly by popular vote. In 1800, ten of the fifteen used legislative selection. By 1832, only South Carolina retained this practice.

The trend was also toward statewide election of an entire slate of electors. States that had chosen their electors within legislative districts converted to a winner-take-all system in order to maximize their voting power in the Electoral College. This change, in turn, created the possibility that there could be a disparity between the popular and electoral vote. A candidate could be elected by winning the popular vote in the big states by small margins and losing the smaller states by large margins.

The next disputed election did not occur until 1876. In that election Democrat Samuel J. Tilden received the most votes. He had 250,000 more popular votes and 19 more electoral votes than his Republican rival, Rutherford B. Hayes. Nonetheless, Tilden fell one vote short of a majority in the Electoral College. Twenty electoral votes were in dispute. Dual election returns were received from Florida (four votes), Louisiana (eight votes), and South Carolina (seven votes). Charges of fraud and voting irregularities were made by both parties. The Republicans, who controlled the three state legislatures, contended that Democrats had forcibly prevented newly freed slaves from voting. The Democrats, on the other hand, alleged that many nonresidents and nonregistered people had participated. The other disputed electoral vote occurred in the state of Oregon. One Republican elector was challenged on the grounds that he held another federal position (postmaster) at the time he was chosen and thus was ineligible to be an elector.

Three days before the Electoral College vote was to be officially counted, Congress established a commission to examine and try to resolve the dispute. The electoral commission was to consist of fifteen members: ten from Congress (five Republicans and five Democrats) and five from the Supreme Court. Four of the Supreme Court justices were designated by the act (two Republicans and two Democrats), and they were to choose a fifth justice. David Davis, a political independent, was expected to be selected, but on the day the commission was created, Davis was appointed by the Illinois legislature to the U.S. Senate. The Supreme Court justices then picked Joseph Bradley, an independent Republican. Bradley sided with his party on every issue. By a strictly partisan vote, the commission validated the credentials of all the Republican electors, thereby giving Hayes a one-vote margin of victory in the Electoral College.[17]

Before 2000, the only election in which the winner of the popular vote was beaten in an undisputed Electoral College vote occurred in 1888. Democrat Grover Cleveland had a plurality of 95,096 popular votes, but only 168 electoral votes compared with 233 for Republican Benjamin Harrison. Cleveland's loss of Indiana by about 3,000 votes and New York by about 15,000 led to his defeat.

Although all other leaders in the popular vote have won a majority of electoral votes, shifts of just a few thousand popular votes in a few states could have altered the results of other elections. In 1860, a shift of 25,000 in New York from Abraham Lincoln to Stephen A. Douglas would have denied Lincoln a majority in the Electoral College. A change of less than 30,000 in three states in 1892 would have given Harrison another victory over Cleveland. In 1916, Charles Evans Hughes needed only 3,807 more votes in California to have beaten Woodrow Wilson. Similarly, Thomas E. Dewey could have denied Harry S Truman a majority in the Electoral College with 12,487 more California votes in 1948. A change of less than 9,000 in Illinois and Missouri in 1960 would have meant that John F. Kennedy lacked an Electoral College majority. In 1968, a shift of only 55,000 votes from Richard M. Nixon to Hubert H. Humphrey in three states (New Jersey, Missouri, and New Hampshire) would have thrown the election into the House — a House controlled by Democrats. In 1976, a shift of only 3,687 in Hawaii and 5,559 in Ohio would have cost Jimmy Carter the election.[18]

Not only could the results of these elections have been affected by very small voter shifts in a few states, but in 1948, 1960, 1968, and 1992, there was the added possibility that the Electoral College itself would not be able to choose a winner. In each of these elections, third-party candidates or independent electoral slates threatened to secure enough votes to prevent either of the major candidates from obtaining a majority. In 1948, Henry Wallace (Progressive Party) and Strom Thurmond (States' Rights Party) received almost 5 percent of the total popular vote, and Thurmond won 39 electoral votes. In 1960, fourteen unpledged electors were chosen in Alabama and Mississippi.[19] In 1968, Governor George Wallace of Alabama, running on the American Independent Party ticket, received almost 10 million popular votes, 13.5 percent of the total, and 46 electoral votes. In 1992, independent H. Ross Perot received 19.7 million popular votes (18.9 percent of the total vote) but none in the Electoral College.[20] In 1996, he received 8.1 million votes (8.4 percent of the total), but again no electoral votes. Ralph Nader received only 3 percent of the vote in 2000. Nonetheless, it is clear that close competition between the major parties, combined with a strong third party movement, provides the Electoral College with its most difficult test.

THE POLITICS OF ELECTORAL COLLEGE VOTING

The Electoral College is not neutral. No system of election can be. The way votes are aggregated does make a difference. It benefits some of the electorate and adversely affects others.

The Electoral College usually works to the advantage of the majority; more often than not, it has exaggerated the margin of the popular vote leader. Bill Clinton received only 43 percent of the popular vote in 1992 but 69 percent of the electoral vote; in 1996, he received 49 percent of the popular vote (54.6 percent of the two party vote) and 70.4 percent of the electoral vote. Similarly in 1968, Richard Nixon won only 43.4 percent of the popular vote but 56 percent of the electoral vote. Jimmy Carter's election in 1976 resulted in a smaller disparity. He won 50.1 percent of the popular vote and 55 percent of the electoral vote. In 1980, Ronald Reagan received 51 percent of the popular vote but a whopping 91 percent of the electoral vote.

Why does the Electoral College usually enhance the margin of the popular vote winner? The reason has to do with the winner-take-all system of voting that has developed in most states. In almost every instance the presidential and vice presidential candidates who receive a plurality of the popular vote within the state get all its electoral votes. This translates into a larger percentage of the Electoral College vote than it would with a direct popular vote.[21] Since 1924, the plurality winner who received more than 53.5 percent of the two party vote received over 75 percent of the electoral vote.[22]

Although the Electoral College has usually enhanced the margin of the popular vote winner, from time to time it has also led to the defeat of the candidate with the most popular votes. On three occasions in the nineteenth century — 1824, 1876, and 1888 — the plurality winner was a loser in the Electoral College.

The Electoral College contains a number of built-in biases. One of them has already been mentioned — it tends to enhance the margin of victory of the candidate with the largest popular vote. In addition to benefiting the candidate with the most votes, it increases the influence of the largest states, not only because of the number of electoral votes they cast but because the votes are almost always cast in a bloc.[23] Moreover, the advantage that the citizens of the largest states receive increases in proportion to their states' population. (See Figure 1–1 for the relative advantage large populations confer on the states.) This large-state advantage is

FIGURE 1–1 ★

STATE SIZE ACCORDING TO POPULATION: THE 2000 ELECTORAL VOTE*

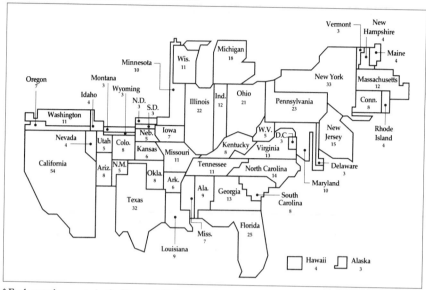

* Each state has a vote in the Electoral College equal to the number of its representatives plus two.
Source: New York Times, December 28, 1990, A9.

why candidates spend a larger share of their campaign time and resources in these states.

By giving an edge to the larger and more competitive states, the Electoral College also works to benefit groups that are geographically concentrated within those states and have cohesive voting patterns. Those who live in urban areas have a particular advantage. Jewish and Hispanic voters and certain immigrant populations fall into this category. Rural voters do not. In general, African Americans are disadvantaged by the Electoral College because of their high concentration in small- and medium-sized southern states.[24]

There is also an offsetting gain for the very smallest states which receive a minimum of three electoral votes regardless of their size. This increases the voting power of sparsely populated states such as Wyoming, Nevada, and Alaska. For example, if Wyoming's 2000 voting age population of approximately 353,000 were divided by its three electoral votes, there would be one elector for every 117,666 people. Dividing California's population of 24,222,000 by the fifty-four electoral votes yields one elector for every 448,555 people.[25] Medium-sized states are comparatively disadvantaged.[26]

Additionally, the Electoral College works to benefit the two major parties.[27] The reason it does so is that the winner-take-all system within states, when combined with the need for a majority within the college, makes it difficult for third parties to accumulate enough votes to win an election.

Which of the major parties is advantaged by the Electoral College has been much debated. Before Bill Clinton's victories in 1992 and 1996, the conventional wisdom held that the Republicans had an advantage. They could increasingly depend on support from the smaller Mountain States, which exercised influence disproportionate to their population because of the two electors they received for their Senate representation.[28] The solid South was considered another bastion of Republican strength. Combined, the Mountain and southern states gave the Republicans a larger and more dependable block of votes than the Democrats received from the few states that consistently voted for them, states like West Virginia, Minnesota, and Rhode Island, as well as the District of Columbia.

The problem the Republicans faced is that about half of the larger states (such as New York, Michigan, Pennsylvania, and California) seemed to lean more to the Democrats. When the winner-take-all votes of these states are considered, these larger states exercise disproportionate influence. Bill Clinton won six of the big eight in 1992 and seven of eight in 1996, losing only Texas, but Gore won only five in 2000. Victories in these states are all but essential for Democrats to overcome the advantages Republicans have in the South, and in the Rocky Mountain region and other states in the West.

Regardless of whether the Electoral College benefits the Republicans or the Democrats, it definitely disadvantages third-party candidates. To have any effect, these minor party candidates must have support that is geographically concentrated, as George Wallace's was in 1968 and Strom Thurmond's was in 1948, rather than more broadly distributed across the country, as Henry Wallace's was in 1948 and H. Ross Perot's was in 1992 and 1996.

Given the limitations on third parties, their most realistic electoral objectives would seem to be to defeat one of the major contenders rather than to elect their own candidate. In 1912, Theodore Roosevelt's Bull Moose campaign split the Republican party, thereby aiding the candidate of the Democratic party, Woodrow Wilson. More recently, third-party and independent candidates have cost the major parties votes but do not appear to have changed the outcome of elections. Truman's loss of Michigan and New York in 1948 apparently was a consequence of Henry Wallace's Progressive Party candidacy, and George Wallace in 1968 probably denied Richard Nixon forty-six more electoral votes from the South. However, George Wallace's 11.4 percent of the Missouri vote and his 11.8 percent in Ohio probably hurt Hubert Humphrey more than Nixon and may explain the loss of these two states by the Democratic candidate. Ford's narrow victory in Iowa in 1976 (632,863 to 619,931) may be partially attributed to the 20,051 votes Eugene McCarthy received as an independent candidate, votes that very likely would have gone to Carter had McCarthy not run. Surveys of voters in 1992 and 1996 indicate that Perot drew slightly more support from Republicans and in 2000 Nader drew more from Democrats, although both got the bulk of their votes from independents.[29]

The impact of third parties is more than simply a question of numbers. It affects the psychology of voting — should one vote for a candidate who has little chance of winning a majority of the electoral vote. In 1980, the Carter and Reagan campaigns appealed to voters sympathetic to John Anderson on the first of these grounds. They urged them not to waste their vote on a candidate who could not win. This "wasted vote" appeal undercut Anderson's ability to raise money and garner political support. In 1992, however, the perception that independent Ross Perot could not win may have had the opposite effect, encouraging those who wished to cast a protest vote to do so without fear of electing their protest candidate president.[30] In 1996, however, the wasted vote appeal, reinforced by Perot's poor showing in public opinion polls, helped reduce his proportion of the vote to less than half of what he received four years earlier. Similarly in 2000, Ralph Nader's vote may have been reduced by the closeness of the Gore-Bush contest and the Gore campaign's appeal for the Nader vote in key states.

SUMMARY

The quest for the presidency has been and continues to be influenced by the system designed in Philadelphia in 1787. The objectives of that system were to protect the independence of the institution, to ensure the selection of a well-qualified candidate, and to do so in a way that was politically expedient. It was intended to be consistent with the tenets of a republican form of government.

Although many of the objectives are still the same, the system has changed significantly over the years. Of all the factors that have influenced these changes, none has been more important than the advent of political parties. This development created an additional first step in the process — the nomination—which has influenced the selection and behavior of electors and has affected the operation and the beneficiaries of the Electoral College itself.

The nomination process is necessary to the parties, whose principal interest is to get their candidates elected. At first, members of Congress, meeting in partisan caucuses, decided on the nominees. On the basis of common friendships and shared perspectives, they reached a consensus and then used their influence to mobilize support for it. In effect, the system provided for legislative selection of the president in violation of the letter and spirit of the Constitution.

The caucus method broke down with the weakening of the parties, the demise of the Federalists, and the factionalization of the Republicans. It was never restored. In its place developed a more decentralized mode of selection reflective of the increasing sectional composition of the parties.

The new nomination process, controlled by state leaders, operated within the framework of a brokered national convention. There was little rank-and-file participation — the wheeling and dealing were done for the party's electorate, not by them. Demands for greater public involvement eventually opened the system, thereby reducing the influence of state leaders and decreasing the dependence of candidates on them. Power eventually shifted from the political leaders to the candidates themselves, with the people making the final judgment.

Similar trends, rooted in the development of parties and the expansion of suffrage, affected the way in which the electors were selected and how they voted. Instead of being chosen on the basis of their qualifications, electors were selected on the basis of their politics; instead of being elected as individuals, they were elected as part of a slate of electors; instead of exercising independent judgment, the electors became partisan agents who were morally and politically obligated to support their party's choice. The predictable soon happened: bloc voting by electors in states.

The desire of the populace for greater participation also had an effect. It accelerated the movement to choose electors directly by the people, which resulted in an increased likelihood of the electoral vote's reflecting, even exaggerating, the popular vote. Prior to the 2000 election, there were only three times in U.S. history that the plurality winner was not elected; however, the shift of a very small number of votes in a few states could have altered the results of other elections, most recently in 1960, 1968, 1976, and 2000. This situation has raised doubts about the adequacy of the system.

The equity of the Electoral College itself has also come into question. The way it works benefits the larger and the more competitive states. Within those states, the groups that are better organized, more geographically concentrated, and more cohesive in their voting behavior seem to enjoy the greatest advantage. Their vote is maximized by the winner's taking all the state's electoral votes and the state's having a larger share of the total Electoral College. Candidates keep this size factor in mind when planning and conducting their campaigns.

In summary, the electoral system has been decisive and efficient, but questions about its equity remain. It does not jeopardize the president's independence. In fact, it may do just the opposite; it may isolate the selection of president and vice president too much from that of Congress. It permits a partisan choice but recently has not contributed to the strength of the party inside or outside the government. It facilitates participation in the nomination process but has not raised the level of public involvement in general elections. The winning candidate often obtains only a bare majority or plurality of the voters, who, in recent elections, have constituted barely half the voting-age population. Thus, only about one out of every four adults of voting age cast their ballots for the winner, hardly the mandate we might expect or desire in a democracy nor one that is sufficient for governing effectively as Clinton found out, much to his dismay, early in his first term in office.

WHERE ON THE WEB?

All sites listed on the "Where on the Web?" pages of this book are linked at the Bedford/St. Martin's Web site, <http://www.bedfordstmartins.com>.

General Links for Presidential Elections

- **C-SPAN: Road to the White House 2000**
  http://www.cspan.org
  Contains up-to-date information about the campaign.
- **WhiteHouse 2000**
  http://www.niu.edu/newsplace/whitehouse.html
  Jokes, candidates, commentary, and the latest news articles.
- **Web White & Blue**
  http://www.webwhiteblue.org
  Site devoted to the use of emerging technologies in elections.
- **Yahoo**
  http://www.yahoo.com/Full_Coverage/US/Presidential_Elections_2000/
  Another comprehensive link for campaign news and information.

The Electoral System

- **Federal Election Commission**
  http://www.fec.gov
  Easily accessible data on election turnout, voting, and money.
- **National Archives and Records Administration; Office of the Federal Register**
  http://www.nara.gov/fedreg/elctcoll/index.html
  You can access federal laws and presidential documents on this site as well as statistics on past presidential elections and information on the Electoral College.
- **Congress**
  http://thomas.loc.gov
  Gain access to Congress from this site. You can link to reports, committee hearings, pending legislation, laws for the current and recent past Congresses. Contains Library of Congress reports.
- **White House**
  http://www.whitehouse.gov
  Provides information on the activities of the president and vice president: what they say, who they meet, and their positions on current issues.
- **World Media**
  http://www.worldmedia.fr/USelections
  Maps of the Electoral College for past presidential elections.

EXERCISES

1. Get up-to-speed on the Electoral College by accessing and reviewing "A Procedural Guide to the Electoral College" at the National Archives site <http://www.nara.gov/fedreg/elctcoll/index.html> and then answer the question, to what extent do the procedures really matter?
2. During the last presidential election both major party candidates spoke of electoral reform. Search their Web sites <http://www.algore2000.com> and <http://www.georgebush.com>, if they are still accessible, or the White House Web site <http://www.whitehouse.gov> and the political parties' sites <http://www.rnc.org> and <http://www.democrats.org> if they are not, to find proposals for changing the way we go about electing a president. Then go to the congressional Web site at <http://thomas.loc.gov> to see whether any of these proposals or ideas have been introduced as legislation. List those which you believe have the greatest and least chance of becoming public policy and explain the reasons for your decision.

SELECTED READING

Abbot, David W., and James P. Levine. *Wrong Winner: The Coming Debacle in the Electoral College.* New York: Praeger, 1991.

Banzhaf, John F. III. "One Man, 3,312 Votes: A Mathematical Analysis of the Electoral College." *Villanova Law Review* 13 (Winter 1968): 303–346.

Berns, Walter, ed. *After the People Vote: A Guide to the Electoral College,* rev. ed. Washington, D.C.: American Enterprise Institute, 1992.

———. "Third Party Candidates Face a High Hurdle in the Electoral College," *The American Enterprise* (January/February 1996): 48–49.

Best, Judith. *The Choice of the People? Debating the Electoral College.* Lanham, Md.: Rowman & Littlefield, 1996.

Bickel, Alexander M. *Reform and Continuity: The Electoral College, the Convention, and the Party System.* New York: Harper & Row, 1971.

Brunell, Thomas, and Bernard Grofman, "The 1992 and 1996 Presidential Elections: Whatever Happened to the Republican Electoral College Lock?" *Presidential Studies Quarterly* (Winter 1997): 134–138.

Destler, I. M. "The Myth of the Electoral College Lock." *PS* (September 1996): 189–193.

Glennon, Michael J. *When No Majority Rules: The Electoral College and Presidential Succession.* Washington D.C.: Congressional Quarterly, 1993.

Hardaway, Robert M. *The Electoral College and the Constitution: The Case for Preserving Federalism.* Westport, Conn.: Praeger, 1994.

Longley, Lawrence D., and James D. Dana, Jr. "The Biases of the Electoral College in the 1990s." *Polity* 25 (Fall 1992): 123–145.

———, and Neal R. Peirce. *The Electoral College Primer.* New Haven, Conn.: Yale University Press, 1996.

Rabinowitz, George, and Stuart Elaine MacDonald, "The Power of the States in U.S. Presidential Elections," *American Political Science Review* 80 (March 1986): 65–87.

Roseboom, Eugene H. *A History of Presidential Elections.* New York: Macmillan, 1957.

Smith, Eric R. A. N., and Peverill Squire. "Direct Election of the President and the Power of the States." *Western Political Quarterly* 40 (March 1987): 29–44.

Sundquist, James. *Constitutional Reform and Effective Government.* Washington, D.C.: Brookings Institution, 1986.

United States Senate, Committee on the Judiciary. *The Electoral College and Direct Election.* Hearings, 95th Cong., 1st sess. Washington, D.C.: Government Printing Office, 1977.

———, Committee on the Judiciary. *Direct Popular Election of the President and Vice President of the United States.* Hearings, 95th Cong., 1st sess. Washington, D.C.: Government Printing Office, 1979.

NOTES

1. Gouverneur Morris, *Records of the Federal Convention,* ed. Max Farrand (New Haven, Conn.: Yale University Press, 1921), 2, 33.

2. The first proposal for direct election was introduced in a very timid fashion by James Wilson, delegate from Pennsylvania. James Madison's *Journal* describes Wilson's presentation as follows: "Mr. Wilson said he was almost unwilling to declare the mode which he wished to take place, being apprehensive that it might appear chimerical. He would say however at least that in theory he was for an election by the people; Experience, particularly in N. York & Massts, shewed that an election of the first magistrate

by the people at large, was both convenient & successful mode." Farrand, *Records of the Federal Convention*, 1, 68.

3. So great was the sectional rivalry, so parochial the country, so limited the number of people with national reputations, that it was feared electors would tend to vote primarily for those from their own states. To prevent the same states, particularly the largest ones, from exercising undue influence in the selection of both the president and vice president, this provision was included. It remains in effect today.

4. George Mason declared, "Nineteen times out of twenty, the President would be chosen by the Senate." Farrand, *Records of the Federal Convention*, 2, 500. The original proposal of the Committee on Unfinished Business was that the Senate should select the president. The delegates substituted the House of Representatives, fearing that the Senate was too powerful with its appointment and treaty-making powers. The principle of equal state representation was retained. Choosing the president is the only occasion on which the House votes by state.

5. Thomas R. Marshall, *Presidential Nominations in a Reform Age* (New York: Praeger, 1981), 19.

6. Quoted in Neal R. Peirce and Lawrence D. Longley, *The People's President* (New Haven, Conn.: Yale University Press, 1981), 36.

7. Marshall, *Presidential Nominations*, 20.

8. Ibid., 21.

9. Louis Maisel and Gerald J. Lieberman, "The Impact of Electoral Rules on Primary Elections: The Democratic Presidential Primaries in 1976," in *The Impact of the Electoral Process*, ed. Louis Maisel and Joseph Cooper (Beverly Hills, Calif.: Sage Publications, 1977), 68.

10. Until the passage of the Twentieth Amendment, which made January 3 the date when members of Congress took their oaths of office and convened, it was the second session of the preelection Congress that convened after the election. This made it a lame-duck session.

11. Quoted in Lucius Wilmerding, *The Electoral College* (New Brunswick, N.J.: Rutgers University Press, 1953), 32.

12. There were 106 members of the House (58 Federalists and 48 Republicans). On the first ballot, the vote of those present was for Burr, 53–51.

13. In those days being secretary of state was considered a stepping-stone to the presidency. With the exception of Washington and John Adams, all the people who became president had first held this position.

14. Peirce and Longley, *People's President*, 51.

15. Marquis James, *The Life of Andrew Jackson* (Indianapolis: Bobbs-Merrill, 1938), 439.

16. He captured the majority of electoral votes in two of these states because the electors were chosen on a district rather than statewide basis. William R. Keech, "Background Paper," in *Winner Take All: Report of the Twentieth Century Fund Task Force on Reform of the Presidential Election Process* (New York: Holmes & Meier, 1978), 50.

17. The act that created the commission specified that its decision would be final unless overturned by both houses of Congress. The House of Representatives, controlled by the Democrats, opposed every one of the commission's findings. The Republican Senate, however, concurred. A Democratic filibuster in the Senate was averted by Hayes's promise of concessions to the South, including the withdrawal of federal troops. Tilden could have challenged the findings in court but chose not to do so.

18. Richard M. Scammon and Alice V. McGillivray, *America Votes* 12 (Washington, D.C.: Congressional Quarterly, 1977), 15.

19. In Alabama, slates of electors ran against one another without the names of the presidential candidates appearing on the ballot. The Democratic slate included six

unpledged electors and five loyalists. All were elected. The unpledged electors voted for Senator Harry Byrd of Virginia, while the loyalists stayed with the Kennedy-Johnson ticket. In Mississippi, all eight Democratic electors voted for Byrd.

20. He came in second in two states in 1992, Maine and Utah. In 1996, Perot did not come in second in any state.

21. Thomas Brunell and Bernard Grofman, "The 1992 and 1996 Presidential Elections: Whatever Happened to the Republican Electoral College Lock?" *Presidential Studies Quarterly* (Winter 1997): 134–138

22. I. M. Destler, "The Myth of the Electoral Lock," *PS* (September 1996): 491.

23. Theoretically, two states, Maine and Nebraska, will not always vote as a bloc because they do not select all their electors on an at-large basis. Two are chosen at-large and the remaining ones are elected in each of the states' congressional districts. Since these states have enacted their electoral laws, however, they have cast all their electoral votes for the same candidate.

24. Lawrence D. Longley and James D. Dana, Jr., "The Biases of the Electoral College in the 1990s," *Polity* 25 (Fall 1992): 140–145.

25. Federal Election Commission, "FEC Announces 2000 Presidential Spending Limits," March 1, 2000, 2–3.

26. Longley and Dana, "The Biases of the Electoral College in the 1990s," 134. There are two other, less obvious, biases in the Electoral College. The distribution of electoral votes is calculated on the basis of the census, which occurs every ten years. Thus, the college does not mirror population shifts within this period. Nor does it take into account the number of people who actually cast ballots. It is a state's population, not its turnout, that determines the number of electoral votes it receives, over and above the automatic three.

27. James C. Garand and T. Wayne Parent, "Representation, Swing, and Bias in U.S. Presidential Elections, 1872–1988," *American Journal of Political Science* 35 (November 1991): 1024, 1029.

28. John E. Berthoud, "The Electoral Lock Thesis: The Weighting Bias Component," *PS* (June 1997): 189–193.

29. Voter News Service, "Exit Poll," November 6, 1996.

30. For a discussion of motivations for voting for independent and third-party candidates, see Steven J. Rosenstone, Roy L. Behr, and Edward H. Lazarus, *Third Parties in America: Citizen Response to Major Party Failure* (Princeton, N.J.: Princeton University Press, 1984).

2

CAMPAIGN
FINANCE

INTRODUCTION

Running for president is very expensive. In the 1995–1996 election cycle, $453.8 million was spent by the Democratic, Republican, and Reform Parties' candidates in their quest for the presidential nomination and election.[1] The 1999–2000 election cycle was even more expensive. The Committee for Responsive Politics estimates that $3 billion was spent on federal elections in 2000. Of that amount, a little over $500 million was expended by or on the presidential candidates. The parties spent $877 million, while group issue ads accounted for about $300 million and congressional races, the remainder.

The magnitude of these expenditures poses serious problems for presidential candidates, who must raise considerable sums during the preconvention struggle, closely monitor their expenses, make important allocation decisions, and conform to the intricacies of finance laws during both the nomination and general election campaigns, as well as answer to party leaders who must solicit, distribute, and spend millions on behalf of their candidates for national office. Moreover, such large expenditures raise important issues for a democratic selection process. This chapter explores some of these problems and those issues.

The chapter is organized into five sections. The first details the costs of presidential campaigns, paying particular attention to the increase in expenditures since 1960. The next section looks briefly at the contributors, the size of their gifts, and the implications of large donations for a democratic election. What happens when the individual's right to give conflicts with the majority's desire to set limits and have its elected representatives level the playing field? Who prevails? Congressional attempts to control spending and subsidize elections are discussed in the third section. The fourth section examines the impact of campaign finance laws on revenues and expenditures in presidential campaigns and on the party system. In the final section, the relationship between campaign spending and electoral success is explored. Can money buy elections? Have the big spenders been the big winners?

THE COSTS OF CAMPAIGNING

Candidates have always spent money in their quest for the presidency, but it was not until they began to campaign personally across the country that these costs rose sharply. In 1860, Abraham Lincoln spent an estimated $100,000. By the turn of the century, those costs had escalated. William McKinley reputedly raised and spent between $6 and $7 million in his 1896 campaign for the presidency compared to William Jennings Bryan's paltry $650,000.

With the advent of the electronic campaign following World War II, campaign costs soared once again. In 1960, John Kennedy and Richard Nixon each spent a hundred times the amount Lincoln spent one hundred years earlier. In the twelve years following the 1960 general election, expenditures increased from about $20 million to over $90 million, an increase that far outstripped the inflation rate during that period. Table 2–1 lists the costs of the major party candidates in presidential elections from 1860 to 1972, the last general election in which campaign spending by major party candidates was unrestricted.

Prenomination costs have risen even more rapidly than those in the general election (see Table 2–2). Until the 1960s, large expenditures were the exception, not the rule, for gaining the party's nomination. General Leonard Wood spent an estimated $2 million in an unsuccessful quest to head the Republican ticket in 1920. The contest between General Dwight D. Eisenhower and Senator Robert A. Taft in 1952 cost about $5 million, a total that was not exceeded until 1964, when Nelson Rockefeller and Barry Goldwater together spent approximately twice that amount.

Since 1968, preconvention expenditures have generally exceeded those in the general election. The increasing number of primaries, caucuses, and candidates has been largely responsible for the rise. In the 1950s, these preconvention contests were optional; since the 1970s, they have been mandatory. Even incumbent presidents may have to enter them, and they must spend money even when they are *not* challenged. In 1984, the Reagan campaign committee spent almost $28 million during the nomination period, much of it on voter registration drives for the general election; in 1992, George Bush spent over $27 million in defeating Pat Buchanan, a conservative newspaper columnist who had not previously sought public office. In 1996, Bill Clinton spent almost $35 million running unopposed for the Democratic nomination while four years later George W. Bush raised over $117 million and spent almost $95 million by the end of the campaign.

Why is it so expensive to run for president today? It costs money to raise money, something candidates have to do during their precandidacy phase, during the phase when they are officially seeking their party's nomination and, increasingly, during the presidential election as well. Identifying potential donors and supporters, contacting them, and getting them to contribute, as well as to the

TABLE 2–1 ★

COSTS OF PRESIDENTIAL GENERAL ELECTIONS, MAJOR PARTY CANDIDATES, 1860–1972

Year	Democrats		Republicans	
1860	Stephen Douglas	$50,000	Abraham Lincoln*	$100,000
1864	George McClellan	50,000	Abraham Lincoln*	125,000
1868	Horatio Seymour	75,000	Ulysses Grant*	150,000
1872	Horace Greeley	50,000	Ulysses Grant*	250,000
1876	Samuel Tilden	900,000	Rutherford Hayes*	950,000
1880	Winfield Hancock	335,000	James Garfield*	1,100,000
1884	Grover Cleveland*	1,400,000	James Blaine	1,300,000
1888	Grover Cleveland	855,000	Benjamin Harrison*	1,350,000
1892	Grover Cleveland*	2,350,000	Benjamin Harrison	1,700,000
1896	William Jennings Bryan	675,000	William McKinley*	3,350,000
1900	William Jennings Bryan	425,000	William McKinley*	3,000,000
1904	Alton Parker	700,000	Theodore Roosevelt*	2,096,000
1908	William Jennings Bryan	629,341	William Taft*	1,655,518
1912	Woodrow Wilson*	1,134,848	William Taft	1,071,549
1916	Woodrow Wilson*	2,284,950	Charles Evans Hughes	2,441,565
1920	James Cox	1,470,371	Warren Harding*	5,417,501
1924	John Davis	1,108,836	Calvin Coolidge*	4,020,478
1928	Alfred Smith	5,342,350	Herbert Hoover*	6,256,111
1932	Franklin Roosevelt*	2,245,975	Herbert Hoover	2,900,052
1936	Franklin Roosevelt*	5,194,751	Alfred Landon	8,892,972
1940	Franklin Roosevelt*	2,783,654	Wendell Willkie	3,451,310
1944	Franklin Roosevelt*	2,169,077	Thomas Dewey	2,828,652
1948	Harry Truman*	2,736,334	Thomas Dewey	2,127,296
1952	Adlai Stevenson	5,032,926	Dwight Eisenhower*	6,608,623
1956	Adlai Stevenson	5,106,651	Dwight Eisenhower*	7,778,702
1960	John Kennedy*	9,797,000	Richard Nixon	10,128,000
1964	Lyndon Johnson*	8,757,000	Barry Goldwater	16,026,000
1968[†]	Hubert Humphrey	11,594,000	Richard Nixon*	25,042,000
1972	George McGovern	30,000,000	Richard Nixon*	61,400,000

* Indicates winner.

[†] George Wallace spent an estimated $7 million as the candidate of the American Independent Party in 1968.

Source: Herbert E. Alexander, *Financing Politics* (Washington, D.C.: Congressional Quarterly, 1984), 7. Copyrighted material printed with permission of Congressional Quarterly Inc.

TABLE 2–2 ★

COSTS OF PRESIDENTIAL NOMINATIONS, 1964–2000 (IN MILLIONS OF DOLLARS)

Year	Democrats	Republicans
1964	(uncontested)	$10.0
1968	$25.0	20.0
1972	33.1	*
1976	40.7	26.1
1980	41.7	86.1
1984	107.7	28.0
1988	94.0	114.6
1992	66.0†	51.0
1996	46.1	187.0
2000	95.9	232.7

* During a primary in which Richard M. Nixon's renomination was virtually assured, Representative John M. Ashbrook spent $740,000 and Representative Paul N. McCloskey spent $550,000 in challenging Nixon.

† Estimates based on Alexander and Corrado, *Financing the 1992 Elections*, Tables 2–1 and 2–4.

Sources: 1964–1972, Herbert E. Alexander, *Financing Politics* (Washington, D.C.: Congressional Quarterly, 1976), 45–47; 1976–1984, Federal Election Commission, "Reports on Financial Activity, 1987–88," *Presidential Pre-Nomination Campaigns* (August 1989), Table A–7, 10; Herbert E. Alexander, "Financing the Presidential Elections" (paper presented at the Institute for Political Studies in Japan, Tokyo, Japan, September 8–10, 1989), 4, 10; Herbert E. Alexander and Anthony Corrado, *Financing the 1992 Elections* (Armonk, N.Y.: Sharpe, 1995). Federal Election Commission, "Presidential Campaign Disbursements" (inception through July 31, 2000).

polls, is expensive. Moreover, candidates are forced to campaign simultaneously in several states. To do so, they need to use the electronic media, design advertisements, and purchase time to air them. This too is costly.

Mass Media. When campaigns were conducted in the written press, expenses were relatively low. Electioneering, as conducted within a highly partisan press environment before the Civil War, had few expenses other than for the occasional biography and campaign pamphlet printed by the party and sold to the public at less than cost.

With the advent of more active public campaigning toward the middle of the nineteenth century, candidate organizations turned to buttons, billboards, banners, and pictures to symbolize and illustrate their campaigns. By the beginning of the twentieth century, the cost of this type of advertising in each election exceeded $150,000, a lot of money then but a minuscule amount by contemporary standards.[3]

In 1924, radio was employed for the first time in presidential campaigns. The Republicans spent approximately $120,000 that year, whereas the Democrats spent only $40,000.[4] Four years later, however, the two parties together spent more than $1 million. Radio expenses continued to equal or exceed a million dollars per election for the next twenty years.[5]

Television emerged as a vehicle for presidential campaigning in 1952. Both national party conventions were broadcast on television as well as radio. Although there were only 19 million television sets in the United States at that time, almost one-third of the people were regular television viewers.

The number of households with television sets rose dramatically over the next four years. By 1956, an estimated 71 percent had television, and by 1968 the figure was close to 95 percent; today it exceeds 98 percent, with most homes having two or more sets. Cable and satellite subscribers have increased to more than two out of three households.

The first commercials for presidential candidates appeared in 1952. They became regular fare thereafter, contributing substantially to campaign costs. Film biographies, interview shows, political rallies, town meetings, and election eve telethons were all seen with increasing frequency.

In 1948, no money was spent on television by either party's candidate. Twenty years later, $13 million was expended for television advertising, approximately one-fourth of the total cost of the campaign. By 1996, television expenses were approximately $100 million. Although significant, however, this amount pales by comparison with what major corporations such as AT&T, Coca Cola, Proctor and Gamble, and McDonald's spent on advertising during the Olympics of that year.

Polling. The use of other modern technology has also increased expenditures. In 1968, Democrats Hubert Humphrey and George McGovern spent a combined $650,000 on polling, whereas in 1972, the Nixon campaign alone spent more than $1.6 million.[6] In 1996, these expenses totalled almost $4.5 million for Clinton and Dole in the presidential nomination and election campaigns; in 2000, they were even greater for the major party contenders.[7]

Fund-Raising. Finally, the costs of fund-raising have increased. In the past, candidates depended on a relatively small number of major contributors from whom they could personally solicit the funds they needed. Today, most of them depend on a relatively large number of smaller contributors. Although the average size of the contribution has increased in recent years, the proportion of the adult population giving money to candidates has declined. In the 1990s, only about 4 percent of the population contributed to campaigns.[8] The need for private funds combined with the declining proportion of givers has forced candidates to devote considerable time, money, and effort to fund-raising activities.

Dwight Eisenhower was the first presidential candidate to make use of the direct mail technique to raise money. His letter to *Reader's Digest* subscribers promising to go to Korea to end the war generated a substantial financial return for his campaign. Unable to obtain support from their parties' regular contributors, Barry Goldwater in 1964 and George McGovern in 1972 targeted appeals to partisans and other sympathizers. Their success in winning their party's nomination, coming from well behind in the preelection polls, combined with changes in the law that prohibited large gifts yet ultimately required more spending, has made direct mail solicitation essential for parties and candidates alike. In 1992, Pat Buchanan depended on it to raise $4 million. Robert Dole raised about 30 percent of his funds from direct mail in 1996. Bill Clinton's first direct mail effort brought in $2 million. Deducting the costs of the mailing but adding government matching funds, the Clinton campaign's profit was a hefty $3.6 million.[9]

Three major issues arise from the problems of large expenditures. One pertains to the donors. Who pays, how much can they give, and what do they get for their money? A second relates to the costs. Are they too high, and can they be controlled without impinging on First Amendment freedoms? The third concerns the impact of spending on the election itself. To what extent does it improve a candidate's chances of winning? The next section turns to the first of these questions — private sources of financial support and attempts to regulate them.

THE SOURCES OF SUPPORT

Throughout most of U. S. electoral history, parties and candidates have depended on large contributions. In the midst of the industrial boom at the end of the nineteenth century, the Republicans were able to count on the support of the Astors, Harrimans, and Vanderbilts; while the Democrats looked to financier August Belmont (American representative of the Rothschild banking interests) and inventor-industrialist Cyrus McCormick. Corporations, banks, and life insurance companies soon became prime targets of party fund-raisers. The most notorious and probably most adroit fund-raiser of this period was Mark Hanna. A leading official of the Republican Party, Hanna owed most of his influence to his ability to obtain substantial political contributions. He set quotas, personally assessing the amount that businesses and corporations should give. In 1896, and again in 1900, he was able to obtain contributions of $250,000 from Standard Oil. Theodore Roosevelt personally ordered the return of some of the Standard Oil money in 1904 but accepted large gifts from magnates E. H. Harriman and Henry C. Frick.[10] Roosevelt's trust-busting activities during his presidency led Frick to remark, "We bought the son of a bitch and then he did not stay bought."[11]

Sizable private gifts remained the principal source of party and candidate support until the mid-1970s. In 1972, Richard Nixon and George McGovern raised an estimated $27 million from fewer than two hundred individual contributors.[12] In general, the Republicans benefited more than the Democrats from wealthy contributors, known in the campaign vernacular as "fat cats." Only in 1964 was a Democrat — incumbent Lyndon B. Johnson, who enjoyed a large lead in the preelection polls — able to raise more money from large donors than his Republican opponent, Barry Goldwater.

The reluctance of regular Republican contributors to support the Goldwater candidacy forced his organization to appeal to thousands of potential supporters through direct mail. The success of this effort — raising $5.8 million from approximately 651,000 people — showed the potential of a popular appeal for funds and shattered an unwritten "rule" of politics that money could not be raised through the mail. In 1968, Alabama Governor George Wallace, running as a third-party candidate, solicited the bulk of his funds in this fashion as have other lesser-known candidates since then.

Despite the use of mass mailings and party telethons to broaden the base of political contributors in the 1960s, dependence on large donors continued. In 1964, more than $2 million was raised in contributions of $10,000 or more. Eight years later, approximately $51 million was collected in gifts of this size or larger. Some gifts were in the million-dollar range.

The magnitude of these contributions, combined with the heavy-handed tactics of the Nixon fund-raisers in 1971–72, brought into sharp focus the difficulty of maintaining a democratic selection process that was dependent on private funding.[13] Reliance on large contributors who did not wish to be identified, the inequality of funding between parties and candidates, and the high cost of campaigning, especially in the mass media, all raised serious issues. Were there assumptions implicit in giving and receiving? Could elected officials be responsive to individual benefactors and to the general public at the same time? Put another way, did the need to obtain large contributors and keep them "happy" affect decision making in a manner that was inconsistent with the tenets of a democratic society — that all people have equal influence on the selection of and access to public officials? Did the high cost of campaigning, in and of itself, eliminate otherwise qualified candidates from running? Were certain political parties, interest groups, or individuals consistently advantaged or disadvantaged by the distribution of funding? Had the presidency become an office that only the wealthy could afford — or that only those with wealthy supporters could seek?

FINANCE LEGISLATION

Reacting to these issues, Congress in the 1970s enacted far-reaching legislation designed to reduce dependence on major donors who contribute large amounts of money, discourage illegal contributions, broaden the base of public support, and control escalating costs at the presidential level. Additionally, the Democratic Congress that passed these laws wanted to equalize the funds available to the Republican and Democratic nominees. Finally, the legislation was designed to buttress the two-party system, making it more difficult for minor candidates to challenge the major parties' nominees for elective office successfully.

One law, the Federal Election Campaign Act of 1971 (FECA), set ceilings on the amount of money presidential and vice presidential candidates and their families could contribute to their own campaigns and the amount that could be spent on media advertising. It allowed unions and corporations to form political action committees (PACs), consisting of their members, employees, and stockholders, to solicit voluntary contributions to be given to candidates or parties or to fund the group's election activities. The FECA also established procedures for the public disclosure of all contributions over a certain amount.

A second statute, the Revenue Act of 1971, created tax credits and deductions to encourage private contributions. It also provided the basis for public funding by creating a presidential election campaign fund. Financed by an income tax checkoff provision, the fund initially allowed a taxpayer to designate one dollar of federal income taxes to a special presidential election account.

These laws began a period of federal government regulation of national elections. The history of that regulation is a history of good intentions built on political compromise but marred by unintended consequences of the legislation and its implementation, caused by candidates and parties circumventing the letter and spirit of the law to gain electoral advantage.

Partisan compromises in the enactment of campaign finance legislation were evident from the outset. Although the original funding provision was enacted in 1971, it did not go into effect until the 1976 presidential election. Most Republicans had opposed the policy of government financial support and regulation. In addition to conflicting with their general ideological position that the national government's role in the conduct of elections be limited, it offset their party's traditional fund-raising advantage. President Nixon was persuaded to sign the bill only after the Democratic leadership agreed to delay the year in which the law became effective until after Nixon ran for reelection in 1972.

There was also a short but critical delay in the effective date for the disclosure provision of the other 1971 campaign finance act. Signed by the president on February 14, 1972, it was scheduled to take effect in sixty days. This delay precipitated a frantic attempt by both parties to tap major donors who wished to remain anonymous. It is estimated that the Republicans collected $20 million, much of it pledged beforehand, during this period. Of this money, approximately $1.5 million came in forms that could not be easily traced.

Even after the disclosure provision went into effect, violations were numerous. Moreover, pressure on corporate executives by Nixon campaign officials, resulted in a long list of "gifts" that seemed to be in violation of the ban on contributions by corporations and labor unions. The spending of funds on "dirty tricks" and other unethical and illegal activities, such as the break-in of the Democratic National Committee's headquarters, further aroused public ire and eventually resulted in new and even more stringent legislation.

Congress responded by amending the FECA. New provisions, passed in 1974, included public disclosure provisions, contribution ceilings for individuals and groups, spending limits for the campaigns, federal subsidies for major party candidates in the nomination process, and complete funding for them in the general election. It also limited the amount candidates could contribute to their own campaign and the amount that others could spend independently on their behalf. The limits on media advertising were removed. Finally, the 1974 amendments established a six-person commission — the Federal Election Commission (FEC) — to enforce the law, of which two members were to be appointed by the president and four by Congress.

The 1974 amendments were highly controversial. Critics immediately charged a federal giveaway, a raid on the treasury. Opponents of the legislation also argued that the limits on contributions and spending violated the constitutionally guaranteed right to freedom of speech, that the funding provisions unfairly discriminated against third-party and independent candidates, and that appointment of four commissioners by Congress violated the principle of separation of powers.

One year after the amendments were enacted, the Supreme Court declared some portions of the law unconstitutional.

In the landmark decision of *Buckley v. Valeo* (424 U.S. 1, 1976), the Court upheld the right of Congress to regulate campaign expenditures but negated two principal parts of the law: the overall limits on nonparty spending, and the appointment by Congress of four of the six election commissioners. The majority opinion contended that by placing restrictions on the amount of money an individual or group could spend during a campaign, the law directly and substantially restrained freedom of speech, a freedom protected by the First Amendment to the Constitution. The Supreme Court did allow limits on contributions to candidates' campaigns, however, and limits on expenditures of those candidates who accepted public funds but not those who refused these funds. In doing so, the justices acknowledged that large, often secret, contributions and rapidly increasingly expenditures did pose problems for a democracy, problems that Congress could address.

The Court's decision required that the election law be amended once again. It took Congress several months to do so. In the spring of 1976, during the presidential primaries of that year, amendments were enacted that continued public funding of the presidential nomination and election campaigns, based on a figure of $10 million in 1974 to be adjusted for inflation, but did so on a voluntary basis. Candidates did not have to accept government funds, but if they did, they were limited in how much they and others could contribute to their own campaigns and how much those campaigns could spend. The Federal Election Commission was reconstituted with all six members to be nominated by the president and appointed subject to the advice and consent of the Senate. The law required that three commissioners be Democrats and three be Republicans, a formula for indecisiveness based on partisan division.

In 1979, additional amendments to the FECA were passed. Designed to reduce the reporting requirements of the law, these amendments raised the minimum contribution and expenditure that had to be filed from $100 to $200. To encourage voluntary activities and higher voter turnout, they also permitted party committees to raise and spend an unlimited and unreported amount of money on party-building activities such as on registration and getting out the vote.

Known as the *soft money provision*, this amendment created a gigantic loophole in the law. It permitted — even encouraged — national parties to solicit large contributions and distribute the money to their state and local affiliates as they saw fit. It was not until 1992 that the FEC imposed reporting requirements on all soft-money contributions over $200, the total amount of money that the national party allocated to the states, and the individual expenses they spent on soft-money operations.

The amendments to the FECA enacted in 1979 also increased the base grant for nominating conventions of the major parties to $3 million. In 1984, this was subsequently increased to $4 million, an amount that is now adjusted for inflation.

The last change in finance legislation occurred in 1993, when the Democratic Congress raised the individual taxpayer's donation from $1 to $3. This increase, approximately equal to the inflation that had occurred over the twenty-year period, was necessitated by an expected shortfall in funds. In 1980, 28.7 percent of the returns (in which people owed taxes to the government) designated that $1 or $2 (depending whether the return was individual or joint) go to the election fund; by the mid-1990s, the percentage designating tax dollars into the fund had declined to less than 13 percent, and it has continued to decline.[14] (For a summary of the key provisions of the law, see Box 2–1, "Key Provisions of Campaign Finance Legislation." For guidelines on how to obtain information from the FEC, see Box 2–2, "How to Get Information from the Federal Election Commission.")

BOX 2–1 ★

KEY PROVISIONS OF CAMPAIGN FINANCE LEGISLATION

Public Disclosure: All contributions of $200 or more must be identified. All expenditures of $200 or more must be reported. Campaign committees are also required to file periodic reports before the election and a final report after it.

Contribution Limits: In any election, including a primary, contributions from an individual cannot exceed $1,000 to a single candidate, $20,000 to a national political party committee, and $5,000 to other political committees, with the total not to exceed $25,000 in any one year.

    Personal contributions from candidates or their immediate families are limited to $50,000 at the prenomination stage and to $50,000 in the general election if a candidate accepts federal funds. Candidates who do not accept federal funds are not limited to what they can contribute to their own campaign. Individuals and political action committees can spend an unlimited amount on their own for candidates of their choice, provided they do not consult or communicate in any way with the candidate's campaign organization.

Campaign Expenses: Candidates who accept public funding cannot spend more than $10 million in their quest for the nomination and $20 million in the general election plus a cost-of-living increment calculated from the base year of 1974. In 2000, the limits were $33.8 million in the postconvention period plus a 20 percent increment for fund-raising ($6.8 million), another 15 percent for compliance to FEC rules ($5.1 million) for a total of $45.7 million. In the general election, the major party candidates were able to spend about $67.6 million; however, they could also raise additional money from private donors to pay for accounting and legal costs to comply with the law, the General Election Legal and Accounting Fund.

    There are also specific spending limits in the states for nomination expenditures. These limits are based on the size of the voting-age population in the state. They ranged from a low of $675,600 in the smallest states to a high of $13,091,507 in California. Candidates who do not accept federal funds have no limit on their expenditures. Additionally, the national parties can spend $.02 per citizen of voting age in support of their presidential and vice presidential candidates. State and local parties can, however, spend unlimited amounts on voluntary efforts to get out the vote.

Matching Funds: Major party contenders who raise $5,000 in twenty states in contributions of $250 or less, a total of $100,000, are eligible to receive matching grants during the prenomination period, which begins January 1 of the year in which the election occurs. Only the first $250 of each contribution is matched. In 1996, the government provided almost $56 million in matching funds; in 2000, it provided over $60 million.

With three party nomination conventions eligible for federal funds and with the money that has to be set aside for candidates in the general election, the FEC had another shortfall in the presidential election campaign fund for the 2000 nomination process, which lasted until mid-June.

Communication Notices: All authorized advertisements by candidates' organizations must state the name of the candidate or agent who authorized them. All nonauthorized advertisements must identify the person who made or financed the ad and his or her organizational affiliation, if any.

Compliance Procedures: The Federal Election Commission has authority to investigate possible violations, hold hearings, and assess certain civil penalties. Its decision may be appealed to U. S. District Courts. The Justice Department retains the authority for criminal investigation and prosecution.

BOX 2–2 ★

HOW TO GET INFORMATION FROM THE FEDERAL ELECTION COMMISSION

The FEC makes a wealth of data available to the public. You can access much of it from the FEC's on-line Web site <http://www.fec.gov>. Its home page gives the following menu options:

Citizens Guide to Contributions and the Law
Using FEC Services
Financial Information about Candidates, Parties, and PACs
Help for Candidates, Parties, and PACs
About Elections and Voting
News Releases, Media Advisories
View Contributions and Financial Reports by Presidential and House
    Campaigns, Parties, and PACs
Additional options may be added in the near future.

In addition, the commission has an automated FlashFax service that operates twenty-four hours a day, seven days a week. More than three hundred documents, including reporting forms, statistical studies, and rules and regulations, can be faxed quickly and without cost to you. Just call the FlashFax automated telephone line at (202) 501-3413 to request up to three documents per call.

If you do not know the number of a document or whether a document with the information you want exists, call the FEC's Public Records Office at (800) 424-9530. The FEC will also mail documents directly to you, usually without charge.

The increase in taxpayer contributions, which went into effect in 1994, provided sufficient money to fund the 1996 elections although over the first few months matching grants had to be distributed on a pro rata basis because the election funds had not been completely replenished. A pro rata distribution occurred again in 2000. The FEC initially matched eligible contributions on a pro rata basis of 50 percent. It was not until June 2000 that candidates received their full amount. Had leading candidate and money raiser, George W. Bush, not declined federal funds, the shortfall would have been greater and the initial pro rata payout less.

THE IMPACT OF THE LAW

Campaign finance legislation has had a significant impact on presidential elections. It has affected the base of contributors, the modes of solicitation, and the objects of spending. It has changed the role of the government, modifying the relationship between the party and its nominees, and influencing the strategies and tactics of the campaign.

Revenue

Individual Contributors. One of the most important objectives of the law was to reduce the influence that a small number of major contributors had on the presidential nomination and election. To some extent it has succeeded, particularly in the nomination phase of the process. No longer can candidates depend on a few wealthy friends to finance their quest for their party's nomination. The $1,000 limit on individual donors, which is not subject to a cost-of-living adjustment, the $250 ceiling on matching grants, and the eligibility requirements for federal funds have made the solicitation of a large number of contributors absolutely essential, more so now than in the past. Not only are campaigns increasingly expensive but the purchasing power of today's dollar is approximately one-third of what it was in 1976. Candidates thus need more than three times the number of donors than they did when the law first went into effect. Table 2–3 lists the total amount of individual contributions in the 1996 preconvention period.

In addition to gifts from individuals, which are the largest single source of revenues, candidates have found other ways to supplement their campaign funds. They can provide some of their own money. There is no restriction on the amount of their personal funds that can be spent in the years prior to the election, until their candidacy is formally established. At the point of candidacy, a $50,000 personal contribution limit is imposed if a candidate accepts federal funds. There is no personal limit for the candidate who does not accept federal funds. Thus, in 1992, H. Ross Perot was able to spend over $63 million of his own money on his campaign in lieu of accepting government funds. In 1996, he chose to accept federal funds and thus was limited to $50,000. He spent more than $8 million, however, to secure the Reform party nomination, fund its nominating conventions, and get the party on the ballot in all fifty states for the general election. The single largest personal contributor was Steve Forbes, who spent close to $38 million of his own fortune in 1996 and more than $48 million in 2000 on his unsuccessful attempts to win the Republican nomination.

TABLE 2–3 ★

PRENOMINATION REVENUES OF MAJOR PARTY CANDIDATES IN 2000 (THROUGH JULY 31, 2000)

Candidate	Federal Matching Funds	Individual Contributions Minus Refunds	PAC Contributions Minus Refunds	Other Revenues	Adjusted Campaign Total
Democratic					
Bradley	$12,462,045	$29,270,589	$0	$409,931	$42,142,565
Gore	$15,317,872	$33,871,206	$0	$13,667	$49,202,745
LaRouche	$1,184,372	$3,319,038	$590	$1,658	$4,505,658
Total Democrats	$28,964,289	$66,460,833	$590	$425,256	$95,850,968
Republicans					
Alexander	$0	$2,301,747	$80,383	$703,501	$3,085,631
Bauer	$4,632,803	$7,553,317	$6,000	−$55,572	$12,136,548
Bush	$0	$91,331,951	$1,960,060	$1,174,330	$94,466,341
Dole	$0	$5,001,635	$118,292	$7,905	$5,127,832
Forbes	$0	$5,752,150	$0	$42,392,826	$48,144,976
Hatch	$0	$2,124,707	$173,016	$255,000	$2,552,723
Kasich	$0	$1,702,668	$77,224	$1,411,191	$3,191,083
Keyes	$3,325,340	$7,663,253	$10,100	$1,059	$10,999,752
McCain	$14,467,788	$28,143,613	$405,599	$2,030,937	$45,047,937
Quayle	$2,087,748	$4,083,201	$43,200	$103,546	$6,317,695
Smith	$0	$1,522,128	$17,070	$75,000	$1,614,198
Total Republican	$24,513,679	$157,180,370	$2,890,944	$48,099,723	$232,684,716
Others					
Buchanan	$3,852,247	$6,651,221	$1,000	$31,967	$10,536,435
Hagelin	$314,135	$755,319	$0	$110,526	$1,179,980
Nader	$100,000	$1,319,434	$0	$44,133	$1,463,567
Browne	$0	$1,217,198	$0	$31,000	$1,248,198
Total Others	$4,266,382	$9,943,172	$1,000	$217,626	$14,428,180
Grand Total	$57,744,350	$233,584,375	$2,892,543	$48,742,605	$342,963,864

Source: Federal Election Commission, September 2000.

Borrowing money from financial institutions is also allowed. The law permits candidates to obtain loans (if they can), provided that the terms of payment are clear and that the money is lent in accordance with regular business practices. Most major party candidates borrow money. They have to do so. The increasing number of early primaries and caucuses have forced them to get as much up-front money as soon as possible.[15] In March 1992, the Clinton campaign borrowed $1.4

million from an Arkansas bank to have sufficient funds for the Super Tuesday southern regional primaries that occurred in early March. In 1996, Clinton had no need to borrow money, but the Democratic National Committee did so in order to finance the party's early generic advertising. Borrowing continued in 2000.

Funds raised but not spent by candidates in their campaigns for other offices, such as for the Senate, House of Representatives, or a state governorship, can be used in their quest for the presidential nomination. Senator Phil Gramm moved $5 million from his previous Senate campaigns into his presidential election fund for the 1996 campaign while John McCain transferred $2 million from his Senate account to fund the initial stages of his 2000 campaign for the Republican nomination.

Although $1,000 is the maximum individual gift, voluntary goods and services are unrestricted. Artists and musicians, in particular, can generate considerable revenue for candidates by offering their time and talent. Concerts, and to a lesser extent art sales, have become excellent sources of revenue. One thousand dollar-a-plate dinners have become a particularly popular way to bring in large amounts of money early in the nomination process. Phil Gramm launched his presidential bid for the 1996 Republican nomination with a Texas barbecue that raised $4.1 million. Clinton raised almost $6 million in one week of fund-raising dinners and galas in June 1995. The same fund-raising pattern repeated itself during the 2000 nomination contest, only it began earlier. By the end of 1999, Democrats Al Gore and Bill Bradley had raised the maximum allowed by law for candidates who received matching funds. George W. Bush had raised over $69 million. (See Box 2–3, "Al Gore's Profitable Trip to the Big Apple" and Box 2–4, "The Money Race for the 2000 Nomination.")

Nonparty Groups and Other Organizations. Although election law prohibits corporations and labor unions from making direct contributions to political campaigns, it does allow their employees, stockholders, or members to form PACs and fund them through voluntary contributions. These groups can directly affect the presidential selection process in four ways: by endorsing a candidate, by giving up to $5,000 to a single candidate, by spending an unlimited amount of money *independently* for or against a candidate, and by communicating to their members and then using their organization to turn out voters.

Surprisingly, direct donations to the presidential candidates are their least important source of revenue. They receive only a small portion of their contributions from PACs, if they accept those contributions at all. George W. Bush banked the most money from PACs, but it constituted only 2 percent of the total amount he received. Neither Bill Bradley nor Al Gore accepted PAC donations in 2000.

Leadership PACs. PACs have proven to be so important that presidential candidates now regularly form their own in the precandidacy stage of their campaign. Known as *leadership PACs,* they have been used primarily to fund organizational activities, build support, and defray travel and other expenses of candidates in the years preceding the presidential election. In addition, money is often given to

BOX 2–3 ★

AL GORE'S PROFITABLE TRIP TO THE BIG APPLE

Vice President Al Gore has proven to be a skilled fund-raiser. Here's how Ceci Connolly, a reporter for the *Washington Post*, describes his three-hour trip to New York in March 1999 which netted pledges of $1.5 million for Gore's 2000 presidential campaign:

> On a blustery evening in early March, the vice president's motorcade is racing from event to event on Manhattan's Upper East Side. It's a familiar tour of the names and addresses that make up the New York Democratic fund-raising circuit.
>
> First stop, the Park Avenue apartment of Christopher Williams, president and CEO of Williams Capital Group, where Gore meets with 20 African American supporters who have volunteered to raise $5,000 apiece for his campaign. . . .
>
> After 20 minutes, it's off to Restaurant Daniel, and a bite with 32 high-tech and entertainment executives who will raise $10,000 apiece.
>
> "This is a group of wonderful friends," Gore says, "and I am grateful for your willingness to be so involved in this presidential campaign."
>
> Handshakes, and then he's out the door again, this time heading to the Fifth Avenue apartment of Steve Rattner and the evening's highest-powered collection: Each of the 40 guests has pledged to raise $35,000.
>
> "I want to tell you all how grateful I am," says the vice president, "for your support, friendship, your advice, your encouragement and for you to be here at this event at the very beginning of my campaign for president."
>
> Forty minutes later, Gore is aboard Air Force 2 for the quick flight home to Washington.

Source: Ceci Connolly, "The $55 Million Man," *Washington Post Magazine,* April 4, 1999, 25.

other candidates for their campaigns in the midterm elections. This money is intended to generate reciprocal support for the presidential nominee later on.

One of the earliest and most successful of these leadership PACs was Citizens for the Republic. Started in 1977, this organization had within a year raised $2.5 million and spent $1.9 million on operations. Most of this money was used for fund-raising, travel, and other expenses of the PAC's principal speaker, Ronald Reagan. In the process of raising money, the organization developed a list of more than 300,000 contributors. This list was purchased for a nominal fee by the Reagan campaign committee. The Reagan PAC became the prototype for other presidential candidates.

Leadership PACs have become a critical fund-raising instrument. They allow candidates to tap potential donors several times, once during each year of a PAC's existence, and then again after their formal candidacy has been declared. The advent of this type of PAC has effectively elongated the presidential selection process by encouraging candidates to create their own PAC and involving them in campaign activities in the year or two before the election cycle begins.[16] As of 1998, most of the major contenders for their party's 2000 nomination had created their own leadership PAC.

Senator Robert Dole is a good example of a presidential candidate who benefited from the prepresidential campaign activities of his PAC, Campaign America. Not only did Dole receive endorsements from many of the Republican officials to whom his PAC had contributed in their previous campaigns, but his presidential organization began its own fund-raising efforts with a list of 500,000 contributors to his PAC. Al Gore is another. In 1997, he organized Leadership 98 with the primary purpose of raising money for Democratic candidates in 1998. By 1999, however, the PAC refocused its efforts on Gore's precandidacy activities for the 2000 presidential nomination.

In addition to leadership PACs, candidates have also established advocacy PACs in states such as Virginia that do not limit the size of contributions. Money raised by these PACs cannot be used in federal campaigns, but it can be spent on issue advocacy, polling to gauge public reaction to this advocacy, as well as expenses which are incurred in the promotion of its views. Lamar Alexander raised several million dollars in this manner and spent it testing policy appeals for his 2000 presidential campaign. Dan Quayle, Gary Bauer, and Pat Buchanan also established Virginia PACs to promote their ideas.

Alexander had tried another tactic four years earlier. He founded a nonprofit corporation, the Republican Exchange Satellite Network, that produced and distributed monthly television shows about public policy, starring Alexander. Funding for the network, raised from private donors, was not subject to reporting requirements or contribution limits of the Federal Election Campaign Act. Thus, Alexander was able to obtain relatively large sums of money from a few wealthy individuals. Additionally, he was able to go back to these same donors for more limited contributions and for help in soliciting other donations once his presidential campaign officially began in 1995.[17]

Matching Funds and Government Grants. In addition to individuals and non-party groups, a third source of money is the government itself. Presidential candidates can receive government matching grants for the nomination process and outright support for the general election. In 2000, these federal subsidies and grants amounted to over $60 million. Figure 2–1 shows matching fund grants since 1976. Since then, Democratic candidates have received about $149 million compared with $159 million for the Republicans through 2000. Bill Clinton has been the largest beneficiary, receiving $25 million in 1992 and $26 million four years later.

Here's how matching grants work. After they have filed as a candidate, eligible federal candidates who receive individual contributions up to $250 in the year of or in the year before the election can match those contributions by an equal amount from the federal election fund in the calendar year of the election. To be eligible, candidates must raise $5,000 in twenty states in contributions of $250 or less, a total of $100,000.

FIGURE 2–1 ★

MATCHING GRANTS, 1976–2000
(IN MILLIONS OF DOLLARS)

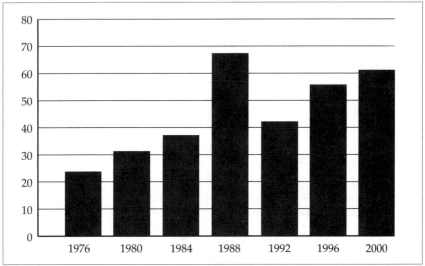

Source: Federal Election Commission, *The Presidential Public Funding Program* (April 1993), 9; updated from data supplied by the Federal Election Commission through September 30, 2000.

Remaining eligible for matching funds is somewhat harder than qualifying to receive them because of the 10 percent rule, a requirement that candidates receive at least 10 percent of the vote in two consecutive primaries in which they are entered. If they are entered in more than one primary on a given day, they need to win 10 percent in only one of them. Failing to receive 10 percent negates their eligibility for federal funds until such time as they receive at least 20 percent of the vote in a subsequent primary.[18] This rule helps front-running candidates and adversely affects those who are lesser known or may be minority candidates. Twice during the 1984 campaign Jesse Jackson lost his eligibility for matching funds, only to regain it later. Consequently, to ensure their continued eligibility, marginal candidates have tended to avoid nonessential contests.[19]

Minor party candidates are also eligible for matching funds if they seek their party's nomination. Lenora Fulani, New Alliance Party, and John Hagelin, Natural Law Party, qualified in 1992 and Hagelin qualified again in 1996 and 2000, as did Pat Buchanan (Reform Party) and Ralph Nader (Green Party), but the amount they received was minimal compared to candidates for major party nominations. Nonetheless, the eligibility of minor party candidates has led to the criticism that this provision encourages candidates to run who have no chance of winning, wasting taxpayers' money in the process.

In general, the matching-fund provision does provide greater opportunities for lesser-known aspirants to seek their party's nomination, but it has not substantially reduced the financial advantage that nationally recognized candidates have.

Moreover, it encourages all candidates to begin their fund-raising well before the election in order to qualify as soon as possible. When Robert Dole announced his candidacy for the 1996 Republican nomination, his organization mailed 1.5 million letters to potential donors asking for contributions; similarly, Al Gore authorized a mailing to 850,000 people requesting donations shortly after he established an exploratory committee for the 2000 Democratic nomination.[20]

Convention and Election Grants. Federal funding is also extended to the major parties for their national nominating conventions. The convention grant in 1996 was $12,364,000 for each party; in 2000 it was $13,512,000. The Reform Party received $2.5 million, an amount based on its percent of the vote in the last election. Parties may also seek convention funding from the cities and states in which the event occurs. These state and local supplements can be substantial.

Once the major party candidates have been officially chosen, they are eligible for a direct grant for the general election. In 1996, $61.8 million was given to the Republican and Democratic candidates; in 2000, it was $67.6 million. The actual dollar figure is calculated in the election year by the FEC on the basis of the rate of inflation.

To be eligible for federal funds, major party candidates must agree to limit their campaign expenditures to the amount of the grant. To comply with the law, they cannot accept private contributions except those designated for accounting and legal fees. Minor party candidates, who may receive private contributions, are also eligible for federal funds in amounts equal to the proportion of the vote they receive, provided it is at least 5 percent of the total. Had Perot accepted federal funds in 1992, he would have received $25.96 million, 47 percent of the amount the major party candidates were given; however, he would have received it *after* the election was over. Automatically eligible for federal funds in 1996 because of the size of the vote he received in 1992, Perot got $29 million; in 2000, the Reform Party nominee, Pat Buchanan, was eligible for $12.6 million from the campaign fund, but the small vote he received makes the party ineligible for federal funds in 2004.[21]

When Perot decided not to accept federal funds in 1992, he was exempted from the $50,000 limit on personal contributions. His campaign was also exempted from the overall spending limits to which the major party candidates were subject. Perot's campaign expenditures totaled $68.4 million compared to $55.2 for Clinton and Bush (plus their legal and accounting expenses which are not subject to this limit). Most of Perot's campaign revenue in that election, $63.3 million, came from his own personal fortune. Because he chose to accept federal funds in 1996, Perot could not use more than $50,000 of his own money, but he could raise additional funds to bring his total amount up to the level of the two major party candidates. His campaign, however, conducted only a modest fund-raising effort.

For other independent and third-party candidates who do not have the personal wealth or organizational support to finance their presidential efforts, who need federal funds, and who are still constrained by the limits on personal ($50,000), individual ($1,000), and nonparty group ($5,000) contributions, the law makes it very difficult to raise sufficient money to mount an effective campaign. In other words, the FECA works to the advantage of those who enacted it — the candidates and organizations of the two major parties.

In the seven presidential elections since the law went into effect, Democratic primary and presidential candidates have received a total of $638 million and their Republican counterparts have received about $659 million. In contrast, only $50 million have gone to minor party or independent candidates.

Hard and Soft Money. Direct federal grants to the candidates are not their only source of funds. They can also benefit from the money political parties raise and spend. The parties broke all records for revenue and expenditures in 2000.

There are two classifications of money that the parties can raise: hard and soft. Hard money is subject to individual and group contribution limits; soft money is not; hard money can be used by the party to promote its presidential and vice presidential candidates by name; soft money cannot. Each of the major parties could spend $13.7 million on behalf of their presidential candidates in 2000. Soft money may not be spent directly on the presidential candidates, though it may be used to benefit them indirectly through party-building activities such as issue advocacy, generic advertising, and registering potential supporters and getting them out to vote. It may also be used to pay for the administrative expenses incurred by the party in conducting these activities, as well as direct support for state and local candidates.

In the first two presidential elections after the soft money amendment was enacted, the Republicans enjoyed a large advantage. Since 1988, their lead has continued. The Republicans raised a total of $554.7 million in hard and soft money while the Democrats raised $345.5 million in the 1995–1996 election cycle. Both figures were up considerably in the 1999–2000 cycle. From January 1, 1999 to October 18, 2000, the Republicans raised $506 million ($295 million in hard money and $211 million in soft money), while the Democrats raised $372 million ($173 million in hard money and $199 million in soft money).[22]

Although the national parties solicit most of the soft money, they distribute a substantial portion of it to their state and local affiliates. They do not do so out of charity. Since the expenditures of the national party on its candidates for federal office are strictly limited by law, giving soft money to the state parties and suggesting that they spend some of it on "educational campaigns" that benefit all of the party's candidates, including those who seek national office, is a tactic that both national committees used to increase their spending and thereby circumvent the limits of the law. State parties can sponsor generic advertisements in which policy positions of the candidates and the parties are discussed and evaluated but no specific recommendation about whom to vote for is made. It can be used for party-building activities such as operating telephone banks, printing and distributing campaign literature, and recruiting field organizers and other political operatives.

Apparently it is also legal for the national parties in conjunction with their presidential candidates to direct these state activities, going so far as to indicate which advertisements should be bought and when and where they should be aired, or at least so a 1998 FEC ruling seems to suggest. This practice, used aggressively by both parties in 1996, was challenged by FEC auditors after the election as an illegal activity; the auditors recommended that millions of dollars ($7 million for Clinton-Gore and $17.7 million for Dole-Kemp) be repaid to the federal treasury. But the commission, consisting of three Democrats and three

Republicans, disagreed the law had been violated and did not support the repayments. The commission's decision has precipitated a no-holds-barred race to acquire millions for generic advertising in 2000, a race in which both major party candidates have aggressively participated, as did President Clinton.[23] Record sums of soft money were raised in 2000.

The parties are not the only groups that can raise and spend soft money. Political action committees, even those established by candidates, can do so. Steve Forbes established such a PAC, Americans for Hope, Growth, and Opportunity, in 1997. The organization which supports issues that Forbes has proposed in his presidential campaigns such as a flat tax and school choice raised more than $13 million from 140,000 donors, until it was terminated in 1999.[24]

There are other ways to circumvent the spending limits in the nomination process. Since 1992, both parties' presidential candidates have depended on the state parties to pay for staff who were based in the states. This arrangement has enabled the major party candidates to operate with relatively small national staffs, reducing their administrative overhead and their need to fund large grassroots organizations and permitting them to devote much of the public funds to media advertising.

The amount raised and the inducements offered have engendered considerable media scrutiny, public and partisan criticism, and Senate and House investigations of improper and unethical campaign finance activities. The Democrats were forced to return millions of dollars to contributors whose status to make legal contributions could not be established. Only American citizens, foreign nationals who are residents in the country, and U.S. subsidiaries of foreign-owned companies and corporations can make contributions. However, according to a 1998 U.S. District court decision, this prohibition does *not* apply to soft money contributions.[25]

The president and vice president were also accused of abusing the perquisites of their office in soliciting money for their reelection campaign. Clinton was even charged with making policy decisions to benefit his contributors, including foreign policy decisions that some Republicans claimed may have adversely affected national security.[26] (See Box 2–4, "The Money Race for the 2000 Nomination.")

BOX 2–4 ★

THE MONEY RACE FOR THE 2000 NOMINATION

The money race for the 2000 presidential election began two years before the nomination when George W. Bush and Al Gore mapped their initial strategies and began to assemble their fund-raising teams. Both patterned their plans on Bill Clinton's successful money-raising operation for his renomination and reelection.

THE CLINTON MODEL

The Clinton strategy was designed to achieve three objectives: to demonstrate the president's strength within his party, to reduce the money available for any potential challenger, and to provide his campaign with maximum flexibility in presenting its message and in countering any Republican criticism.

The campaign's financial target — $37 million by the end of 1995, the maximum amount permitted by law — was easily achieved through a combination of $1,000-a-plate-dinners, a direct mail campaign to 1992 contributors, and the recruitment of two hundred well-heeled and well-connected Democrats who each promised to raise $50,000 for the campaign.

But Clinton and his fellow Democrats did not stop here. They solicited millions more in soft-money contributions to pay for generic advertising for the president and other Democratic candidates. It was this effort that got the president, vice president, and other Democratic fund-raisers into trouble. Not only did the party fail to screen its donations to make sure that they were legal, but the fund-raisers took advantage of their control of the White House to host potential contributors. Those in the $50,000 to $100,000 range were treated to intimate dinner parties with the president, sleepovers in the Lincoln bedroom, invitations to state dinners with foreign dignitaries, even rounds of golf with Clinton, and trips on Air Force One. Those who made smaller donations were rewarded with dinners with the vice president, coffee hours at the White House, meetings with cabinet officials, and participation on U.S. trade missions led by the secretary of commerce. Clinton and Gore were heavily involved in these activities. The president attended ninety events during the election year alone, including a birthday celebration which netted the Democrats $10 million.[27] The vice president made fifty-two solicitation telephone calls from his White House office and attended thirty-nine fund-raising events including one held at a Buddhist temple (see photograph on p. 51).[28]

Naturally, the Republicans were outraged by these activities, particularly the use of the public office for partisan purposes. Their party officials and elected leadership protested, but in vain. Ultimately, Republicans employed their control of Congress to raise their own soft money, eventually netting more than the Democrats actually raised. Nonetheless, after the election, Republican leaders in Congress launched official inquiries into the alleged campaign finance illegalities. The congressional hearings, however, failed to generate much public reaction against the president and his party at that time. Nevertheless, residual anger toward politicians of both parties surfaced during the 2000 campaign largely as a consequence of John McCain's appeal to end special interest politics and support of campaign finance reform such as the bill he cosponsored in the Senate (the McCain-Feingold bill).

THE REPUBLICAN CONTEST WITH GEORGE W. BUSH AS THE BIG WINNER

George W. Bush's fund-raising strategy was straightforward. In late 1998 and early 1999, he invited prominent Republicans to Austin, Texas, for informal discussions over lunch. Those who expressed support for Bush's candidacy were invited to join a team of "pioneers," a group of individuals who each promised to raise $100,000 once Bush gave the word that he probably would be a candidate. When an exploratory Bush for President committee was established in the spring of 1999, the pioneers went to work. In just twenty-eight days, they raised a whopping $7.6 million.[29] This torrential fund-raising pace continued throughout the year, with the campaign netting almost $70 million in revenues — the most ever raised by a single presidential candidate.[30]

The size of Bush's war chest helped his campaign in several ways. It was interpreted by the press as a sign of his candidacy's strength. Not only was Bush acknowledged as the Republican front-runner, but his success in fund-raising indicated that he was way ahead of the pack. As a consequence, Bush receive more press coverage and gained greater recognition of his front-runner status, which in turn, generated more contributions.

In addition, the money enabled Bush to establish a relatively large organization of political consultants and campaign operatives, set up field operations in many states, gain political endorsements and the organizational support of other Republicans, and engage in extensive advertising.

Money also afforded Bush more flexibility in designing his campaign strategy than any other Republican candidate, with the possible exception of millionaire Steve Forbes. Only he and Forbes could afford to launch multistate efforts; the rest of the field had to concentrate almost entirely on the early contests. Moreover, because Bush raised so much money, he did not accept federal funds, and thus was not subject to state spending limits as were those who needed the matching grants.

Finally, Bush's large financial lead discouraged other presidential hopefuls from continuing when they found themselves unable to raise anywhere near the amount Bush had in the bank. In short, Bush's money served to thin out the Republican field faster than the primaries and caucuses. It clearly established the significance of the pocketbook vote.

Only Steve Forbes could match Bush's war chest. As long as Forbes continued in the race, he spent lavishly, at or above Bush's level. But Forbes's money could not overcome his image as unelectable. His campaign was mercifully short-lived.

John McCain was not in as dire financial straits as the other Republican candidates. Although he had not raised much more money than they had, he was helped by his decision not to contest Iowa and by the $2 million he was able to transfer from previous Senate campaigns to his presidential effort. This money got him through the pre–New Hampshire period. Once McCain was able to demonstrate his electability by winning big in New Hampshire, he got a large fund-raising bump. Enough money flowed to his campaign to enable him to compete with Bush in the next round of primaries, but never on a completely even keel. McCain had much less to spend on the big state primaries in New York, California, and Ohio on SuperTuesday and practically no funds to spend on the other contests that day or after, had he continued. Money was not the only reason McCain lost, but it contributed to his defeat.

THE DEMOCRATIC CONTEST WITH AL GORE PERCEIVED AS THE LOSER

Al Gore was not able to achieve the kind of money advantage that Bill Clinton enjoyed and that he, as Clinton's heir apparent, was expected to have. His campaign did raise almost $9 million in the first quarter of 1999, but donations declined thereafter. The press quickly interpreted this decline as a lack of enthusiasm for Gore as well as the product of a poorly run fund-raising effort. In October 1999, Gore shook up his sagging campaign, changed top personnel and moved them to Nashville, and began to spend more time "stroking" large donors.[31] His efforts paid off. He eventually raised the maximum amount permitted by law. But he got no advantage from this success. Trailing Bush in the hypothetical election polls, having less money to spend than Bradley, appearing increasingly vulnerable to his Democratic challenger and presumptive Republican opponent, Gore's financial difficulties became a media metaphor for a disappointing campaign. In the eyes of the press, and to some extent, the public, Gore was in the process of losing more than the money race.

Fund-raising was an important component of Bradley's strategy. His plan was to challenge Gore's inevitable renomination by first illustrating his popularity and viability with dollars. Using his contacts from professional basketball, the Wall Street investment community, and Silicon Valley, he matched Gore's bankroll, even exceeding it in the fourth quarter of 1999. Because Bradley did not have an organization of the size and experience of Gore's, he did not incur the same administrative expenses. He ended 1999 with more money in the bank than Gore. His financial success was perceived by the news media as a indication of his strength and Gore's weakness. But Bradley was not able to take advantage of this perception. His financial resources were insufficient to overcome his own limitations as a candidate: his personal reserve and standoffishness, his overly idealistic policy goals accompanied by vague proposals, and especially his inability to relate to core Democratic constituents — African Americans, Latinos, women, and organized labor. In the end it was these limitations, not lack of money, that doomed his candidacy.

In short, a variety of funding sources are available for major party presidential aspirants. These sources, necessitated by the low limits on individual and group contributions which have not been adjusted for inflation, permit political parties, nonparty groups, and wealthy individuals to use their resources to promote the candidate of their choice. The availability of and need for this money has forced those seeking the presidency to spend an increasing amount of time raising money, particularly in the year preceding the nomination. Despite the intent of the FECA to reduce the burdens of this activity and give candidates more time to campaign, much of their initial effort must be devoted to fund-raising.

Expenditures

The additional sources of revenue are necessary because campaign costs keep rising with more candidates seeking their party's nomination and with greater use of the mass media to reach voters. Moreover, in most elections these increases have exceeded the rate of inflation.

The crunch in expenditures represents the greatest problem for candidates at the initial stages of the nomination process. The need to gain recognition, get a boost, or maintain a lead has prompted candidates of both parties to spend much of their money early, well before the first contest is held, and to focus their attention on the states that have the first caucuses and primaries.

As small states, Iowa and New Hampshire have low spending limits. The desire to be free of these limits led three Republican aspirants, John Connally, Steve Forbes, and George W. Bush to reject matching funds in 1980, 1996, and in 2000.

Because of this high early spending, most campaigns are forced to accept government funds and then use their ingenuity to circumvent the state spending limits. In doing so, they have employed a variety of "legal" tactics and some not-so-legal ones. It has become common practice for campaign workers to commute to the early small states from neighboring ones, thus allowing the campaign to allocate only a portion of its expenses to the state in which the early primary would be held. Another legal technique is to use national phone banks to canvas voters within these states. Television ads, particularly those directed at New Hampshire, are aired on Boston television, where 85 percent of the cost can be applied to the Massachusetts limit.[32]

Other questionable tactics include encouraging friendly groups to design and air their own commercials, set up telephone banks, and mount other grassroots activities in support of the campaign. PACs are allowed to communicate with their members but not under the direction or indirect auspices of a candidate's official campaign or party organization. Yet they do have an impact on the campaign. Republicans for Clean Air spent $2.5 million to help George W. Bush. The AFL-CIO ran $21 million of issue ads from January 1999 to August 31, 2000 to help Democrats in general and Al Gore in particular.[33]

In addition to the expenditure ceilings in states based on voting-age population, there is an overall prenomination spending limit. In 2000, it was $40.5 million plus an additional 15 percent for compliance with the FEC's reporting requirements. (See Table 2–4.)

TABLE 2–4 ★

PRESIDENTIAL SPENDING LIMITS AND COLAS
FOR THE DEMOCRATIC AND REPUBLICAN PARTIES,
1976–2000 (IN MILLIONS)

	Unadjusted Limit 1974 Base Year	1976	1980	1984	1988	1992	1996	2000
COLA*	—	9.1%	47.2%	102%	123%	128%	131%	134%
Primary election limit[†]	$10	$10.9	$14.7	$20.2	$23.1	$27.6	$31.0	$33.8
General election limit[‡]	$20	$21.8	$29.4	$40.4	$46.1	$55.2	$61.8	$67.6
Party convention limit[§]	$2	$2.2	$4.4	$8.1	$9.2	$11.0	$12.4	$13.5
Party general election limit (2¢ × voting-age population adjusted by COLA)	—	$3.2	$4.6	$6.9	$8.3	$10.3	$11.6	$13.7

* COLA is the cost-of-living adjustment, which the Department of Labor annually calculates using 1974 as the base year.

† Primary candidates receiving matching funds must comply with two types of spending limits: a national limit (listed in this table) and a separate limit for each state. The state limit is $200,000 or 16¢ multiplied by the state's voting-age population, whichever is greater. (Both amounts are adjusted for increases in the cost of living.) The maximum amount of primary matching funds a candidate may receive is half of the national spending limit. In addition, candidates may spend up to 20 percent of their primary election limit on fund raising.

‡ Legal and accounting expenses to comply with the law are exempt from this limit. These funds may be raised through private contributions.

§ This limit has been raised twice by legislation: once in 1979 and once in 1984.

Source: Federal Election Commission, *Annual Report, 1984* (June 1, 1985), 8–9, updated by the author with data supplied by the Federal Election Commission. For 2000, see Federal Election Commission, "Record," April 2000, 10.

As the campaign progresses candidates do bump up to the total spending ceiling, but since the contests have been effectively settled fairly early in the calendar year, the overall limits have not been as much of a problem as the limits in Iowa and New Hampshire. The overall limits would have been a problem for McCain had he stayed in the race after March 7. They were also a problem for Dole in 1996, but only after he had effectively secured the Republican nomination. Dole had spent within $1.5 million of the maximum amount prior to his nomination by the Republicans by the end of March. He thus had little money left with which to campaign between April and the August 11th start of the Republican national convention. In contrast, his opponent, Bill Clinton, had between $16 and $20 million that he had to spend prior to the Democratic convention in late August.

To survive politically in these circumstances, the Dole nomination campaign sold its computer equipment for $1.4 million to the Dole election committee to pay for staff and the candidate's travels until the Republican convention. As mentioned previously, Dole was also dependent on generic advertising by the Republican Party to counter the Democratic advertising campaign during this period. Both prospective nominees in 2000 were also dependent on their party's soft-money advertisements in key states.

With the concentration of primaries and caucuses on the same days at the beginning of the nomination process, the only way for candidates to reach voters in a number of states during the same time period is through the mass media. Television advertising, in particular, is one of the most expensive forms of communication. Its use increases the costs of running for the major contenders, who will need to raise large sums of money *before* the first primary or caucus is held. Along with operating costs and fund-raising, advertising is a principal source of campaign expenditures.

Independent expenditures have also played a role in the nomination and general election processes although their impact appears to be declining. In 1980, $13.7 million was reported to the FEC as being spent independently on the presidential campaign. In 1984, this figure reached a high point of $17.5 million, with ideological groups spending the bulk of this money. Since 1984, independent spending has declined substantially. In 1996, it was $1.4 million, a tiny fraction of the total expenditures for the presidential election.

When independent expenditures were more significant, they benefited Republicans more than Democrats. The largest differential was in 1984 when $16.3 million was spent on behalf of Ronald Reagan or against Walter Mondale compared with $1.2 expended for Mondale or against Reagan. The proportions have continued to favor the Republicans even though the expenditures in this category have been decreasing. The decline is one consequence of the soft-money loophole which permits individuals and groups to increase their contributions to party and nonparty groups whose "educational," nonpartisan election activities reflect the concerns of these contributors.

But these activities in turn have raised other issues such as illegal collusion among the parties, candidates, and like-minded groups, groups whose advocacy benefits one side over the other. In 1996, the FEC charged that the Christian

Questionable Fund-Raising Activity In April 1996, Vice President Al Gore appeared at a ceremony and fund-raiser at a Buddhist temple in Los Angeles where illegal contributions were made to the Democratic Party. Gore claimed that he did not know the event was a fund-raiser; the party was forced to return the money. *(Photo Source: AP/Wide World Photos)*

Coalition violated the law by coordinating its nonpartisan advocacy advertising with the Republican Party and its candidates, but a federal court dismissed the charges. The Republicans made similar accusations against organized labor in 1996 when union dues financed a $35 million campaign in seventy-five key congressional districts primarily for Democratic candidates.

There have been numerous other allegations about illegal campaign finance activities. Republicans claimed that a Democratic Party fund-raiser in a Buddhist temple in Los Angeles in which Vice President Gore participated violated the law because of that religious institution's nonpartisan status as a tax exempt organization precluded its use for a partisan fund raiser. Questions were also raised about the $5,000 contributions from monks who had taken a vow of poverty and thus probably did not have much, if any, personal wealth. None of the monks were prosecuted, however, and the Democrats returned the money but the accusation plagued Gore throughout his 2000 presidential campaign.[34]

Competition between Parties and Their Candidates

The FECA created competition within and between the major parties and their nominees. This competition was not the intent of the law, but it has been a consequence of it. By providing funds directly to individuals who seek major party nominations, the law facilitates candidacies and candidate organizations within the national parties, thereby initially fractionalizing those parties. The organization of the successful candidate is not dismantled after the nomination; it is expanded and may compete with the regular party organization. On the other hand, the 1979 amendments have encouraged the national parties to mount extensive soft money, fund-raising efforts and distribute much of that money to the state parties thereby making those parties more dependent on the national parties for money. This dependency has contributed to the strengthening of the national parties, as have the rules imposed on the state parties in the presidential nominating process.

MONEY AND ELECTORAL SUCCESS

The relationship between money and electoral success has spurred considerable debate in recent years and generated much anger by those who believe unequal resources undermine the democratic character of the U.S. electoral process. Is the conventional wisdom correct? Do those with more money have an advantage? Do they usually win?

The simple answer is usually "yes," but the longer answer is more complicated. First, who has or gets the money? Second, what difference does the money make in the election?

Two types of candidates tend to have disproportionate resources at their disposal: those who are personally wealthy and those who are well-known public figures. Money can buy recognition as it did for Steve Forbes in 1996; it gave him a chance that he otherwise would not have had. But obviously, it cannot, in and of itself, buy a victory. Similarly, front-runners, such as Robert Dole in 1996, George Bush in 1988, and his son George W. Bush in 2000, can raise more money because they are perceived as likely to win and that money in turn contributes to their likelihood for success. Although it increases the odds, especially for winning their party's nomination, it does not make that nomination inevitable.

The task is harder and more difficult for non-front-runners. They have to establish their viability as candidates. The best way and perhaps the only way to accomplish this is to do surprisingly well early and thereby gain media coverage in time to use that coverage to raise additional funds as John McCain did in 2000. However, the need to do well early creates another money problem — having sufficient funds to spend in the first round of caucuses and primaries. Even if they are successful as McCain was, they may still face an uphill financial battle with a wounded but wealthier front-runner. Yet such candidates have few other options. The failure to do better than expected and/or to gain the coverage necessary to "change" public expectations will likely doom non-front-runners financially, which makes their defeat almost inevitable.[35]

The second money issue pertains to the difference money makes in the vote. Have candidates with the largest bankrolls generally been victorious? In the general elections at the presidential level, the answers seem to be yes, but it is difficult to determine precisely the extent to which money contributed to victory or simply flowed to the likely winner.

Between 1860 and 1972, the winner outspent the loser twenty-one out of twenty-nine times. Republican candidates have spent more than their Democratic opponents in twenty-five out of twenty-nine elections. The four times they did not, the Democrats won. The trend has continued if independent expenditures, partisan communications, and soft money are considered. In the 1980s, considerably more was spent on behalf of Republican nominees than for their Democratic opponents. In the 1990s, the Democrats benefited from substantial expenditures by organized labor to mobilize their members, but their total spending was still less than the Republicans.

What do all these trends suggest? The pattern of greater spending and electoral victories indicates that money contributes to success, but potential success also attracts money. Having more funds is an advantage, but it does not guarantee victory. The fact that heavily favored incumbent Richard Nixon outspent rival George McGovern more than 2 to 1 in 1972 does not explain McGovern's huge defeat, although it probably portended it. On the other hand, Hubert Humphrey's much narrower defeat by Nixon four years earlier was partially influenced by Humphrey's having spent less than $12 million, compared with more than $25 million spent by Nixon. The closer the election, the more the disparity in funds can make a difference.

Theoretically, campaign spending should have a greater impact on the nomination process than on the general election and at the beginning of the process rather than at the end. According to political scientists Michael Robinson, Clyde Wilcox, and Paul Marshall, money matters most when the candidates are least known to the voters, when they do not receive a lot of news coverage, and when paid advertising, which, of course, is expensive, can bring recognition and enhance images.[36]

As the nomination process progresses, as candidates become more easily recognized by the public, the expenditure of funds is not as critical to electoral success. What money buys is recognition, but it may not buy much more. It certainly does not guarantee success, as Phil Gramm and Steve Forbes found out in 1996 and Forbes and Bill Bradley discovered in 2000. Once the nomination is decided, however, money can still be a factor especially if there are several months until the national nominating conventions. This is the lesson that Dole learned in 1996, and the reason Bush continued to raise money in 2000.

Is the expenditure of funds by candidates an important consideration in the general election? Most candidates believe it to be. The 2000 election was characterized by extensive fund-raising by both parties with the aid and support of their presidential nominees. But whether spending more money on more advertising or additional grassroots activities made a difference is difficult to say.[37]

SUMMARY

Campaign finance became an important aspect of presidential elections by the end of the nineteenth and the beginning of the twentieth centuries. In recent years, however, it has become even more important as costs have escalated. Expanded use of high technology and multiple channels of communication to reach the voters has been primarily responsible for the increase.

With few exceptions, candidates of both major parties turned to large contributors, the so-called fat cats, for financial support in the early and mid-twentieth century. Their dependence on a relatively small number of large donors, combined with spiraling costs, created serious problems for the democratic selection process. The 1972 presidential election, with its high expenditures, "dirty tricks," and illegal campaign contributions, vividly illustrated some of these problems and generated public and congressional support for rectifying them.

In the 1970s, Congress enacted and amended the Federal Election Campaign Act to bring donors into the open and to prevent their exercising undue influence on elected officials. By placing limits on contributions, controlling expenditures, and subsidizing the election, Congress hoped to make the selection process less costly and more equitable. It also established the Federal Election Commission to monitor activities, oversee compliance, and prosecute offenders.

The legislation has been only partially successful. It has increased the importance of having a large base of contributors during the preconvention period but has not eliminated the impact of large donors on the parties' and candidates' efforts in the general election. It has limited the expenditures of individual campaigns in both the nomination process and general election but has not reduced the amount of money spent on presidential elections. It has produced greater equity by its limits on contributions and expenditures and by its federal subsidies, but has not achieved equity among candidates or between parties in either phase of the electoral process. It has provided greater opportunities for those candidates who lack national recognition, but it has not lessened the advantages that national recognition can bring to those who seek their party's nomination. It has benefited major party candidates in the general election but has fractionalized their parties during the nomination. It has weakened the party leaderships' control over their nomination process and over their conduct of the general election campaign, but it has also enhanced the strategic value of the national parties' fund-raising, particularly their solicitation of soft-money contributions. It has encouraged the formation and involvement of nonparty groups, but it has also increased the importance of state and local party organizations on the campaigns of their candidates for national office.

Finally, the law has contributed to knowledge about the conduct of campaigns. Gifts and expenditures of candidates are now part of the public record. This information can be used by candidates to develop strategy, by the news media to cover the election and expose illegal activities, and by academicians and other analysts to explain the outcome. The publicizing of actions that violate the letter and spirit of the law has forced candidates and their parties to find other, legal means to circumvent the campaign limits and has led to the virtual breakdown of the campaign finance system. This breakdown has further disillusioned the electorate.

WHERE ON THE WEB?

- **Center for Responsive Politics**
  http://www.crp.org or http://www.opensecrets.org
  A nonpartisan, public interest group that is concerned with the conduct of federal elections, particularly how money is raised and spent. Publishes alerts, press releases, and major studies on campaign finance.
- **Common Cause**
  http://www.commoncause.org
  Another public interest group that is concerned with large and unreported contributions and expenditures and has continually urged campaign finance reform.
- **Destination Democracy**
  http://www.destinationdemocracy.org
  Sponsored by the Benton Foundation, this public interest group debates the various changes that have been proposed to make the electoral system more democratic and less beholden to special interests.
- **Federal Election Commission**
  http://www.fec.gov
  The first stop for any study of campaign finance, the FEC collects and disseminates data on contributions and expenditures for candidates seeking federal office as well as for parties and PACs.

EXERCISES

1. Present a summary of revenue and expenditures of the candidates who sought their party's presidential nomination in 2000. Get these data from the FEC at <http://www.fec.gov>. To what extent do these figures explain the outcome of the presidential nominations in 2000?
2. Look at the pattern of hard and soft money contributions to the political parties. To what extent are the parties circumventing the limits on federal expenditures by their solicitation and use of soft money?
3. Take the Road Test on the Destination Democracy Web site <http://www.destinationdemocracy.org>. Where did you end up? What did you learn that was most surprising/interesting?
4. Note the proposals for campaign finance reform that were debated by the 106th Congress <http://thomas.loc.gov>. Which of these proposals became law and which didn't; why? What do you think the 107th Congress will do about campaign finance reform?

SELECTED READING

Alexander, Herbert E., and Anthony Corrado. *Financing the 1992 Election.* Armonk, N. Y.: Sharpe, 1995.

Corrado, Anthony. *Paying for Presidents: Public Financing in National Elections.* New York: Twentieth Century Fund Press, 1993.

Corrado, Anthony, Thomas E. Mann, Daniel Ortiz, Trevor Potter, and Frank Sorauf. *Campaign Finance Reform: A Source Book.* Washington, D.C.: Brookings Institution, 1997.

Damore, David F. "A Dynamic Model of Candidate Fund-Raising: The Case of Presidential Nominating Campaigns." *Political Research Quarterly* (June 1997): 343–364.

Haynes, Audrey A., Paul-Henri Gurian, and Stephen F. Nichols, "The Role of Candidate Spending in Presidential Nomination Campaigns." *Journal of Politics* (February 1997): 213–235.

Magleby, David B., and Candice J. Nelson. *The Money Chase: Congressional Campaign Finance Reform.* Washington, D.C.: Brookings Institution, 1990.

Robinson, Michael, Clyde Wilcox, and Paul Marshall. "The Presidency: Not for Sale." *Public Opinion* II (March/April 1989): 49–53.

Sabato, Larry J. *PAC Power.* New York: Norton, 1985.

Sorauf, Frank J. *Money in American Elections.* Glenview, Ill.: Scott Foresman, 1988.

Stephenson-Horne, Marilee. "The Road to Hell: Unintended Consequences of Unwise Federal Campaign Finance Reforms." *Northern Kentucky Law Review* 17 (Spring 1990): 547–570.

Wayne, Stephen J. "Interest Groups on the Road to the White House: Traveling the Hard and Soft Routes." In *The Interest Group Connection,* edited by Paul S. Herrnson, Ronald G. Shaiko, and Clyde Wilcox, 65–79. Chatham, N.J.: Chatham House, 1998.

Wilcox, Clyde. "Financing the 1988 Prenomination Campaigns." In *Nominating the President,* edited by Emmett H. Buell, Jr. and Lee Sigelman, 91–118. Knoxville: University of Tennessee Press, 1991.

NOTES

1. Center for Responsive Politics, "The Big Picture — 1996," <http:www.crp.org/pubs/bigpicture/overview>, November 11, 1998.

2. Ruth Marcus, "U.S. Campaigns Fuel $3 Billion in Spending," *Washington Post,* November 6, 2000, A1, 12.

3. Herbert E. Alexander, "Making Sense about Dollars in the 1980 Presidential Campaigns," in *Money and Politics in the United States,* ed. Michael J. Malbin (Washington, D.C.: American Enterprise Institute/Chatham House, 1984), 24.

4. Edward W. Chester, *Radio, Television, and American Politics* (New York: Sheed & Ward, 1969), 21.

5. Herbert E. Alexander, *Financing Politics,* 3rd ed. (Washington, D.C.: Congressional Quarterly, 1984), 11–12.

6. Herbert E. Alexander, "Spending on Presidential Campaigns" in *Electing the President: A Program for Reform,* ed. Robert E. Hunter (Washington, D.C.: Center for Strategic and International Studies), 61.

7. "How Clinton and Dole Spent $232 Million," *Washington Post,* March 31, 1997, A19.

8. National Election Studies, Inter-University Consortium for Political and Social Research, Center for Political Studies, University of Michigan.

9. Bob Woodward, *The Choice* (New York: Simon & Schuster, 1996), 144.

10. This brief discussion of the sources of political contributions is based primarily on Alexander, *Financing Politics*, 55–59.

11. Quoted in Jasper B. Shannon, *Money and Politics* (New York: Random House, 1959), 35.

12. Herbert E. Alexander and Brian Haggerty, *Financing the 1984 Election* (Lexington, Mass.: Lexington Books, 1987), 148.

13. In 1972, the chief fund-raiser for the Nixon campaign, Maurice Stans, and Richard Nixon's private attorney, Herbert Kalmbach, collected contributions, some of them illegal, on behalf of the president. They exerted strong pressure on corporate executives, despite the prohibition on corporate giving. Secret contributions totaling millions of dollars were received, and three special secured funds were established to give the White House and the Committee to Reelect the President (known as CREEP) maximum discretion in campaign expenditures. It was from these funds that the "dirty tricks" of the 1972 campaign and the Watergate burglary were financed.

14. Federal Election Commission.

15. Those who do not do well and are forced out early are often saddled with sizable debts. Frequently, for the sake of party unity and to obtain the backing of their opponents, party nominees promise to try to help pay off their rivals' debts.

16. It costs more to engage in prospective fund-raising, going to people who have not contributed for donations, than to go back to those who have. Sometimes, in fact, the costs of prospective fund-raising can exceed the dollar return. This is one of the reasons that prospective candidates wish to shift these costs to a leadership PAC rather than have them come out of the campaign fund-raising budget and thus detract from the total amount that can be spent prior to the convention. Having a mailing list in hand also helps obtain money for the critical start-up costs of the campaign.

17. Jason DeParle, "The First Primary," *New York Times Magazine,* April 16, 1995, 33.

18. The FEC sought to impose still another eligibility rule — how matching funds had been spent in the past. The commission denied matching funds to Lyndon LaRouche in 1992 on the grounds that his campaign had misused such funds in a previous election. LaRouche, who had been convicted and jailed for engaging in fraudulent fund-raising practices, appealed the FEC's decision and won. On July 2, 1993, the U.S. Court of Appeals ruled that the law did not give the FEC authority to prejudge how a candidate would use his government funds — that was up to the voters. LaRouche received over $1.2 million in matching funds in 2000.

19. Candidates can also notify the FEC that they wish to exclude certain primaries from the 10 percent rule and not campaign in those states even though their names may appear on the ballot.

20. Ceci Connolly, "Huge Money Chase Marks 2000 Race," *Washington Post,* February 28, 1999, A7.

21. Federal Election Commission, "Record," April 2000, 10.

22. At the end of the first eighteen months of the 1999–2000 election cycle, Democratic and Republican Party committees had raised $256 million in soft money alone with the Republicans besting the Democrats $137.4 million to $118 million. Susan Schmidt, "Soft Money Contributions to Parties Hit $256 Million," *Washington Post,* September 8, 2000, A7.

23. Clinton raised $26.5 million in one fund-raising event in 2000, the most ever raised in a single night. The high for the Republicans was $21 million that year. Common Cause, "Election Ear," June 1, 2000, <http://www.commoncause.org>.

24. Jill Abramson, "Unregulated Cash Flows Into Hands of P.A.C.'s for 2000," *New York Times,* November 29, 1998, A1, 45.

25. Robert Suro and Bill Miller, "Judge: 'Soft Money' Not Covered by Foreign Political Donor Ban," *Washington Post,* October 10, 1998, A3.

26. The sale of satellite technology to the Chinese was especially criticized by Republicans. Senate Majority Leader Trent Lott called for a special investigator to examine the decision in the light of State Department opposition to it. The head of the company that was allowed to sell the technology made a $100,000 contribution to the Democrats.

27. Alison Mitchell, "Clinton Pressed Plan to Reward Donors," *New York Times*, February 26, 1997, A1,18.

28. Bob Woodward, "Gore was 'Solicitor-in-Chief' in '96 Reelection Campaign," *Washington Post*, March 2, 1997, A18; Alison Mitchell, "Gore's Fund-Raising Cast a Political Shadow," *New York Times*, March 3, 1997, A1,12. Ceci Connolly, "The Gore Machine," *Washington Post Magazine*, April 4, 1999, 22.

29. Don Van Natta, Jr. "Early Rush of Contributions Opened Floodgates for Bush," *New York Times*, January 31, 2000, A20. Don Van Natta, Jr. "Bush Is Hardly a Passive Fund-Raiser." *New York Times*, May 16, 2000, A20.

30. Susan Glasser, "Bush Raised $69 Million, Spent $37 Million in '99," *Washington Post*, February 1, 2000, A4.

31. John M. Broder and Katharine Q. Seelye, "Gore Campaign Responds to Money Crunch," *New York Times*, November 20, 1999, A9.

32. Beginning with the 1992 nomination process, the FEC took these practices into account by liberalizing its cost allocation policy. It permitted candidates to allocate expenses if they pertained to media, mailings, telephoning, polling, and overhead. Moreover, the commission allowed up to 50 percent of the expenses to be considered fund-raising and thus entirely exempt from the state spending limits.

33. Erika Falk, "Issue Advocacy Advertising Through the Presidential Primary 1999–2000 Election Cycle," Annenberg Public Policy Center, University of Pennsylvania, September 20, 2000.

34. Beaulieu of America, a large carpet manufacturer, was not as fortunate as the Buddhist monks. Accused of funneling $36,000 in illegal contributions to Lamar Alexander's 1996 campaign, the company entered into a plea-bargaining agreement with the government in which it agreed to pay a $1 million fine and civil penalties to be determined by the FEC. Kevin Sack, "Campaign Finance Case Costs a Carpet Company $1 Million," *New York Times*, December 2, 1998, A23.

35. David F. Damore, "A Dynamic Model of Candidate Fundraising: The Case of Presidential Nominating Campaigns," *Political Research Quarterly* (June 1997): 343–364.

36. Michael Robinson, Clyde Wilcox, and Paul Marshall, "The Presidency: Not for Sale," *Public Opinion* II (March/April 1989): 51.

37. In an examination of campaign advertising spending by Bush in 1988, a group of political scientists found an *inverse* relationship between advertising costs and public support for the candidates. They write, "When Bush spent more in one week than he had in the previous week, the size of his lead actually grew smaller." Audrey A. Haynes, Paul-Henri Gurian, and Stephen M. Nichols, "The Role of Candidate Spending in Presidential Nomination Campaigns," *The Journal of Politics* (February 1997): 213–225.

CHAPTER

THE POLITICAL ENVIRONMENT

3

INTRODUCTION

The nature of the electorate influences the content, images, and strategies of the campaign and affects the outcome of the election — an obvious conclusion to be sure, but one that is not always appreciated. Campaigns are not conducted in ignorance of the voters. Rather, they are calculated to appeal to the needs and desires, attitudes and opinions, and associations and interactions of the electorate.

Voters do not come to the election with completely open minds. They come with preexisting views. They do not see and hear the campaign in isolation. They observe it and absorb it as part of their daily lives. In other words, their attitudes and associations affect their perceptions and influence their behavior. Preexisting views make it important for students of presidential elections to examine the formation of political attitudes and the patterns of social interaction.

Who votes and who does not? Why do people vote for certain candidates and not others? Do campaign appeals affect voting behavior? Are the responses of the electorate predictable? Political scientists have been interested in these questions for some time. Politicians have been interested for even longer.

A great deal of social science research and political savvy have gone into finding the answers. Spurred by the development of sophisticated survey techniques and methods of data analysis, political scientists, sociologists, and social psychologists have uncovered a wealth of information on how the public reacts and the electorate behaves during a campaign. They have examined correlations between demographic characteristics and voter turnout. They have explored psychological motivations, social influences, and political pressures that contribute to voting behavior. This chapter examines some of their findings.

It is organized into three sections. The first discusses who votes. Describing the expansion of suffrage in the nineteenth and twentieth centuries, the section then turns to recent trends. Turnout is influenced by partisan, economic, and social factors. It is also affected by laws that govern elections and by circumstances of the vote itself, such as interest in the election, the closeness of the contest, the effectiveness of the campaign, and even the weather on election day. The impact of these variables on the decision of whether or not to cast a ballot at all is the principal focus of this section.

The second and third sections of the chapter study influences on the vote. First, the partisan basis of politics is examined. How have political attitudes changed over the years and how do they affect the ways people evaluate the campaign and shape their actual voting decisions? Models of voting behavior are presented and then used to help explain contemporary voting patterns.

Next, the social basis of politics is analyzed. Dividing the electorate into distinct and overlapping demographic, socioeconomic, and religious groupings, this section deals with the relationship of these groupings to voting behavior. It places primary emphasis on the formation of party coalitions during the 1930s and their evolution through the 1990s into the twenty-first century.

The final part of this chapter looks to the future. What is happening to the electoral coalitions of the two major parties? Are they going through a period of realignment or dealignment? Are voters becoming more independent in their allegiances and their voting decisions? Recent research provides some answers to these questions.

TURNOUT

Who votes? In one sense, this is a simple question to resolve. Official election returns indicate the number of voters and the states, even the precincts, in which the votes were cast. By easy calculation, the percentage of those eligible who actually voted can be determined. In 1992, 55.2 percent of the voting-age population cast ballots in the presidential election; in 1996, 49.0 percent voted, in 2000 it was about 50.7 percent.[1] (See Table 3–1 for turnout in other presidential elections.)

For campaign strategists and political analysts, however, more information than simple percentages of the proportion of the population that voted is needed. In planning a campaign, it is necessary to design and target appeals to attract specific groups of voters. In assessing the results, it is also essential to understand how particular segments of the electorate responded. By evaluating turnout on the basis of demographic characteristics and partisan attitudes, strategists and analysts alike obtain the information they need to make sophisticated judgments.

Voting turnout has varied widely over the years. In the first national election, only about 11 percent of the potentially eligible population participated. The presidential vote was even smaller, since most of the electors were designated by the state legislatures and not chosen directly by the people.

In the early period from the end of the eighteenth century until 1824, voters constituted only about 20 to 25 percent of those who were eligible to vote in most states. Without parties or a tradition of participation in politics, the public deferred to the more politically prominent members of the society.[2]

TABLE 3-1 ★

SUFFRAGE AND TURNOUT

Year	Total Adult Population (including aliens)*	Total Presidential Vote	Percentage of Adult Population Voting
1824	3,964,000	363,017	9.0
1840	7,381,000	2,412,698	33.0
1860	14,676,000	4,692,710	32.0
1880	25,012,000	9,219,467	37.0
1900	40,753,000	13,974,188	35.0
1920	60,581,000	26,768,613	44.0
1932	75,768,000	39,732,000	52.4
1940	84,728,000	49,900,000	58.9
1952	99,929,000	61,551,000	61.6
1960	109,672,000	68,838,000	62.8
1964	114,090,000	70,645,000	61.9
1968	120,285,000	73,212,000	60.9
1972	140,777,000	77,719,000	55.5
1976	152,308,000	81,556,000	53.5
1980	164,595,000	86,515,000	52.6
1984	174,447,000	92,653,000	53.1
1988	182,600,000	91,602,291	50.2
1992	189,044,000	104,426,659	55.2
1996	196,507,000	96,277,564	49.0
2000	206,000,000	105,000,000	51.0

* Restrictions based on sex, age, race, religion, and property ownership prevented a significant portion of the adult population from voting in the nineteenth and early twentieth centuries. Of those who were eligible, however, the percentage casting ballots was often quite high, particularly during the last half of the nineteenth century.

Sources: Population figures for 1824 to 1920 are based on estimates and early census figures that appear in Neal R. Peirce, *The People's President* (New York: Simon & Schuster, 1968), 206. Population figures from 1932 to 1984 are from the U.S. Department of Commerce, Bureau of the Census, *Statistical Abstract of the United States* (Washington, D.C.: Government Printing Office, 1987), 250. Figures for 1988 and 1992 were compiled from official election returns supplied by the Federal Election Commission. Data for 1996 based on official elections returns from the Federal Election Commission, revised October 1997. Data for 2000 based on estimated returns as of November 30, 2000.

Turnout increased in the 1820s, however, spurred by a political reform movement. Known as Jacksonian Democracy, this movement advocated greater public participation in the electoral process. By the 1830s, 50 to 60 percent of the eligible electorate voted. With the rise of competitive, mass-based parties in the 1840s and their campaigns appealing to voters, turnout increased to 80 percent and remained within the 70 to 80 percent range for the next fifty years in all regions except the South.[3] There, the rise of one-party politics following the Civil War, the disfranchisement of African Americans after the withdrawal of federal troops, and the introduction of various impediments to voting such as poll taxes, literacy tests, and "private" primaries in which only whites could participate, plus the imposition of more restrictive residence requirements, all substantially reduced the proportion of those who voted.

Although the size of the electorate continued to grow, the percentage of those eligible who actually voted did not. Populated by thousands of immigrants, who initially spoke little English, the size of the eligible electorate increased but the proportion of those voting decreased. Similarly, the enfranchisement of women in 1920 had much the same effect. In 1924, only 44 percent of the electorate voted. Within a period of thirty years, turnout had declined almost 40 percent.[4]

Although voter turnout grew moderately during Franklin Roosevelt's presidency and the post–World War II era, it began to decline again following the 1960 presidential election, an election in which 64 percent voted. With the exception of 1992, the trend has been downward. In the 1996 presidential election, fewer than half of those eligible voted. In nonpresidential elections the proportion of eligible voters participating is even lower, in the range of 40 percent or less for midterm elections. In 1998, it was only 36 percent.

What has caused the decline in voter turnout since 1960? Why do so many people choose not to vote? Does low turnout indicate voter satisfaction or alienation? Does it contribute to stability or create conditions for instability within the democratic political system? What party and which programs benefit and which groups suffer when so many people do not vote? These questions are addressed in an examination of turnout and its implications for the political system.

The Expansion of Suffrage

The Constitution empowers the state legislatures to determine the time, place, and manner of holding elections for national office. Although it also gives Congress the authority to alter such regulations, Congress did not do so until the Civil War. Thus, the states were free to restrict suffrage, and most did. In some states, property ownership was a requirement for exercising the franchise; in others, a particular religious belief was necessary. In most, it was essential to be white, male, and over twenty-one.[5]

By the 1830s, most states had eliminated property and religious restrictions, thereby extending suffrage to approximately 80 percent of the adult white male population.[6] The Fifteenth Amendment, ratified in 1870, removed race and color as qualifications for voting. In theory, it enabled all nonwhite males to vote. In practice, it enfranchised those in the North and border states but not those in the South, where a series of restrictive voting laws combined with social pressure to prevent African Americans from voting in large numbers for another hundred years. In every southern state, a majority of eligible African Americans were not registered to vote until the mid- to late 1960s.[7]

Following the Civil War, both the number of eligible voters and the percentage of actual voters increased. More competition between the parties contributed to this higher level of participation, as did the absence of registration procedures and the use of secret ballots in some states.

In the twentieth century, the passage of the four constitutional amendments expanded the voting-age population still further. In 1920, women received the right to vote at the national level (Nineteenth Amendment) although some states and territories had granted women suffrage earlier.[8] In 1961, the District of Columbia was granted three electoral votes, thereby extending the franchise to its residents in presidential elections (Twenty-third Amendment); in 1964, the collection of a poll tax was prohibited in national elections (Twenty-fourth Amendment); in 1971, suffrage was extended to all citizens eighteen years of age and older (Twenty-sixth Amendment).

Moreover, the Supreme Court and Congress began to eliminate the legal and institutional barriers to voting. In 1944, the Court outlawed the white primary.[9] In the mid-1960s, Congress, by its passage of the Civil Rights Act (1964) and the Voting Rights Act (1965), banned literacy tests in federal elections for all citizens who had at least a sixth-grade education in a U.S. school. Where less than 50 percent of the population was registered to vote, federal officials were sent to facilitate registration. No longer was drawn-out and costly litigation necessary to ensure the right to vote. Amendments to the Voting Rights Act have also reduced the residence requirement for presidential elections to a maximum of thirty days.

The expansion of suffrage has produced more voters. It has enlarged the electorate, but initially that enlargement also contributed to the smaller percentage of that electorate who voted. The reason for the smaller percentage is that newly enfranchised voters cast ballots less regularly than those who have previously enjoyed the right to vote.

It takes time to develop the practice of voting. For example, although women received the right to vote in 1920, the proportion of women who voted was less than the proportion of men who cast ballots for another fifty-six years. By 1980, however, the rate at which women and men turned out to vote was approximately the same. Since 1988, women have been slightly more likely to vote than men, between 2 and 3 percent more likely.[10]

Concern has been voiced about the relatively low turnout of voters in the United States compared with other democratic countries. As Table 3–2 demonstrates, voting turnout is much higher in most European democracies than in the United States.

If the percentage of those registered who actually vote is the basis for comparison, the United States fares better, but it still trails numerous other democratic countries.[11] Unlike many other countries, the United States does not impose penalties on those who fail to register and vote; nor does it have a national system for automatic registration as do many other democracies. Election day is a workday in the United States whereas in most other countries, it occurs on Sunday or on a national holiday.

In 1993, Congress responded to the registration problem by enacting legislation that requires states to allow people to register by mail or at the time they obtain or renew their driver's license.[12] The motor-voter bill, as it is called, also states that registration materials should be available at certain agencies that provide social services such as welfare offices and those that serve the disabled. The law took effect in 1995 and voter registration has increased since then. By 1998,

TABLE 3–2 ★

International Voter Turnout (in percentages)

Country	Year	Type of Election	Turnout of Registered Voters
Argentina	1995	Presidential	80.9
Australia	1998	Lesislative	95.2
Austria	1998	Presidential	74.4
Belgium	1999	Parliamentary	90.5
Brazil	1998	Presidential	78.5
Canada	1997	General	67.0
Germany	1996	Parliamentary	67.5
India	1998	Parliamentary	62.0
Israel	1999	Parliamentary	78.7
Japan	1995	Parliamentary	44.5
Mexico	2000	Presidential	60.0
Poland	1995	Presidential	64.7/68.2*
Russia	2000	Presidential	67.8
Turkey	1995	Parliamentary	87.1
United States	1996	Lesislative	36.0 of VAP[†] 51.5 of registered voters
	2000	Presidential	51.0

*Two rounds.

[†] VAP — Voting-age population.

Source: Federal Election Commission, <http://www.fec.gov/votregis/InternaTO.htm>, July 20, 2000; "Turning Out the Vote," *Washington Post*, November 4, 2000, A17.

70.15 percent of the voting-age population was registered to vote with 43 percent of the new registrants completing their forms at motor vehicles bureaus.[13] (See Box 3–1, "Registering to Vote," page 65.)

Two groups, the youngest eligible voters and the poorest, were expected to increase their electoral participation the most as a result of this law. Although eighteen- to twenty-four-year-olds have traditionally had the lowest registration rates (only about 40 percent), they have much higher driving rates (85 percent have driving licenses). By making registration available at the same time and place where people get or renew their driving licenses, it was thought that the law could double the number of registered voters in the lowest age cohort. Similarly, by making registration available at centers for public assistance, the legislation could also help increase the proportion of poorer people who register to vote.[14]

If the proportion of younger voters and poorer voters increased, the Democrats would probably be helped more than the Republicans, at least that was what some Republican governors feared who tried to delay the implementation of the motor-voter bill in their states.

Making it easier to register to vote was expected to increase voting turnout, but in 1996 and 1998 it did not. Turnout actually declined in both elections — in

---

BOX 3–1 ★

Registering to Vote

It is easy to register to vote. You can now do so by mail using a national registration form developed by the Federal Election Commission. There are several ways to do so.

1. Contact your state's chief election official. In most states, it is the secretary of state; in some, it is the head of the Board of Elections; in a few, it may be the lieutenant governor.

   Simply request a registration form, complete it, and return it to the address indicated. If you are uncertain whom to contact, call the Federal Election Commission (FEC) on its toll-free number (800) 424–9530 to find out. The FEC also has a Web site <http://www.fec.gov> from which you can access the national registration form, download it, and print it on standard paper. About half the states will accept downloaded copies of this form or photocopies of it as registration applications. Others require an official state form which can be obtained by mail or will be available in state offices. Unfortunately, you cannot register on-line, at least not yet.

2. Go to your nearest motor vehicle office in your home state. Complete the form, and give it to the appropriate person at the office.

3. Access the Web site of an organization called Rock-the-Vote <http://www.rockthevote.org/main-register.html>. You will be asked to complete some basic information. The group will then transmit this information to a central clearinghouse, which will print it on an application card and mail it to you in about two weeks along with the address of the office in your state to which it should be mailed. If you register in this way, the group will also send you a reminder to vote a few days before the election.

1996, it was 49 percent; in 1998, it was 36 percent — even though voter registration increased. Why? The answer relates primarily to the campaign itself and to the environment in which it occurred. People were more content in 1996 than they were four years earlier; they were less interested in the campaign and more likely to believe that President Clinton would win easily. These factors combined to depress turnout. There is another reason that turnout has declined particularly among African-American males. Almost 1.5 million of the 10.4 million African-American men who have been convicted of a felony are ineligible to vote in fourteen states permanently and in all but three states (Maine, New Hampshire, and Vermont) during the time they are incarcerated.[15]

Other Influences on Turnout

There are also psychological, social, and political influences on who comes out to vote. Interest in the election, concern over the outcome, feelings of civic responsibility, and sense of political efficacy (the belief that one's vote really counts) are factors that influence voting.[16]

TABLE 3-3 ★

TURNOUT, 1964–1996
(NUMBERS IN THOUSANDS; CIVILIAN NONINSTITUTIONAL POPULATION)

Region, Race, Hispanic Origin, Gender, and Age	Presidential Elections of								
	1996	1992	1988	1984	1980	1976	1972	1968	1964
United States									
Total, voting age	193,651	185,684	178,098	169,963	157,085	146,548	136,203	116,535	110,604
Percent voted	54.2	61.3	57.4	59.9	59.2	59.2	63.0	67.8	69.3
White	56.0	63.6	59.1	61.4	60.9	60.9	64.5	69.1	70.7
Black	50.6	54.0	51.5	55.8	50.5	48.7	52.1	57.6	58.5†
Hispanic origin*	26.7	28.9	28.8	32.6	29.9	31.8	37.5	(NA)	(NA)
Male	52.8	60.2	56.4	59.0	59.1	59.6	64.1	69.8	71.9
Female	55.5	62.3	58.3	60.8	59.4	58.8	62.0	66.0	67.0
18 to 24 years	32.4	42.8	36.2	40.8	39.9	42.2	49.6	50.4‡	50.9‡
25 to 44 years	49.2	58.3	54.0	58.4	58.7	58.7	62.7	66.6	69.0
45 to 65 years	64.4	70.0	67.9	69.8	69.3	68.7	70.8	74.9	75.9
65 years and over	67.0	70.1	68.8	67.7	65.1	62.2	63.5	65.8	66.3

Northeast, Midwest, and West

Total, voting age	125,571	122,025	117,373	112,376	106,524	99,403	93,653	81,594	78,174
Percent voted	55.3	62.5	58.9	61.6	61.0	61.2	66.4	71.0	74.6
White	57.4	64.9	60.4	63.0	62.4	62.6	67.5	71.8	74.7
Black	51.4	53.8	55.6	58.9	52.8	52.2	56.7	64.8	72.0†

South

Total, voting age	68,080	63,659	60,725	57,587	50,561	47,145	42,550	39,941	32,429
Percent voted	52.2	59.0	54.5	56.8	55.6	54.9	55.4	60.1	56.7
White	53.4	60.8	56.4	58.1	57.4	57.1	57.0	61.9	59.5
Black	50.0	54.3	48.0	53.2	48.2	45.7	47.8	51.6	44.0†

NA — Not available.

* Hispanics may be of any race.

† Black and other races in 1964.

‡ Prior to 1972, data are for people twenty-one to twenty-four years of age with the exception of those aged eighteen to twenty-four in Georgia and Kentucky, nineteen to twenty-four in Alaska, and twenty to twenty-four in Hawaii.

Source: Current Population Reports, Series P20, Nos. 143, 192, 253, 322, 370, 405, 440, 466, and the November 1996 Current Population Survey. Taken from "Voting and Registration in the Election of November 1996," by Lynne M. Casper and Loretta E. Bass, U.S. Census Bureau <http://www.census.gov/prod/3/98pubs/p20–504.pdf>, April 2, 1999; 2000 data are based on estimates from exit poll conducted by the Voter News Service.

Naturally, people who feel more strongly about the election are more likely to get involved. Those with more intense partisan feelings are more likely to have this interest, more likely to participate in the campaign, and more likely to vote on election day. Voters are also more likely than nonvoters to believe that their participation in elections makes a difference.[17] For many, voting becomes a civic responsibility, the result of a personal conviction, even a habit. The more people have done it in the past, the more likely they will do it in the future. Table 3–3 provides empirical support for the proposition that the newly eligible vote with less regularity than those who have previously exercised their franchise. Voting turnout increases with age up to about seventy-five years old.

What are the reasons that young people vote less often? They are more mobile and have fewer economic interests and looser political ties to the community in which they live. Moreover, many young people have not yet developed the habit of voting or, in some cases, even of identifying with a political party.

Similarly, advances in medicine have prolonged life and increased the number of senior citizens. Those over seventy-five vote with less regularity, primarily for reasons of health. In short, the increasing proportion of the electorate in the youngest and oldest age groups has contributed to lower voter turnout, but other factors, such as the weakening of partisan attitudes, have contributed as well.

Other democratic characteristics related to turnout are education, income, and occupational status. As people become more educated, as they move up the socioeconomic ladder, as their jobs gain in status, they are more likely to vote. Education is the most important of these variables. It has a larger impact than any other single social characteristic.[18] As Table 3–3 demonstrates, the higher the level of education, the greater the percentage voting.

The reason education is so important is that it provides the skills for processing and evaluating information; for perceiving differences among the parties, candidates, and issues; and for relating these differences to personal values and behavior. Education also affects personal success. It increases a person's stake in the system, interest in the election, and concern over the outcome. Since the lesson that voting is a civic responsibility is usually learned in the classroom, schooling may also contribute to a more highly developed sense of responsibility about voting. Finally, education provides the knowledge and confidence to overcome voting hurdles — to register on time, to file absentee ballots properly, and to mark the ballot or use the voting machine or punch-hole ballot correctly on election day.[19]

Given the relationship of education to turnout, why should the rate of turnout have declined since 1960 when the general level of education in the United States was rising? One explanation for this trend has been the increasing number of younger voters who entered the electorate, the so-called Generation Xers, and their lack of "social connectedness."[20] Related is the increase in the proportion of the population who are resident aliens and thus cannot vote, and of those who are eligible, the increasing proportion of the population who are single and who do not attend religious services regularly. People who are married and those who are active within their church or synagogue generally evidence stronger community ties than those who are not; these ties, in turn, motivate voting.

There are other attitudinal factors. The weakening of partisan attitudes, the growth of political cynicism and apathy among the electorate, particularly among those in the lower socioeconomic groups, and the declining sense of political effi-cacy that people can make a difference in what the government does or does not do have all contributed. Before examining each of these factors, however, it is important to understand that the decline in turnout occurred despite increasing education levels and not because of them. Professors Paul R. Abramson, John H. Aldrich, and David W. Rohde estimate that turnout would have declined three times as much had education levels *not* increased.[21]

For the last three decades of the twentieth century, the strength of partisan loyalties declined, while the proportion of the electorate identifying themselves as independent grew. Since party allegiances are a motivation for voting, the weaken-ing of partisan attitudes contributed to the decrease in turnout. Moreover, parties have become less important influences on the campaign and provide less sturdy linkage to voters.

As the parties have become more personalized and factionalized and as cam-paigns become more candidate centered, the election becomes more confusing to more voters. The difficulty people have in deciding whose election would be most beneficial to them has contributed to nonvoting, particularly among those with less education, who tend to have less information and less highly developed ana-lytical skills.

During this period, people also became more disillusioned about the political system and, correspondingly, less confident that their vote mattered, or that they could change the way government works or public officials behave. This lower sense of efficacy has also depressed the vote. Abramson and colleagues argue that about two-thirds of the decline in turnout from 1960 can be attributed primarily to the combined effects of weaker partisan affiliation and feelings of less political effectiveness.[22]

A class bias also exists in voting that is related to negative feelings people have about their own ability to influence events and the trust they place in political leaders. The decline in turnout has been greatest among those in the lowest socio-economic groups, thereby enlarging the participation gap between the haves and have-nots.[23] This gap has produced an electorate that is less representative of the population as a whole, an electorate that is better educated and has higher incomes than the general public. To the extent that government responds to the electorate rather than to the general population, its policies take on a "have" coloration.

This class bias in voting produces a tragic irony in American politics. Those who are most disadvantaged, who have the least education, and who need to change conditions the most actually participate the least. Those who are the most advantaged, who benefit from existing conditions and presumably from the public policy that contributes to those conditions, vote most often. These trends in vot-ing behavior work to reflect, even to perpetuate, the status quo.

Generational and racial divisions accentuate the problem. Younger people and racial minorities are disproportionately found in the lower socioeconomic strata. There is a difference in turnout between white and African Americans, with whites voting at higher levels than African Americans.

Demographic characteristics may suggest patterns in turnout, who votes and why, but these characteristics are also affected by the electoral environment. In 1992, for example, turnout increased by 5 percent. If the demographic factors were fairly constant then what explains the increase? The recession of 1991–1992 may have energized some of those adversely affected by it; Perot's candidacy appealed to independents who are generally less interested in politics and less likely to vote; and new media formats reached and informed new voters. Singularly and together, these factors momentarily reversed the downward cycle in the proportion of the electorate that voted in that election.

In short, campaigns and electoral environments matter. They affect who comes out to vote. Compared to 1992, people in 1996 were less interested and excited about an election that received much less media coverage. Is it any wonder that turnout declined in that election?[24] The closeness of the 2000 election and extensive turn-out-the-vote activities by both campaigns increased the proportion voting in 2000, particularly in the key battleground states where much of the campaign was focused. For the country as a whole, turnout was estimated at about 51 percent.

Turnout and Partisanship

Turnout has partisan implications as well. Since the Democratic Party draws more of its electoral support from those in the lower socioeconomic groups, those with less formal education, and those with fewer professional opportunities, lower turnout tends to hurt that party more than the GOP. In 1992 and 1996, however, it did not. The increase in turnout was greater among Democrats than Republicans, thereby eliminating the partisan advantage the Republicans usually have from turning out a larger proportion of their partisans to vote.[25]

Republicans have also benefited from their party's greater financial resources, which have enabled them to mount more effective campaigns to identify and register new voters. They have had the resources to employ an individualized, targeted approach to get out their vote, whereas the Democrats with help from organized labor and African-American and Hispanic organizations have generally utilized a strategy that directs mass appeals to these key Democratic blocs of voters.

Despite the demographic differences between voters and nonvoters, some evidence suggests that results of recent presidential elections would not have been any different had more people voted. Nonvoters surveyed after recent elections indicated that they preferred the winner by approximately the same percentage as the national averages in these elections. One reason that nonvoters follow the dominant mood of the electorate is that they tend to be influenced by shorter-term factors that affect the outcome of the election, perhaps even more so than voters whose partisan allegiances can more readily resist these short-term forces. To understand the impact of partisanship on turnout we turn to the partisan basis of politics.

THE PARTISAN BASIS OF POLITICS

Why do people vote as they do? Considerable research has been conducted to answer this question. Initially, much of it was done under the direction of the Center for Political Studies at the University of Michigan. Beginning in 1952, the center began conducting nationwide surveys during presidential elections.[26] An objective of these national election studies has been to identify the major influences on voting behavior. A random sample of the electorate is interviewed before and after each election. Respondents are asked a series of questions designed to reveal their attitudes toward the parties, candidates, and issues. On the basis of their answers to these questions, researchers have amassed a wealth of data to explain the voting behavior of the U.S. electorate.

A Model of the U.S. Voter

One of the earliest and most influential theories of voting behavior based on the Michigan survey data was presented in a book entitled *The American Voter* (1960).[27] The model on which the theory is based assumes that individuals are influenced by their partisan attitudes and social relationships in addition to the political environment in which the election occurs. In fact, these attitudes and those relationships condition the impact of that environment on individual voting behavior.

According to the theory, people develop attitudes early in life, largely as a consequence of interacting with their families, particularly their parents. These attitudes, in turn, tend to be reinforced by neighborhood, school, and religious associations. The reasons they tend to be reinforced lie in the psychological and social patterns of behavior. Psychologically, it is more pleasing to have beliefs and attitudes supported than challenged. Socially, it is more comfortable and safer to associate with "nice," like-minded people — those with similar cultural, educational, and religious experiences — than with others. This desire to increase one's "comfort level" in social relationships explains why the environment for most people tends to be supportive much of the time.[28]

Attitudes mature and harden over the years. The older people become, the less amenable they are to change. They are more set in their ways. Consequently, their behavior is more predictable. Political attitudes are no exception to this general pattern of attitude formation and maintenance. They too are developed early in life, are reinforced by association, grow in intensity, and become more predictable with time.

Of all the factors that contribute to the development of a political attitude, an identification with a political party is the most important. It affects how people see campaigns, how they evaluate candidates, and how they vote on election day. Party identification operates as a conceptual framework, a lens through which the campaign is understood and evaluated. It provides cues for interpreting the issues, for judging the candidates, and for deciding whether and how to vote. The stronger these attitudes, the more compelling the cues; conversely, the weaker the attitudes, the less likely they will affect perceptions during the campaign and influence voting on election day.[29]

When identification with a party is weak or nonexistent, other factors, such as the personalities of the candidates and their issue positions, are correspondingly more important. In contrast to party identification, which is a long-term stabilizing factor but one that can be changed over time, candidate and issue orientations are shorter term, more variable factors, often shifting from election to election.

As elections have become more candidate centered, so too is partisanship more influenced by the image of the party's nominee. It is a two-way relationship. Party helps shape the image of the candidate, and candidates affect the image of the party. Moreover, the impact of candidates on partisan images can extend beyond the election itself.[30]

Candidate images turn on performance and policy dimensions. People form general impressions about candidates on the basis of what they know about the candidates' personal experiences, their leadership capabilities, and their character. For an incumbent president seeking reelection, accomplishments in office provide much of the criteria for evaluating how well the president has done. Other characteristics, such as trustworthiness, integrity, empathy, and candor, are also important. How important they are depends on the nature of the times. Following a presidency besmirched by scandal, such as Nixon's and Clinton's, integrity, credibility, and character assume more importance than at other times. For the challenger, it is the potential for office as demonstrated by experience, knowledge, confidence, and assertiveness, plus a host of personal qualities that help determine qualifications for a leadership position such as president.[31]

Candidates' stands on the issues, however, seem less critical than do their partisanship and performance in office. The principal explanation for downgrading the importance of issues has been the low level of information and awareness that much of the electorate possesses. To be important, issues must be salient. They must attract attention — they must hit home. Without personal impact, they are unlikely to be primary motivating factors in voting. To the extent that issue positions are not known or distinguishable between the principal candidates, their respective personal images become a stronger influence on the vote.

Ironically, that portion of the electorate who can be more easily persuaded — weak partisans and independents — tend to have the least information.[32] Conversely, the most committed tend to be the most informed. They use their information to support their partisanship.

The relationship between degree of partisanship and amount of information has significant implications for a democratic society. The traditional view of a democracy holds that information and awareness are necessary to make an intelligent judgment on election day. However, the finding that those who have the most information are also the most committed, and that those who lack this commitment also lack the incentive to get more information, has upset some of the assumptions about the motivation for acquiring information and using it to vote intelligently.

A More Refined Theory of Voting

The model of voting behavior first presented in 1960 has engendered considerable controversy. Critics have charged that the theory presumes that most of the electorate is uninformed and vote habitually rather than rationally. One well-known political scientist, the late V. O. Key, even wrote a book dedicated to "the perverse and unorthodox argument . . . that voters are not fools."[33] Key studied the behavior of three groups of voters between 1936 and 1960: switchers, stand-patters, and new voters. He found those who switched their votes to be interested in and influenced by their own evaluation of policy, personality, and performance. In this sense, Key believed that they exercised an intelligent judgment when voting.

Key's conclusion that most voters were not automatons and that most of their voting decisions were not solely or even primarily the product of their psychological dispositions and social pressures is accepted today by most students of electoral behavior. Even though voters may have limited information, they use it to arrive at reasoned political judgments. They take into account their present situation, their beliefs about government, and their assessments of how the country is doing under its current leadership and will do in the future. In the words of political scientist, Samuel Popkin:

> They consider not only economic issues but family, residential, and consumer issues as well. They think not only of their immediate needs, but also of their needs for insurance against future problems; not only about private good but also about collective goods.[34]

How do they do this? What criteria do they use in making judgments?

Morris Fiorina, in his provocative study *Retrospective Voting in American National Elections* (1981), tries to answer these questions. Utilizing a rational choice model adopted from economics, Fiorina argues that voting decisions are calculations people make on the basis of their accumulated political experience. They make these calculations by assessing the past performance of the parties and their elected officials in light of the promises they made and political events that have occurred. Fiorina calls this a *retrospective evaluation*.[35]

Retrospective evaluations are not only important for influencing voting in a given election, they are also important for shaping partisan attitudes, which Fiorina defines as "a running tally of retrospective evaluations of party promises and performance."[36] In other words, the running tally is a summary judgment of how well the parties and their leaders have done and are doing.

As a political attitude, partisanship is fairly stable. It can change but usually does not do so quickly. Nonetheless, changes in partisan attitudes have taken place over the last three decades and these changes have had an impact on voting behavior.

Partisan Voting Patterns

The initial model of voter behavior was based on research conducted in the 1950s. Since that time, the U.S. electorate has experienced a divisive, unsuccessful war in Southeast Asia; a cohesive, successful one in the Persian Gulf; an end to the Cold War; a major scandal (Watergate) that led to the resignation of a president and the impeachment and acquital of another president; other scandals involving public officials, from cabinet secretaries to members of Congress, in their private behavior and in the exercise of their public responsibilities; large-scale social movements for extending equal rights and opportunities to women, racial and ethnic minorities, and those with same sex orientations; and periods of economic recession, inflation, and prosperity. Naturally, these events and the reaction of government officials to them have had an impact on the partisan attitudes of the electorate.

Three major trends stand out. First, over the last half of the twentieth century, there has been a reduction in the percentage of the voting-age population who identify with a party and, concurrently, an increase in the percentage of self-proclaimed independents. That increase occurred primarily in the 1970s, with the Democratic party the big loser. Second, there has been a decline in the strength of partisan identities. Third, there has been a shift in partisan loyalties, with the Democratic party losing and the Republican party gaining adherents. Each of these changes has important long- and short-term implications for electoral politics in America.

Table 3–4 lists the percentage of party identifiers and independents. As the table indicates, during a forty-eight-year period from 1952 to 2000, there has been a 13-percent decline in people who identify with a political party and a 16-percent increase in the number of self-proclaimed independents. Most of this shift occurred after 1964. The table also suggests that the decline was principally in the strong partisan category during the 1970s.

Although partisanship has weakened, with some strong partisans becoming weaker partisans and weak partisans considering themselves independents, how independently voters actually behave on election day is another matter. Truly independent voting has increased far less rapidly than has independent identification by the electorate. In other words, a sizable portion claim that they are independent but continue to vote for candidates of the same party. They appear in Table 3–4 as independent but leaning in a partisan direction.[37]

The decline in partisanship and the growth of independents have produced a more volatile and manipulable electorate. With weaker partisan allegiances and more independent identifiers, campaigns, candidates, and issues seemingly have become more important influences on the vote.

Partisan Deviations

There has been a dramatic rise in split-ticket voting. According to Arthur H. Miller and Martin P. Wattenberg, about three times as many people divide their vote today as did in the 1950s.[38] The defections come primarily from weak partisans. Figure 3–1 presents the rates of defection among party identifiers from 1952 through 1996.

Defections from partisan voting patterns have tended to help the Republicans more than the Democrats. Without votes from Democratic defectors, the GOP could not have won a majority of the presidential elections between 1952 and 1996. Much of the help, however, has been short term. Although the Republicans have won seven elections at the presidential level since 1952, they still do not command the loyalty of even a plurality of the electorate. In 1992 and in 1996, defections among Republicans were actually higher than among Democrats.

The gap between self-identified Republicans and Democrats has narrowed, however. In 1952, the Democrats enjoyed a 20-percent advantage in party identification. Twenty years later that advantage had declined to 18 percent. The 1980s witnessed an even greater reduction in the partisan differential. By 1984, the parties were at rough parity with one another, and they have remained so since then although the Democrats still hold a slight advantage in party identifiers but less when turnout is taken into account.

Partisan ties have also become weaker than they were thirty or even twenty years ago. The weakening of partisan loyalties, in turn, has produced more candi-

TABLE 3–4 ★

PARTY IDENTIFICATION, 1952–2000* (IN PERCENTAGES)†

Party Identification	1952	1956	1960	1964	1968	1972	1976	1980	1984	1988	1992	1996	2000
DEMOCRAT	47	44	45	52	45	41	40	41	37	36	35	38	34
Strong	22	21	20	27	20	15	15	18	17	18	17	18	19
Weak	25	23	25	25	25	26	25	23	20	18	18	20	15
INDEPENDENT‡	23	23	23	23	30	35	37	34	34	36	39	34	39
Leaning Democrat	10	6	6	9	10	11	12	11	11	12	14	14	13
Nonpartisan	6	9	10	8	11	13	15	13	11	11	12	8	11
Leaning Republican	7	8	7	6	9	11	10	10	12	13	13	12	11
REPUBLICAN	27	29	30	25	25	23	23	23	27	28	26	29	27
Strong	14	14	14	14	15	13	14	14	15	14	15	13	14
Weak	13	15	16	11	10	10	9	9	12	14	11	16	13
APOLITICALS "Don't know"/other	4	4	3	1	1	1	1	2	2	2	1	1	4

* The survey question was "Generally speaking, do you usually think of yourself as a Republican, a Democrat, an Independent, or what?" If Republican or Democrat, "Would you call yourself a strong (R) (D) or a not very strong (R) (D)?" If Independent, "Do you think of yourself as closer to the Republican or Democratic party?"

† Percentages may not equal 100 due to rounding.

‡ The people who fall into this category are those who declare themselves to be independent, but in follow-up questions indicate that they may lean in a partisan direction.

Sources: National Election Studies (NES), Inter-University Consortium for Political and Social Research, Center for Political Studies, University of Michigan, 1952–1996; data for 2000 comes from Campaign 2000 Typology Survey conducted by Princeton Survey Research Associates, August 24–September 10, 2000, for the Pew Research Center for the People & the Press, September 14, 2000.

FIGURE 3-1 ★

DEFECTION RATE AMONG PARTY IDENTIFIERS, 1952–1996*

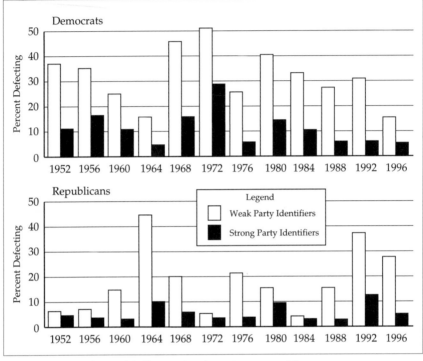

* Includes partisans who voted for Perot or the other major party candidate.

Source: National Election Studies (NES), Inter-University Consortium for Political and Social Research, Center for Political Studies, University of Michigan, 1952–1996.

date-oriented voting and, to a lesser extent, more issue-oriented voting, especially at the presidential level. Why have these trends developed?

The reaction to Vietnam and Watergate and to the credibility gaps and political abuses of the so-called imperial presidents generated feelings of mistrust and hostility that were directed at politicians and their parties. Those who became eligible to vote, particularly during the 1970s were less willing to identify with a political party. The unhappiness with the major parties has continued.[39]

A second reason for the decline in partisan allegiances has been the lowering of the voting age to eighteen. Over the last thirty years, the percentage of the electorate twenty-four years of age and under has nearly doubled. Since party identification tends to develop and harden over time, the influx of younger voters has contributed to the weakening of partisan loyalties and growth of independents. This trend may change as the electorate gets older.

A third factor has to do with contemporary modes of campaigning. In the past, political parties provided the organizations, planned campaigns, and made partisan appeals. In doing so, they trumpeted their own cause. Today, candidates' organizations direct their own campaigns. In doing so, they focus attention on the candidates' personal attributes and policy agenda rather than the party's.

Nonetheless, it is premature to write an obituary for partisanship and its impact on the electorate. The proportion of the population who continues to identify with a party remains significant and that identification either directly or indirectly influences people's voting behavior.[40] There continues to be a strong relationship between perceived partisanship and presidential voting. In 2000, 86 percent of self-identified Democrats voted for Gore and 91 percent of people who considered themselves Republicans voted for Bush.

To summarize, partisanship has weakened but not disappeared. It is not as strong an influence on how people evaluate candidates or issues, and ultimately on how they vote, as it once was. Correspondingly, short-term factors, such as the candidates, issues, and economic and social environment, are more important. The combination of these campaign-specific factors with partisan attitudes help explain election outcomes.

But that is not all. When individuals develop attitudes and opinions, they are also influenced by the associations they have with others, by the groups with which they are affiliated. In the next section we turn to these groups — to the parties' electoral coalitions, how those coalitions have changed, and how those changes have affected the parties and their electoral prospects.

THE SOCIAL BASIS OF POLITICS

The New Deal Realignment

Political coalitions form during periods of partisan realignment. The last time a classic realignment occurred was in the 1930s. Largely as a consequence of the Great Depression, the Democrats emerged as the dominant party.[41] Their coalition, held together by a common economic belief that the government should play a more active role in dealing with the nation's economic problems, supported Franklin Roosevelt's New Deal program. Those who saw government involvement as a threat to the free enterprise system opposed much of Roosevelt's domestic legislation. They remained Republican in attitude and voting behavior.

The Democrats became the majority party during this period by expanding their base. Since the Civil War, the Democrats had enjoyed support in the South. White Protestants living in rural areas dominated the southern electorate; African Americans were largely excluded from it. Only in the election of 1928, when Al Smith, the Catholic governor of New York, ran as the Democratic candidate, was there a sizable southern popular and electoral vote for a Republican candidate at the presidential level. Being a Catholic and an opponent of prohibition made Smith unacceptable to many white Protestant fundamentalists who lived in the South.

As a group, Catholics also voted Democratic before the 1930s. Living primarily in the urban centers of the North, they became increasingly important to the Democrats as their numbers grew in the population. Poor economic and social conditions, combined with the immigrant status of many Catholics, made them dependent on big-city bosses, who were able to deliver a sizable Democratic vote. In 1928, for the first time, a majority of the cities in the country voted Democratic. Catholic support for Smith and the Democratic Party figured prominently in this vote.

The harsh economic realities of the Great Depression enabled Roosevelt to expand Democratic support in urban areas still further, especially among those in the lower socioeconomic strata. Outside the South, Roosevelt's political coalition was differentiated along class lines. It attracted people with less education and income and those with lower-status jobs. Organized labor, in particular, threw its support to Roosevelt. Union members became a core group in the Democratic coalition.

In addition to establishing a broad-based, blue-collar, working-class coalition, Roosevelt also lured specific racial and ethnic groups, such as African Americans and Jewish Americans, from their Republican roots. African Americans, who lived outside of the South, voted Democratic primarily for economic reasons, and Jewish Americans supported Roosevelt's liberal domestic programs and his anti-Nazi foreign policy. Neither of these groups provided the Democratic Party of the 1930s with a large number of votes, but their loyalty to it and long-term impact on it have been considerable.

In contrast, during the same period the Republican Party shrank. Not only were Republicans unable to attract new groups to their coalition, they were unable to prevent the defection of some supporters whose economic situation affected their partisan loyalties and influenced their vote. Although the Republicans did retain the backing of many business and professional people, they lost the support of much of the white Protestant working class. Republican strength remained concentrated in the Northeast, particularly in the rural areas.

Evolving Political Coalitions

The coalition that formed during the New Deal held together, for the most part, until the 1960s. During this period, African Americans and Jewish Americans increased their identification with and support of the Democratic Party and its candidates. Catholics tended to remain Democratic, although they fluctuated more in their voting behavior at the presidential level. Nonsouthern white Protestants continued to support the Republicans.

Some changes did take place, however, mainly along socioeconomic lines. Domestic prosperity contributed to the growth of a larger middle class. Had such a class identified with the Republicans for economic reasons, the Democratic majority would have been threatened. This identification did not occur, however. Those who gained in economic and social status did not, as a general rule, discard their partisan loyalties. The Democrats were able to hold on to the allegiance of a majority of this group and improve their position with the professional and managerial classes, which had grown substantially during this period. The Republicans continued to maintain their advantage with those in the upper socioeconomic strata. The economic improvement in the country had the effect of blurring class distinctions that were evident during the 1930s and 1940s.[42]

Partisan attitudes, however, were shifting in the South. White southerners, particularly those who first voted after 1940, began to desert their party at the presidential level, largely over civil rights issues. In 1948, Harry Truman won 52 percent of the southern vote, compared with Roosevelt's 69 percent four years earlier. Although Adlai Stevenson and John Kennedy carried the South by reduced margins, the southern white Protestant vote for president went Republican for the first time in 1960.

Major shifts in the national electorate began to be evident in the mid-1960s and continued through the 1990s. (See Table 3–5.) The continued defection of southern white Protestants to Republican candidates, not only at the presidential level but at the other levels as well, has been the most significant and enduring of these changes.

Since 1952, the decline in the partisan loyalty of southern whites has been substantial. Then, 85 percent of them identified with the Democratic Party; forty years later, that proportion had shrunk to less than 40 percent with the ratio of Democrats to Republicans in the South declining from approximately six to one to less than two to one.[43] Moreover, in the 1994 midterm elections, Republican congressional candidates won a majority of the southern vote, the first time that has happened since Reconstruction.[44] In subsequent elections, the Republicans maintained their southern majority in the House. The South was also the region of the country that voted most heavily for Dole.

Despite Republican gains in the South, it is still not as solidly Republican today as it was solidly Democratic from 1876 through 1944. According to political scientists Earl and Merle Black, Franklin Delano Roosevelt averaged 78 percent of the southern vote during his four presidential elections compared with 57 percent for Republican presidential candidates from 1972 to 1988.[45]

Beginning in 1988, southern whites have been less apt to vote for the Democratic presidential candidate than have whites in any other region of the country. Arkansas Democrat, Bill Clinton, managed to split the southern vote with Robert Dole in 1996, with each receiving approximately 46 percent. Clinton had a plurality of the vote in the other regions of the country. Had it not been for the growth of the African-American electorate in the South and its overwhelming support for Democratic candidates, the defection of the southern states from the Democratic camp would have been even more dramatic.

Another potentially important shift has been occurring among new voters, particularly younger ones. During the 1980s, a plurality of this group turned to the Republican party after being more Democratic than their elders since the 1950s. In 1984, eighteen- to twenty-nine-year-olds supported Ronald Reagan in his reelection bid just as strongly as did those over thirty. (See Table 3–5.) Their support of George Bush in 1988 was even greater. In 1992, however, the vote of younger Americans more closely reflected national voting trends, and in 1996, they provided Bill Clinton with more support than any other age cohort in the population. In 2000, voters under thirty leaned slightly toward Gore.

While Democrats have lost the allegiance of southern whites at the presidential level and have lost support from southern voters generally, they also saw electoral support dwindle from several of their key coalitions. Organized labor is a good example. In six of the eight presidential elections between 1952 and 1976,

TABLE 3–5 ★

VOTE BY GROUPS IN PRESIDENTIAL ELECTIONS, 1968–2000 (IN PERCENTAGES)

	1968			1972		1976			1980		
	Humphrey	Nixon	Wallace	McGovern	Nixon	Carter	Ford	McCarthy	Carter	Reagan	Anderson
NATIONAL	43.0%	43.4%	13.6%	38.0%	62.0%	50.0%	48.0%	1.0%	41.0%	51.0%	7.0%
Sex											
Men	41	43	16	37	63	53	45	1	38	53	7
Women	45	43	12	38	62	48	51	—	44	49	6
Race											
White	38	47	15	32	68	46	52	1	36	56	7
Nonwhite	85	12	3	87	13	85	15	—	86	10	2
Education											
College	37	54	9	37	63	42	55	2	35	53	10
High school	42	43	15	34	66	54	46	—	43	51	5
Grade school	52	33	15	49	51	58	41	1	54	42	3
Occupation											
Prof. and business	34	56	10	31	69	42	56	1	33	55	10
White collar	41	47	12	36	64	50	48	2	40	51	9
Manual	50	35	15	43	57	58	41	1	48	48	5

Age										
Under 30 years	47	38	15	48	52	53	45	1	47	41	11
30–49 years	44	41	15	33	67	48	49	2	38	52	8
50 years and older	41	47	12	36	64	52	48	—	41	54	4
Religion										
Protestants	35	49	16	30	70	46	53	—	39	54	6
Catholics	59	33	8	48	52	57	41	1	46	47	6
Politics										
Republicans	9	86	5	5	95	9	91	—	8	86	5
Democrats	74	12	14	67	33	82	18	—	69	26	4
Independents	31	44	25	31	69	38	57	4	29	55	14
Region										
East	50	43	7	42	58	51	47	1	43	47	9
Midwest	44	47	9	40	60	48	50	1	41	51	7
South	31	36	33	29	71	54	45	—	44	52	3
West	44	49	7	41	59	46	51	1	35	54	9
Labor Union										
Union families	56	29	15	46	54	63	36	1	50	43	5

(continues)

TABLE 3-5 ★ (continued)

Vote by Groups in Presidential Elections, 1968–2000 (in percentages)

	1984		1988		1992			1996			2000*		
	Mondale	Reagan	Dukakis	Bush	Clinton	Bush	Perot	Clinton	Dole	Perot	Gore	Bush	Nader
NATIONAL	41.0%	59.0%	46.0%	54.0%	43.2%	37.8%	19.0%	50.0%	41.0%	9.0%	48.0%	48.0%	3.0%
Sex													
Men	36	64	44	56	41	37	22	45	44	11	42	51	4
Women	45	55	48	52	46	38	16	54	39	7	49	43	3
Race													
White	34	66	41	59	39	41	20	46	45	9	39	59	4
Nonwhite	87	13	82	18	77	11	12	82	12	6	81	9	5
Education†													
College	39	61	42	58	43	40	17	47	45	8	46	48	4
High school	43	57	46	54	40	38	22	52	34	14	41	51	5
Grade school	51	49	55	45	56	28	16	58	27	15	48	42	4
Age													
Under 30 years	40	60	37	63	40	37	23	54	30	16	43	46	8
30–49 years	40	60	45	55	42	37	21	49	41	10	43	51	3
50 years and older	41	59	49	51	46	39	15	50	45	5	48	43	3

Religion												
Protestants	39	61	42	58	41	41	18	44	50	6	—	—	—
Catholics	39	61	51	49	47	35	18	55	35	10	—	—	—
Politics												
Republicans	4	96	7	93	7	77	16	10	85	5	7	91	1
Democrats	79	21	85	15	82	8	10	90	6	4	85	10	9
Independents	33	67	43	57	39	30	31	48	33	19	37	42	3
Region												
East	46	54	51	49	47	35	18	60	31	9	52	38	6
Midwest	42	58	47	53	44	34	22	46	45	9	43	47	4
South	37	63	40	60	38	45	17	44	46	10	36	56	3
West	40	60	46	54	45	35	20	51	43	6	43	47	6
Labor Union												
Union families	52	48	63	37	—	—	—	—	—	—	58	31	6

* Gallup data in 2000 underestimated Gore's vote in most demographic categories (see Table 8-3, pages 286–287).

† In 2000, categories comprised College, Some college, and No college.

Notes: National figures are based on actual election outcomes, repercentaged to exclude minor third-party candidates. Demographic data are based on Gallup Poll final preelection surveys, repercentaged to exclude "no opinions"; for 2000, data are based on Gallup six-day average, October 31–November 5, 2000, except Region.

Source: Gallup Organization, "Vote By Groups," <http://www.gallup.com/poll/trends>, November 6, 2000; "Final Preelection Poll," November 7, 2000.

this group favored the Democratic candidate by an average of nearly 30 percentage points. In the 1980s, the results were closer although the Democrats still enjoyed an advantage. Labor support for the Democrats has increased in the 1990s. Clinton received 55 percent of the vote from people who lived in union households in 1992 and 59 percent in 1996, while Gore also got 59 percent in 2000. However, as a group, organized labor has declined as a proportion of the total population. Members of union households made up 25 percent of the electorate in 1952; today they constitute only about 15 percent. Thus, the proportion of the vote the Democrats receive from labor has declined.

Catholic allegiance to the Democratic Party has also weakened, declining from its high of 78 percent in 1960 to a low of 39 percent in 1984. Dukakis and Clinton recovered some of these losses. Clinton won 53 percent of the Catholic vote in 1996, helped by his considerable support within the Hispanic community. Gore had a slightly smaller percentage. In general, Catholics as a group now seem more susceptible to candidate-centered and issue-specific appeals than they were when their partisan identification was stronger.[46] Clinton's and Gore's positions on Social Security, Medicare, education, and the environment apparently helped with Catholic voters and, surprisingly, so did their pro-choice position on abortion.[47]

Jewish voters have evidenced a much smaller decrease in their Democratic partisan sympathies and voting behavior, although as a group Jews have declined as a proportion of the population. But they have remained loyal to the Democratic Party. Approximately two-thirds of this group identify with the Democratic Party, and three-fourths have voted for its presidential candidates since 1928. The only election since World War II in which a majority of Jews did not vote Democratic occurred in 1980 when only 47 percent cast ballots for President Carter. Independent candidate John Anderson was the principal beneficiary of this defection, winning 14 percent of the Jewish vote. As a group, Jewish Americans returned to their traditional voting patterns after that election. Contributing to their support for the Democratic candidates has been the party's liberal position on social issues and, in 2000, the nomination of Joseph Lieberman as the Democratic vice presidential candidate.

The Democratic electoral coalition has also retained and even increased its support among other key groups, notably African Americans and Hispanics. Today, more than 75 percent of African Americans consider themselves Democrats, with less than 10 percent considering themselves Republicans compared to the late 1950s when almost 25 percent considered themselves Republican.[48] While other groups have weakened their loyalty to the Democrats, African Americans have increased theirs. In general, the smaller the Democratic vote, the larger the African-American proportion of it. In 1980, one out of four Carter voters came from this group; from 1984 to 1992, one out of five voted for the Democratic presidential candidate; in 1996, one out of six Clinton voters was African American; in 2000, Gore received the support of nine out of ten African-American voters.[49]

But there has been a flip side to this African-American support. Democratic positions on social issues, particular civil rights, that appeal to African Americans have alienated some white working-class voters whose support for the Democrats has declined over the last three decades.[50]

Hispanic voters have also become an important component of the Democrats' electoral coalition, particularly as that group expands within the population. With the exception of Cuban Americans concentrated in south Florida, a majority of Hispanic voters identify with the Democratic Party and two-thirds of them tend to vote for its candidates on a regular basis. Clinton received the support of almost three out of four Hispanic voters in 1996, and Gore, almost two out of three in 2000.

Since 1980, there have been discernible differences in the partisan identities and electoral voting patterns of men and women. This differential has produced a "gender gap," with women more likely to identify with and vote Democratic and men more likely to prefer the Republican Party and its candidates. The gap had been in the range of 4 to 11 percent until 1996, when it rose to 17 percent; in 2000, it was 22 percent. It is larger among whites than nonwhites, larger among those in the higher socioeconomic brackets than in lower groups, and larger among those with more formal education than less.[51] It is also greater among those who are unmarried than those who are married and those without children than those with them.

In the light of these shifts, how can the composition of the major political parties be described today? Table 3–6 presents a demographic profile of the major parties. As Table 3–6 indicates, the Democrats have become a diverse party in which ethnic and racial minorities and, increasingly, women constitute core constituencies. Democrats still receive overwhelming support from those with the lowest incomes and those who live in the cities. However, the relatively small size of the latter two groups compared with the population as a whole and their lower turnout make them less important components of the total electorate than they were in the past. The same can be said for organized labor which continues to vote Democratic but now accounts for a smaller percentage of the electorate. Southern whites have exited in the largest proportions, but the Democrats have picked up support in the Northeast. Additionally, those voters who came of age during the Roosevelt presidency remain the party's most loyal age group but their children and grandchildren do not share their strong Democratic allegiances.

Although the Democrats' New Deal coalition has eroded, the groups within that coalition, with the exception of southern whites, have not become Republican. They have simply provided less support for the Democrats. Although the Republican Party has gained adherents, it has not done so by virtue of a major exodus of groups from one party to the other, except in the South.

As a party, the Republicans have become more white, more middle class, more suburban, and more male. They have gained support in the South and Southwest, the so-called Sunbelt. Additionally, they have gained adherents from white evangelical Christian groups that had supported the Democratic Party and voted for its candidates through 1976. By the end of the 1980s, a plurality of this group thought of themselves as Republican, with 80 percent voting for George Bush in 1988, 63 percent in 1992, 65 percent for Dole in 1996, and 80 percent for Bush in 2000. White evangelicals now constitute a core bloc within the Republican party's electoral coalition almost as important to the GOP as African Americans are to the Democrats.[52]

The shift of white evangelical Christians, who constitute approximately one-fourth of the population, to the Republican Party has offset some of the reduction

TABLE 3–6 ★

REPUBLICAN AND DEMOCRATIC PARTY PROFILES, 2000

	Republicans and Independents Who Lean Republican (in percentages)	Democrats and Independents Who Lean Democratic (in percentages)
Gender		
Male	53	43
Female	47	57
Age		
18–29	21	20
30–49	43	40
50–64	19	21
65+	15	18
Race		
White	93	75
Black	3	19
Other nonwhite	4	6
Education		
Postgraduate degree	12	13
Undergraduate degree	14	11
Some college	37	29
No college	38	47
Household Income		
$75,00 and over	22	15
$50,000–74,999	21	16
$30,000–49,000	24	25
$20,000–29,999	12	14
Less than $20,000	15	23
Region		
East	20	25
Midwest	24	22
South	33	31
West	22	21
Type of Community		
Urban	23	31
Suburban	53	45
Rural	24	24
Political Ideology		
Conservative	54	22
Moderate	36	46
Liberal	8	26

TABLE 3–6 ★ *(continued)*

REPUBLICAN AND DEMOCRATIC PARTY PROFILES, 2000

	Republicans and Independents Who Lean Republican (in percentages)	Democrats and Independents Who Lean Democratic (in percentages)
Religion		
Protestant	44	34
Roman Catholic	24	25
Greek Orthodox	1	1
Mormon	3	1
Other Christian	6	6
Jewish	1	3
Church or Other Holy Place Attendance		
Weekly	33	33
Semimonthly	26	20
Seldom	16	14
Never	17	21
Marital Status		
Married	61	50
Living together	5	7
Never married	16	20
Widowed/divorced/separated	17	23
Children		
Yes	39	35
No	61	65
Employed		
Full-time	56	53
Part-time	7	8
Retired	17	22
Homemaker	8	7
Student	6	4
Unemployed	4	3
Union Member		
Yes	12	18
No	87	81

Source: Gallup Poll, July 30–August 11, 2000 (based on surveys conducted between March and July 2000, which included over 10,000 interviews), <http://www.gallup.com/poll/releases/pr000811.asp>.

in Republican support from mainline Protestants, particularly those with liberal social views. The presidential votes of members of this group have declined in the 1990s, as has their identification with the Republican Party. In general, regular churchgoers within both evangelical and mainline Protestant groups are more Republican in their party identification and voting behavior than those who do not attend regularly. Nonchurchgoers, those who think of themselves as secular and rarely attend religious services, have become the least Republican group of all.[53] The contemporary Republican Party thus consists of racial and religious majorities, those in the higher socioeconomic brackets, and those in the professional and managerial ranks.

What conclusions can we draw about the social basis of politics today? It is clear that the old party coalitions have evolved and, in the Democrats' case, weakened. Today, voters seem to be less influenced by group cues. They exercise a more independent judgment on election day, a judgment that is likely to be influenced by factors that condition the environment in which the election occurs and by the campaign itself.

A New Partisan Majority?

Will there be a new partisan realignment? Will the GOP emerge as the new majority? The answer is still unclear, but two basic trends stand out: one relates to the contemporary dealignment of the partisan attitudes of the electorate over time; the other pertains to the narrowing of the gap that has developed between Democratic and Republican identifiers.

Dealignment. Dealignment is a weakening in the attachments people feel toward political parties. It has produced more split-ticket voting, which helped Republican presidential candidates more than their Democratic counterparts in the 1970s and 1980s but not in the 1990s. It has also led more people to think of themselves as independents. Dealignment, in short, enabled the Republicans to win an electoral majority when their party was still in the minority, particular during the period from 1968 to 1980. It also enabled independent candidate Ross Perot to receive 19 percent of the vote in 1992 but less than half that percentage in 1996.

Realignment. There is some evidence that a gradual, partial, partisan realignment may have occurred, with the Republican Party the principal beneficiary. This realignment, however, seems to be less meaningful and less extensive than the one that took place in the 1930s. With the exception of white southerners who have switched their allegiances from Democratic to Republican, it has not involved wholesale shifts from one electoral coalition to another in the rest of the country.[54] Nor has it involved overwhelming proportions of new voters who ally themselves with one party.

A partisan realignment that occurs during an era of weaker partisan attachments for adherents to both parties may not have the same impact as one that occurs during a period in which partisan loyalties are stronger and more predictive of the vote. If people generally have less confidence in parties and weaker partisan allegiances, then their affiliation is not likely to matter as much. In the words of Martin Wattenberg, a keen student of partisan attitudes and behavior, "such a realignment is hollow when the two parties involved continue to have a weak image in the public mind and an uncertain role in the future of American government."[55]

SUMMARY

The electorate is not neutral. People do not come to campaigns with completely open minds. Rather, their preexisting attitudes and accumulated experiences color their perceptions and affect their judgments, much as stimuli from the campaign affect those attitudes and experiences.

Of the political beliefs people possess, partisanship has the strongest impact on voting. It provides a perspective for evaluating the campaign and for deciding whether and how to vote. It is also a motive for being informed, for being concerned, and for turning out to vote.

Since 1960, and with the exception of 1992, there has been a decline in the proportion of the population who voted. This decline can be partially attributed to the weakening of party ties, to the increasing proportion of younger voters, and to the cynicism and apathy of the population as a whole.

Partisan attitudes have also eroded since the 1960s. The percentage of people identifying with a party has declined. One consequence has been the increasing importance of short-term factors on voting. A second related one has been more split-ticket ballots. The weakening of partisan ties has produced a vote that either party can win. It has produced a presidential vote that has less carryover to congressional and state elections. Presidential coattails have not been evident since 1980. The electorate has become more volatile and less predictable.

Group ties to the parties have also loosened. Partisan coalitions have shifted. The Democratic Party, which became dominant during the New Deal period, has lost the support of a majority of southern whites in presidential and congressional elections and has suffered defections from other groups. That some of these groups have also declined as a proportion of the population or have lower-than-average turnout has further aggravated the Democrats' problem. Racial minorities, such as African Americans and Hispanics, however, have retained their loyalty to the Democrats as have Jewish Americans. Women have become much more supportive of Democratic candidates and men more supportive of Republicans. Those with secular views have become more Democratic and those with sectarian views more Republican.

Naturally, the Republicans have benefited from the fraying of the Democrats' electoral coalition. Looser partisan ties have given them greater electoral opportunities. The Republicans have gained in the South, benefited from the increased social and economic conservatism of a growing middle and upper-middle class, and made strides among younger voters. Although they won seven of the twelve presidential elections between 1952 and 1996, thus far they have not been able to expand their electoral coalition into a partisan plurality much less majority.

These changes within the political environment have important implications for presidential politics. The weakening of partisan attitudes and the splintering of the New Deal coalitions augur a new era in electoral politics. It is clear that a dealignment has occurred. It is not clear whether a realignment is occurring or, if it is, how important that realignment will be to the future of American politics. Partisan attitudes seem to be less compelling influences on voting behavior than they were in the past.

WHERE ON THE WEB?

- **Democracy Network**
  http://www.dnet.org
  A public interest site sponsored by the education fund of the League of Women Voters on which you can find out candidate positions on the issues as well as connect to grassroots groups on a variety of salient issues.
- **Democratic National Committee**
  http://www.democrats.org
  Information on Democratic Party history, rules, convention, and campaigns. Links to Democratic youth and state party affiliates.
- **League of Women Voters**
  http://www.lwv.org
  Information on candidates, their positions, and how to register and vote.
- **Republican National Committee**
  http://www.rnc.org
  Information on Republican Party history, rules, convention, and campaigns. Links to Republican youth and state party affiliates.
- **Rock-the-Vote**
  http://www.rockthevote.org
  An organization whose goal is to encourage young people to register and vote. Enables you to fill out a registration form on-line, as well as obtain an absentee ballot.
- **Project Vote Smart**
  http://www.vote-smart.org
  An organization that provides a wealth of information on candidates and their issue positions and evaluates their performance in office.

EXERCISES

1. If you are a U.S. citizen, eighteen years of age or older, and haven't already done so, register to vote by accessing FEC at <http://www.fec.gov> and downloading the national voter registration form, completing it, and sending it to your state, or access Rock-the-Vote at <http://www.rockthevote.org/main_register.html> and provide them with information to begin the registration process.
2. Indicate all the services that the major parties are providing their candidates in the general election by accessing their sites and going through their menu of services. Which of these services do you think will be most helpful to the presidential candidates?

3. Become a chief political strategist for a prospective third-party or independent presidential candidate by participating in the Web-based case study developed by the Kennedy School of Government <http://www.ksg.harvard.edu/case/3pt> if that study is still available on the school's Web site.
4. Describe the composition of the major parties' electoral coalitions. On the basis of your description, locate interest groups that represent these types of supporters. Access their sites and note what they have done to mobilize their members and sympathizers in the 2000 campaign.

SELECTED READING

Black, Earl, and Merle Black. *The Vital South: How Presidents Are Elected.* Cambridge, Mass.: Harvard University Press, 1992.

Box-Steffensmeier, Janet M., and Renee M. Smith, "The Dynamics of Aggregate Partisanship." *American Political Science Review* (September 1996): 567–580.

Burnham, Walter D. "The Turnout Problem." In *Elections American Style,* edited by A. James Reichley, 97–133. Washington, D.C.: Brookings Institution, 1987.

Campbell, Angus, Philip E. Converse, Warren E. Miller, and Donald E. Stokes. *The American Voter.* New York: Wiley, 1960.

Carmines, Edward G., and James A. Stimson. *Issue Evolution: Race and the Transformation of American Politics.* Princeton, N.J.: Princeton University Press, 1989.

Clubb, Jerome M., William H. Flanigan, and Nancy H. Zingale. *Partisan Realignment: Voters, Parties, and Government in American History.* Boulder, Colo.: Westview Press, 1990.

Keith, Bruce E., David B. Magleby, Candice Nelson, and Elizabeth Orr. *The Myth of the Independent Voter.* Berkeley: University of California Press, 1992.

Ladd, Everett Carll, Jr., with Charles D. Hadley. *Transformations of the American Party System.* New York: Norton, 1978.

Leege, David, and Lyman A. Kellstedt. *Rediscovering the Religious Factor in American Politics.* New York: Sharpe, 1993.

Lyons, William, and Robert Alexander. "A Tale of Two Electorates: Generational Replacement and the Decline of Voting in Presidential Elections." *Journal of Politics* 62 (November 2000): 1014–1034.

McCann, James A., Randall W. Partin, and Ronald B. Rapoport, "Presidential Nomination Campaigns and Party Mobilization: An Assessment of Spillover Effects." *American Journal of Political Science* (August 1996): 756–767.

Miller, Warren E. "Party Identification, Realignment, and Party Voting: Back to the Basics," *American Political Science Review* 85 (June 1991): 557–570.

Nardulli, Peter F., Jon K. Dalager, and Donald E. Greco, "Voter Turnout in U.S. Presidential Elections: A Historical Overview and Some Speculation." *PS* (September 1996): 480–490.

Nie, Norman H., Sidney Verba, and John R. Petrocik. *The Changing American Voter.* Cambridge, Mass.: Harvard University Press, 1976.

Niemi, Richard G., and Herbert F. Weisberg. *Controversies in Voting Behavior.* 3rd ed. Washington, D.C.: Congressional Quarterly, 1993.

Piven, Frances Fox, and Richard A. Cloward. *Why Americans Don't Vote.* New York: Pantheon, 1988.

Popkin, Samuel L. *The Reasoning Voter: Communication and Persuasion in Presidential Campaigns.* Chicago: University of Chicago Press, 1991.

Rapoport, Ronald B. "Partisanship Change in a Candidate-Centered Era." *Journal of Politics* (February 1997): 185–199.

Tate, Katherine. "Black Political Participation in the 1984 and 1988 Presidential Elections." *American Political Science Review* 85 (December 1991): 1159–1176.

Teixeira, Ruy A. *The Disappearing American Voter.* Washington, D.C.: Brookings Institution, 1992.

Wattenberg, Martin P. *The Decline of American Political Parties: 1952–1988.* Cambridge, Mass.: Harvard University Press, 1990.

White, John Kenneth, and William D'Antonio. "The Catholic Vote in '96." *The Public Perspective* (June/July 1997): 45–48.

Wolfinger, Raymond E., and Steven J. Rosenstone. *Who Votes?* New Haven, Conn.: Yale University Press, 1980.

NOTES

1. Calculating turnout on the basis of voting-age population results in a lower percent for a country such as the United States that has high immigration rates, and as a result, many resident aliens living within its borders. Resident aliens are not citizens and cannot vote. See Samuel L. Popkin and Michael McDonald, "Turnout's Not as Bad as You Think," *Washington Post,* November 5, 2000, B1, 2.

2. Ronald P. Formisane, "Deferential-Participant Politics: The Early Republic's Political Culture, 1789," *American Political Science Review* 68 (June 1974): 473–487.

3. Walter Dean Burnham, "The Turnout Problem," in *Elections American Style,* ed. A. James Reichley (Washington, D.C.: Brookings Institution, 1987), 112–116.

4. Peter F.Nardulli, Jon K. Dalager, and Donald E. Greco, "Voter Turnout in U.S. Presidential Elections: An Historical View and Some Speculation," *PS* (September 1996): 480.

5. Although some states initially permitted all landowners to vote, including women, by 1807 every one of them limited voting to men. Michael X. Delli Carpini and Ester R. Fuchs, "The Year of the Woman: Candidates, Voters, and the 1992 Election," *Political Science Quarterly* 108 (Spring 1993): 30.

6. Ibid.

7. Earl Black and Merle Black, *The Vital South: How Presidents Are Elected* (Cambridge, Mass.: Harvard University Press, 1992), 217.

8. The territory of Wyoming was the first to grant women the vote in 1867.

9. In the case of *Smith v. Allwright* (321 U.S. 649, 1944), the Supreme Court declared the white primary unconstitutional. In its opinion the Court rejected the argument that parties were private associations and thus could restrict participation in their selection processes.

10. In 1992, women were about 2.1 percent more likely to vote than men. In 1996, this percentage increased to 2.7 according to the Census Bureau's Current Population Survey. Paul R. Abramson, John H. Aldrich and David W. Rohde, *Change and Continuity in the 1996 Elections* (Washington, D.C.: Congressional Quarterly, 1998), 75.

11. David P. Glass, Peverill Squire, and Raymond E. Wolfinger, "Voter Turnout: An International Comparison," *Public Opinion* 5 (December/January 1984): 49–55.

12. Approximately half the states had motor-voter laws of their own prior to the enactment of federal legislation.

13. Federal Election Commission, "The Impact of the National Voter Registration Act on the Administration of Elections for Federal Office, 1997–1998," <http://www.fec.gov/pages/9798NVRAexec.htm>.

14. "Record Numbers Register under 'Motor Voter' Law," *Washington Post*, March 27, 1996, A16; "20 Million 'Motor Voters,'" *New York Times*, October 16, 1996, A15.

15. In addition, thirty-two states prohibit those on parole from voting and twenty-nine prohibit those on probation. Fox Butterfield, "Many Black Males Barred from Voting," *New York Times*, January 30, 1997, A12. Michael A. Fletcher, "Voting Rights for Felons Win Support," *Washington Post*, February 22, 1999, A1, 6.

16. Angus Campbell, Philip E. Converse, Warren E. Miller, and Donald E. Stokes, *The American Voter* (New York: Wiley, 1960), 102.

17. A survey of voters and nonvoters conducted during March 1996 found no differences in the levels of trust and confidence in government between these groups. This is an interesting finding because of the conventional wisdom that political alienation contributes to apathy and nonvoting. This survey found higher levels of information about the election and stronger partisan beliefs as factors that differentiated voters from nonvoters. Richard L. Berke, "Nonvoters Are No More Alienated than Voters, A Survey Shows," *New York Times*, May 30, 1996, A21.

18. Raymond E. Wolfinger and Steven J. Rosenstone, *Who Votes?* (New Haven, Conn.: Yale University Press, 1980), 13–26.

19. Ibid., 18–20, 35–36.

20. Ruy Teixeira describes "social connectedness" as the "interpersonal, community, and general social ties [that] provide a substantial proportion of an individual's motivation to vote." *The Disappearing American Voter* (Washington, D.C.: Brookings Institution, 1992), 36. He adds that demographic characteristics that usually reflect connectedness are marital status, church attendance, and age. Ibid., 37. See also Abramson, Aldrich, and Rohde, *Change and Continuity in 1992*, 115.

21. Paul R. Abramson, John H. Aldrich, and David W. Rohde, *Change and Continuity in 1996* (Washington, D.C.: Congressional Quarterly, 1998), 80.

22. Ibid., 84.

23. Abramson, Aldrich, and Rohde, *Change and Continuity in 1992*, 118.

24. For a good discussion of the effect of demographic characteristics and campaigns on the electorate see Robert A. Jackson, "A Reassessment of Voter Mobilization," *Political Research Quarterly* (June 1996): 331–349.

25. Abramson, Aldrich, and Rohde argue that Clinton benefited more from converting 1988 Bush supporters to his cause than from the increasing Democratic turnout in 1996. Abramson, Aldrich, and Rohde, *Change and Continuity in 1996*, 86.

26. Actually, a small interview-reinterview survey was conducted in 1948, but the results were never published. In contrast to the emphasis on political attitudes of the large-scale interview projects in the 1950s, the project in 1948 had a sociological orientation.

27. Campbell, Converse, Miller, and Stokes, *The American Voter*, 102.

28. Ibid., 146–152.

29. Ibid., 133–136. Party identification is determined by the following question: "Generally speaking, do you usually think of yourself as a Republican, Democrat, an Independent, or what?" To discern the strength of the identification, a second question is asked (if Republican or Democrat): "Would you call yourself a strong (R) (D) or a not very strong (R) (D)?"; (if Independent): "Do you think of yourself as closer to the Republican or Democratic party?" In examining the concept of party identification, Michigan

analysts have stressed two dimensions: direction and strength. Others, however, have criticized the Michigan model for overemphasizing party and underemphasizing other factors, such as social class, political ideology, and issue positions. For a thoughtful critique, see Jerrold G. Rusk, "The Michigan Election Studies: A Critical Evaluation," (paper presented at the annual meeting of the American Political Science Association, New York, September 3–6, 1981).

30. Janet M. Box-Steffensmeier and Renee M. Smith, "The Dynamic of Aggregate Partisanship," *American Political Science Review* (September 1990): 567–580; Ronald B. Rapoport, "Partisanship Change in a Candidate-Centered Era," *Journal of Politics* (February 1997): 185–199.

31. For a more extensive discussion of desirable presidential images, see Chapter 6 of this book and Benjamin I. Page, *Choices and Echoes in Presidential Elections* (Chicago: University of Chicago Press, 1978), 232–265.

32. Campbell, Converse, Miller, and Stokes, *The American Voter*, 143 and 547. Independents who lean in a partisan direction tend to be better informed than those who do not. These independent leaners have many of the characteristics of party identifiers including loyalty to the party's candidates. They do not, however, identify themselves as Republicans or Democrats.

33. V. O. Key, Jr., *The Responsible Electorate* (Cambridge, Mass.: Harvard University Press, 1966), 7.

34. Samuel L. Popkin, *The Reasoning Voter* (Chicago: University of Chicago Press, 1991), 43.

35. Morris P. Fiorina, *Retrospective Voting in American National Elections* (New Haven: Conn.: Yale University Press, 1981), 65–83.

36. Ibid., 84.

37. For an analysis of independents and their voting patterns, see Bruce E. Keith, David B. Magleby, Candice Nelson, and Elizabeth Orr, *The Myth of the Independent Voter* (Berkeley: University of California Press, 1992).

38. Arthur H. Miller and Martin P. Wattenberg, "Policy and Performance Voting in the 1980 Election," (paper presented at the annual meeting of the American Political Science Association, New York, September 3–6, 1981).

39. A CBS News/*New York Times* poll fielded nine days before the 1994 midterm election found 57 percent of those surveyed felt the country needed a new political party. See *New York Times,* November 3, 1994, 8A. A poll conducted for the Times Mirror Center for the People and the Press during the period April 6–9, 1995, found similar results.: "News Release," Times Mirror Center for the People and the Press, 66.

40. Warren E. Miller, "Party Identification, Realignment, and Party Voting: Back to the Basics," *American Political Science Review* 85 (June 1991): 559.

41. This description of the New Deal realignment is based primarily on the discussion in Everett Carll Ladd, Jr. with Charles D. Hadley, *Transformations of the American Party System* (New York: Norton, 1975), 31–87.

42. Ibid., 93–104.

43. Black and Black, *The Vital South*, 27.

44. Thomas B. Edsall, "Huge Gains in South Fueled GOP Vote in '94," *Washington Post,* June 27, 1995, A8.

45. Ibid.

46. Lyman A. Kellstedt, John C. Green, James L. Guth, and Corwin E. Schmidt, "Religious Voting Blocs in the 1992 Election: Year of the Evangelical?" *Sociology of Religion* 55 (1994): 307–326; Robert B. Fowler and Allen D. Hertzke, *Religion and Politics in America: Faith, Culture, and Strategic Choice* (Boulder, Colo.: Westview Press, 1995).

47. John Kenneth White and William D'Antonio, "The Catholic Vote in Election '96," *The Public Perspective* (June/July 1997): 45–48.

48. Everett Carll Ladd, "The 1992 Vote for President Clinton: Another Brittle Mandate?" *Political Science Quarterly* 108 (Spring 1993): 4. For a discussion of turnout among African Americans in 1984 and 1988, see Katherine Tate, "Black Political Participation in the 1984 and 1988 Presidential Elections," *American Political Science Review* 85 (December 1991): 1159–1176.

49. Abramson, Aldrich, and Rohde, *Change and Continuity in 1996,* 104.

50. For an extended discussion of the impact of race on the Democratic Party, see Robert Huckfeldt and Carol Weitzel Kohfeld, *Race and the Decline of Class in American Politics* (Urbana: University of Illinois Press, 1989).

51. Abramson, Aldrich, and Rohde, *Change and Continuity in 1996,* 96.

52. The conservative policy orientation of this group has also colored the Republicans' position on some important and divisive social issues. For an excellent discussion of the religious right and its impact on the 1992 election see Kellstedt, Green, Guth, and Smidt, "Religious Voting Blocs in the 1992 Election: The Year of the Evangelical?" (paper presented at the annual meeting of the American Political Science Association, Washington, D.C., September 1–4,1993).

53. Ibid., 7, 8, 11, 18, and 21.

54. Miller, "Party Identification," 562.

55. Martin P. Wattenberg, *The Decline of American Political Parties, 1952–1988* (Cambridge, Mass.: Harvard University Press, 1990).

PART II

THE
NOMINATION

THE RACE FOR DELEGATES

4

INTRODUCTION

Presidential nominees are selected by the delegates to their party's national convention. The way those delegates are chosen, however, influences the choice of nominees. It also affects the influence of the state and its party leadership.

Procedures for delegate selection are determined by state law. Today, these procedures also have to conform to the general guidelines and rules established by the national parties. Prior to the 1970s, they did not. Under the old system, statutes passed by the state legislature reflected the needs and desires of the political leaders who controlled the state. Naturally, these laws were designed to buttress that leadership and extend its clout.

Primary elections in which the party's rank and file chose the delegates were discouraged, co-opted, or even circumvented. Favorite son candidates, tapped by the leadership, prevented meaningful contests in many states. Although primaries were held, many of them were advisory; the actual selection of the delegates was left to caucuses, conventions, or committees, which were more easily controlled by party officials. There were also impediments to potential delegates getting on the ballot: high fees, lengthy petitions, and early filing dates. Winner-take-all provisions gave a great advantage to the organization candidate, as did rules requiring delegates to vote as a unit.

Popular participation in the selection of convention delegates is a relatively recent phenomenon in the history of national nominating conventions. It was the Democrats who took the lead in encouraging their partisans to become involved in the nomination process by adopting a series of reforms that affected the period during which delegates could be selected, the procedures for choosing them, and ultimately their behavior at the convention. Although these Democratic Party rules limited the states' discretion, they did not result in uniform primaries and caucuses. Considerable variation still exists in how delegates are chosen, how the vote is apportioned, and who participates in the selection.

This chapter explores these rules and their consequences for the nomination process. It is organized into four sections. The first details the changes in party rules. The second considers the legal challenges to these rules and the Supreme Court's decisions on these challenges. The third section examines the impact of the rules changes on the party and the electorate, and the fourth discusses how the rules have affected the candidates and how those candidates have responded with strategies designed for today's participatory nomination politics.

REFORMING THE NOMINATION PROCESS

Historically, states set their own rules for nominating candidates with relatively little guidance from the national party. Some rules discouraged popular involvement; others encouraged it but made no effort to translate the public's opinion of the candidates into delegate support for them. In very few states was the delegation as a whole representative, demographically or ideologically, of the party's electorate within that state.

Democratic Party reforms have attempted to change this situation. The party had two principal objectives in altering its rules to promote more internal democracy. Democrats wanted to encourage greater rank-and-file participation and to select delegates who were more representative of the party's supporters. The problem has been how to achieve these goals and still win elections.

The Democratic Party has gone through two stages in reforming its delegate selection procedures. During the first, 1968–1980, it adopted a highly structured set of national rules aimed at achieving its two principal aims: greater participation and more equitable representation. It imposed these rules on the states. Since that time the party has modified these rules to improve the chances of its nominees in the general election. Unlike the Democrats, the Republican Party has mandated very few national rules on its state parties although an advisory commission on the party's nomination process urged it to do so for 2004.[1] Republican state parties, however, have been affected by Democratic reforms, particularly in states whose legislatures were controlled by the Democrats when their primaries and caucuses were established.

Democratic Rules, 1968–1980

The catalyst for the rules changes was the tumultuous Democratic convention of 1968, a convention in which Senator Hubert Humphrey won the nomination without actively campaigning in the party's primaries. Yet the primaries of that year were very important. They had become the vehicle by which Democrats could protest the Johnson administration's conduct of the war in Vietnam.

Senator Eugene McCarthy, the first of the antiwar candidates, had challenged Lyndon Johnson in the New Hampshire primary. To the surprise of many political observers, McCarthy received 42.4 percent of the vote, almost as much as the president, who got 49.5 percent.[2] Four days after McCarthy's unexpectedly strong showing, Senator Robert Kennedy, brother of the late president and political rival of Johnson, declared his candidacy for the nation's highest office. With protests against the war mounting and divisions within the Democratic Party intensifying, Johnson bowed out, declaring that he did not want the country's involvement in Southeast Asia to become a divisive political issue.

Johnson's withdrawal cleared the way for Hubert Humphrey, the vice president, to run. Humphrey, however, waited almost a month to announce his intentions. His late entrance into the Democratic nomination process intentionally precluded a primary effort since filing deadlines had expired in most of the states. Like Johnson, Humphrey did not want to become the focal point of antiwar protests. Nor did he have the grassroots organization to match McCarthy's and Kennedy's. What he did have was the support of most national and state Democratic leaders, including the president.

The last big-state primary in 1968 was California's. In it, Kennedy scored a significant victory, but during the celebration that followed, he was assassinated. His death left McCarthy as the principal antiestablishment, antiwar candidate, but he was far short of a convention majority. Despite the last-minute entrance of Senator George McGovern, who hoped to rally Kennedy delegates to his candidacy, Humphrey won the nomination easily. To make matters worse for those who opposed Humphrey and the administration's war efforts, an amendment to the party platform calling for an unconditional end to the bombing of North Vietnam was defeated. McCarthy and Kennedy delegates felt victimized by the nomination process and the resulting nomination of Humphrey. They were angry. They demanded reform and eventually got it. A divided convention approved the establishment of a party committee to reexamine the rules for delegate selection with the goals of providing greater participation by the rank and file and more equitable representation.

Compounding the divisions within the convention were demonstrations outside the hall. Thousands of youthful protesters, calling for an end to the war, congregated in the streets of Chicago. The police, under direction from Mayor Richard Daley to maintain order, used strong-arm tactics to disperse the crowds. Clashes between police and protesters followed. Television news crews filmed these confrontations, and the networks showed them during their convention coverage. The spectacle of police beating demonstrators further inflamed emotions and led to calls for party reform, not only from those who attended the convention but from those who watched it on television.

After the election, a commission, chaired initially by Senator George McGovern, was appointed to study procedures for electing and seating convention delegates and to propose ways of improving them. The commission recommended that delegate selection be a *fair reflection* of Democratic sentiment within the state and implicitly, less closely tied to the wishes of state party leaders. Rules to make it easier for individuals to run as delegates, to limit the size of the districts from which they could be chosen, and to require that the number of delegates elected be proportional to the popular vote that they or the candidates to whom they were pledged received, were approved by the party. A requirement that delegates be chosen no earlier than the calendar year of the election was also approved.

Additionally, Democrats tried to prevent independents and, especially, partisans of other parties, from participating in the selection of Democratic delegates. The difficulty, however, was to determine who was a Democrat, since some states did not require or even permit registration by party. When implementing this rule, the national party adopted a very liberal interpretation of Democratic affiliation. People identifying themselves as Democrats at the time of voting, or those requesting Democratic ballots, were viewed as Democrats. This process of identification effectively permitted crossover voting, allowing Republicans or independents to cross over and vote in the Democratic primaries in some states. The only primaries that the Democratic rules effectively prohibited were *open primaries,* those in which voters are given the ballots of both major parties, discard one, and vote the other.

In addition to translating public preferences into delegate selection, another major objective of the reforms was to equalize representation on the delegations themselves. Three groups in particular — African Americans, women, and youth — had protested their underrepresentation on party councils and at the conventions. Their representatives and others who were sympathetic to their plight pressed hard for more power and better representation for women and minorities. The reform commission reacted to these protests by proposing a rule requiring that all states represent these particular groups in reasonable relationship to their presence in the state population. Failure to do so was viewed as prima facie evidence of discrimination. In point of fact, the party had established quotas.

Considerable opposition developed to the application of this rule during the 1972 nomination process, and it was subsequently modified to require that states implement affirmative action plans for those groups that had been subject to past discrimination.[3] The Democrats went one step further with respect to women. Beginning with its 1980 nominating convention, they required that each state delegation be equally divided between the sexes.

Still another goal of the reforms, to involve more Democrats in the selection process, was achieved not only by the fair reflection rule but by making primaries the preferred method of delegate selection. To avoid a challenge to the composition of their delegation, states switched to primaries in which delegates were elected directly by the people.[4]

Caucuses in which party regulars selected the delegates were still permitted, but they, too, were redesigned to encourage greater rank-and-file participation. (See Box 4–1, "The Iowa Caucus: How It Works.") No longer could state party leaders vote a large number of proxies for the delegates of their choice. Caucuses had to be publicly announced with adequate time given for campaigning. Moreover, they had to be conducted in stages, and three-fourths of the delegates had to be chosen in districts no larger than those for members of Congress.

Other consequences, not nearly so beneficial to the goal of increased participation, were a lengthening of the process, escalation of its costs, candidate fatigue, public boredom, and party division. Since the contests at the beginning of the quest for the nomination received the most attention from the news media,

BOX 4–1 ★

THE IOWA CAUCUS: HOW IT WORKS

DATE	STAGES
February	1. Caucuses are held in 2,166 precincts to choose more than 1,500 delegates to ninety-nine county conventions.
March	2. Conventions are held in counties to choose 3,000 delegates to the five congressional district conventions.
May	3. Conventions are held in congressional districts to elect district-level delegates to national party conventions. The same delegates also attend the state convention.
June	4. State conventions elect at-large delegates to national party convention. Democrats also select their state party and elected official delegates.

PROCEDURES FOR THE FIRST-ROUND PRECINCT CAUCUSES

Democrats: Only registered Democrats who live in the precinct and can vote may participate. Attendees are asked to join preference groups for candidates. A group must consist of at least 15 percent of those present to be viable. Nonviable groups are dissolved, and those who were members of them may join other viable groups. Much lobbying occurs at this stage of the meeting. Delegates are allocated to candidates strictly on the basis of the group's proportion to the caucus as a whole.

Republicans: Attendees, who must be eligible to vote but do not have to be registered as Republicans, cast a presidential preference vote by secret ballot, which is tabulated on a statewide basis. Delegates to the county convention are then selected by whatever method the caucus chooses, either by direct election (winner-take-all) or proportionally on the basis of the straw vote.

candidates, and public alike, states began moving their primaries forward, "front-loading" the schedule and forcing candidates to start their campaigns in the year prior to the election, another trend that has continued and intensified in recent elections.

Primaries and caucuses affected the type of delegate selected as well. They made it more difficult for elected officials and party leaders automatically to attend the nominating conventions. To participate, they too had to run as delegates. This, in turn, forced them to endorse a candidate or run as an unpledged delegate. Some chose not to do so, and others supported unsuccessful candidates. As a consequence the number of party leaders who attended the national nominating conventions following the adoption of the rules changes declined substantially. The absence of these leaders generated and extended cleavages between the nominees and their electoral coalitions on one hand and the party's organization and its leadership on the other.

These cleavages created serious problems, adversely affecting the chances of the party's nominees in the general election, and if successful, in governing the country. During the presidential campaign, the divisiveness impaired a unified organizational effort, tarnished the images of party candidates, and increased partisan defections. After the election, it made establishing an agenda and building a majority coalition more difficult.

In short, the early party reforms produced unintended consequences. These consequences — the proliferation of primaries, the lengthening of the process, the divisiveness within the party, the poor representation of elected leaders, and, most importantly, the failure to win elections and govern successfully — prompted the Democrats to reexamine and modify their rules for delegate selection beginning in the 1980s.

Democratic Rules, 1981–Present

After each presidential election, party commissions, composed of a cross section of party officials, interest group representatives, and supporters of leading candidates for the nomination, have met and proposed a series of rules for the next party nomination. Each commission has tinkered with the rules.

The changes that have been made fall into three categories: those that affect the time frame and procedures of the selection process, those that affect the representation of public officials and party leaders, and those that govern the behavior of delegates at the convention itself.

The objective of the original reforms, to encourage participation by rank-and-file party supporters and to reflect their sentiment in the allocation of delegates, was impeded by three problems:

1. The states that held their primaries and caucuses early seemed to exercise disproportionate influence. This situation created an incentive for other states to front-load the process, for candidates to expend most of their resources at the beginning of the campaign or as soon as they got them, and for participants to turn out more regularly in March than in May.

2. A relatively small percentage of the vote in a state, known as a *threshold*, was needed for candidates to win delegates. This small percentage encouraged multiple candidacies, factionalizing the party and providing an incentive for those without national experience, reputation, and even party ties to run. By obtaining the votes of as little as 15 percent of those who participated in a primary or caucus, relatively unknown candidates could win delegates, gain public recognition, and use this recognition to build a constituency and become a national figure.

3. The application of the proportional voting rule in some instances did not fairly reflect the popular vote. And even in instances in which it did, the rule produced unintended and undesirable consequences for the national party, for its state affiliates, and for the candidates seeking the nomination. For the national party, proportional voting extended the nomination process, disadvantaging it and its nominees in the general election. For the state parties, proportional voting diffused power and reduced the

collective influence of party officials. For the candidates, proportional voting sometimes discouraged them from investing resources in districts that were highly competitive and from which they could gain only minimal advantage and encouraged them to concentrate on less competitive districts in which they enjoyed the most support. This concentration of resources adversely affected turnout.

To modify the first of these problems, the party has imposed a "window" during which primaries and caucuses can be held. Initially, the official period extended from the second Tuesday in March to the second Tuesday in June. Beginning in 1992, it was moved one week earlier to the first Tuesday in March, but continued until the second Tuesday in June.

What to do with those states, such as Iowa and New Hampshire, where laws require that they choose their delegates before others, has been a perennial issue. Believing that it could not conduct its own selection process in these states, the national party decided that the best it could do was establish the window and grant these states an exception.[5]

Front-loading still remains a problem, however, more so now than ever. In 1992, twenty-four states held Democratic primaries or the first round of their caucus selection process and fifteen states held Republican primaries or caucuses by the second Tuesday of March, choosing approximately one-third of all the Democratic delegates and almost 37 percent of all the Republican delegates.

There was greater front-loading in 1996. Almost two-thirds of the convention delegates were selected within a forty-four-day period beginning mid-February and continuing through March 26, 1996.

In 2000, the nomination process became more front-loaded than ever. California, New Jersey and New York moved their primaries to the first Tuesday in March when other states in the Northeast also voted, resulting in the selection of one-half of both parties' delegates by that date. By the end of the second Tuesday, about two-thirds of the delegates had been chosen. (See Appendix D for the dates and results of the 2000 primaries and caucuses.)

Another change has been the modifications to the so-called fair reflection rule. One modification affected the minimum percentage of the vote necessary to be eligible for delegates; the other pertained to the methods by which the primary vote is converted into delegates. After some experimenting with the minimum vote necessary to receive delegates, the Democrats settled on a 15 percent threshold.

The party also requires that candidates receive delegates in Democratic primaries solely on the basis of the proportion of the vote they receive.[6]

Another reform was the addition of party leader and elected official delegates (PLEOs), known as *superdelegates*. Unhappy with the decreasing number of its party leaders and elected officials who attended the convention as delegates in the 1970s, the party wished to ensure that its leadership participated in conventions that selected its nominees. The absence of this leadership, particularly national elected officials, was thought to have contributed to the lack of support that the nominees received during the campaign and after the election. Jimmy Carter's difficulties in dealing with Congress were cited as evidence of the need for closer cooperation between congressional party leaders and their presidential standard-bearer.

To facilitate closer ties, the Democrats established a new category of *add-on* delegates to be composed of PLEOs. One group of these add-on delegates, chosen from designated party leaders (including all members of its national committee) and from those who held high elected positions in government (including all Democratic governors and members of Congress plus a number of other national, state, and local officials), were to be unpledged. It was thought that this group of distinguished Democrats might be in a position to hold the balance of power if the primaries produced a mixed verdict and the convention remained divided. Additionally, the party also provided for the selection of pledged add-on delegates equal to 15 percent of the state's base delegation. (See Table 4–1.)

Although these superdelegates have not been in a position to broker a divided convention, they have had an impact on the delegate selection process, an impact that reinforces the front-runner's advantage.[7] Naturally this advantage has incurred criticism from non-front-runners who desire the selection process to be open and not dominated by national legislators and party officials. A proposal by Jesse Jackson to decrease the number of PLEOs by eliminating the automatic inclusion of members of the party's national committee, however, was rejected by the Democratic National Committee in 1990. Eighteen percent of the delegates in 1996 were superdelegates, approximately the same percent as in 2000.

Finally, the Democrats have reversed a rule adopted in 1980 that delegates who are publicly committed must vote for the candidate to whom they are pledged. Democratic delegates today can vote their consciences, although when they are initially selected as pledged delegates, they must sign an advanced pledge of presidential preference to assure that they are supporters of the candidates to whom their seats are allocated. Under the circumstances, it is unlikely that many delegates will change their minds at the convention, unless their candidate encourages them to do so.

Republican Rules

The Republicans have not changed their rules after each recent national convention as the Democrats have. Nor can they do so. It is the Republican convention itself that approves the rules for choosing delegates for the next Republican convention. Under normal circumstances, these rules cannot be altered by the Republican National Committee or by special commissions the party creates.

Republicans, however, have been affected by the Democratic rules changes in several ways. Since state legislatures enact laws governing party nominations, and since the Democrats controlled many of these legislatures in the 1970s and 1980s when these laws were enacted, they literally forced some of their reforms on the Republicans. Moreover, the Republicans have also made changes of their own to eliminate discrimination and prevent a small group from controlling the nomination process. A committee of delegates and organizations, appointed in 1969, recommended that delegate selection procedures encourage greater participation in states that used conventions to pick their delegates; that more information about

TABLE 4–1 ★

DELEGATE SELECTION RULES

	Democrats	Republicans
Rank-and-file participation	Open to all voters who wish to participate as Democrats.	No national rule.*
Apportionment of delegates within states	75 percent of base delegation elected at congressional district level or lower; 25 percent elected at-large on proportional basis.	No national rule; may be chosen at large.
Party leaders and elected officials delegates	Current members and former chairs of the national committee, all Democratic members of Congress, former House Speakers and minority leaders and Senate party leaders, current and past presidents and vice presidents, all Democratic governors.	None.
Composition of delegations	Equal gender division; no discrimination; affirmative action plan required with goals and time tables for specified groups (African Americans, Native Americans, and Asian/Pacific Americans).	No gender rule but each state is asked to try to achieve equal gender representation. "Positive action" to achieve broadest possible participation required.
Time frame	First Tuesday in March to second Tuesday in June. Exceptions: Iowa, New Hampshire, and Maine.	No national rule.
Allocation of delegates	By proportional vote. Only in primaries or caucuses.	May be selected in primaries, caucuses, or by state committee on basis of proportional vote or by direct election within congressional districts or on an at-large basis.
Threshold	15 percent.	No national rule.
Delegate voting	May vote their conscience.	No national rule.
Enforcement	Automatic reduction in state delegation size for violation of time frames, allocation, or threshold rules.	Each state party to enforce its own rules, although certain types of disputes may be appealed to the national party.

* Republican national rules prescribe that selection procedures be in accordance with the laws of the state.

these procedures be promulgated to the party's electorate; and that voting by proxy be prohibited. These recommendations, adopted by the 1972 Republican convention, remain in effect today.

Unlike the Democrats, the Republicans have not chosen to mandate national guidelines for their state parties. Although they do not have a window period during which all primaries and caucuses must be held, their nominations process is still heavily front-loaded, too much so from the perspective of the party's national committee. To encourage states to hold their nomination contests later in the cycle, the national committee introduced an incentive plan for 2000. States that held their primary or caucus between March 15 to April 14, were entitled to 5 percent more delegates on their convention delegation, from April 15 to May 14, they got 7.5 percent more, and on or after May 15, the number of allocated delegates increased by 10 percent. The plan had few takers, however, prompting the national committee to appoint an advisory commission to study the current process, noting its impact on partisan participation and representation. The commission, chaired by former senator and party chairman Bill Brock, recommended changes to improve how the party selects its presidential candidate. One of the proposals put forth by the commission was the implementation of a population-based nominating system in which states would be placed in one of four groups, based on size, rather than geography. The states in each group would hold their primary or the first stage of their caucus selection on the same day. The group containing the least-populated states would go first and the one with the largest states last. The dates on which the four groups would hold their nomination contests would be spaced approximately one month apart, beginning on the first Tuesday in March.

Opposition to the plan quickly developed. Republican leaders from large states were fearful that the nominee would be effectively determined before they had a chance to vote. George W. Bush's campaign manager, Karl Rove, and others expressed concern about the added costs to the candidates if they had to compete for four months, much less the wear and tear they would encounter.[8] With Bush opposing the change, the rules committee of the Republican convention voted against implementing the plan.

Whereas the Democrats prescribe a minimum threshold to receive delegate support, the Republicans do not. Their threshold varies from state to state. Whereas the Democrats impose proportional voting, the Republicans do not. They permit winner-take-all voting within districts or within the state. Such a voting system greatly advantages front-runners, who can win the large states. In the last closely contested Republican nomination in 1988, George Bush won 59 percent of the popular vote in states holding some type of winner-take-all voting on Super Tuesday but won 97 percent of the delegates, giving him an almost insurmountable lead over his principal opponent that year, Robert Dole. In 1996, Dole, the Republican front-runner, was similarly advantaged and built a huge delegate lead in the winner-take-all states. As part of its recommendations to improve the delegate selection process, the party's advisory commission on nomination reform proposed that all delegates be allotted to candidates on a proportional basis, but the rules committee of the 2000 convention did not approve the change.

Finally the Republicans do not have special categories of delegates for party leaders and elected officials, although their state and national leaders have traditionally attended Republican conventions in greater proportion than their Democratic counterparts. Nor do the Republicans require that 50 percent of each state delegation be women. Since the 1980s, the proportion of women at Republican conventions has ranged from a low of 29 percent to a high of 44.

A summary of delegate selection rules for the 2000 nomination appears in Table 4–1.

THE LEGALITY OF PARTY RULES

As previously mentioned, party reforms, to be effective, must be enacted into law. Most states have complied with the new rules. A few have not, sometimes resulting in confrontation between these states and the national party. When New Hampshire and Iowa refused to move the dates of their respective primary and caucuses into the Democrats' window period in 1984, the national party backed down. But previously, when Illinois chose its 1972 delegates in a manner that conflicted with new Democratic rules, the party sought to impose its rules on the state.

In addition to the political controversy that was engendered, the conflict between the Democratic National Committee and Illinois also presented an important legal question: which body — the national party or state — was the higher authority? In its landmark decision *Cousins v. Wigoda* (419 U.S. 477, 1975), the Supreme Court sided with the national party. The Court stated that political parties were private organizations with rights of association protected by the Constitution. Moreover, choosing presidential candidates was a national experience that states could not abridge unless there were compelling constitutional reasons to do so. Although states could establish their own primary laws, the party could determine the criteria for representation at its national convention.

Crossover voting in open primaries prompted still another court test between the rights of parties to prescribe rules for delegate selection and the rights of states to establish their own election law. Democratic rules prohibit open primaries. Four states had conducted this type of election in 1976. Three voluntarily changed their law for 1980. The fourth, Wisconsin, did not. It permitted voters, who participated in the primary, to request the ballot of either party. The national party's Compliance Review Commission ordered the state party to design an alternative process. It refused. The case went to court. Citing the precedent of *Cousins v. Wigoda*, the Supreme Court held in the case of *Democratic Party of the U.S. v. Wisconsin ex. rel. La Follette* (450 U.S. 107, 1981) that a state had no right to interfere with the party's delegate selection process unless it demonstrated a compelling reason to do so. It ruled that Wisconsin had not demonstrated such a reason; hence, the Democratic Party could refuse to seat delegates who were selected in a manner that violated its rules.[9]

A recent decision by the Supreme Court, *California Democratic Party v. Jones* (99-401, 2000) reiterated that judgment. The Court invalidated California's "blanket" primary system which voters had approved in a 1996 ballot initiative.

The new procedure required that state officials provide a uniform ballot in which voters, regardless of their partisan affiliation, could vote for any candidate of any party for any elected position. Naturally, the parties were upset by the possibility that their nominees could be determined by people who did not consider themselves as partisans of their party. Four state parties, including the Democrats and Republicans, went to court to challenge the constitutionality of the initiative. They claimed that it violated their First Amendment right to freedom of association. The Supreme Court agreed. Its majority opinion held that the blanket primary system represented "a clear and present danger" to the parties and was therefore unconstitutional.

Although these Court decisions have given the political parties the legal authority to design and enforce their own rules, the practicality of doing so is another question. Other than going to court if a state refuses to change its election law, a party, particularly a national party, has only two viable options: require the state party to conduct its own delegate selection process in conformity to national rules and penalize it if it does not do so, or grant the state party an exemption so that it can abide by the law of the state. In 1984, the Wisconsin Democratic Party was forced by the national Democratic Party to adopt a caucus mode of selection since the Republican-controlled legislature refused to change the state's open primary system. Turnout declined in the Wisconsin caucus. Subsequently, the Democrats have given Wisconsin and Montana, another state with a tradition of open primaries, exemptions to the closed primary rule.

Despite the intraparty agitation over open primaries and others in which partisans are permitted to cross over and vote for candidates of the other party, there is evidence to suggest that this fear of heavy crossover voting may be overblown. One study of sixteen primaries on Super Tuesday in 1988 found little evidence of this phenomenon occurring.[10] In 2000, however, John McCain received a substantial portion of his votes from independents and Democrats, and to a lesser extent, Bill Bradley got independents to support his candidacy as well. (See Tables 4–4 and 4–5, pages 141–143.)

The party rule that seems to have had more of an impact on the nomination process, particularly on how the candidates allocate their resources, is the apportionment of delegates among the states.[11] Here the Republicans have had more controversy than the Democrats. The formula Republicans use to determine the size of each state delegation is complex. It consists of three criteria: statehood (six delegates), House districts (three per district), and support for Republican candidates elected within the previous four years (one for a Republican governor, one for each Republican senator, one if the Republicans won at least half of the congressional districts in one of the last two congressional elections, and a bonus of four and one-half delegates plus 60 percent of the electoral vote if the state voted for the Republican presidential candidate in the last election). Additionally, the party's incentive system in 2000 added delegates to those states which held their caucus or primary after March 15.

This apportionment formula, particularly the bonus rule for voting Republican, effectively discriminates against the larger states in two ways. First, it awards many of the bonus delegates to a state without regard to its size. Thus, the voting strength of the larger states is proportionally reduced by the bonuses while that of the smaller states is increased. Second, since the larger states are more competitive, they are less likely to be awarded bonus delegates on a recurring basis. Particularly hard hit are states in the Northeast and on the Pacific Coast which have gone Democratic in recent elections. The Ripon Society, a moderate Republican organization, has twice challenged the constitutionality of this apportionment rule, but it has not been successful.

The Democratic apportionment formula, which results in larger conventions than the Republicans, has also been subject to some controversy, but not in recent nominations.[12] Table 4–2 lists the apportionment of Republican and Democratic convention delegates.

TABLE 4–2 ★

DELEGATE APPORTIONMENT, 1996 AND 2000

State	Democrats*		Republicans	
	1996	**2000**	**1996**	**2000**
Alabama	66	63	40	44
Alaska	19	19	19	23
Arizona	52	55	39	30
Arkansas	47	47	20	24
California	424	435	165	162
Colorado	58	61	27	40
Connecticut	67	67	27	25
Delaware	21	22	12	12
District of Columbia	33	33	14	15
Florida	178	186	98	80
Georgia	91	92	42	54
Hawaii	30	33	14	14
Idaho	23	23	23	28
Illinois	193	190	69	74
Indiana	88	88	52	55
Iowa	56	57	25	25
Kansas	42	42	31	35
Kentucky	61	58	26	31
Louisiana	71	73	30	29
Maine	32	33	15	14
Maryland	88	95	32	31
Massachusetts	114	118	37	37
Michigan	156	157	57	58
Minnesota	92	91	33	34
Mississippi	47	48	33	33

TABLE 4–2 ★ *(continued)*

Delegate Apportionment, 1996 and 2000

| | Democrats* | | Republicans | |
State	1996	2000	1996	2000
Missouri	93	92	36	35
Montana	24	24	14	23
Nebraska	34	32	24	30
Nevada	26	29	14	17
New Hampshire	26	29	16	17
New Jersey	122	124	48	54
New Mexico	34	35	18	21
New York	289	294	102	101
North Carolina	99	103	58	62
North Dakota	22	22	18	19
Ohio	172	169	67	69
Oklahoma	52	52	38	38
Oregon	57	58	23	24
Pennsylvania	195	191	73	78
Rhode Island	32	33	16	14
South Carolina	51	52	37	37
South Dakota	22	22	18	22
Tennessee	83	81	38	37
Texas	229	231	123	124
Utah	31	29	28	29
Vermont	22	22	12	12
Virginia	97	95	53	56
Washington	90	94	36	37
West Virginia	43	42	18	18
Wisconsin	93	92	36	37
Wyoming	19	18	20	22
American Samoa	6	12	4	4
Democrats abroad	9	9	—	—
Guam	6	12	4	4
Puerto Rico	58	61	14	14
Virgin Islands	4	12	4	4
Unassigned superdelegates*	—	13	—	—
Totals	4,289	4,370	1,990	2,066

* Includes Democratic National Committee, Democratic members of Congress, governors, and other distinguished party leaders.

Source: Democratic and Republican National Committees.

THE IMPACT OF THE RULES CHANGES

The new rules adopted by the parties have produced some of their desired effects. They have opened up the nomination process by allowing more people to participate. They have increased minority representation at the conventions. But they have also decreased the influence of state and national party leaders over the selection of delegates, ultimately weakened the power of party leaders in the presidential electoral process, and have exacerbated divisions within the parties.

Turnout

One objective of the reforms was to involve more of the party's rank and file in the delegate selection process. This goal has been partially achieved. In 1968, before the reforms, only 12 million people participated in primaries, approximately 11 percent of the voting-age population (VAP). In 1972, the first nomination contest after changes were made, that number rose to 22 million. In 1988, it peaked. With two contested nominations, turnout increased to 35.1 million, approximately 21 percent of the VAP. It remained relatively high in 1992, dipped in 1996, and rose again in 2000. Approximately 36 million people voted in the most recent primaries, about 15 percent of the VAP; 35.3 million voted in one of the major parties' primaries.[13] More than 20 million participated in forty-three Republican primaries, the most ever for the GOP, compared to only 14.7 million for the Democrats.[14]

The level of participation also varies. It has always been greater in primaries than caucuses. In Iowa, which held the first caucus, only about 4 percent of the VAP participated, despite extensive media coverage.

Turnout tends to be greater in states that hold their contests earlier than in those that hold them later in the process and greater in those in which there is more competition than in states in which there is less. New Hampshire generally has a high turnout; in 2000, 54 percent of the state's eligible population voted in the Republican primary.[15] South Carolina and Michigan also had unusually high Republican turnout because of the attention given to the Bush-McCain contest. Approximately 19 percent of the VAP voted in both states' Republican primaries.

Not only does turnout vary among states, it also varies among population groups within them. The better-educated, higher-income, older members of society vote more often than do younger, less-educated, and poorer people. In general, the lower the turnout, the greater the demographic differences between voters and nonvoters. Although this pattern of participation has persisted in recent elections, the success of the Jackson campaigns in 1984 and 1988 in attracting minority voters and, to a much lesser extent, the campaign of Pat Robertson in 1998 which appealed to white, evangelical Protestants muted some of the differences that had existed between primary voters and their party's electorate in the elections in which Jackson and Robertson ran.

There have also been claims that primary voters tend to be more ideologically extreme in their political beliefs than the average party voter, with Democrats being more liberal and Republicans more conservative than their party as a whole. Strong empirical evidence has not been found to support this contention although studies have shown southern Democrats who participate in their party's primary tend to be more moderate than the southern electorate as a whole.[16] In general for most of the country, primary voters do not appear to be more ideologically extreme than people who vote in the general election, but convention delegates who represent them do.[17]

Representation

A principal goal of the reforms was to make the national nominating convention more representative of those who identified with the party. Before 1972, the delegates were predominantly white, male, and well educated. Mostly professionals whose income and social status placed them considerably above the national mean, they were expected to pay their own way to the convention. Large financial contributors, as well as elected officeholders and party officials, were frequently in attendance.

In 1972, the demographic profile of convention delegates began to change. The proportion of women rose substantially. Youth and minority participation, especially in Democratic conventions, also increased. Since 1976, when the Democrats changed from a quota system to an affirmative action commitment, the representation of minorities has remained fairly constant. The percentage of women has increased, largely as a consequence of the Democratic rule that half the delegates be women. But attendance by those under age thirty, who have been removed from the specified minorities list, has declined.

Despite the changes in composition, the income and educational levels of the delegates have remained well above the national average. Most of the delegates have much more formal education than do their party's rank and file.

It is more difficult to determine the extent to which ideological and issue perceptions of recent delegates differed from those of their predecessors and from the electorate as a whole. In general, convention delegates tend to be more conscious of issues than their party's rank and file, with Republican delegates being more conservative than Republicans as a whole, and Democratic delegates more liberal than Democrats are generally.

Surveys of the ideological perspectives of convention delegates at recent conventions support these generalizations. They reveal clear distinctions between the delegates of the major parties. (See Table 4–3.) Moreover, the issue stands of the delegates tend to confirm the ideological cleavage. Republican and Democratic delegates consistently take more conservative and liberal positions, respectively, on a range of policy matters. If these positions were plotted on an ideological continuum, they would appear to be more consistent (or ideologically pure) than the partisan electorate they represent and much more consistent (or pure) than the general public.

The delegate selection process seems to have contributed to the purity of these perspectives by encouraging activists, who have less of a tie to the party and more of a tie to a candidate and that candidate's ideological and issue positions, to get involved and run for delegate. To the extent that this trend has resulted in the election of more issue purists and fewer partisan pragmatists, compromise in government has become more difficult. One objective of the creation of superdelegates by the Democrats was to reverse the trend of party fragmentation.

TABLE 4–3 ★

THE IDEOLOGY OF NATIONAL CONVENTION DELEGATES,
1976–1996

Ideology	1976 Dem.	Rep.	1980 Dem.	Rep.	1984 Dem.	Rep.	1988 Dem.	Rep.
Liberal	40%	3%	46%	2%	48%	1%	43%	0%
Moderate	47	45	42	36	42	35	43	35
Conservative	8	48	6	58	4	60	5	58

Ideology	1992 Dem.	Rep.	1996 Dem.	Rep.	General Population (1996)
Liberal	47%	1%	43%	0%	16%
Moderate	44	28	48	27	47
Conservative	5	70	5	66	32

Sources: CBS News Delegate Surveys, 1976 through 1980. Characteristics of the public are average values from seven CBS News/*New York Times* polls, 1980. Warren J. Mitofsky and Martin Plissner, "The Making of the Delegates, 1968–1980," *Public Opinion* (December–January 1980): 43. Reprinted with the permission of American Enterprise Institute. The 1984 and 1988 data for delegates and public opinion supplied by CBS News from its delegate surveys and reprinted with permission of CBS News; 1992 data published in the *New York Times* (July 13, 1992), B6, and the *Washington Post* (August 16, 1992), A19. The 1996 data is from *New York Times*/CBS News Delegate Survey as published in the *New York Times*, August 26, 1996, A12. This table also appears in Stephen J. Wayne, G. Calvin Mackenzie, David M. O'Brien, and Richard L. Cole, *The Politics of American Government,* 3rd ed. (New York: St. Martin's, 1999), 375.

In summary, despite the reforms, there continue to be differences between the ideological and demographic characteristics of convention delegates and those of their party members and of the electorate as a whole. Convention delegates reflect some demographic characteristics of their party's rank and file more accurately than in the past, but they are not necessarily more ideologically representative. In fact, delegates have tended to exaggerate the differences between the beliefs and attitudes of Republicans and Democrats. Whether this trend makes contemporary conventions more or less representative is difficult to say. One thing is clear: it is difficult to achieve representation, reward activism, maintain an open process, unite the party, and win elections, all at the same time.

Party Organization and Leadership

Although increasing turnout and improving representation have been two desired effects of the reforms, weakening the state party structures and their leadership has not. Yet this development seems to have been an initial consequence of the increasing number of primaries. By promoting internal democracy, the primaries helped devitalize party organizations already weakened by new modes of campaigning and party leadership already weakened by the loss of patronage opportunities and the growth of social services by state and local governments. Although the growth of caucuses and primaries has enhanced participation in the general election by enlarging the pool of people who are more likely to become active, stay involved, and vote, it has also contributed to struggles for control of the party organization and ultimately produced more divisions within it.[18] Moreover, the rules changes have encouraged the proliferation of candidates, which in turn has led to the creation of separate electoral organizations that can rival the regular party organization.

The power of elected party leaders has also been weakened. No longer able to control their state's delegation, party officials now have to compete with the supporters of the successful candidate for influence over the campaign. State party organizations and state party leaders, however, continue to exercise influence. The soft money they have been given by the national parties or have solicited on their own has provided them with more opportunities to influence the election. The increasing importance of providing funds and organizational support for the presidential candidates has also benefited these state party officials.

The nominees are affected as well. Political scientists have argued that the more divisive the nomination process, the more likely that it will adversely affect the successful nominee's chances in the general election.[19] Other factors such as the quality of the candidates themselves and the particular environment in which the election occurs also affect the final general election results.[20]

Nonetheless, a divisive nomination process is rarely an asset for the successful nominee; usually it is a liability. Undergoing rigorous and critical examination by one's partisan opponents can damage a nominee's image at the beginning of the general election campaign. Candidates who avoid a challenge for the nomination do not have to contend with this problem. However, it often is the potential vulnerability of a candidate that encourages others to seek the nomination in the first place. Challenges and perceived vulnerability go hand-in-hand.

Winners and Losers

Rules changes are never neutral. They usually benefit one group at the expense of another. Similarly, they tend to help certain candidates and hurt others. That is why candidates have tried to influence the rules and why the rules themselves have been changed so frequently. Candidate organizations and interest groups have put continuous pressure on the Democratic Party to amend the rules to increase their own clout in the selection process.

Clearly, the prohibition of discrimination, the requirement for affirmative action, and the rule requiring an equal number of men and women in state delegations have improved representation for women and minorities. These changes also have reduced the proportion of white males. For candidates seeking their party's nomination, this change has necessitated that slates of delegates supporting a candidate be demographically balanced to ensure that a multitude of groups are included.

The openness of the process and the greater participation by the party's rank and file have encouraged those who have not been party regulars to become involved and have created opportunities for outsiders to seek their party's nomination. Businessman Steve Forbes (1996 and 2000), ministers Jesse Jackson (1984) and Pat Robertson (1988), columnist Pat Buchanan (1992, 1996, and 2000), and former Senator Paul Tsongas (1992), and to some extent even governors Michael Dukakis (1988) and Bill Clinton (1992), as well as former Senator Bill Bradley and Senator John McCain (both in 2000) have literally come out of political nowhere to run initially for their party's nomination.

On the other hand, the continuing front-loading of the process has given those with national reputations great advantages. The more the process concentrates the number and location of primaries at the beginning of the delegate selection process, the more those who have access to the largest amounts of money and the most political endorsements, particularly from governors who control their state party organizations, are likely to benefit.

All of this has affected the candidates' quest for the nomination and their ability to govern if elected. It has made campaigning more arduous and governing more difficult. Take Bill Clinton, for example. To win in 1992 he made many promises such as lowering taxes for the middle class, ending discrimination against homosexuals in the military, and admitting Haitian refugees into the United States. Once in office, he soon found that he could not redeem these promises and had to delay, modify, or abandon them. Moreover, he had to endure character accusations that continued to plague him throughout his presidency. Although all of Clinton's problems cannot be attributed to the nomination process, some of them can be. The point is that the quest for the nomination and what it takes to win may ultimately weaken a president by hyping performance expectations and then generating discontent when these expectations cannot be realized.

CAMPAIGNING FOR DELEGATES

Rules changes, finance laws, and television coverage have affected the strategies and tactics of the candidates. Prior to the 1960s, entering primaries was optional for leading candidates and necessary only for those who did not enjoy party support or national recognition. Today, entering primaries is essential for everyone, even an incumbent president. No longer can a front-runner safely sit on the sidelines and wait for the call. The winds of a draft may be hard to resist but, more often than not, it is the candidate who is manning the bellows.

In the past, candidates carefully chose the primaries they entered and concentrated their efforts where they thought they would run best. Today, they have much less discretion, particularly at the beginning of the process, when gaining press coverage is essential. The distribution of delegates in a number of states provides incentives for campaigning in as many states as possible for as long as possible.

Strategy and tactics have naturally evolved. There are now new answers to the old questions: when to declare, where to run, how to organize, what to claim, and how to win. Before 1972, it was considered wise to wait for an opportune moment in the spring of the presidential election year before announcing one's candidacy. Adlai Stevenson did not announce his intentions until the Democratic convention. John F. Kennedy made his announcement two months before the New Hampshire primary. It was also considered wise to restrict primary efforts, obtain the backing of the state party leaders, and work through their organizations. The successful candidates were those who could unify the party. They took few chances. The object of their campaign was to maintain a winning image.

Basic Strategic Guidelines

Plan Far Ahead. Much of the conventional wisdom is no longer valid. Today, it is necessary for all candidates to plan their campaigns early — very early. Creating an organization, devising a strategy, and raising the amount of money necessary to conduct a national campaign all take time. These needs prompted George McGovern to announce his candidacy for the 1972 presidential nomination in January 1971, almost a year and a half before the Democratic convention, and Jimmy Carter to begin his quest in 1974, two years before the 1976 Democratic convention. Similarly, President Clinton began planning his reelection campaign following the Democrat's defeat in the 1994 midterm elections although he never formally announced his candidacy in order to convey the impression that his actions and decisions during this period were motivated solely by the needs of his office, not his candidacy. (See Boxes 4–3 and 4–4 for a description of the nomination strategies of the principal candidates in 2000, on pages 136 and 145.)

Candidates for their party's nomination in 2000 began forming their prenomination organizations in 1998 prior to the midterm elections. Al Gore established Leadership '98 ostensibly to raise money for other Democrats but also to lay the groundwork for his presidential campaign in 2000. Similarly, Republican presidential hopeful, George W. Bush, began to plan his campaign in 1998 and formed an exploratory committee in the spring of 1999. He and other GOP aspirants made numerous trips to Iowa and New Hampshire in the two years before the 2000 race officially got under way.

Concentrate Efforts in the Early Contests. Doing well in the initial caucuses and primaries and qualifying for matching funds are the principal aims of most candidates today. The early contests are particularly important for lesser-known aspirants, less for the number of delegates they can win than for the amount of publicity they can generate and the public recognition they can gain as a consequence.

By tradition the first official selection of delegates occurs in Iowa. Jimmy Carter in 1976, George Bush in 1980, and Gary Hart in 1984 got great boosts from their unexpectedly good showings in this state. Conversely, Ronald Reagan in 1980, John Glenn in 1984, and George Bush in 1988, and Robert Dole in 1996, were hurt by their disappointing performances. In 2000, Iowa simply confirmed the front-runner's advantage that Bush and Gore each enjoyed over their rivals.

Doing well in Iowa can enhance the fortunes of a lesser-known candidate. A good example was Gary Hart's performance in 1984. He received only 16.5 percent of the Democratic vote, compared with front-runner Walter Mondale's 48.9 percent, former nominee George McGovern's 10.3 percent, and Senator John Glenn's 3.5 percent. But Mondale's victory was expected; Hart's second-place finish was not. As a consequence, Hart shared the media spotlight with Mondale but

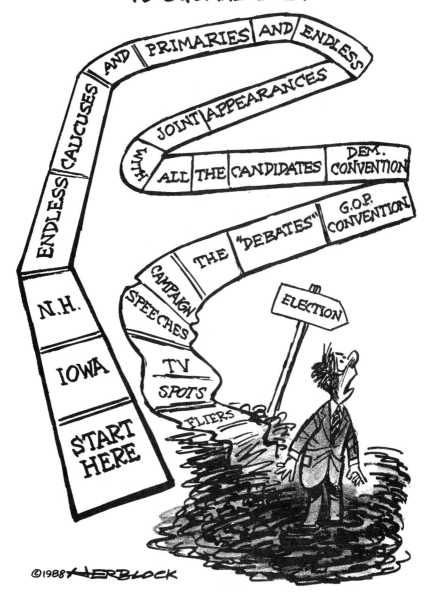

Source: Herblock, *Washington Post*, November 1, 1988, A18.

profited from more laudatory coverage. Similarly, Pat Robertson's surprising second-place finish ahead of Vice President George Bush in 1988 in Iowa and Pat Buchanan's strong challenge to Dole in 1996 generated favorable media coverage for them. Their gain was at the expense of Bush and Dole.[21]

The Iowa caucus has been more important for lesser-known candidates than for front-runners. The victories of Carter (1976), Bush (1980), and Hart (1984) gave these candidates opportunities to establish their credentials, opportunities which they might not have had in a big state primary. Although a defeat or poor showing by a front-runner such as happened to Reagan, Bush, and Dole in 1980, 1988, and 1996 respectively may dimish their luster, it does not necessarily terminate their candidacy. They will have other opportunites. But for lesser-known non-front-runners, a loss or poor showing in Iowa may be the beginning of the end.[22]

The importance of the Iowa caucus has diminished in recent presidential campaigns because of the front-loading of the nomination process. With New Hampshire nine to ten days later and an increasing number of primaries occurring in early or mid-March, there is simply not enough time to parlay success in Iowa into raising more money. Yet candidates continue to spend more time and money not less in this first caucus contest.

Iowa "winners" face another problem. Expectations of their future performance increase and media coverage tends to become more negative. Professor Craig Allen Smith describes the Iowa caucuses as "a Venus fly-trap for presidential candidates," a description he embellishes in the following manner:

> Dramatic logic lures them to the sticky leaves of the precinct caucuses where, prodded by journalists and Iowans, they pour more and more of their time, money, people, and strategic options into the gaping mouth of the plant until, at the very moment of victory, it snaps shut on their ability to win subsequent contests. Iowa provides no significant delegates, its New Hampshire momentum is soon reversed, its Super Tuesday momentum is transient, and the resources it devours are rarely recovered.[23]

After Iowa, attention turns to New Hampshire, traditionally the first state to hold a primary in which the entire electorate participates. Candidates who do surprisingly well in this primary have benefited enormously. Eugene McCarthy in 1968, George McGovern in 1972, Jimmy Carter in 1976, Gary Hart in 1984, Bill Clinton in 1992, Pat Buchanan in 1996, and John McCain in 2000 all gained visibility and credibility from their New Hampshire performances, although none had a majority of the vote and only Carter and McCain had pluralities. Bill Clinton actually came in second with 25 percent of the vote in 1992, 8 percent less than former Massachusetts, and New Hampshire neighbor, Senator Paul Tsongas. Clinton's relatively strong showing, however, in the light of allegations of marital infidelity and draft dodging made his performance more impressive in the eyes of the news media than Tsongas's expected win. Similarly, John McCain's impressive victory in 2000 over front-runner George W. Bush by 18 percent elevated him overnight from just another candidate to serious contender.

FIGURE 4–1 ★

NEWS COVERAGE OF THE PRESIDENTIAL NOMINATIONS, 1988–2000

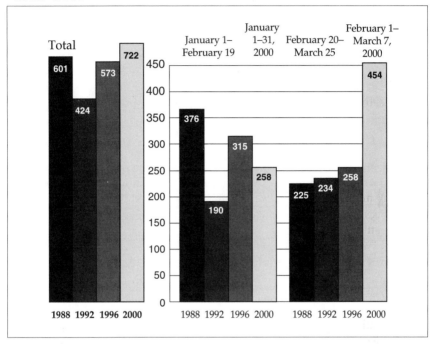

Note: Based on number of election stories on the ABC, CBS, and NBC evening news programs.

Source: "The Parties Pick Their Candidates," *Media Monitor* VI (March 1992): 2; "The Bad News Campaign," *Media Monitor* X (March/April 1996): 1–3; "Campaign 2000 — The Primaries," *Media Monitor* XIV (March/April 2000): 1–3.

Like Iowa, New Hampshire also receives extensive media attention. Together with Iowa, it usually accounts for the bulk of prenomination television coverage on the national news. (See Figure 4–1.) Is it any wonder that candidates spend so much time, money, and effort in these early contests?

For non-front-runners there are few options other than to contest these initial contests. Unless they can demonstrate their voter appeal, they are not likely to gain the financial and organizational support, much less the press coverage, necessary to mount a serious challenge to the front-runner.

Al Gore and John McCain tried a variation of this strategy, Gore in 1988 and McCain in 2000. Both skipped the Iowa caucus and concentrated on other early primaries where they believed they would run stronger; Gore focused on the southern regional primaries while McCain concentrated first in New Hampshire, then in his home state of Arizona, and then South Carolina and Michigan. McCain gained a short-term advantage from this strategy, largely on the basis of his victories in New Hampshire and Michigan, but Gore did not.

Although the early contests are extremely important, particularly for those who lack a national following, the odds of doing well are not great. A failure to stand out frequently forces candidates to drop out, usually because they are unable to raise sufficient money to continue or see the handwriting on the wall. Steve Forbes left the 2000 Republican contest on February 10th after he received only 15 percent of the vote in New Hampshire and 20 percent in Delaware, two states in which his campaign had targeted and spent considerable resources.

On the other hand, doing surprisingly well in these early contests is no guarantee of success. Pat Buchanan won New Hampshire in 1996, but little after that. McCain's surprisingly large victory over George Bush in 2000 extended his campaign for five more weeks before he was effectively forced to terminate his efforts.

For front-runners, the needs and opportunities are different. The early caucuses and primaries present a situation in which their resources can be used to eliminate or preclude competition, demonstrate electability, perhaps even invulnerability, and build a delegate lead. Winning confirms the front-runner's status, losing jeopardizes it. While recovery is possible, as Ronald Reagan demonstrated in 1980, Walter Mondale in 1984, George Bush in 1988, Bob Dole in 1996, and George W. Bush in 2000, an early loss can raise questions about a front-runner's viability, questions that may linger for the general election.

Raise and Spend Big Bucks Early. Having a solid financial base at the outset of the nomination process provides a significant strategic advantage. It allows a presidential campaign to plan ahead, to decide where to establish its field organizations and how much media advertising to buy, as well as where and on which groups to focus that advertising. It is no coincidence that those candidates who raise and spend the most money tend to do best.[24]

The impact of early money is particularly significant for candidates who do not begin the quest for their party's nomination with a national reputation, candidates such as Michael Dukakis in 1988 and Bill Clinton in 1992. The ability to raise relatively large amounts of money early, particularly in comparison with one's rivals gives a candidate an edge in gaining media recognition, building organizational support, raising even more money, and discouraging potential rivals from entering the race. In fact, the amount of money raised is frequently viewed by the press as a harbinger of future success or failure in the primaries.

Democrats Michael Dukakis (1988), Bill Clinton (1992), Al Gore (2000), and Republicans George Bush (1988), Robert Dole (1996), and George W. Bush (2000) used their superior fund-raising to build and staff large organizations in the early primary and caucus states, develop and target their media to key groups, and focus their personal efforts on campaigning, whereas most of their principal opponents lacked the resources to do so competitively.

Early money is considered important for several reasons. It buys recognition for those who need it. Steve Forbes bought that recognition in 1996 with the expenditure of more than $42 million, much of it his own money. But public recognition also brings increased scrutiny by the news media and increased criticism by the other candidates.

Early money also buys legitimacy. The press evaluates the credibility of candidates in part on the basis of how much money they can raise and how willing people are to contribute. Candidates who cannot raise much money are not usually taken seriously by the news media and by other potential contributors, even if they are well known, as was Elizabeth Dole in 2000. Six of the twelve Republican candidates for the 2000 nomination were forced to terminate their quest for their party's nomination three months *before* the first caucus and primary. All cited financial reasons for their withdrawal. On the other hand, Bill Bradley's campaign was given a boost in the eyes of the news media when he was able to match Al Gore's fund-raising during 1999 and the beginning of 2000, even though Bradley had not demonstrated any vote-getting ability.

The most important reason for having early money is that it gives a candidate the most flexibility in deciding where and how to campaign. Without such resources candidates have little choice but to compete in Iowa, New Hampshire, and other early contests in which most of their competitors are also running, thereby decreasing their odds of winning. The early expenditure of funds can build support, win delegates, generate momentum, and result in an early knockout of one's opponents.

There are two negatives to early spending. With overall limits placed on expenditures for candidates who accept federal funds, which is usually everyone but multimillionaires or those with access to significant financial resources, money can run out even if the competition stays in. This was more of a problem when the primaries and the caucuses were not all clustered at the beginning of the nomination process as occurred in the 1970s then it is today. But today's early spender faces another problem similar to the one Bob Dole ran into in 1996. His early expenditure of funds helped ensure his victory, but it also left him vulnerable to attack without money to reply in the period after he had effectively won the nomination but before he was officially anointed as the candidate at the party's convention in midsummer. George W. Bush lost a lot of his initial fund-raising advantage by spending almost all the money he raised during the competitive phase of the Republican nomination process. He ended that phase of the process with a smaller war chest than his Democratic rival, Al Gore. However, because he did not accept federal funds, he could raise additional sums while Gore, who had reached his maximum, could not.

Two principal consequences follow from the need for early money: the financial campaign in the years before the nomination has assumed greater importance than in the past, and non-front-runners are disadvantaged even more than they were previously unless they are independently wealthy. The odds against a little-known outsider using Iowa, New Hampshire, and the other early states to obtain the resources necessary to compete seriously for the nomination have increased in recent years.

Gain Media Attention. Candidates cannot win if they are not known. Gaining recognition is most important at the beginning of the nomination process when the electorate starts to pay some attention to the contests that loom ahead.

Since lesser-known aspirants are not as likely to have large war chests, unless they are independently wealthy or have substantial sums left over from previous campaigns, they need free media. Their problem is that coverage and public recognition go hand-in-hand. Better-known candidates get more coverage because they are more likely to do better, hence they are more newsworthy. It is not news when a long shot loses; it is news when a front-runner does. On the other hand, when a long shot does well in raising money, gaining endorsements, drawing crowds, winning straw votes and especially delegates, the press follows the story of the "conquering hero."

Take the Bradley-Gore and McCain-Bush challenges for example. In 1999, Al Gore and George W. Bush were the big television news, measured in terms of coverage they received. Bush was the focus of eighty-six stories on the evening news compared to fifty-six for all his Republican competitors combined. Similarly, Gore was the subject of seventy-three stories while his opponent, Bill Bradley, was featured in forty.[25]

Coverage became more balanced as the caucuses and primaries approached. From January 1 to January 31, 2000, the day of the New Hampshire primary, McCain and Bradley received almost as much attention on the evening news as did Gore and Bush. From New Hampshire until the nomination was effectively decided, they continued to attract similar amounts.[26] (See Figure 4–2.)

FIGURE 4–2 ★

TELEVISION COVERAGE OF THE CANDIDATES IN THE 2000 CAMPAIGN

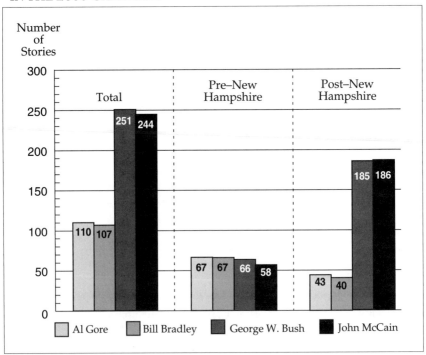

Note: Based on the number of stories on the ABC, CBS, and NBC evening news. More than one candidate may be featured in a story.

Source: "Campaign 2000 — The Primaries," *Media Monitor* XIV (March/April 2000): 2.

What can non-front-runners do to gain more coverage? They stage events, fax a stream of seemingly endless press releases to most local media outlets, leak controversial information about their opponents, and create opportunities and encourage invitations to appear on talk/entertainment programs on radio and television. Here's how Pat Buchanan's 1996 campaign manager described a typical day in Iowa before that state held the first nominating caucus:

> Gregg [Mueller, the press secretary] and Pat would get up at about five in the morning, get some coffee, get in the minivan, and go from one TV station to the other, in the local market, wherever they had morning shows and they would do a live segment on every morning television show.
>
> Then they'd come back to the hotel, read through the newspapers and at 10 A.M. we'd go out and do our theme event for the day — drive whatever our message was, get out a press release, which we faxed out everywhere and let that, hopefully, resonate into the newspapers.
>
> At noon, we'd go back to the television stations, if they would have us, or else we'd drive into a new market . . . all the time that they would be driving the van, Greg would have Pat on the cell phone doing radio interviews . . . Buchanan would literally go from one station to the other to the other, go back to the hotel, maybe take a nap in the afternoon, then you go out at 5 P.M. and you do the evening TV stations. If you literally saturated the local TV market, you try to get to the next one. You try to maximize the amount of time you could get on TV in a state while you were there.[27]

Participating in debates against their political opponents has become increasingly important for most candidates. In 2000, there were thirteen debates among the Republican contenders and eight among the Democrats. The debaters focused on issues of concern to the party's core supporters: taxes, foreign policy, and social issues such as abortion for the Republicans and health care, education, race relations, and campaign finance reform for the Democrats.[28]

Debates are important because they spark local interest. When combined with media advertising and newsworthy events, they educate voters, primarily those in the states that hold early contests. At the national level these local debates, which may be aired nationally on cable news and/or C-SPAN and occasionally, the Public Broadcasting System, are much less newsworthy and receive only a fraction of the audience that the presidential debates get in the fall. As a consequence, they do not have much national impact unless one of the candidates makes a major faux pas.

In general, there was a decline in the amount of time given to news coverage of the 2000 nomination process on the commercial television broadcast networks, even though the number of candidate stories actually increased. (See Figure 4–1.) There has been an even steeper decline in the number of people who regularly watch these shows that helps explain why public interest in the presidential selection process has also declined.[29]

Beginning in November 1999, the Shorenstein Center of the Press, Politics, and Public Policy at Harvard University conducted weekly polls measuring public interest. Researchers designed a Voter Interest Index based on whether people are following the campaign closely and whether they have thought, talked, or seen a

FIGURE 4–3 ★

Voter Involvement Index, November 1999–August 2000

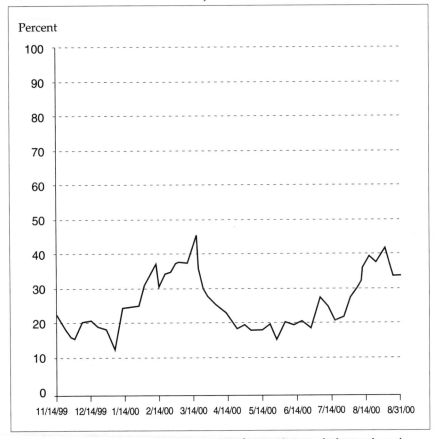

Note: Index is calculated by averaging the responses to four questions — whether people say they are currently paying close attention to the campaign, whether they are thinking about the campaign, talking about it, and following it in the news.

Source: Joan Shorenstein Center on the Press, Politics, and Public Policy, Harvard University, Vanishing Voter Project.

news story about it the previous day. Figure 4–3 plots that index over the course of the 2000 nomination cycle, showing that interest was highest during the competitive phase of the nomination, particularly in those states that held primaries during this period, and after that in the summer when both parties held their national nominating conventions.[30]

With campaign news sources more dispersed, candidates must pay close attention to what viewers are watching. Increasingly, they must design and present their own messages via paid advertising. Free media is not sufficient nor is favorable coverage. John McCain and Bill Bradley both received a higher percentage of positive spin than their front-running opponents — Bradley, prior to New Hampshire, and McCain after New Hampshire.[31]

Advertisements remain one of the most effective ways to communicate with voters. Studies have shown that people tend to retain more information from candidate commercials than they do from the broadcast networks' evening news.[32] As a result, campaigns continue to spend the bulk of their revenues on political advertisements.

BOX 4–2 ★

THE AIR WARS OF 2000: THE NOMINATIONS

A critical component of the nomination campaign was conducted electronically, over the airways, on cable, via satellite, and over the Internet. Most of the campaigns spent well over half their funds on designing, targeting, and presenting their messages in the form of advertisements. The first round of political advertising for the 2000 nomination took place in the campaign preseason during 1999. The ads were primarily positive and optimistic and largely biographical, with an emphasis on broad-based goals not detailed policy proposals. They were designed to introduce candidates to the voters as nice guys who would do good.

The radio and television campaigns, which were conducted primarily over local media and cable, began in June 1999 when Steve Forbes reintroduced himself to the Republican electorate as a social conservative, a proponent of a flat income tax, and a political and Washington outsider who would curb the appetite of the big government, big spending, politicians.

Other Republican hopefuls soon followed Forbes onto the airways. They presented biographical ads which trumpeted their credentials, public record, and policy goals. Some, like Dan Quayle, Orrin Hatch, and Elizabeth Dole, stressed their experience in government as well as their conservative credentials. Others, like Gary Bauer and Robert Smith, stated their strong convictions on social and national security respectively.

Front-runner George W. Bush presented himself as a kind and upbeat person, an outsider who could moderate the divisive partisanship that has characterized Washington politics during the Clinton presidency. Promising to return decency, integrity, and moral virtue to the Oval Office, Bush emphasized the positive. "I'm going to run a campaign that is hopeful and optimistic and very positive," he said. His ads, which pictured him as a highly successful governor who cut taxes, reduced spending, improved public education and cut welfare rolls in Texas, ended with a reaffirmation of the image Bush wished to present to the American people. "George W. Bush. A compassionate conservative. A fresh start for America."[33]

John McCain's ads stressed his military experience in Vietnam and his crusade against special interest politics as illustrated by the following excerpt from one of his frequently aired commercials:

Announcer: "He was a young Navy pilot who volunteered for duty in Vietnam and was shot down over Hanoi. Lieutenant Commander John McCain, dragged off by an angry mob. When found to be the son and grandson of admirals, was offered early release; he refused. McCain's commitment to country and fellow prisoners brought him repeated beatings and five and a half years in prison. . . . Navy officer, congressman, senator, taking on the establishment. And defying special interests. And never forgetting those heroes with whom he served. Today John McCain is ready to lead America into the new century. His mission: to fundamentally reform government. More experience and more courage than anyone. Ready to be president and leader of the free world."[34]

McCain campaigned as a reformer and as a Reagan Republican. "Here's some straight talk," he said in one of his ads, "I'm a Reagan Republican. I'll tear up the 44,000 page tax code that benefits special interests; stop the outrageous waste and pork barrel spending. . . . Give me your vote, and we'll give you back your government."[35]

On the Democratic side, Gore initially emphasized his role as an experienced vice president who would promote and protect traditional Democratic Party values. When his campaign foundered in the fall of 1999, his ads presented him in more human terms, working summers on the farm in Tennessee in his youth, exposing crime as a young investigative reporter, and serving his country in the Army in Vietnam as well as during his many years of public service.

Bill Bradley painted himself as a humble, low-key person, motivated by his desire to serve his country and make it a better place for more people and qualified to do so by his success as a Rhodes scholar, Olympic gold medalist, professional basketball player, and U.S. senator. Bradley's commercials emphasized his goals of universal health care, racial equality, and unparalleled educational opportunities but did not contain many details of how he would achieve these objectives.

As the primaries and caucuses neared and the campaign heated up, so did the advertisements. They become more confrontational, although not to the extent that they had been in previous nomination cycles. Residual press and public negativity toward attack advertising slowed the introduction of negative ads in the 2000 campaign, but such ads began to appear in greater frequency before the New Hampshire primary approached, and they continued to be aired until the nomination process was effectively decided.[36]

Bush and McCain were particularly critical of each other in their television spots. Bush's ads referred to McCain's temper and questioned his loyalty to Republican policy, such as his opposition to across-the-board tax cuts. McCain's votes against appropriations for mass transportation, home heating oil subsidies, and breast cancer research were cited as evidence of his insensitivity to problems outside his state.[37]

McCain responded by angrily accusing Bush of distorting his record, of "talking like Clinton," and of being just another politician who could not be trusted. Bush "hit the roof" when McCain's ad made the Clinton comparison. Here are excerpts from two of their ads.

THE McCAIN AND BUSH NEGATIVE ADVERTISEMENTS

McCain

Picture: Senator McCain in blue suit and red tie.

Audio: McCain talking

I guess it was bound to happen. Governor Bush's campaign is getting desperate, with a negative ad about me. The fact is, I'll use the surplus money to fix Social Security, cut your taxes, and pay down the debt. His ad twists the truth like Clinton. We're all pretty tired of that. As president, I'll be conservative and always tell you the truth. No matter what.

Bush

Picture: Banners with McCain picture interspersed.

Audio: Announcer talking

It's disappointing. Friday, John McCain promised to stop running a negative campaign. Then Sunday he attacked Governor Bush on national television with false charges on campaign finance. . . .

Governor Bush supports comprehensive reform that would outlaw foreign, corporate, and union money to political parties. Senator McCain? Five times he voted to use your taxes to pay for political campaigns. Governor Bush will devote the surplus to priorities: a strong military, education, Social Security, and tax cuts.[38]

Bush's complaints about McCain's negativity combined with the impact of his ads questioning McCain's positions on a range of conservative issues placed the senator on the defensive. Believing that his own ads undercut the image he was trying to project as a straight-talking political reformer, McCain pulled his confrontational ads before the South Carolina primary with much public fanfare, replacing them with positive ones that lauded his accomplishments, qualifications, and agenda and defensive ads that denied Bush's accusations.

Bush and the outside groups that supported his candidacy, however, continued to air commercials that attacked McCain. Ads that were sharply critical of the senator's statements on abortion were aired in that state as well as in Michigan and Virginia. These ads were reinforced by telephone campaigns that questioned McCain's Republican credentials on a range of social issues. Even more controversial than the calls was the $2.5 million worth of ads in New York, California, and Ohio that savaged McCain's environmental record. Sponsored by Republicans for Clean Air, a PAC financed by Texas millionaire Sam Wyly, a close friend and financial supporter of George W. Bush, the ads claimed that McCain voted against solar and renewable energy while Bush improved air quality in Texas by clamping down on coal-burning electric power plants.[39]

By contrast, the Democratic confrontational ads were less inflammatory on the surface, but no less critical in content. Bradley chided Gore for his inconsistency over the years on abortion, gun control, and tobacco, suggesting that Gore adopted and then changed his position for political purposes. In reiterating his Democratic credentials, Gore in turn accused Bradley of quitting the Senate when his party lost control rather than staying to fight for what he believed, voting for Ronald Reagan's budget, and supporting private school vouchers, another Republican policy position.[40]

When Gore's ads seemed to be having an impact, lowering Bradley's standing in the polls, Bradley hit back. He defended his record, criticized Gore, and aired testimonials from such well-known sports stars as Michael Jordan and public officials as Senator Daniel Patrick Moynihan (D-NY) and Bob Kerrey (D-NE) supporting his character and candidacy.

The ad wars of the 2000 nomination process took their intended toll. Bush's ads seem to convince Republicans that he was a good human being and safe on their issues, while McCain was temperamental, unpredictable, and had his own issue agenda, which was different than the party's. Gore's commercials raised questions about Bradley's loyalty to the party and his command of the issues, while they trumpeted Gore's qualifications as an experienced vice president, a Democratic partisan, and appropriate heir to the Clinton-Gore presidency.

Develop a Deep and Wide Organization. The concentration of primaries and caucuses also requires that candidates create a deep and wide organization, one that can attend to the multiple facets of the campaign and do so in many states simultaneously. But doing so has become increasingly difficult with the front-loading of the primaries, even for well-financed candidates. As a consequence the deep organization rarely extends beyond the early states and in those states it must also be supplemented by group activity, such as with the pro-life and Christian coalition groups which helped Pat Buchanan in 1996 and George W. Bush in 2000, and organized labor which aided Al Gore, particularly in Iowa and New Hampshire. All the candidates who survive these contests must supplement their organizations with volunteers who may be encouraged by their victories or by the organizations of state parties if those parties can be persuaded to support them.

George Bush benefited enormously from the backing and organizational support of state parties in New Hampshire, South Carolina, and Illinois in 1988, as did his son in the early contests in Iowa, South Carolina, and Virginia in 2000. Similarly, Bill Clinton owed his first primary victory in Georgia in 1992 to the active campaign of Governor Zell Miller and his party organization.

The major task of any organization is to mobilize voters. Media coverage alone usually does not suffice. Having an organization in the field is deemed especially important in caucus states in order to get supporters and sympathizers to the precinct meetings which are less well-known than the voting places where people cast their primary ballots and also vote in the general election. In both caucuses and primaries, telephone banks must be established, door-to-door canvassing undertaken, and appropriate material mailed or hand delivered. It is also necessary to create the impression of broad public support and generate excitement. These activities involve a large grassroots effort. A major assumption of the Robertson campaign in 1988 was that the 3 million people who signed petitions urging him to run for president would be a continuing source for voluntary campaign activities and for fund-raising which they were until Robertson's chances appeared futile.

Eugene McCarthy, George McGovern, and to a lesser extent Bill Bradley recruited thousands of college students to ring doorbells, distribute literature, and get supporters out to vote in 1968, 1972, and 2000. Jimmy Carter had his "Peanut Brigade," a group of Georgians who followed him from state to state in 1976. Jesse Jackson effectively used African-American churches to recruit volunteers and raise money for his presidential campaigns in 1984 and 1988. Pat Buchanan had his greatest success in caucus states in 1992 and 1996 where his passionate and committed supporters could control local meetings and state conventions. In fact, the only states in which Buchanan received a majority of the delegates were caucus states.

Monitor Public Opinion. With intentions clear, money in hand, media events organized, and an organization in place, it is necessary to ascertain public sentiment, appeal to it, and try to manipulate it. To achieve these goals, polling and focus groups are considered essential. However, they did not become part and parcel of the nomination process until the middle of the twentieth century.

Republican Thomas E. Dewey was the first to have private polling data available to him when he tried unsuccessfully to obtain the Republican nomination in 1940. John F. Kennedy was the first candidate to engage a pollster in his quest for the nomination. Preconvention surveys conducted by Louis Harris in 1960 indicated that Hubert Humphrey, Kennedy's principal rival, was potentially vulnerable in West Virginia and Wisconsin. On the basis of this information, the Kennedy campaign decided to concentrate time, effort, and money in these predominantly Protestant states. Victories in both helped demonstrate Kennedy's broad appeal, thereby improving his chances for the nomination.

Today, all major presidential candidates commission their own polls. These private surveys are important for several reasons. They provide information about the beliefs and attitudes of voters, their perceptions of the candidates, and the kinds of appeals that are apt to be most effective, as well as which ones seem to be working. Bill Clinton used polls to great advantage in 1992 to develop and target an economic appeal and to respond to allegations about his personal character. He used them even more intensely to reposition himself and launch his reelection bid following the Democrats' debacle in the 1994 midterm elections. The entire Clinton advertising campaign in 1995 and 1996 was developed and monitored through careful and constant White House polling.

Focus groups have become increasingly important. They are used to gauge the public's reaction to words and phrases as well as to evaluate the potential impact of candidate appeals on voters. According to Clinton's 1996 political strategist Dick Morris, he and his aides crafted the president's media advertising on the basis of focus group reactions:

> We prepared several different rough versions of the ads, call animatics, which [pollster] Mark Penn would arrange to test at fifteen shopping malls around the nation. After the Republicans began to attack us in their own ads, Penn tested the opposition ad and our reply at the same time to measure their relative impact. Penn's staffers would set themselves up in a mall and invite shoppers one by one to fill out a short questionnaire about Clinton, Dole, and their own political views. Then they would show the voters the ad we wanted to test. Afterward the shopper would fill in the same questionnaire and Penn would measure any changes in opinion. . . .
>
> Based on the mall tests, we decided which ad to run and whether to combine it with elements from ads that did not do as well. We worked for hours to make the ad fit thirty seconds. Then we'd send the script to Doug Sosnik, the White House political director, who gave it to the president for his OK.[41]

The Bush and Gore campaigns engaged in similar efforts in 2000. (See Box 4–4 on page 145.)

Telephone polling can also be a guise for getting out the vote, for pushing a vote, or even for suppressing one. In 1992, Bush supporters in New Hampshire countered Pat Buchanan's criticism with a telephone campaign directed at women who were read statements that Buchanan had made about their fitness to have a career. The choice of the statement was designed to produce a negative effect. Similarly, in 2000, supporters of McCain and Bush raised questions about their opponents' religious tolerance to get out their own religious supporters.[42]

Poll results can also be used to build momentum, increase morale, and affect media coverage. The amount of coverage is important because the more coverage candidates have, particularly during the early months, the more volunteers they can attract and the more money they can raise. The benefits of appearing to be popular and electable suggest why candidates have also used their private polls for promotional purposes. A good example is Nelson Rockefeller, who tied his quest for the Republican nomination in 1968 to poll data. Since he did not enter the primaries, Rockefeller's aim was to convince Republican delegates that he, not Richard Nixon, would be the strongest candidate. Private surveys, conducted for Rockefeller in nine large states, five important congressional districts, and the nation as a whole one month before the Republican convention, indicated that he would do better against potential Democratic candidates than Richard Nixon. Unfortunately for Rockefeller, the final Gallup preconvention poll, fielded two days after former President Dwight Eisenhower endorsed Nixon, did not support these findings. The Gallup results undercut the credibility of Rockefeller's polls as well as of another national poll that had Rockefeller in the lead and thus effectively ended his chances for the nomination.

Another use of private polls is to raise money. Contributors are more motivated to give to candidates who stand a reasonable chance of winning. Thus, the release of poll data to potential donors and even to the news media is often designed to demonstrate a candidate's electability.

Although polls directly affect a candidate's strategy, tactics, and fund-raising, their impact on the general public is less direct and much less pronounced. Despite the fear of many politicians, there are few empirical data to suggest that polls generate a bandwagon effect, a momentum for a candidate that causes people to jump on board. There is, however, some evidence of a relationship between a candidate's standing in the polls, success in the primaries, and winning the nomination. What is unclear is whether the public opinion leaders win because they are more popular or whether they are more popular initially because they are better known and ultimately because they look like winners.

Design and Target a Distinctive Appeal. The information obtained from polls and focus groups is used to create and sharpen leadership images and to target these images to sympathetic voters. In designing an appeal, candidates must first establish their credentials, then articulate a general approach, and finally discuss specific policy problems and solutions. For lesser-known candidates, the initial emphasis must be on themselves and their relevant experience.

With a few notable exceptions — Vice President Al Gore and Governor George W. Bush — most of the candidates in the 2000 presidential campaign were not well-known to the general public at the outset of the nomination process. In September 1999, as candidates began to organize their campaigns and vie for attention, only Gore and Bush were recognized by more than 15 percent of the voters as candidates.[43] For the rest, name recognition and image creation became their first and essential task.

The increasing front-loading of the primaries and caucuses added to the plight of these lesser-known aspirants. At a time when only a small portion of the people were paying close attention to news about the campaign, most of these non-front-running candidates who were not independently wealthy had to gain recognition in order to obtain sufficient money, media, and volunteers to run a viable campaign. Half of the Republican aspirants were unable to do so and thus were forced to drop out, claiming a lack of funds, even before the election year began.

As the Republican race narrowed to a two-person contest, the policy emphases of the principal candidates became clearer. Bush, who had begun his campaign as a main street Republican, one who could unify the various factions within his party, became more conservative, emphasizing his plan to cut taxes and his support of the social policy positions of the Christian coalition. In contrast, McCain emphasized his independence, his reform agenda with campaign finance at its center, and his credentials as a Reagan Republican.

On the Democratic side, the policy differences were narrower. Al Gore pointed to his experience as vice president in a successful administration. Desiring to share credit for the administration's accomplishments, Gore indicated some of his contributions, such his leading role in advocating and overseeing the administration's policies designed to build an information superhighway. However, an off-the-cuff remark on television, "I took the initiative in creating the Internet," embarrassed him and illustrated his propensity to exaggerate his own importance.[44] Bill Bradley spoke about the need for reform in health care, improving race relations, and ending child poverty. He presented himself as a nontraditional candidate who was motivated to do what was right, not what was politically correct.

In general, the candidates' issue positions and image projections did reach voters. The Annenberg Public Policy Center at the University of Pennsylvania, which studied these policy agendas and image projections in 2000, found that overall, "people gained greater awareness and knowledge of the candidates and their positions as the primary season progressed. Knowledge gains were higher in states with primaries in which the candidates actively campaigned than in states without candidate activity."[45]

The state exit polls also indicated that the candidates "hit" their targets although some, obviously, were more successful than others. (See Tables 4–4 and 4–5, pages 141–143.) The Annenberg Center's study noted that people had a clearer understanding of McCain's position on campaign finance reform than they did of Bradley's on health care. Bradley, nonetheless, proved to be quite successful, energizing inactive Democrats and independents, at least initially. McCain was even more successful in mobilizing independents and some Democrats to support his candidacy.[46]

Annenberg researchers also examined the impact of political endorsements and campaign attacks on the electorate. They concluded that endorsements and attacks can inform voters and influence their behavior on election day. Not only were people aware of candidate endorsements by prominent officials in their states, but that these endorsements carried weight and were a factor affecting their vote. Similarly, attacks, particularly those that became items in the news, also had an effect. Criticism of McCain for voting against breast cancer research and of Bradley for his overly ambitious and expensive health care plan were cited as examples by the study.[47]

In short, what candidates say and do matters. Candidate appeals and attacks inform and influence the electorate. They may not be the only factors that affect the election's outcome, but they do make a difference.

In addition to the advertising, a staple of contemporary presidential campaigns, other methods are also used to reach voters. These include video news releases produced by the candidates, satellite interviews with local news media, and telephone, specifically the use of a toll-free number, to raise money and gain volunteers.

One of the distinctive aspects of nomination campaigns in the 1990s and in 2000 has been the propensity of candidates to circumvent the national media. They have done so in a variety of ways. The Clinton campaign in 1992, for example, distributed between 25,000 and 30,000 videotapes about the candidate to New Hampshire Democrats.[48] Video news releases were also given to local media by several of the candidate organizations. Some of the local stations even used them on their news shows without revealing the source.[49]

Satellite technology has also been used extensively. In 1992, nearly half of the local news media conducted interviews with the candidates compared with only 20 percent four years earlier.[50] Since 1992, candidates have taken advantage of free television on national talk-entertainment shows as well as news shows.

The Internet has also become another vehicle, and an increasingly important one, through which policy positions are stated and argued, and financial appeals are made. (See "Where on the Web," pages 151–152.) John McCain collected over $7 million in donations using his Web site, most of it after his surprisingly strong showing in New Hampshire.[51] Soliciting volunteers, communicating with supporters, and making information available to the press and other interested parties are some of the other ways in which candidates have used their Web sites as a campaign tool.

The Internet has generated problems as well. Squatters have used the names of actual and potential candidates to register Web addresses and then demanded large sums from the campaigns to give them up. Parody sites and linkages have mushroomed on the Net. Unsubstantiated rumors can be circulated so widely and rapidly that they become news. Security has also become a problem as Web sites become targets of political opponents and hackers who wish to damage a candidate by invading the site.

All of these factors — timing, finance, organization, and communications — affect the quest for delegates. They help shape the candidates' strategies and tactics for the nomination. Generally speaking, there have been two successful contemporary prototypical strategies, one for lesser-known aspirants, the other for front-runners. Jimmy Carter used the first of these strategies successfully in his quest for the nomination in 1976. In his run four years later, Carter adopted the second. Since that time, most of the principal contenders have employed one of these strategies or a variation of them in their attempts to win their party's nomination.

The Non-Front-Runner Strategy: Stepping-Stones to Prominence

Non-front-runners lack the resources for victory: money, media, and organization. Their objective must be to obtain them and to do so as quickly as possible. The only way to do this is to run hard and fast at the outset, entering the early contests, doing well, gaining media attention, demonstrating electability, generating momentum, and eventually building a delegate base.

Jimmy Carter pursued such a strategy in 1976; it has since become the non-front-runner model. Hamilton Jordan, Carter's campaign manager, designed the basic game plan two years before the election. He described the early preconvention strategy as follows:

> The prospect of a crowded field coupled with the new proportional representation rule does not permit much flexibility in the early primaries. No serious candidate will have the luxury of picking or choosing among the early primaries. To pursue such a strategy would cost that candidate delegate votes and increase the possibility of being lost in the crowd. I think that we have to assume that everybody will be running in the first five or six primaries.
>
> A crowded field enhances the possibility of several inconclusive primaries with four or five candidates separated by only a few percentage points. Such a muddled picture will not continue for long as the press will begin to make "winners" of some and "losers" of others. The intense press coverage which naturally focuses on the early primaries plus the decent time intervals which separate the March and mid-April primaries dictate a serious effort in all of the first five primaries. Our "public" strategy would probably be that Florida was the first and real test of the Carter campaign and that New Hampshire would just be a warm-up. In fact, a strong, surprise showing in New Hampshire should be our goal which would have tremendous impact on successive primaries.[52]

The goal was achieved. Dubbed the person to beat after his victories in the Iowa caucuses and New Hampshire primary, Carter, with his defeat of George Wallace in Florida, overcame a disappointing fourth place in Massachusetts a week earlier and became the acknowledged front-runner. The Carter effort in 1976 became the strategic plan for George Bush in 1980, Gary Hart in 1984, and John McCain in 2000.

Doing well in the early caucuses and primaries is important but no longer has the payoff it had for Carter. The front-loading of the selection process has reduced the "bump" that Iowa and New Hampshire can give to a victorious non-front-runner. Yet, such candidates have few other options to increase their name recognition and at the same time demonstrate their viability as serious candidates for their party's nomination. And a win in the early caucuses and primaries, no matter how slight, confounds the odds, surprises the news media, embarrasses the front-runner, and energizes the non-front-runner's candidacy. (See Box 4–3, "Non-Front-Runner Strategies in 2000.") Media coverage expands; fund-raising is made easier; volunteers join the organization; endorsements become more likely; and momentum can be generated, at least in the short run.[53]

BOX 4–3 ★

NON-FRONT-RUNNER STRATEGIES IN 2000

McCAIN'S "STRAIGHT-TALK" CHALLENGE

A hero, a renegade, very much his own person, but one who had little public recognition, political support, and financial backing, McCain's challenge to George W. Bush turned out to be one of the big surprises and the biggest news story of the 2000 nominations.

McCain started slowly. He had a small staff, little money, and responsibilities that kept him in the Senate for much of the 1999 preseason. Moreover, he lacked the credentials of successful Republican nominees in the past. He was not considered a party loyalist; he had not previously run a national campaign; he had few political endorsements, few major financial backers, and no discernible grass-roots support. What he did have, however, was a leadership image from his service in Vietnam, his outspoken campaign against special interests, pork barrel legislation, and soft money, and his strong support for a national tobacco settlement. McCain exuded confidence and conviction, two traits that were to take him far in his campaign.

McCain did not begin his presidential quest until December 1999, well after most of his Republican rivals. With limited resources, McCain had no choice but to target the early primaries as stepping-stones to the nomination. However, he did make one strategic decision that worked to his advantage — not to contest the first caucus in Iowa. This decision enabled him to conserve his resources and avoid an in-the-pack finish. As attention shifted to New Hampshire, he was the only Republican who had not lost to George W. Bush. This fact alone earned him media notoriety.

McCain's campaign organization was smaller and more informal than George W. Bush's.[54] Unlike Bush who followed his handlers' advice religiously, McCain was very much his own campaign manager. He called the shots. Hating to read set speeches, he liked to engage in free-floating, unscripted discussions of his issues: campaign finance reform, special interest politics, reduction of the national debt, and a strong, flexible national defense. The image he presented was that of a straight shooter, an antipolitician, who like Jimmy Carter, pledged, "I will always tell you the truth."[55] Reputed to be temperamental and prone to angry outbursts by his opponents, McCain acknowledged his emotions and claimed that they reflected the strength of his convictions and his penchant for straight talk.

McCain's appeal to patriotism, public service, and political reform resonated well with Republicans in New Hampshire, as well as independent voters and Democrats around the country. Core Republicans, however, were not as moved by his rhetoric. Most strong Republican loyalists still thought in terms of the language, themes, and policies that President Reagan and his disciples championed: a smaller and less intrusive national government, tax cuts, and conservative social values. None of these were at the top of McCain's priorities.

During his campaign, Senator McCain had excellent relations with the press. In fact, he was a media favorite. The access he gave to reporters, the no-nonsense image he conveyed, and the competition he generated in the Republican campaign resulted in expansive coverage of his campaign and a more favorable press than Bush received from the New Hampshire primary until Super Tuesday.[56]

McCain's game plan was to do well in New Hampshire, gain media attention, become George W. Bush's principal challenger, and then use the recognition he would receive from a victory in the first primary to raise money, gain volunteers, and produce momentum for the next contest. The plan worked splendidly. McCain won 48 percent of the New Hampshire vote compared to Bush's 30 percent and Forbes's 13 percent. His unexpectedly large victory put Bush on the defensive, hastened the departure of other candidates (Bauer after New Hampshire and Forbes after Delaware), and upped the ante for the next contest in South Carolina. McCain's impressive win also gave him a big financial boost. He raised an additional $2 million following the New Hampshire primary, much of it from appeals on his Web site.[57]

After an intervening caucus in Delaware in which only Forbes and Bush competed and that received scant media coverage, McCain turned his attention to South Carolina. With the state's Republican establishment supporting Bush, with religious conservatives comprising a major bloc of voters, with pro-tobacco groups active in the state, McCain faced big odds. Complicating his effort were negative advertising campaigns waged by his opponents — George W. Bush, antiabortion and pro-tobacco groups, religious conservatives, and even a group that supported flying the Confederate flag over the state capital.

The campaigns against McCain were largely confrontational and personal. They focused on the senator's position on the issues, his congressional voting record, his loyalty to the Republican party, even rumors about his private life. Many of the campaigns were conducted at the grassroots level. Millions of voters were contacted by phone and mail. The Bush campaign alone reached an estimated 1 million people in the final two days before the vote.[58]

Initially, McCain countered with negative ads of his own against Bush. However, when the press made negativity an issue, McCain abruptly pulled his attack ads and pledged not to go negative again. But his pledge seemed to have little impact on the outcome. Bush won handily, gaining an overwhelming proportion of the Christian Coalition vote. (See Table 4–5, page 142.)

The contest then moved to more friendly territory for McCain, his home state of Arizona and Michigan, a state in which religious conservatives were not as strong. McCain was also helped in Michigan by the law that permitted independents and Democrats to cross over and vote in the Republican primary. Although the establishment Republicans in Arizona and Michigan endorsed Bush, although the Bush campaign spent considerable sums on media advertising in both states ($2 million in Arizona alone), and although conservative antiabortion and antitax groups actively opposed his candidacy,[59] McCain was able to overcome this opposition by appealing to independent and Democratic voters. He won both contests.

At this point, McCain looked viable. His campaign was raising money. He was appealing to a cross-section of voters. In fact, hypothetical polls against the likely Democratic candidate, Al Gore, actually showed McCain running stronger than George W. Bush. This fact provided support for McCain's claim that he, not George W. Bush, was Al Gore's worst nightmare.

The next three contests, the Washington and Virginia primaries and caucus election in North Dakota, proved disappointing to McCain and essentially undercut his earlier wins. In none of these states was he able to overcome Bush's lead among Republicans, the only voters who could participate. Nor did his positive advertising achieve nearly the impact that Bush's negative advertising did. And looking ahead to Super Tuesday, Bush's large war chest put him in a much stronger position to compete in the twelve primaries and two first-round caucuses that were to be held that day.

Behind in the polls and unable to match Bush's money and organization, McCain took a tactical gamble. Speaking in an area of Virginia known for its religious fundamentalism, McCain denounced two of the state's most prominent fundamentalist ministers, Jerry Falwell and Pat Robertson, calling them "agents of intolerance" and "forces of evil."[60] His remarks, which he was forced to modify, serve to unite the Christian Coalition against him and brought out an unusually large vote from this group, but did not appear to help McCain with more moderate Republican voters.[61] (See Table 4–5.)

With his campaign on the rocks, McCain ran as best he could on Super Tuesday. Although he won four out of the five New England primaries, he lost everywhere else, including the delegate-rich states of California, Ohio, and New York. In each of these big states, the Republican establishment combined with outside groups to mobilize a sizable pro-Bush, anti-McCain vote. With his opponent's delegate lead all but insurmountable, McCain announced he would reevaluate his campaign. The race was over.

Though he lost, McCain gained stature from his defeat. He had attracted independent and Democratic voters. In every state in which he competed, McCain received a much higher percentage of the votes of self-declared independents than did Bush. He also got more Democratic support in states in which cross-over voting was permitted. Among Republicans, he was weaker. In general, the more conservative the voter the less likely that voter would cast a ballot for McCain. But his biggest weakness was among the religious right. This group voted overwhelmingly for George W. Bush. Each of these trends is documented in the state exit polls and illustrated in Table 4–5.

Nonetheless, McCain's issue of campaign finance reform, his diatribe against special interest politics, even his proposals to pay down the national debt rather than give tax relief to all voters, resonated with the American electorate. He had become a new force in Republican party politics, a leader whom George W. Bush would have to acknowledge.

BRADLEY'S NONTRADITIONAL CHALLENGE

Bill Bradley's challenge was unexpected; his campaign, unconventional; and his candidacy, quixotic. Desiring to put government and public policy on a more moral and egalitarian foundation, Bradley espoused a variety of goals that seemed to place him to the ideological left of Gore and into the liberal, big government wing of his party.

Bradley presented himself as a candidate who disdained politics as usual, a man of deep convictions. His image as an antipolitician appealed to those who had grown increasingly cynical about the motives, decisions, and actions of people who made a career of electoral politics. His earnestness, genuineness, and self-effacing manner contrasted sharply with Gore's inside-Washington style and political image.

Bradley's campaign style was unique as well. He jealously guarded his privacy, refusing to discuss even his own religious beliefs. He was also reluctant initially to criticize his opponent or engage in the give-and-take that characterizes contemporary politics. Bradley emphasized the positive, how much better America could become if more people benefited from the country's prosperity.

At first, the press and public found Bradley's image refreshing, his fund-raising ability surprising, and his rise in the polls startling. Who would have expected this candidate to mount such an effective challenge to an incumbent vice president? As long as Bradley's image as a citizen not a politician, a person with whom the average American could identify and trust, remained the story of his campaign, he did well.

Bradley's problem, however, was that he could not move beyond this image. In fact, that image initially immobilized him. When his Democratic credentials were attacked and his policies critically evaluated in face-to-face debates with Gore and by Gore's political advertising, Bradley took the high road. Rather than attacking Gore, he defended himself and his policies. His defensive posture, however, made him appear passive and timid in comparison to the aggressiveness of his opponent.

Being a nice guy also limited Bradley's ability to exploit Gore's vulnerabilities: the vice president's tendency to exaggerate, his involvement in the Democratic Party's campaign finance scandal, and his defense of the president in the Monica Lewinsky affair. By the time Bradley began to question Gore's veracity and judgment, the vice president's campaign had rebounded from its early doldrums.

The first caucus and primary were very important for Bradley. As a challenger, he had to demonstrate that he could win. Putting a lot of effort into the Iowa caucus, Bradley spent seventy-five days in the state in 1999, much more than Gore, and he was there for most of month preceding caucus on January 24, 2000. Bradley also spent the maximum legal amount of $2.2 million, more than half of which went into television advertising. Four hundred, mostly young, campaign volunteers combed the state for potential supporters, but Bradley's organization could not match organized labor's and the Iowa State Education Association which turned out a large caucus vote for Gore.[62]

Despite Bradley's effort, he failed to generate much excitement and support in the state. Hurt by his health care plan which Iowa Democrats perceived as too costly, by his vote against flood relief for Iowa in 1993, and by a low turnout, the senator only received a little more than one-third of the vote, a disappointing showing given the time and resources he put into the state.

Bradley's Iowa loss weakened his New Hampshire campaign. Not only did it call into question his status as a serious challenger to Gore, but it cut into his organizing effort because he had to move his grassroots operation from New Hampshire to Iowa. By the time he and his operatives returned to the state, Bradley's lead in the polls had all but vanished, and he lacked sufficient time to turn things around. Again, he had to battle the AFL-CIO in addition to Gore's campaign regulars. Labor organizers contacted every union household not once but seven times to bring out the prolabor, pro-Gore vote.[63]

Although the New Hampshire vote was closer than in Iowa, Bradley still lost. Other than a popularity contest in the state of Washington, there was no other Democratic contest scheduled until the first Tuesday in March when twelve primaries and two, initial-round caucuses were to be held. With the news media turning their attention to the Republican contests occurring in the interim, Bradley lost visibility. Although he kept campaigning, he did not pick up steam. His staff was becoming increasingly frustrated. Polls showed him losing ground to Gore.[64] The die was cast. On Super Tuesday, March 7th, Bradley was defeated in all the contests he entered. He officially ended his candidacy two days later.

Bradley lost for several reasons. His diffident manner, ephemeral style, and unassuming personality raised questions of image — whether this decent person could be a strong, decisive, and effective leader. Bradley just didn't connect with core Democratic voters.[65] He also did not respond quickly enough and with sufficient vigor to Gore's charges in their face-to-face debates and to television advertisements in which his policy stands and Senate votes were criticized. When Bradley finally began to question his opponent's integrity, credibility, and more conservative policies, he became just another politician in the eyes of many Democrats. His uniqueness had faded.

Nor could Bradley's organization compete with Gore's. The senator's young volunteers were no match for the seasoned and skilled organizers of organized labor and Democratic Party professionals who helped Gore. Bradley operated as his own campaign director, but his loner style made it difficult for his campaign staff to plan far ahead. Usually, one to four events were held per day, with many of them occurring after the evening newscasts.[66] Bradley also kept reporters at a distance, even traveling separately from them.[67]

The Democratic challenger was also hurt by Republican John McCain's candidacy, particularly McCain's appeal to independent voters and weak Democrats. Although both he and McCain championed similar causes, it was McCain, not Bradley, who was seen as the leader on them.

Bradley had another problem that McCain did not. He had to contend with a Democratic electorate that was more complacent, more approving of the Clinton-Gore administration, and much less upset with its scandals than were the people to whom McCain appealed. McCain's voters were more angry, and they showed it by turning out to vote. Bradley's supporters were not, and they turned out in smaller numbers.

Although people saw Bradley as distant, they also perceived him as a man of convictions and a person with new ideas. For those Democrats who were cynical about the political process, upset with the moral and ethical shortcomings of the Clinton administration, or critical of its moderate, incremental policies, Bradley's candidacy was refreshing. For most core Democrats, however, it was not. He did not win the vote of self-declared Democrats in any of the states in which he competed against Gore. Bradley did better among independent voters, although not as well as McCain. Ideology did not seem to be the factor it was for the Republicans, but the absence of labor support clearly was. Bradley lost the vote of union households by a margin of two or three to one. These trends among those who voted in the Democratic primaries are illustrated in Table 4–4.

On the other hand, early losses for non-front-runners doom their candidacy, forcing them to withdraw, usually on the pretext of having insufficient funds to continue.[68] There is no prize for coming in second, except perhaps a prime-time convention speech. News media often speculate that candidates who demonstrate some popular appeal would make good vice presidential candidates, but the fact of the matter is that successful nominees rarely choose their opponents to run with them. The only recent exception to this rule was Reagan's selection of Bush — not his first choice — in 1980.

TABLE 4–4 ★

THE GORE-BRADLEY COMPETITION:
A PROFILE OF THE PRIMARY ELECTORATE (IN PERCENTAGES)

	Iowa		New Hampshire		California		New York		Ohio		Rhode Island	
	G	B	G	B	G	B	G	B	G	B	G	B
Party												
Democratic	(82) 66	29	(56) 59	41	(85) 82	17	(80) 70	29	(77) 80	19	(60) 65	33
Independent	(17) 39	42	(40) 41	56	(13) 64	35	(18) 46	50	(21) 52	43	(38) 43	55
Ideology												
Liberal	(49) 61	34	(54) 50	49	(50) 75	24	(54) 62	38	(42) 72	25	(50) 50	48
Moderate	(42) 60	30	(38) 50	47	(42) 84	16	(35) 70	29	(49) 75	25	(39) 63	35
Conservative	(9) 64	23	(8) 47	49	(8) 83	17	(10) 63	34	(10) 60	28	(11) 0	0
Union Household												
Yes	(33) 69	24	(22) 60	38	(26) 83	16	(40) 70	30	(46) 74	22	(33) 62	34
No	(67) 57	35	(77) 47	51	(74) 79	20	(60) 61	38	(54) 71	28	(67) 52	46

	Missouri		Massachusetts		Maryland		Maine		Connecticut		Vermont	
	G	B	G	B	G	B	G	B	G	B	G	B
Party												
Democratic	(78) 70	28	(67) 67	33	(80) 74	23	(62) 60	36	(77) 60	38	(58) 60	39
Independent	(16) 44	51	(29) 53	43	(16) 42	48	(29) 43	53	(20) 39	54	(39) 49	50
Ideology												
Liberal	(48) 65	33	(55) 57	41	(52) 68	29	(57) 52	45	(52) 55	43	(68) 55	45
Moderate	(43) 67	31	(37) 64	32	(37) 71	25	(35) 58	37	(37) 60	36	(27) 53	46
Conservative	(9) 0	0	(8) 64	30	(12) 46	40	(8) 0	0	(12) 41	53	(5) 0	0
Union Household												
Yes	(26) 65	32	(29) 63	33	(29) 73	22	(27) 55	42	(35) 57	38	(20) 54	45
No	(74) 65	33	(71) 59	39	(71) 65	31	(73) 54	41	(65) 54	44	(80) 55	43

Note: Parentheses indicate proportion of the total state population.

Source: Voter News Survey Exit Poll as reported by CNN at <http://cnn.com/ELECTIONS/2000/primaries.html>.

TABLE 4–5 ★

THE BUSH-MCCAIN COMPETITION: A PROFILE OF THE PRIMARY ELECTORATE (IN PERCENTAGES)

	Iowa		New Hampshire		Delaware		South Carolina		Michigan		Arizona	
	B	**M**	**B**	**M**	**B**	**M**	**B**	**M**	**B**	**M**	**B**	**M**
Party												
Democratic	(2) 0	0	(4) 13	78	(2) 0	0	(9) 18	79	(17) 10	82	(2) 0	0
Republican	(83) 44	3	(53) 41	38	(80) 56	21	(61) 69	26	(48) 66	29	(80) 41	56
Independent	(15) 29	10	(41) 19	62	(18) 26	45	(30) 34	60	(35) 26	67	(18) 20	72
Ideology												
Liberal	(6) 41	6	(13) 24	67	(8) 33	47	(10) 34	63	(17) 16	78	(9) 19	77
Moderate	(20) 47	13	(36) 26	60	(30) 48	36	(29) 37	59	(37) 33	64	(28) 25	72
Conservative	(73) 40	2	(51) 35	37	(62) 53	18	(61) 69	26	(45) 60	31	(62) 43	51
Religious Right												
Yes	(37) 33	1	(16) 36	26	(24) 54	12	(34) 68	24	(27) 66	25	(26) 44	48
No	(57) 47	7	(80) 28	54	(72) 48	31	(61) 46	52	(67) 36	60	(69) 33	64

	Virginia		California		New York		Ohio		Rhode Island		Missouri	
	B	**M**	**B**	**M**	**B**	**M**	**B**	**M**	**B**	**M**	**B**	**M**
Party												
Democratic	(8) 11	87	(2) 0	0	(3) 0	0	(7) 30	66	(6) 0	0	(10) 21	76
Republican	(63) 69	28	(82) 63	32	(74) 57	38	(69) 68	28	(40) 57	42	(61) 72	21
Independent	(29) 31	64	(16) 50	41	(23) 33	58	(24) 37	56	(53) 24	72	(29) 43	49
Ideology												
Liberal	(12) 27	69	(6) 59	39	(14) 41	50	(14) 54	40	(13) 18	80	(12) 43	52
Moderate	(33) 35	62	(33) 44	54	(35) 43	53	(39) 46	51	(39) 27	72	(33) 42	55
Conservative	(55) 69	27	(61) 66	29	(51) 58	35	(37) 68	26	(48) 48	48	(56) 71	20
Religious Right												
Yes	(19) 80	14	(17) 73	17	(15) 62	28	(23) 74	19	(11) 68	27	(24) 72	15
No	(77) 45	52	(79) 56	39	(80) 47	47	(73) 52	44	(85) 32	65	(70) 52	42

TABLE 4–5 ★ *(continued)*

THE BUSH-MCCAIN COMPETITION: A PROFILE OF THE PRIMARY ELECTORATE (IN PERCENTAGES)

	Massa-chusetts		Maryland		Maine		Connecticut		Vermont	
	B	M	B	M	B	M	B	M	B	M
Party										
Democratic	(8)	8 88	(3)	0 0	(3)	0 0	(3)	0 0	(8)	19 81
Republican	(37)	54 43	(69)	66 27	(66)	63 33	(72)	56 39	(50)	51 44
Independent	(54)	21 75	(28)	33 59	(31)	33 62	(26)	25 69	(42)	23 74
Ideology										
Liberal	(20)	16 82	(11)	41 51	(14)	40 57	(14)	20 74	(19)	29 69
Moderate	(40)	27 71	(34)	43 53	(35)	40 54	(39)	43 54	(37)	24 74
Conservative	(40)	46 48	(55)	67 23	(51)	64 32	(47)	57 36	(44)	50 44
Religious Right										
Yes	(8)	46 44	(22)	71 15	(21)	73 19	(13)	61 29	(14)	63 31
No	(85)	29 68	(75)	51 43	(75)	45 50	(83)	44 51	(82)	31 65

Note: Parentheses indicate proportion of the total state vote.

Source: Voter News Survey Exit Poll, as reported by CNN at <http://cnn.com/ELECTIONS/2000/primaries.html>.

Other Non-Front-Runner Approaches: Using the Campaign as a Pulpit

Jesse Jackson was not a typical non-front-runner in 1984 and 1988, and, to some extent, neither were Pat Robertson in 1988, Jerry Brown and Pat Buchanan in 1992, 1996, and 2000, and Gary Bauer and Alan Keyes in 2000. Jackson and Brown did not employ the prototypical challenger strategy although Robertson, Buchanan, Bauer, and Keyes did. Most of these candidates could not afford large paid organizations or extensive paid media. Robertson, Buchanan, and to a lesser extent Bauer relied more heavily on advertisements and in Robertson's case, a paid field organization. What all these candidates had in common, however, was a large cadre of grassroots supporters but little realistic chance of winning their party's nomination. Why then did they campaign for it?

They each had several overlapping objectives: to use the campaign as a pulpit for presenting their ideas and as a vehicle for mobilizing their constituencies to promote the interests of those who were not well represented in the party and its hierarchy, to be considered as members of that hierarchy with considerable political power, and to influence the party and its platform. Bay Buchanan, Pat's sister and campaign manager, described why her brother ran in 1992:

> There were a number of reasons why we were going to run, the least of which is that we wanted to win. . . . First, we felt very strongly that the President was the heir to the Reagan legacy, that he had taken the country in a certain direction, and it was assumed it was the direction the conservatives would have taken. Pat thought that we needed a spokesperson to represent conservatives, to say this *isn't* the direction we think is in the best interest of conservatives. . . . Second was eminent domain. David Duke, who had been made a national figure, was speaking about some of those issues that we thought were ours legitimately. He was being made the ultimate spokesperson for conservatives, a development which was going to do incredible damage to the conservative movement. . . . The third was to actually move the President, force him to keep to the issues that we felt were right and proper for the Reagan legacy.[69]

To achieve their objectives, each of these candidates needed above all else to campaign. They also needed to demonstrate their political strength by winning elections if they were to remain active candidates. Jackson and Brown continued their campaign right up to the Democratic convention although it was obvious that they would not be their party's nominee; Robertson and Buchanan dropped out, but not before gaining notoriety for their policy positions. Facing other socially conservative candidates, Buchanan decided to drop out of Republican contention in 2000 and try for the Reform Party's nomination, and with it, $12.6 million in federal funds as well as ballot access in a majority of the states.

Others have also used the campaign to focus attention on themselves and their ideas. Ellen McCormick ran as an antiabortion candidate for the Democratic nomination in 1976. Lyndon LaRouche has used the Democratic primaries since 1980 as a pretext for expounding his philosophy and gaining additional publicity. George McGovern entered the 1984 nomination sweepstakes, Gary Hart reentered in 1988, and Dan Quayle in 2000 in large part to participate in the public forum generated by the campaign and to try to resuscitate their damaged political images and reputations.[70]

With television a primary vehicle for conducting a large-scale nomination campaign, and with candidates having distinctive perspectives and appeals attracting public attention, it is likely that the preconvention process will continue to be used for podium purposes in addition to realistically seeking the nomination.

The Front-Runner Strategy: Amassing Delegates

For front-runners the task is different. They do not need to gain recognition or establish their credentials. They do need to maintain their credibility and electability and extend their constituencies. Their strategy is simple and straightforward — acquire as many delegates as quickly as possible, build an insurmountable lead, and do not allow an early loss to discourage supporters.

The principal advantages front-runners have occur at the beginning of the process. A key element of their strategy must be to maximize these advantages.

They need to make use of the benefits of a superior organization, financial base, media coverage, political endorsements, and volunteer efforts to overwhelm their opposition. The front-loading of the primaries provides added impetus to strike a knockout blow in the early rounds, when the lesser-known opponents are least able to compete with them. Scott Reed, Dole's campaign manager, describes how this scheduling advantages the front-runner:

> [I]f we were well funded and well organized, we'd be able to take advantage of the condensed period. We also recognized that even if we did stumble early in New Hampshire or Iowa — and we recognized in early January that we might — it would be very difficult for somebody else to capitalize with the next six, seven, or eight primaries happening so quickly. We were the only campaign that had gone out and registered actual delegates to run in all the other states; the other campaigns had missed a few states here and there.[71]

Walter Mondale pursued this front-runner strategy in 1984, George Bush did so in 1988 and again in 1992, and Robert Dole in 1996. Michael Dukakis and Bill Clinton used variations of this approach in 1988 and 1992. They all spent heavily up front, had large paid staffs, and sought (and received) political endorsements. These resources produced early payoffs — delegate leads that encouraged most of their opponents to drop out and gave them as front-runners a hedge against any future losses against the candidates who remained.

Front-runners Al Gore and George W. Bush adopted similar strategies in their respective quests for their party's nomination in 2000. Both raised large sums of money, obtained political endorsements from most of their party's elected elite, ran as the presumptive nominee, and won. George W. Bush's image as the popular, unifying candidate was damaged by John McCain's challenge while Al Gore's position as the consensus Democratic candidate was not by Bill Bradley's. Gore beat Bradley in every contest; Bush lost to McCain in the Northeastern states as well as in Arizona and Michigan.

For candidates who are unchallenged, the nomination strategy is obviously different. They can use their resources to launch their presidential campaign as Reagan did in 1984 and Clinton in 1996. The key here is to have the resources at the beginning of the nomination cycle to discourage challengers and have the flexibility to reply to critics. (See Box 4–4, "Front-Runner Strategies in 2000.")

BOX 4–4

FRONT-RUNNER STRATEGIES IN 2000

GEORGE W. BUSH: THE CONSENSUS CANDIDATE

Bush's large war chest and extensive endorsements from elected Republican leaders allowed him to pursue a typical front-runner strategy. The campaign was to be run everywhere in order to demonstrate the candidate's broad popular appeal to a diverse set of constituents from the traditional social and economic conservatives to more moderate Republicans and independent voters. Running as a moderate with strong conservative roots, Bush tried to project the image of a consensus builder, a popular governor, an outsider and reformer capable of broadening the Republican's electoral coalition and softening the party's hard-nosed conservatism. In fostering such an image, Bush took pains to distinguish himself from official Washington, his policy orientation from that of the congressional Republicans, and his moral principles, character, and personal behavior from the scandal-plagued Clinton-Gore administration.

In the summer of 1999, Bush criticized the GOP's congressional tax cut initiative (which President Clinton later vetoed) as well as other policy positions that congressional Republicans advocated. But in doing so, he was careful not to offend anyone. Bush avoided divisive issues, refused to take a position on flying the Confederate flag over the statehouse in South Carolina, equivocated when asked whether he would appoint openly gay people to his administration, and would neither embrace nor repudiate the social policy positions of the Christian right.[72]

His was a highly scripted, play-it-safe, avoid-mistakes-at-all cost, campaign run by a close-knit group of political strategists who had helped Bush in his gubernatorial elections and policy advisers who had served his father during the elder Bush's years in office.[73]

The candidate's speeches were carefully crafted with themes and language that resonated with his audiences. In his standard stump speech, he talked about "responsibility, compassion, and love." Words such as *dreams, heart, love,* and especially *children* were sprinkled liberally throughout his prepared remarks.[74] Bush contrasted his personal ethic with Clinton's in a line that brought roars of approval from his Republican audiences: "Should I be fortunate enough to become your president, when I put my hand on the Bible, I will swear to not only uphold the laws of the land, I will swear to uphold the honor and the dignity of the office to which I have been elected, so help me God."[75] To his Christian fundamentalist supporters, he talked about his own sinful past, his day of reckoning when he stopped drinking and faced his marital responsibilities, the support he received from his renewed faith in the teachings and ministry of Jesus Christ whom Bush acknowledged to have had the greatest philosophical influence on his life

Bush's speeches were reinforced by symbols. The candidate campaigned in Latino, African-American, and Asian neighborhoods to illustrate his broad-based appeal; he appeared with Catholic clergy and at church events to counter an undercurrent that he was anti-Catholic;[76] he wore a pink ribbon in his lapel to express his concern about breast cancer at the same time his political advertising was accusing his principal opponent, John McCain, of voting against funds for cancer research.[77]

Little was left to chance. The Bush campaign even went so far as to design mock ads attacking his positions, show them to focus groups to discern their candidate's perceived vulnerabilities, and then present response ads to gauge people's overall reaction to them.[78] The Clinton campaign had used the same technique in 1992 and 1996 with great success.

Throughout the competitive phase of the nomination process, the press were kept at a distance. Spokesperson Karen Hughes protected Bush and staunchly defended him. Initially, all the sessions that he held with reporters were "off the record," so that he could not be quoted directly. Misstatements could be corrected.[79]

Once the nomination had been effectively secured, the Bush campaign relaxed the off-the-record rule and made the candidate more accessible to the press.

Avoiding mistakes meant sticking to the script, repeating lines that had proven emotional impact. The contrast between the well-prepared and pretested remarks and his off-the-cuff comments were sometimes startling in their syntax and content.[80] In addition, Bush's tendency to stay by his script also presented a problem: it reinforced the point political pundits, late-night comics, and his opponents in the Republican contest were suggesting — that he was not well informed, did not have many original ideas, was a programmed candidate, a product of his handlers, and lacked the gravitas to be president. Published reports of his mediocre school record and his failed business ventures buttressed this view.

Although Bush did loosen up as his campaign progressed, it was events, not accusations, that forced changes in the strategic plan. John McCain's rise in the public opinion polls and his impressive victory in New Hampshire, combined with the threat he posed to Bush in the next contest in South Carolina, a conservative state that had seemed safe for Bush, drove the Bush campaign to emphasize its core constituency of religious conservatives.

Bush accepted an invitation to address students and faculty at Bob Jones University, a fundamentalist Christian school which at the time did not permit interracial dating and, in fact, had accepted only Caucasians until the federal government mandated integration of its student body. The visit to Bob Jones, the backing from evangelical ministers Pat Robertson and Jerry Fallwell, and the mobilization of Christian Coalition voters helped firm up Bush's support in South Carolina as did the extensive advertising campaign that was launched against Senator John McCain. Bush won the hotly contested primary election, but in the process tarnished his image as a moderate, centrist, reformer.

The tarnish, in turn, was reinforced by Bush's conservative message in the Michigan and Virginia primaries and the support he received from antiabortion and antitax groups. Although he won most of the primaries held on the first Tuesday in March, thereby ensuring the Republican nomination, Bush's lead in the polls over Democratic rival Al Gore had all but dissipated, his policy priorities and positions had become associated with those of the conservative wing of his party, and his positive, people-oriented image had been marred by the negativism of his campaign. The good news for Bush was that he had won the nomination; the bad news was that his candidacy had been weakened in the process: his appeal had been narrowed to core Republicans, the religious right. (See Table 4–5, page 142.) More moderate Republicans, particularly those in the Northeast, were much less supportive of his candidacy. Bush clearly had his work cut out for him.

AL GORE: RUNNING FROM THE VICE PRESIDENCY

Contemporary vice presidents have an advantage when seeking their party's nomination. Not only are they well known, well connected, and usually well versed on policy matters, but they have also been cast in a political role that has them doing favors for their party's candidates and its elected officials. Their quest for the presidential nomination amounts to payback time.

Vice President Al Gore had the additional advantage of serving during a period of economic prosperity and social tranquility at home and U.S. dominance abroad.

Heir apparent to the Clinton presidency, he had the president's enthusiastic endorsement as well as the support of Democratic leaders and rank-and-file partisans. The only negatives were his stereotype as stiff, dull, and uninspiring; his position as number two, a follower not a leader; his penchant for verbal bloopers; and his involvement in a scandal-plagued administration.

Most of the other leading Democratic contenders had opted not to challenge Gore. Only Bill Bradley, who had been out of office and the public eye for three years, did so. Gore thought so little of Bradley's challenge that initially he chose to ignore him and campaign as if he were running in the general election against George W. Bush. Gore did not want to legitimize and elevate Bradley's candidacy; besides he was trailing Bush by double digits in the polls throughout most of 1999.

But Gore's strategy backfired. Bradley succeeded in raising money, increasing his name recognition, and building public support. He gained media coverage, was perceived as an increasingly viable candidate, and moved up in the polls at the same time that Gore and his campaign were getting a bad rap from the press for running an inept campaign. Even Bill Clinton had publically criticized Gore's efforts.[81]

With his bloated campaign organization in disarray, his initial strategy unsuccessful, his image as a politician mired in the politics of Washington and the scandals of the Clinton administration, Gore shook up his campaign's personnel, structure, strategy, and tactics. In May 1999, he announced that a former, high-ranking Democratic congressman, Tony Coehlo, would oversee his presidential effort.[82] Known as a tough, inside-the-beltway politician, Coehlo proceeded to reinvent the campaign, the candidate, and the message. Gore also made a more concerted effort to obtain the endorsements of Democratic Party leaders and elected officials most of whom would be attending the Democratic convention as superdelegates. Additionally, the campaign directed its sights on securing support from the four pillars of the Democratic Party's electoral coalition: organized labor, African Americans, Latinos, and women.

The third change was both symbolic and real. Gore moved the campaign headquarters from K Street in Washington, D.C., where many of the most powerful special interest groups had their offices, to a home base in Nashville, Tennessee. The move was intended to diminish the perceived influence of Washington insiders as well as cut the size and expenses of the staff and eliminate its top-heavy collection of pollsters, image makers, and Democratic campaign consultants who had flocked to Gore as his campaign got under way.[83]

Finally, strategic and tactical adjustments were put into place. The vice president displayed a more human side. Formal speeches were replaced by town meetings in which the candidate would interact with the audience, answering their questions and lingering to chat with them. The candidate shed his coat and tie and rolled up his sleeves to appear more down-to-earth and more approachable. His message became more personal as well.

The focus of the vice president's campaign shifted as well. Bradley rather than Bush became the object of criticism. The senator's voting record and positions on the key issues of health care, gun control, and race relations became Gore's targets of opportunity. Drawing distinctions between himself and his opponent, Gore contrasted Bradley's comprehensive, big-government orientation with his own more tempered, incremental approach. This comparison reinforced, Gore's image as a moderate.

Once his campaign was reorganized, Gore ran impressively. He lashed out at Bradley's failure to seek reelection, his support of Reagan's 1981 budget, and his costly social policy proposals. By doing so, Gore achieved two objectives: to create doubts in the minds of Democrats about Bradley's partisan loyalties and his command of the issues; and to revitalize his image as a fighter, an active leader not a passive follower as his vice presidential stereotype suggested.

Gore's strategy was to contest Bradley everywhere. Tapping the financial and personnel resources at his disposal, he was able to stage a multistate campaign. The concentration of Democratic primaries in early March worked to his advantage as did the absence of other contests between New Hampshire and Super Tuesday, the day on which nearly half of the Democratic delegates were to be selected. Focusing on traditional Democratic themes and issues, Gore maintained a heavy speaking schedule. As his campaign moved onto solid ground with the Democratic electorate, he also began to keep his distance from the press. He held fewer news conferences and avoided the off-the-cuff remarks that had gotten him into trouble in the past.

The strategy of campaigning widely, matching Bradley's spending in the big states, and appealing to core Democratic voters on the basis of traditional party issues, combined with the tactics of being less formal and seeming more comfortable with average Democratic voters proved successful. Gore whipped Bradley in every state, largely on the basis of a strong vote from self-declared Democrats, especially from organized labor. (See Table 4–4, page 141.) By the evening of March 7th, the vice president was in a position to claim victory. He emerged from the primaries stronger than when he entered them. The party had coalesced around him. He had even rivaled Bill Clinton for the news media's attention in early March. But the glow from his victory was to be short-lived.

SUMMARY

The delegate selection process has changed dramatically since 1968. Originally dominated by state party leaders, it has become more open to the party's rank and file as a consequence of the reforms initiated by the Democratic party. These reforms, designed to broaden the base of public participation and increase the representation of the party's electorate at its nominating convention, have affected the Republicans as well, even though the GOP has not chosen to mandate national guidelines for its state parties, as the Democrats have. Supreme Court decisions that give the national parties the authority to dictate rules, new state laws that conform to these rules, and public pressure to reflect popular sentiment and improve representation have led to a greater number of primaries and more delegates selected in them for both parties.

Public participation has increased somewhat although turnout levels have varied with the date of the contest, the level of intraparty competition, the amount of money spent, and other candidate-related factors and is less than one-half of that in the general election. The delegates have been demographically more representative than those of the prereform era. Larger percentages of women and minorities have been chosen. The delegates seem to be more ideologically conscious, consistent, and extreme in their views, however, than do rank-and-file partisans.

There have been other effects, some of them not beneficial to the parties. Candidacies have proliferated. Factions within the parties are more in evidence. These unintended consequences have generated still other reforms, such as the imposition of a window period and the creation of superdelegates, designed to produce more cohesiveness within the party without at the same time abolishing the original goals of reform. They have also been designed to strengthen the influence of party leaders and elected officials.

The strategy for seeking delegates has also been affected by the rules changes. The basic tenets of this strategy include:

1. Plan far ahead.
2. Concentrate efforts in the early contests.
3. Raise and spend big bucks early.
4. Mount a media campaign.
5. Develop a deep and wide organization.
6. Monitor public opinion.
7. Design and target a distinctive appeal.

Although tactical decisions on how to mobilize and allocate sufficient resources to build and maintain delegate support depend on the particular circumstances of individual candidates, the use of new technology, particularly in the arena of mass communications, has revolutionized presidential campaigning and shortened the time frame in which incidents, remarks, and events can make a difference. Computers are used to map and track political advertising; targeted appeals are calibrated to arouse particular emotions in selective political communities; interactive campaigning on the Net and in town meetings is now standard fare. Even voting by mail and on-line is beginning to take hold. All of these technologies are expensive, another reason why having a large war chest has become increasingly important.

In general, there have been two successful prototypes for winning the nomination: the come-from-the-pack approach of the non-front-runners, and the outfront, big bucks, challenge-me-if-you-dare approach of the leading candidates.

Non-front-runners need stepping-stones to the nomination. Their initial goal must be to establish themselves as viable candidates. At the outset, the key is recognition. Over the long haul, it is momentum. Recognition is bestowed by the news media on those who do well in the early caucuses and primaries; momentum is achieved through a series of prenomination victories that demonstrate electability. Together, recognition and momentum compensate for what the non-front-runners lack in reputation and popular appeal. That is why non-front-runners must concentrate their time, efforts, and resources in the first few contests. They have no choice. Winning will provide them with opportunities; losing will confirm their secondary status.

For the front-runners, the task is different and easier. They have to maintain their position as likely nominees, not establish it. This purpose provides them with a little more flexibility at the outset, but it also requires a broad-based campaign with major resources raised and spent early. Front-runners must take advantage of their organizational and financial base to build a quick and insurmountable lead.

In the end, it is the ability to generate a popular appeal among the party's electorate that is likely to be decisive. Only one person in each party can amass a majority of the delegates, and that is the individual who can build a broad-based coalition. Although specific groups may be targeted, if the overall constituency is too narrow, the nomination cannot be won. That is why most candidates tend to broaden and moderate their appeal over the course of the prenomination process and continue to do so in the general election campaign.

WHERE ON THE WEB?

The Nomination Campaign

- **America Online**
  http://www.aol.com/mynews/presidential elections
  A comprehensive source for the latest news on the election.
- **Campaigns and Elections**
  http://www.camelect.com
  A magazine published monthly by *Congressional Quarterly*. Contains up-to-date information on strategy and tactics of candidates.
- **Gallup Poll**
  http://www.gallup.org
  Check this site for up-to-date polling data.
- **National Journal**
  http://www.nationaljournal.com
  There are many news sources for following the presidential primaries and caucuses. The *National Journal*'s site is one of the best.
- **New York Times**
  http://www.nytimes.com
  The *New York Times* prides itself on being a paper of record. You will find much information on the policy positions and speeches of the candidates in this newspaper as well as the latest delegate count and prenomination polls.
- **Yahoo**
  Yahoo.com/elections/presidential2000
  A comprehensive listing of articles on the nomination and election.

The Candidates

Listed below are the Web sites the candidates used during their campaigns. Most deactivate their sites after they conclude their campaign.

Republicans

Lamar Alexander	http://www.lamaralexander.com
Gary Bauer	http://www.Bauer2k.com
Pat Buchanan	http://www.gopatgo2000.org
George W. Bush	http://www.georgebush.com

Elizabeth Dole	http://www.e-dole2000.org
Steve Forbes	http://www.forbes2000.com
Orrin Hatch	http://www.orrinhatch.org
John Kasich	http://www.k2k.org
Allen Keyes	http://www.keyes2000.org
John McCain	http://www.mccainforpresident.org
Dan Quayle	http://www.quayle.org
Robert Smith	http://www.smithforpresident.org

Democrats

| Bill Bradley | http://www.billbradley.com |
| Al Gore | http://www.algore2000.com |

EXERCISES

1. Check the home pages of the two successful candidates. Use the information from their Web sites to compare and contrast the positions of the candidates on the most controversial issues in the campaign. How different are the candidates' positions on these issues?

2. Follow the news of the nomination campaign from the perspective of a major newspaper, television network, and news magazine (see Where on the Web? in Chapter 7, page 263). Is the coverage essentially the same? From which source did you learn the most about strategy and tactics?

3. Analyze the nomination campaign on the basis of the candidates' issue positions, basic appeals, and strategy and tactics. Use Internet sources from the candidates, the new media, and public interest Web sites to obtain the information you need for your analysis.

SELECTED READING

Bartels, Larry M. *Presidential Primaries and the Dynamics of Public Choice.* Princeton, N.J.: Princeton University Press, 1988.

Buell, Emmett H., Jr., and Lee Sigelman, eds. *Nominating the President.* Knoxville: University of Tennessee Press, 1991.

Greer, John G. *Nominating Presidents: An Evaluation of Voters and Primaries.* New York: Greenwood, 1989.

Gurian, Paul-Henri, and Audrey A. Haynes. "Campaign Strategy in Presidential Primaries, 1976–1988." *American Journal of Political Science* 37 (February 1993): 335–341.

Harvard University Institute of Politics, ed. *Campaign for President: The Managers Look at '96.* Hollis, N.H.: Hollis Publishing, 1997.

Magleby, David B. *Getting Inside the Outside Campaign.* Provo, Utah: Brigham Young University, 2000.

Mayer, William G., ed. *In Pursuit of the White House.* Chatham, N.J.: Chatham House, 2000.

Norrander, Barbara. "Ideological Representativeness of Presidential Primary Voters." *American Journal of Political Science* 33 (August 1989): 570–587.

———. "The End Game in Post-Reform Presidential Nominations." *Journal of Politics* 62 (November 2000): 999–1013.

Plissner, Martin, and Warren J. Mitofsky. "The Making of the Delegates, 1968–1988." *Public Opinion* 3 (September/October 1988): 45–47.

Polsby, Nelson W. *The Consequences of Party Reform.* New York: Oxford University Press, 1983.

Shafer, Byron E. *Quiet Revolution: The Struggle for the Democratic Party and the Shaping of Post-Reform Politics.* New York: Russell Sage Foundation, 1983.

Woodward, Bob. *The Choice.* New York: Simon & Schuster, 1996.

NOTES

1. See "A Review of the Republican Process: Nominating Future Presidents," *Advisory Commission on the Presidential Nominating Process,* Republican National Committee, May 2000.
2. McCarthy's name was on the ballot, but the president's was not. The regular Democratic organization in New Hampshire did conduct a campaign to have Democrats write in Johnson's name.
3. The groups that were initially singled out were Native Americans, African Americans, and youth. Subsequently, the list of affected groups has been altered by the addition of Hispanics, Asian/Pacific Americans, and women, and by the deletion of youth. In 1992, the party also added those with physical disabilities to the groups protected against discrimination.
4. Some states still hold a presidential preference vote with a separate election of delegates by a convention. Others connect the presidential vote and delegate selection on an at-large or district basis. By voting for a particular candidate or delegates pledged to that candidate (or both), voters may register their presidential choice and delegate selection at the same time and by the same vote. The number of these primaries has increased as a consequence of the rules changes. A third alternative is to cast separate votes for president and for convention delegates.
5. Iowa and New Hampshire both have state laws that require their contests to be the first caucus and primary, respectively. Democratic party rules take these laws into consideration by the exceptions granted to these two states. The perennial problem for the Democrats, however, has been that other states have also enacted legislation that schedules their nomination contests before the official period begins, thereby forcing Iowa and New Hampshire to move their selection date even further ahead — all in violation of party rules.
6. In 1984, the Democrats had raised the minimum vote needed to obtain delegates to 20 percent in caucuses and up to 25 percent in primaries. This change was designed to advantage nationally known candidates, such as Walter Mondale who was running that year for the Democratic nomination, and reduce the factionalizing effect that a large number of candidates could have on the party. After losing in 1980, the Democrats hoped the change would enable the eventual winner to emerge earlier, be a candidate of national prominence, and be better positioned to challenge the Republicans in the general election.

   Naturally, these changes hurt minority candidates such as Jesse Jackson, whose supporters were concentrated in districts with large minority populations. Although Jackson received votes in majority districts, he was unable to achieve the minimum required percentage in many of them. Thus, his 19 percent of the popular vote translated into only 10 percent of the delegates. Owing to pressure from Jackson and others, the Democrats lowered the minimum threshold in 1988 to 15 percent and have kept it there since then.

Jackson was also victimized by the rule that gave states flexibility in determining proportionality. This flexibility too was eliminated in 1988.

7. The front-runner advantage was particularly evident in 1984 when the rule specified that 80 percent of the Democratic members of Congress were to be chosen and placed in the Party Leaders and Elected Officials (PLEOs) category. Their selection before the caucuses and primaries had occurred prompted complaints that the popular vote had been preempted and that nonestablishment candidates were disadvantaged. The party has subsequently revised its rules to include all Democratic members of Congress, but front-runners have continued to gain disproportionate support from the superdelegates.

8. Will Lester, "GOP Scuttles Primary Plan," Associated Press, July 29, 2000; <http://www.ap.com>.

9. In another decision by the Supreme Court, also involving open primaries, the power of parties (in this case, state parties) to establish rules for nominating candidates was affirmed. In December 1986 the Supreme Court, in the case of *Tashjian v. Republican Party of Connecticut* (107 S. Ct. 544, 1986), voided a Connecticut law that prohibited open primaries. Republicans, who were in the minority in Connecticut, had favored such a primary as a means of attracting independent voters. Unable to get the Democratic-controlled legislature to change the law, the state Republican Party went to court, arguing that the statute violated First Amendment rights of freedom of association. In a 5 to 4 ruling, the Supreme Court agreed, and struck down the legislation.

10. Priscilla L. Southwell, "Open versus Closed Primaries: The Effect on Strategic Voting and Candidate Fortunes (Super Tuesday 1988)," *Social Science Quarterly* 72 (December 1991): 795.

11. Paul-Henri Gurian, "The Influence of Nomination Rules on the Financial Allocations of Presidential Candidates," *Western Political Quarterly* 43 (September 1990): 684.

12. Under the plan used since 1968 and modified in 1976, the Democrats have allotted 50 percent of each state delegation on the basis of the state's electoral vote and 50 percent on the basis of its average Democratic vote in the last three presidential elections. The rule for apportionment was challenged in 1971 on the grounds that it did not conform to the "one person, one vote" principle, but a court of appeals asserted that it did not violate the equal protection clause of the Fourteenth Amendment. The Democratic formula results in even larger conventions than the Republicans.

13. In states in which there were both Republican and Democratic primaries, turnout averaged almost 18 percent according to an analysis by the Committee for the Study of the American Electorate. Steven A. Holmes, "Many Stayed at Home," *New York Times*, September 1, 2000, A18.

14. Federal Election Commission.

15. Linda L. Fowler, Constantine J. Spiliotes, and Lynn VaVreck, "The Role of Issue Advocacy Groups in the New Hampshire Primary," in *Getting Inside the Outside Campaign*, ed. David B. Magleby (Provo, Utah: Brigham Young University, 2000), 31.

16. Earl Black and Merle Black, *The Vital South: How Presidents Are Elected* (Cambridge, Mass.: Harvard University Press, 1992), 268.

17. Barbara Norrander, "Ideological Representativeness of Presidential Primary Voters," *American Journal of Political Science* 33 (August 1989): 570–587.

18. Walter Stone Jr., Lonna Rae Atkeson, and Ronald B. Rapoport, "Turning On or Turning Off? Mobilization Efforts of Participating in Presidential Nominations," *American Journal of Political Science* 36 (August 1992): 688.

19. James I. Lengle, "Divisive Presidential Primaries and the Party Electoral Prospects, 1932–1976," *American Politics Quarterly* 8 (1980): 261–277; James I. Lengle, Diana Owen, and Molly Sonner, "Divisive Nomination Campaigns and Democratic Party Electoral Prospects," *Journal of Politics* 57 (1995): 370–383.

20. Lonna Rae Atkeson, "Divisive Primaries and General Election Outcomes: Another Look at Presidential Campaigns," *American Journal of Political Science* 42 (January 1998): 256–271.

21. S. Robert Lichter, Daniel Amundson, and Richard E. Noyes, *The Video Campaign: Network Coverage of the 1988 Primaries* (Washington, D.C.: American Enterprise Institute, 1988), 95–96.

22. See Peverille Squire, *The Iowa Caucus and the Presidential Nominating Process* (Boulder, Colo.: Westview Press, 1989).

23. Craig Allen Smith, "The Iowa Caucuses and Super Tuesday Primaries Reconsidered: How Untenable Hypotheses Enhance the Campaign Melodrama," *Presidential Studies Quarterly* 22 (Summer 1992): 524.

24. However, Professor Barbara Norrander also notes that in nomination contests between 1976 and 1988 some of the biggest spenders on the Republican side have also been the biggest losers. Pat Robertson and Robert Dole in 1988 are two examples. Norrander found that the Republicans who did win within this period did so regardless of how much money they spent. In short, it appears that the prospective losers tried to compensate for their secondary status by spending more, and it did not work. Barbara Norrander, "Nomination Choices: Caucus and Primary Outcomes, 1976–1988," *American Journal of Political Science* 37 (May 1993): 361.

25. "Campaign 2000 — The Primaries," *Media Monitor* XIV (March/April 2000): 1–2.

26. Ibid., 2.

27. Terence Jeffrey, quoted in *Campaign for President: The Managers Look at '96,* Institute of Politics, Harvard University (Hollis, N.H.: Hollis Publishing Company, 1997), 7–8.

28. Annenberg Public Policy Center, "The Primary Campaign: What Did the Candidates Say, What did the Public Learn, and Did It Matter?" University of Pennsylvania (March 27, 2000): 2–3.

29. Pew Research Center For The People & The Press, "Fewer See Choice of President as Important: Voter Turnout May Slip Again," part 2, (July 13, 2000).

30. Joan Shorenstein Center on the Press, Politics, and Public Policy, "Voter Involvement Index: State Rankings," Harvard University, <http://www.vanishingvoter.org>.

31. "Campaign 2000 — The Primaries," 4.

32. Thomas E. Patterson and Robert D. McClure, *The Unseeing Eye* (New York: Putnam, 1976), 58.

33. Frank Bruni, "The Ad Campaign: Bush Discusses His Candidacy," *New York Times,* September 26, 1999.

34. Howard Kurtz, "Ad Watch," *Washington Post,* October 28, 1999, A11.

35. John Broder, "The Ad Campaign: Donning the Reagan Mantle," *New York Times,* February 26, 2000, A10.

36. Peter Marks, "Negative Campaigning 2000: The Other Guy Did It First," *New York Times,* January 29, 2000, A1, A9.

37. Adam Nagourney and Richard Pérez-Peña, "Bush and McCain Trade Bitter Criticism as Campaigns in New York Gather Steam," *New York Times,* March 3, 2000, A15.

38. Peter Marks, "The Ad Campaign: McCain Launches a New Salvo," *New York Times,* February 9, 2000, A14; Howard Kurtz, "Bush Hits Back on Campaign Reform," *Washington Post,* February 17, 2000, A9.

39. Richard A. Oppel, Jr., with Richard Pérez-Peña, "The Power Broker: Role in Ads Puts Focus on Bush Friend," *New York Times,* March 6, 2000, A14.

40. Howard Kurtz, "Democratic Themes Dominate Airwaves," *Washington Post,* January 9, 2000, A8; Peter Marks, "In New Hampshire Ads, an Audible Warmth," *New York Times,* December 6, 1999, A1, A22.

41. Dick Morris, *Behind the Oval Office* (New York: Random House, 1997), 146–147.

42. Alison Mitchell, "More Complaints About Negative Phone Calls," *New York Times,* February 13, 2000, A27.

43. Pew Research Center For The People & The Press, "The Tough Job of Communicating with Voters," February 5, 2000.

44. In a television interview, Gore took credit for "inventing the Internet" when he meant to say that he had been a principal advocate for extending its utility for the government and to the public. He had also claimed that he and his wife were the role models for Erich Segal's book, *Love Story,* a claim that Segal denied. Gore exaggerated his physical danger as a military reporter in Vietnam and his own accomplishments as a Tennessee journalist. He was also plagued by his representation that there was "no legal authority" which prevented him from making fund-raising calls from his White House office. "Transcript: Vice President Gore on CNN's Late Edition," March 9, 1999, <http://cnn.com>; Katherine Q. Seelye, with John M. Broder, "Questions over Veracity Have Long Dogged Gore," *New York Times,* February 17, 2000, A22.

45. Annenberg Center, "The Primary Campaign," 1, 4–10.

46. Ibid., 1; Annenberg Center for Public Policy, "The 2000 Nominating Campaign: Endorsement, Attacks, and Debates," University of Pennsylvania (July 10, 2000), 6–11.

47. "The 2000 Nominating Campaign," 6–11.

48. David Wilhelm as quoted in Royer, *Campaign for President: The Managers Look at '92* (Hollis, N.H.: Hollis Publishing, 1994), 77.

49. John Pavlik and Mark Thalhimer, "From Wausau to Wichita: Covering the Campaign via Satellite," in *Covering the Presidential Primaries* ed. Martha FitzSimon (New York: Freedom Forum Media Studies Center, 1992), 41.

50. Ibid., 36–37.

51. Neil Munro, "The New Wired Politics," *National Journal* (April 22, 2000): 1260.

52. Hamilton Jordan, "Memorandum to Jimmy Carter, August 4, 1974," in Martin Schram, *Running for President 1976,* (New York: Stein & Day, 1977), 379–380.

53. According to Larry M. Bartels, momentum is a product of personal preferences that are projected onto expectations. Bartels argues that momentum can best be achieved by a little-known candidate who scores unexpected successes in situations where there is no clear front-runner. What happens is that people who have little substantive information about this candidate project their own desires for an ideal candidate onto this new winner. This result increases expectations and contributes to momentum. Larry M. Bartels, "Expectations and Preferences in Presidential Nominating Campaigns," *American Political Science Review* 79 (1985): 804–815.

54. The McCain team included campaign director, Rich Davis, who had served as deputy director of the 1996 Dole campaign, political director John Weaver, a veteran of the 1988 Republican campaign, and Mike Murphy, a political strategist who also worked on Dole's presidential bid. Supplementing the campaign were an array of current and former members of Congress, experienced Washington hands, and policy advisers.

55. Alison Mitchell, "Birth and Death of the 'Straight Talk Express,' From Gamble to Gamble," *New York Times,* March 11, 2000, A8.

56. "Campaign 2000," 4.

57. Ruth Marcus and John Mintz, "Bush Spending Spree Shrinks GOP Cash Gap," *Washington Post,* February 21, 2000, A1, A6.
58. Schuyler Kropf, "Decisive Win Boosts Momentum," *Charleston Post & Courier,* February 20, 2000, A14, as referenced in Bill Moore and Danielle Vinson, "The South Carolina Republican Primary" in Magleby *Getting Inside,* 42.
59. Pat Robertson recorded a telephone message urging Michigan voters to select Bush and the Christian Coalition made 45,000–50,000 calls with Robertson's voice. David Magleby, "Issue Advocacy in the 2000 Presidential Primaries," in Magleby, *Getting Inside,* 14. In addition, Right to Life Groups mailed letters to over 400,000 households in Michigan and operated phone banks which played taped messages criticizing McCain's position on social issues important to the Christian right.
60. Mitchell, "Birth and Death," A8.
61. McCain later claimed that he had been using the words of Luke Skywalker at the end of *Star Wars.* David Von Drehle, "McCain Tries to Erase His 'Evil' Accusation," *Washington Post,* March 2, 2000, A7.
62. Arthur Sanders and David Redlewsk, "Money and the Iowa Caucus," in Magleby, *Getting Inside,* 27.
63. Fowler, et al., "Issue Advocacy in New Hampshire," in Magleby, *Getting Inside,* 30.
64. Richard L. Burke with James Dao, "Aides Fear That Bradley Let Iowa Momentum Slip Away," *New York Times,* January 21, 2000, A22.
65. Despite his emphasis on racial justice, he did not gain much African-American support. He had no labor endorsements. The campaign made little attempt to appeal to Latino voters; no Spanish language messages appeared on his Web site.
66. Mike Allen, "Bradley Campaign's Lost Opportunities Mount," *Washington Post,* February 13, 2000, A12.
67. The *Washington Post* reported that a *Wall Street Journal* reporter covering Bradley found himself seated in front of the candidate on a commercial flight. The reporter introduced himself and asked for a chance to talk with the candidate. Bradley declined and moved his seat. Barton Gellman, Dale Russakoff, and Mike Allen, "Where Did Bradley Go Wrong?" *Washington Post,* March 4, 2000, A7.
68. In 2000, Senator Orrin Hatch dropped out after the Iowa caucus in which he received only 1 percent of the vote. Gary Bauer exited after New Hampshire performances generated little possibility that he could rival the principal Republican challengers. Forbes left after a disappointing performance in the third contest in Delaware, a state in which he had won four years earlier.
69. Bay Buchanan, quoted in Royer, *Campaign for President '92,* 24.
70. Republicans Robert Dornan and Allen Keyes fell into the pulpit candidacy category in 1996 as did Keyes and Bauer in 2000. Each wished to use the nomination campaign as a platform for his issue agenda and ideological perspective as well as a vehicle for extending his own name recognition and political influence.
71. Scott Reed, quoted in *Campaign for President: The Managers Look at '96,* p. 182.
72. The following exchange between Karen Hughes, the campaign's director of communications and Jay Carney, a reporter for *Time* magazine, illustrates the care with which the campaign treated the issue of "gay appointments."

    Hughes: He said, first of all, how would I know? That's not a question he asks.
    Carney: But someone who is openly gay.
    Hughes: It would depend on their agenda. He would expect them to share his philosophy . . . he views that as someone's private business.
    Carney: So the issue would be his sexuality or her sexuality but whether of not they were promoting . . .

Hughes: Again, that's not a question he asks. He's never asked that of prospective employees.

Carney: But if they're out of the closet, if they're open. If he knew.

Hughes: How would he know that? Based on rumor?

Carney: If they have a boyfriend or girlfriend.

Hughes: He would expect people who worked with him to agree with his philosophy and his approach.

Carney: Right. But — you see what I'm saying?

Hughes: You're trying to make me say it the way you want me to say it.

Carney: So the question is, would he appoint somebody who is known to be gay?

Hughes: It's not a question that he would ask.

Howard Kurtz, "Team Bush's Defensive Strategy," *Washington Post,* March 5, 2000, C1, 14.

73. The principal operatives included chief strategist Karl Rove, campaign manager Joe Allbaugh, and communications director Karen Hughes. Bush's policy advisory groups were led by Condoleezza Rice, a foreign policy expert who served on President Bush's National Security Council, Stephen Goldsmith, domestic adviser and former mayor of Indianapolis, and economist Lawrence Lindsay, who had worked in the Reagan and Bush administrations.

74. Linguist Deborah Tannen noted the emotional lexicon that his language contained:

In a speech on tax cuts last month [December 1999], Mr. Bush managed to work in "child" or "children" 11 times. In a speech on faith-based initiatives last summer, it was a dozen times. In a talk in New Hampshire in November [1999], children recur like a mantra 35 times (not counting "kids" and "students") . . .

It's not only the speeches on education that are studded with hearts. Speaking on farm policy in Iowa, Mr. Bush called agriculture "the heart of our economy." Regarding Veterans Day, he told a New Hampshire audience that we must impart veterans stories to the next generation to "raise a monument in their hearts." The speech on faith-based groups contained 7 "hearts" and 11 "loves."

Deborah Tannen, "Bush's Sweet Talk," *New York Times,* January 20, 2000, A23.

75. "Excerpts from Bush's Campaign Speech," *New York Times,* November 1, 1999, A14.

76. Polls did reflect a drop in his support among Catholics after Bush was accused of not condemning the anti-Catholic rhetoric of the President of Bob Jones University. Lydia Saad, "Bush Support Down among Catholic Republicans," Gallup Poll, March 3, 2000, <http://www.gallup.com/poll/release/pr000303.asp>.

77. Frank Bruni, "Using Signals and Cues to Project Bush's Image," *New York Times,* March 19, 2000, A 24.

78. Terry M. Neal, "Bush Team Uses Mock Ads to Test Effect of Forbes Attack," *Washington Post,* October 12, 1999, A5.

79. Kurtz, "Team Bush's Defensive Strategy," C1.

80. Frank Bruni reported a part of a Bush speech on foreign policy, delivered in January in Sioux City Iowa, as follows:

When I was coming up, it was a dangerous world and we knew exactly who the they were. It was us versus them and it was clear who them was. Today, we're not so sure who the they are, but we know they're there.

Frank Bruni, "The Syntax: Bush Follows in the Missteps of His Father," *New York Times,* January 23, 2000, A17.

81. Richard L. Berke, "Clinton Admits to Concerns As Gore Campaign Stumbles," *New York Times,* May 14, 1999, A1.
82. In addition to Coelho, the principal operatives of the Gore campaign were campaign manager Donna Brazile, a veteran organizer, media strategists Carter Eskew, Bob Shrum, and Tad Devine, all of whom had worked on other Democratic campaigns, policy advisers Elaine Kamarck (domestic) and Leon Furth (foreign), both of whom had served as advisers on his vice presidential White House staff, and his eldest daughter, Karenna Gore Schiff.
83. They succeeded in cutting the top-heavy layers of political consultants, pollsters, and media advisers, but were stuck with the $60,000 a month lease that they had taken out on their K Street offices.

5 | LAUNCHING THE PRESIDENTIAL CAMPAIGN: PARTISAN CONSOLIDATION AND PUBLIC RELATIONS

THE SPRING INTERREGNUM: CONSOLIDATING VICTORY AND POSTURING FOR THE ELECTION

The nomination campaign had taken its toll, more so for Bush than Gore. Before the contest had begun, Bush led Gore in the trial heats by 15 to 20 percent. After the competitive phase was over, the race appeared to be a toss-up. On a personal level, Bush still fared well. On a policy level, Gore seemed to have the advantage. Table 5–1 compares public perceptions of the two candidates in mid-March when each had effectively secured his party's nomination.

The Bush Campaign: After the Primaries and on to the Convention

Bush needed to replenish his war chest, mend fences with McCain, and repair his image. The presumptive Republican nominee had no choice but to raise more money. He had spent liberally to defeat Forbes and McCain. In fact, by the end of the competitive phase of the nomination process, Bush was actually in worse financial shape than was his Democratic opponent, Al Gore.[1]

Bush also needed to consolidate his political base by appealing to McCain voters. To do so, he had to reach out to McCain personally and champion his reform issues. Unfortunately for Bush, answers he had given to the *New York Times* on the heels of his Super Tuesday primary victories cast doubt on his willingness to do either. In response to a question about whether McCain raised Bush's awareness of reform issues, Bush answered, "No, he didn't change my views," although he did go on to add that McCain "made me a better candidate. He forced me to play to my strengths better." When asked again whether there

TABLE 5–1 ★

CANDIDATE QUALITIES AND ISSUE POSITIONS (IN PERCENTAGES)

Question: Thinking about the following characteristics and qualities, please say whether you think each one applies more to Al Gore or more to George W. Bush.

Qualities	Bush	Gore
Is a strong and decisive leader	63	52
Can manage the government effectively	64	57
Inspires confidence	56	49
Has strong moral character	74	70
Is someone you would be proud to have as president	53	50
Honest and trustworthy	64	61
Shares your values	52	53
Generally agrees with you on the issues you care about	49	54
Has a vision for the country's future	68	73
Has the knowledge necessary to be president	71	77
Cares about the needs of people like you	51	60

Question: Regardless of which presidential candidate you support, please tell me if you think Al Gore or George W. Bush would better handle each of the following issues.

Issues	Bush	Gore
Crime	51	37
Improving moral climate	49	39
Taxes	48	41
The economy	45	46
Foreign policy	44	46
Guns	42	44
Campaign finance reform	38	43
Education	41	48
Social Security and Medicare	40	49
Health care	34	54
The environment	31	59

Source: "Poll Finds Bush and Gore Closely Matched on Image Ratings," *Gallup Poll*, March 20, 2000, <http://www.gallup.com/poll/releases/pr000320.asp>.

was anything McCain brought to light or on which he changed Bush's opinion, Bush responded as he had previously, "No, not really. We agreed more than we disagreed."[2] Naturally McCain's supporters were not happy with Bush's remarks.

However, McCain had incentives to support the Republican nominee if only to improve his negative image among party leaders and some rank-and-file GOP partisans, a necessity if he were to make another run for presidency in four or eight years. But McCain also needed to maintain his standing as a reformer motivated by his strong beliefs — an individual who would not buckle under to the political establishment, a man above the crowd, a person of heroic stature. Nonetheless, it was not until early May, almost two months later, that Bush and McCain got together to reconcile their differences.

To broaden his appeal, Bush moved toward the policy center. He accentuated the positive, stressing issues of compassion such as education, housing, Medicare, and Social Security — issues that had special appeal to Democrats and women voters and which would help mute the impression left by the competitive primaries that he was a hard-nosed conservative. By promoting Democratic issues, Bush was following the same strategy that Clinton used so successfully in 1995–1996 when he adopted Republican issues of stepped-up crime prevention, a balanced budget, and improved defense for his own campaign.[3]

But Bush also distinguished himself from his Democratic opponent by running ads that focused on the ethical and moral lapses of the Clinton-Gore administration, ads which served indirectly to reinforce the reformer image Bush wished to project.[4] He also emphasized the one policy issue on which most Republicans agreed — the need for a strong military — and deemphasized the social issues that divided Republicans — abortion, school prayer, and gay rights.

Just as important was the Texas governor's urging of an end to Washington's strident ideological politics. His theme of working together and talking quietly with one another was intended to heal divisions within his own party as well as provide a contrast with the partisan Washington environment with which his opponent was associated. Although Bush attacked his Democratic rival, particularly noting Gore's penchant for exaggeration, his flip-flops on the issues, and the contradiction between his promise to eliminate soft money and his active fundraising for the Democrats, his overall message was more positive than negative. And this message was reinforced by Bush's rhetoric and personal style: his conciliatory language, moderate tone, commensensical proposals, and a folksy manner.

To support the friendly, down-to-earth image it wished to project for its candidate, the Bush campaign placed Bush in small-group settings, such as experimental schools for underperforming, underprivileged, or learning-disabled children, neighborhood programs or community centers for troubled teenagers, and assisted living facilities for senior citizens. Bush quietly empathized with those who were having troubles, talked about his goals and values, and explained how his policies would improve their plight. During May and June, the campaign limited itself to only a few media-oriented events per day in the key battleground states.[5]

The messages delivered at Bush's staged events were reinforced by a national advertising campaign aired in the same key states by the Republican National

Committee. Using soft money, much of which was raised by the candidate and his fund-raisers, the Republican generic ads featured the same policy positions that Bush was emphasizing: Social Security investment accounts, tax cuts, economic opportunities for minorities, and school vouchers.

Polls taken at the end of this interim period indicated that Bush had enhanced his leadership image. He had consolidated his Republican base, gained the endorsement of rival John McCain, and energized Republican contributors and rank-and-file supporters. Moreover, he had moderated his policy agenda, moved to the center of the political spectrum, and softened his social conservatism. One sign of his growing stature was the widening lead he enjoyed in the polls over Vice President Al Gore.

The Gore Campaign:
After the Primaries and on to the Convention

For Gore, the task was different but no less difficult. Although he had achieved parity with Bush by mid-March, he still needed to establish his leadership credentials and move out of Clinton's shadow. The primaries had not enabled him to do so fully, in part because Bradley had proven to be a weak challenger and in part because Clinton remained a very active and visible president. Gore also needed to gain credit for the successes of the current administration, the peace and prosperity that had occurred during his eight years as vice president. He also wanted to reduce Bush in size, making him seem more like his father during the economic recession of 1991–1992 than a popular, reformist governor.

Gore, who had successfully improved his standing with the Democratic electorate during the nomination process by attacking Bradley, tried the same tactic with Bush, painting his opponent as a stereotypical Republican, whose policies benefited the rich and powerful such as big tobacco, big oil, and the National Rifle Association. Not only did he wish to tie Bush to special interests, he also wanted to demonstrate his own aggressiveness and strength in taking on these monied, conservative groups.

Bush's father had pursued a similar campaign strategy in the summer of 1988 to get himself out of the shadows of Ronald Reagan and overcome the wimpy image with which he had been saddled.[6] While the elder Bush was successful, Gore was not. In fact, the aggressive strategy backfired by reinforcing the unattractive aspects of his image, that of a no-holds-barred, partisan, Washington politician.

After two months of sagging ratings and a campaign that seemed adrift, Gore changed his tune. He assumed the high road, while other Democrats were given the task of criticizing Bush.[7] In mid-June, the vice president went on a peace and prosperity trip, emphasizing the achievements of the last eight years. However, a number of short-term setbacks — the unexpected resignation of his campaign manager for reasons of health, a spike in oil prices in the Midwest, and the release of an internal Justice department memo that urged Attorney General Janet Reno to appoint a special investigator to look into Gore's involvement in the 1996 Democratic fund-raising scandal — initially undercut his efforts. Although Gore remained behind his Republican opponent, the gap was not large. Going into the parties' national nominating conventions, polls indicated that a significant proportion of the electorate had not yet made up their minds for whom they would vote.

NATIONAL NOMINATING CONVENTIONS

The Preliminaries

With the national nominating conventions approaching, both candidates played the role of anointed leaders, ready to carry their party's standard in the fall election. Their campaigns went to great lengths to orchestrate the public events leading up to their coronations. While past conventions had evidenced divisions within the parties, the 2000 conventions projected unity, conveyed enthusiasm, and appealed to mainstream voters.

Bush continued to follow a careful, calculated, play-it-safe approach. He opposed changes to the traditional positions the party took in its platform so as not to alienate any of the core Republican supporters. He chose a running mate who was acceptable to all major party factions, Dick Cheney, whose Washington qualifications as a former chief of the White House staff under President Ford, member of Congress, and defense secretary during his father's administration supplemented the younger Bush's outsider appeal and his executive experience. Bush let it be known that he wanted an upbeat, people-oriented convention that emphasized positive imagery. As the poll leader going into the conventions, he and his staff did not want to rock the boat or break his momentum.

In contrast, Gore needed a boost. He needed to enhance his leadership image and differentiate himself from Clinton. At the same time, he wanted credit for the policy successes of the administration of which he was a part. The first step in achieving the leadership objective was his surprising choice of Senator Joseph Lieberman, a Democrat from Connecticut, as his running mate. The selection of the devout, orthodox Jewish senator captured media attention. Bush and Cheney fell from public view. Moreover, Gore won praise for his courageousness in choosing Lieberman; he helped insulate himself from the scandals of the Clinton administration by designating a vice presidential nominee who had become associated with moral and ethical issues; and he reinforced his own ideological perspective as a moderate by selecting a senator who was in many ways more conservative than he was.

Like Bush, Gore also wanted his convention to be a public relations springboard for him and his party. He wanted an event to establish his personal independence and a podium from which to articulate the themes he intended to emphasize in the general election. Democratic convention leaders obliged by scripting and orchestrating their convention to achieve Gore's desired effect.

The Tradition

National nominating conventions were at one time important decision-making bodies. Conventions were used to decide on the party's nominees, platforms, and rules and procedures, as well as provide a podium for launching presidential campaigns. Today, however, conventions are theater, pure and simple. They are ritual, part of the American political tradition. What they are not is nearly as newsworthy as they were in bygone days.

Prior to 1956, majorities were constructed within conventions to make the critical decisions. Party leaders, who exercised considerable control over the selection of their state delegations, debated among themselves. Once they agreed on the candidates, they directed their delegates to vote in favor of their particular choice.

The last brokered conventions occurred in 1952. That year, Democratic and Republican leaders wheeled and dealed in "smoke-filled rooms" to select Governor Adlai Stevenson of Illinois and General Dwight Eisenhower as their respective nominees. Since those conventions, the delegate selection process has dictated the nominees.

Another indication of the decline of the brokered convention has been first-ballot phenomena that have characterized recent conventions. In fact, since 1924, when the Democrats took 103 ballots to nominate John W. Davis, there have been only four conventions (two Democratic and two Republican) in which more than one ballot has been needed to choose a presidential nominee. In 1932, the Democrats held four roll calls before they agreed on Franklin Roosevelt, and took three in 1952 to nominate Adlai Stevenson. In 1940, Republican Wendell Willkie was selected on the eighth ballot, breaking a deadlock among Thomas Dewey, Arthur Vandenberg, and himself. Eight years later, Dewey was nominated on the third ballot.

A variety of factors have reduced the convention's decision-making capabilities. The broadcasting of conventions by radio and later by television has detracted from the delegates' ability to bargain with one another effectively. It is difficult to compromise before a television camera, especially during prime time. Public exposure has forced negotiations off the convention floor and even out of "leaky" but no longer "smoke-filled" committee rooms.

Size is another factor that has affected the proceedings. Conventions used to be relatively small. In 1860, 303 delegates nominated Democrat Stephen Douglas, and 466 chose Republican Abraham Lincoln. Today, the participants run into the thousands. Table 5–2 lists the number of delegate votes at Democratic and Republican conventions since 1940. When alternates and delegates who possess fractional votes are included, the numbers grow even more. In 2000, the Republicans had 2,066 delegates and the same number of alternates, while the Democrats had 4,370 delegates, some casting fractions of a vote, and 610 alternates.[8]

Because of the large number of delegates, divisions within the parties tend to be magnified. These divisions, in turn, have produced the need for more efficient control over the convention's operation. For the party leaders and the prospective nominee, the task has become one of orchestration; their goal is to conduct a huge pep rally replete with ritual, pomp, and entertainment — a made-for-TV production. From the perspective of the party and its nominees, the convention now serves primarily as a launching pad for the general election. Finally, and most importantly, the party's electorate now determines the convention delegates, not

TABLE 5–2 ★

DELEGATE VOTES AT NOMINATING CONVENTIONS, 1940–2000

Year	Republicans	Democrats
1940	1,000	1,100
1944	1,059	1,176
1948	1,904	1,234
1952	1,206	1,230
1956	1,323	1,372
1960	1,331	1,521
1964	1,308	2,316
1968	1,333	2,622
1972	1,348	3,016
1976	2,259	3,008
1980	1,994	3,331
1984	2,234	3,933
1988	2,277	4,160
1992	2,210	4,286
1996	1,990	4,289
2000	2,066	4,370

Source: Richard C. Bain and Judith H. Parris, *Convention Decisions and Voting Records,* 2nd ed. (Washington, D.C.: Brookings Institution, 1973), Appendix C. Updated by author from data supplied by the Republican and Democratic National Committees.

the state party leaders and elected officials. This determination occurs well in advance of the convention, is publically known, and preordains the outcome. As a consequence, conventions have effectively lost their decision-making power and instead become decision-ratifying bodies characterized more by pomp and circumstance and less by substance.

The next section examines the official convention before most political outcomes were dictated by the nomination process and before television made a public relations spectacular inevitable.

The Official Proceedings

Preliminary decisions on the convention are made by the party's national committee, usually on the recommendation of its chair and appropriate convention committees. An incumbent president normally exercises considerable influence over many of these decisions: the choice of a convention city, the selection of temporary and permanent convention officials, and the designation of the principal speakers. Both the Democrats and the Republicans have traditionally turned to national party leaders, primarily members of Congress, to fill many of the positions. The technicalities of scripting and staging the event are left to entertainment professionals, media consultants, pollsters, and party officials with national campaign experience.

In choosing a site, many factors are considered: the size, configuration, and condition of the convention hall, transportation to and from it, financial inducements, the political climate, the geographic area, and the cultural ambiance of the city itself. These factors weighed heavily in the Democrats' choice of Los Angeles for their 2000 convention and the Republicans' choice of Philadelphia for theirs. Both cities are located in states and regions critical to that party's electoral success.

Speeches. Over the years, both parties have organized their conventions with similar schedules, daily themes, and speeches (lots of them) by party leaders, elected officials, celebrities, and occasionally, ordinary citizens. Of these speeches, the keynote address and the formal acceptance of the nomination by the candidates and their running mates are usually the most important and newsworthy.

The keynote address, which occurs early in the convention and in past years used to kick it off, has been designed to unify the delegates, smoothing over any divisions that may have emerged during the preconvention campaign, and to rouse them and the public for the coming election. The address ritually trumpets the achievements of the party, eulogizing its heroes and criticizing the opposition for its ill-conceived programs, inept leadership, and general inability to cope with the nation's most pressing problems. The keynoter for the party that does not control the White House sounds a litany of past failures and suggests that the country needs new leadership. Naturally, the keynoter for the party in office reverses the blame and praise. Noting the accomplishments of the administration and its unfinished business, the speaker urges a continuation of the party's effective leadership and policy successes.[9]

The tone of the speech, however, can vary considerably. In 1984, Governor Mario Cuomo of New York, the Democratic keynoter, sounded a sober theme. Describing the United States as a tale of two cities, he chided the Reagan administration for pursuing policies that benefited the rich at the expense of the poor. In contrast, Ann Richards, then treasurer of Texas, gave a more folksy, upbeat, and humorous address in 1988. Criticizing George Bush for being aloof, insensitive, and uncaring, she concluded sarcastically, "he can't help it. He was born with a silver foot in his mouth."[10] The Republicans did not designate a keynote speaker at their 2000 convention. The Democrats did, Representative Harold Ford Jr. of Tennessee, Gore's home state.

In recent years, there have been other newsworthy speeches. Pat Buchanan gave one of his rousing campaign speeches on opening night of the 1992 Republican convention. Endorsing the president for reelection, Bush's former challenger unleashed a scathing attack on the Democrats and Bill Clinton. The delegates loved the speech, but the news media saw it as harsh and mean-spirited conservative rhetoric.[11] In contrast, former President Reagan's speech in which he effectively passed the torch to his vice president, George Bush, was lauded for its eloquence and optimism. President Clinton's address to the 2000 Democratic convention was also a pass-the-torch speech in which the president noted the accomplishments of his administration and pointed to Al Gore as the best person to continue that successful policy legacy.

In recent conventions it has also become customary to give the potential or actual first lady an opportunity to address the convention to provide an "inside" perspective on the character, qualifications, and achievements of the prospective nominee. Elizabeth Dole and Hillary Clinton both gave speeches at the 1996 conventions as did Laura Bush and did Tipper Gore in 2000.

Reports from the major committees (credentials, rules, and platform) are usually on the agenda early in the convention. Often the product of lengthy negotiations, these reports to the convention represent the majority's voice on the committees and are usually ratified without change by the convention delegates. For a minority to present its views, 25 percent of the committee must concur in the minority report. Membership on the committees tends to reflect support for the candidates in the convention as a whole. Thus, when the majority is unified and effectively coordinated, there is little the minority can do, as was the case in 1992 and 1996 for both parties.

Another day traditionally is devoted to the presidential nomination and balloting. In an evenly divided convention, this period is clearly the most exciting. Much ritual has surrounded the nomination itself. In early conventions, it was customary for delegates simply to rise and place the name of a candidate in nomination without a formal speech. Gradually, the practice of nominating became more elaborate. Speeches were lengthened. Ritual required that the virtues of the candidate first be extolled before the candidate's identity was revealed. Today, with public speculation beginning months before and the selection of the nominee a foregone conclusion, the practice of withholding the name has been abandoned.

Demonstrations normally follow the practice of placing a person's name in nomination. The advent of television, however, has changed the nature of these demonstrations. No longer spontaneous, they are now carefully staged and timed to indicate enthusiasm for the nominee but also to keep convention events moving during the prime-time viewing hours.

Once nominations have been made, the balloting begins. The secretary of the convention calls the roll of states in alphabetical order, with the chair of each delegation announcing the vote. A poll of the delegation may be requested by any member of that delegation. Beginning in 1988, the Democrats have used an electronic system to ensure a fast and accurate count. After the delegation is polled, the chair records the vote of the state on a terminal connected to the podium.

Formally selecting the vice presidential nominee usually is the next order of business. In their early years, nominating conventions evidenced some difficulty in getting candidates to accept the vice presidential nomination. Because of the low esteem in which the office was held, a number of prominent individuals, including Henry Clay and Daniel Webster, actually refused it. In Webster's words, "I do not propose to be buried until I am really dead and in my coffin."[12]

Today, the vice presidency is coveted, especially as a stepping-stone to the presidency. In the twentieth century alone, six vice presidents have become president through succession (either death or resignation); two, Richard Nixon and

George Bush, have been elected to the presidency (although Nixon was not elected directly from the vice presidency); and two others, Hubert Humphrey and Walter Mondale, have been presidential candidates.

Despite the appeal of the vice presidency, it is almost impossible to run for it directly. There are no vice presidential primaries and no government matching funds for vice presidential candidates. Only one "vote" really counts — the presidential nominee's. Since the prospective nominee normally has sufficient delegates to control the convention, the presidential standard-bearer can and does dictate the selection. Although most delegates accept the recommendation, there have been a sprinkling of protest votes over the years by delegates who do not like the person selected or who wish to use the vice presidential nomination to signify their opposition to a policy position or perspective that the presidential nominee has adopted.

Only once in the last forty years has the convention had to make more than a pro forma decision on the vice presidential nomination. In 1956, Democrat Adlai Stevenson professed to have no personal preference. He allowed the convention to choose between Estes Kefauver and John Kennedy. The convention chose Kefauver, the most popular Democrat in the public opinion polls at the time of his nomination.

In 2000, both major parties' vice presidential nominees made their acceptance speeches on the third night of the convention leaving the fourth and final night to the presidential nominees.

The custom of giving acceptance speeches by the presidential standard-bearers was begun in 1932 by Franklin Roosevelt. Before that time, conventions designated committees to inform the presidential and vice presidential nominees of their decisions. Journeying to the candidate's home, the committees would announce the selection in a public ceremony. The nominee, in turn, would accept in a speech stating his positions on the major issues of the day. The last major party candidate to be told of the nomination in this fashion was Republican Wendell Willkie in 1940.

Today, acceptance speeches can be occasions for great oratory — they are both a call to the faithful and an address to the country. They articulate the principal themes for the general election. Harry Truman's speech to the Democratic convention in 1948 is frequently cited as one that helped to fire up the party. Truman chided the Republicans for obstructing and ultimately rejecting many of his legislative proposals and then adopting a party platform that called for some of the same social and economic goals. He electrified the Democratic convention by challenging the Republicans to live up to their convention promises and pass legislation to achieve these goals in a special session of Congress that he announced he was calling. When the Republican-controlled Congress failed to enact that legislation, Truman was able to pin a "do-nothing" label on it and make that label the basic theme of his successful presidential campaign. Robert Dole's address to the Republican convention in 1996 was also a major unifying speech that energized his campaign at least for a short while.

In 1984, Democratic candidate Walter Mondale made a mammoth political blunder in his acceptance speech. Warning the delegates about the United States budget deficit that had increased dramatically during Reagan's first term, Mondale said that he would do something about it if he were elected president: "Let's tell the truth. Mr. Reagan will raise taxes, and so will I. He won't tell you. I just did." Democratic delegates cheered his candor, directness, and boldness; the public did not. He and his party were saddled with the tax issue throughout the *entire* campaign.

The 2000 acceptance addresses continued the practice of reiterating themes and emphasizing priorities. George W. Bush used his address to reach beyond his core coalitional support. Bush stressed inclusiveness, compassion, and morality, saying he wanted to maximize opportunities for all Americans. He used words such as *promise, moral courage, responsibility,* and *opportunity* to emphasize his moderate tone and unifying spirit. The Republican candidate spoke of broad policy goals but provided few details.

Al Gore sounded a populist theme. After lauding the accomplishments of the last eight years of Democratic control of the White House, Gore proceeded to differentiate himself and his policy goals from those of the Clinton administration. "I stand here tonight as my own man," he said.[13] Gore then went on to provide a litany of policy objectives designed to extend the economic prosperity to those who had not benefited as much during the Clinton years — middle-class, working Americans. In contrast to Bush, Gore was program oriented and issue specific. (See Box 5–1, for "Excerpts from Acceptance Addresses at the 2000 Conventions.")

BOX 5–1 ★

EXCERPTS FROM ACCEPTANCE ADDRESSES AT THE 2000 CONVENTIONS

REPUBLICAN NOMINEE GEORGE W. BUSH (AUGUST 3, 2000)

Criticism of Clinton-Gore

Our current president embodied the potential of a generation. So many talents. So much charm. Such great skill. But, in the end, to what end? So much promise, to no great purpose . . . but instead of seizing this moment [end of the Cold War], the Clinton-Gore administration has squandered it.

Non-Washington Politican

I don't have enemies to fight. And I have no stake in the bitter arguments of the last few years. I want to change the tone of Washington to one of civility and respect.

Compassionate Conservative

On one side [of the wall between haves and have nots] are wealth and technology, education, and ambition. On the other side of the wall are poverty and prison, addiction and despair. . . . We must tear down this wall. Big government is not the answer. But the alternative to bureaucracy is not indifference. It is to put conservative values and conservative ideas into the thick of the fight for justice and opportunity. This is what I mean by compassionate conservatism.

Moral Presidential Leadership

When I put my hand on the Bible, I will swear to not only uphold the laws of our land, I will swear to uphold the honor and dignity of the office to which I have been elected, so help me God.

DEMOCRATIC NOMINEE AL GORE JR. (AUGUST 17, 2000)

Accomplishments of the Administration

Instead of the biggest deficits in history, we now have the biggest surpluses, the highest home ownership ever, the lowest inflation in a generation, and instead of losing jobs, we now have 22 million good new jobs, higher family incomes.

The Future

Now we turn the page and write a new chapter. This election is not an award for past performance. I'm not asking you to vote for me on the basis of the economy we have. I ask for your support on the basis of the better, fairer, more prosperous American we can build together.

Leadership

I stand here tonight as my own man. And I want you to know me for who I truly am. . . . If you entrust me with the presidency, I will fight for you.

Vision of Honor

We will honor hard work by raising the minimum wage. . . . We will honor families by expanding child care and after-school care. . . . We will honor the ideal of equality by standing up for civil rights and defending affirmative action.

Reproductive Choice

I will protect and defend a woman's right to choose. The last thing this country needs is a Supreme Court that overturns *Roe v. Wade.*

GREEN PARTY NOMINEE RALPH NADER (JUNE 25, 2000)

Reinvigorate Democracy

Feelings of powerlessness and the withdrawal of massive numbers of Americans from both civic and political arenas are deeply troubling. This situation has to be addressed by fresh political movement arising from the citizenry's labors and resources and dreams about what America could become at long last. The worsening concentration of global corporate power over our government has turned that government frequently against its own people, denying its people their sovereignty to shape their future.

Constraining Corporate Avarice

The corporate commercialization of our country, our government, our universities, our schools, our youngsters, our very expectation levels continues unabated. Health, safety, justice, education, respect for the environment and future generations are subordinated to boundless greed and commercialism. Much of our foreign policy is driven by unsatiable corporate pressures to sell military hardware to both the Defense Department and directly to foreign dictators.

REFORM PARTY NOMINEE PAT BUCHANAN (AUGUST 12, 2000)

Neo Isolationism
The Cold War is over; it is time to bring American troops home to the United States where they belong and end foreign aid.

International Trade
As for Communist China, we will no longer accept one-sided trade deals, where we buy 40 percent of their exports and they buy 1 percent of ours. And I will tell them: Fellas either you stop this persecution of Christians, and these threats to our friends on Taiwan, and rattling missiles at the United States, or you fellows have sold your last pair of chopsticks in any mall in the United States of America.

Education
The Department of Education is the problem; and the solution to the education crisis is to get God and the Ten Commandments, and discipline back into the public schools, and the federal bureaucrats and federal judges out, and to shut down the Department of Education, and let the building sit there as a monument to the failure and folly of Big Government.

Source: Each of these speeches are available on the campaign Web sites of the candidates as well as from the Associated Press; <http://www.georgebush.com/news.asp>; <http://www.algore2000.com>; <http://www.ralphnader2000.org/press/000625acceptance_speech.html>; <http://www.buchananreform.com/new/speeches/rpusa_acceptance.htm>; <http://wire.ap.org/APnews>.

Before the current nominating system dictated the eventual nominees and gave them operational control over the convention, there were frequent challenges. In one way or another, they involved the leadership, the successful nominees, and their delegates on one hand and the unsuccessful candidates and their supporters on the other. These disputes concerned the credentials of the delegates, the rules of the nomination process and the convention, and the party's campaign platform.

Credentials. All delegates must present proper credentials to participate at national nominating conventions. Disputes over credentials have occurred from time to time. Twice in the twentieth century, Republican conventions have witnessed major credential changes that ultimately determined their nominee. William Howard Taft's victory over Theodore Roosevelt in 1912 and Dwight Eisenhower's over Robert Taft in 1952 followed from convention decisions to seat certain delegates and reject others.[14]

Democratic conventions have also witnessed credentials fights. In 1968 and again in 1972, these challenges were based on allegations that certain party members had been excluded from caucuses and conventions, that certain state delegations did not possess sufficient minority representation, and that some of those delegations were chosen in a manner that did not conform to party rules.[15]

Rules. Rules govern the manner in which the convention is conducted; they also can affect the next delegate selection process four years down the road. In formulating the rules, there is often tension between the desire of the minority to be heard and the interest of the majority, especially the leadership, to run an efficient convention. A humorous incident at the 1956 Republican convention illustrates this tension. In the nomination for vice president, Richard Nixon was expected to be the unanimous choice. A movement to dump him from the ticket, led by perennial candidate Harold Stassen, had failed. When the roll of states was called for nominations, a delegate from Nebraska grabbed the microphone and said he had a nomination to make. "Who?" said a surprised Joseph Martin, chair of the convention. "Joe Smith," the delegate replied. Martin did not permit the name of Joe Smith to be placed in nomination, although the Democrats were later to contend that any Joe Smith would have been better than Nixon.

For the most part, convention rules have not caused much wrangling. Those that have generated the most controversy have concerned voting for the party's nominees. Until 1936, the Democrats operated under a rule that required a two-thirds vote for winning the nomination. James K. Polk's selection in 1844 was a consequence of Martin Van Buren's failure to obtain the support of two-thirds of the convention, although Van Buren had a majority. The two-thirds rule in effect permitted a minority of the delegates to veto a person they opposed.

The Democratic party also permitted the unit rule, a requirement that some states adopted to maximize their voting strength. The rule obligated all members of a delegation to vote for the majority's candidate or position on a pending issue regardless of their own views. Beginning in 1968, the Democratic convention refused to enforce unit voting any longer. The elimination of this majority-take-all principle obviously reduced the probability that state delegations would vote as units and, ultimately, weakened the power of the state party leaders. The Republicans never sanctioned or prohibited unit voting. When the Mississippi Republican delegation decided to vote as a unit at the 1976 convention to enhance its influence and perhaps tip the balance to President Ford, there was little that challenger Ronald Reagan could do or party officials would do.

Among the more recent rules controversies, two stand out. During the 1976 Republican convention, when the Reagan organization proposed a rules change that would have required Gerald Ford to name his choice for vice president before the convention's vote for president, as his opponent, Ronald Reagan had done. Ford's supporters strongly opposed and subsequently beat this amendment. As a consequence, there was no way for Reagan to shake the remaining delegates loose from Ford's coalition.

The other occurred at the 1980 Democratic convention. At issue was a proposed requirement that delegates vote for the candidate to whom they were publicly pledged at the time they were chosen to attend the convention. Trailing Jimmy Carter by about six hundred delegates, Ted Kennedy, who had previously supported this requirement, urged an open convention in which delegates could vote their consciences rather than merely exercise their commitments. This change in the rules would have required rejection of the pledged delegate rule. Naturally, the Carter organization favored the rule and lobbied strenuously and successfully for it. The Democrats have subsequently repealed this rule, requiring instead that delegates reflect in good conscience the sentiments of those who elected them.

Platform. Platforms have always been an important part of nominating conventions. They are a collective statement of the party's principal positions and agenda for the fall campaign. As such, they have become targets of opportunity for those who seek to promote their issues and interests. The heterogeneous character of both major political parties has contributed to the battles over the content and wording of the platform. It has also forced the platform drafting process to become more open and provide greater opportunities for those who represent interests within the party to participate.

Two often conflicting aims lie at the heart of the platform-drafting process. One has to do with winning the election, and the other with pleasing the party's core constituency. The goal of accommodating as many people as possible is frequently accomplished by moderating the language and, occasionally, by increasing the level of ambiguity on the most controversial and emotionally charged issues. When appealing to the party's dominant coalition, on the other hand, traditional images have been presented and specific economic and social positions stressed.

Contrary to popular belief, platforms have meaning. They are the party's principal attempt to define itself; to state what it stands for and why its candidates should be elected. Although platforms contain rhetoric and self-praise, they also articulate goals and policy positions that differentiate one party from the other. In an examination of the Democratic and Republican platforms between 1944 and 1976, political scientist Gerald Pomper found that most of the differences were evident in the planks incorporated by one party but not by the other.[16] Over these years the Republicans, who were in the minority during that period, emphasized national security and general governmental matters, whereas the Democrats, the majority party, stressed economic issues, particularly those that pertained to labor and social welfare.

Party platforms are directed to broad constituencies. Each party has traditionally tried to expand its electoral base by appealing to independents and weak partisans of the other party on the basis of popular national issues and values. In addition, each designs its platforms to appeal to as many of the specific groups that compose their electoral coalition as possible.

Beginning in 1988, the Democrats toned down their liberal rhetoric in an attempt to make their platforms more appealing to middle-class voters, disaffected by the party's social policies in the 1970s and 1980s. In contrast, the Republicans have moved to the right, becoming more conservative, more ideological, and more exclusive in the 1980s and 1990s. The GOP position on abortion has been especially divisive for the party.

There have also been substantial differences in content between the party's platforms. (See Box 5–2, "Contrasts in the 2000 Republican and Democratic Party Platforms.") These differences in turn have produced different public policies because elected officials of both parties have a relatively good record of meeting their pledges. Although approximately three-quarters of party platforms are high-sounding rhetoric, about one-fourth contains fairly specific promises. Of these, Pomper found that almost 75 percent have been kept.[17]

BOX 5–2 ★

CONTRASTS IN THE 2000 REPUBLICAN AND DEMOCRATIC PARTY PLATFORMS

REPUBLICANS	DEMOCRATS

Abortion

The Supreme Court's recent decision, prohibiting states from banning partial-birth abortion, shocks the conscience of the nation . . . the unborn child has a fundamental individual right to life which cannot be abridged. We support a human life amendment to the Constitution . . . oppose using public revenues for abortion and will not fund organizations which advocate it.

The Democratic Party stands behind the right of every woman to choose. We believe it is a fundamental constitutional liberty that individual Americans — not government — can best take responsibility for making the most difficult and intensely personal decisions regarding reproduction.

Affirmative Action

We believe rights inhere in individuals, not in groups. We will attain our nation's goal of equal opportunity without quotas or other forms of preferential treatment. . . . No one should be denied a job, promotion, contract, or chance at higher education because of their race or gender.

We have increased funding for Civil Rights enforcement. . . . Al Gore has strongly opposed efforts to roll back affirmative action programs. The Clinton-Gore administration has appointed the most diverse administration in American history.

Campaign Finance Reform

We have one guiding principle in the development of laws to regulate campaigns: Will any particular proposal encourage or restrict the energetic engagements of Americans in elections? Stop the abuses of corporate and labor "soft" money contributions to political parties; enact "paycheck protection" ensuring that no union member is forced to contribute to anybody's campaign; preserve the right of every individual and group to express their opinions and advocate their issues.

We must restore American's faith in their own democracy by providing real and comprehensive campaign finance reform. The McCain-Feingold bill is the very first piece of legislation that a President Al Gore will submit to Congress. . . . And then he will go further. He will insist on tough new lobbying reform, publicly guaranteed TV time for debates and advocacy by candidates, and a crackdown on special interest issue ads.

Education — School Vouchers

We advocate choice in education, not as an abstract theory, but as the surest way for families, especially low-income families, to free their youngsters from the failings of dangerous schools and put them onto the road to opportunity and success.

What America needs are public schools that compete with one another and are held accountable for results, not private school vouchers that drain resources from public schools and hand over the public's hard-earned tax dollars to private schools with no accountability.

Energy

America needs a national energy strategy that will increase domestic supplies of coal, oil, and natural gas. Our country does have ample energy resources waiting to be developed. Environmental concerns are not at the heart of the matter.

From the Redwood forests to the Florida Everglades, . . . we have protected millions of acres of our precious natural lands. We stopped development in America's last wild places. . . . Republicans see them as the playground of the powerful — there for big business to exploit with drilling and mining.

Guns

We defend the constitutional right to keep and bear arms, and we affirm the individual responsibility to safely use and store firearms.

We need mandatory child safety locks, to protect our children. We should require a photo license ID, a full background check, and a gun safety test to buy a new handgun in America.

Health Care

We will promote a health care system that supports, not supplants, the private sector; that promotes personal responsibility in health care decision-making; and that ensures the least intrusive role for the federal government.

We must redouble our efforts to bring the uninsured into coverage step-by-step and as soon as possible. We should guarantee access to affordable health care for every child in America.

Patient's Bill of Rights

We believe that a quick and fair resolution to treatment disputes without going to court is the best result. However, as a last resort, we also support a patient's right to adjudicate claims in court to receive necessary medical care.

Americans need a real, enforceable Patient's Bill of Rights with the right to see a specialist, the right to appeal decisions to an outside board, guaranteed coverage to emergency room care, and the right to sue when they are unfairly denied coverage.

Social Security

Personal savings account must be the cornerstone of restructuring [Social Security]. Each of today's workers should be free to direct a portion of their payroll taxes to investments for their retirement future. Choice is the key. Any new options to retirement security should be voluntary.

To build on the success of Social Security, Al Gore has proposed the creation of Retirement Savings Plus . . . voluntary, tax-free, personally personal controlled, privately managed savings accounts with a governmental match, . . . separate from Social Security.

Tax Cuts

. . . It's time to change the tax system, to make it simpler, flatter, and fairer for everyone. We . . . enthusiastically endorse the principles of Governor Bush's tax cut plan: replace the five current tax brackets with four; double the child tax credit to $1,000; capping

Democrats seek . . . tax cuts that are specifically targeted to help those who need them the most. These tax cuts would let families . . . save for college, invest in their job skills and life-long learning, pay for health insurance, afford child care, eliminate the marthe top marginal rate, ending the death tax, and making permanent the Research and Development credit.

riage penalty for working families, care for the elderly and disabled loved ones, invest in clean cars and clean homes and build additional security for their retirement.

Trade

Free trade must be fair trade, within an open, rules-based international trading system. We will not tolerate the foreign practices, rules, and subsidization that put our exports on an unequal footing.

We need to make the global economy work for all. That means making sure that all trade agreements contain provisions that will protect the environment and labor standards, as well as open markets in other countries.

Source: Republican and Democratic Party Platforms, 2000, <http://www.nc.org/2000/2000platformcontents> and <http://www.dems2000.com/AboutTheConvention.html>.

Strategies and Tactics. There are a number of prizes at nominating conventions. The platform contains some of them. The rules can also be important, but the big prize is the presidential nomination itself. When that is in doubt, all the efforts of the leading contenders must be directed at obtaining the required number of votes to be nominated. When it is not in doubt, the leading contenders can concentrate on uniting the party, articulating their themes, and converting the convention into a huge campaign rally for themselves. In 1976, the Reagan organization focused its attention on winning the nomination; in 1980, it sought to present a united front; in 1984, it orchestrated a coronation ceremony that was repeated by George Bush in 1988 and 1992, Bob Dole in 1996 and George W. Bush in 2000.

In recent Democratic conventions the front-runners have tried to heal the wounds of the nomination contest by appealing to disaffected delegates to join them and the party for the fall campaign. Making peace with his principal opponent in 1998, the Reverend Jesse Jackson, Michael Dukakis conceded the rules changes and some of the platform proposals Jackson wanted in exchange for Jackson's public support of the Democratic ticket at the convention and during the campaign. In 1992, the Clinton campaign appealed to delegates who supported his opponents. One of those opponents, Jerry Brown, refused to release his delegates or endorse the Democratic ticket. As a consequence, the Clinton delegates refused to consider any of his proposals for reform and denied him a prime-time opportunity to address the convention. Clinton faced no disappointed nomination seekers in 1996, nor did Gore in 2000.

A key to success, regardless of the objective, is organization. Recent conventions have seen the operation of highly structured and efficient candidate organizations. Designed to maximize the flow of information, regulate floor activity, and anticipate and control roll call votes, these organizations usually have elaborate communications systems linking floor supporters to a command center outside the convention hall. Key staff members at the command center monitor reports, articulate positions, and make strategic decisions.

In addition to having an effective organization, candidates often have specific goals. For Clinton in 1992, it was to reintroduce himself and discard the party's liberal label. In 1996, it was to present himself as a successful president and as the person best able to lead the country into the twenty-first century. Bob Dole sought to redefine himself and his party as sensitive to the values, needs, and aspirations of the average American. In 2000, George W. Bush reinforced his centrist compassionate image while Al Gore stressed his personal independence and political popularism.

Front-runners tend to avoid taking unnecessary risks at conventions. Compromising where necessary on policy and other issues, the goal of front-runners is to maintain their position on most challenges that could jeopardize their nomination or injure their presidential campaign. For non-front-runners, the task is different. They need to indicate the vulnerability of the front-runner, and to emphasize their own capacity to win. Two tactics have been employed by challengers to accomplish these ends. One is to release polls, such as Rockefeller did in 1968, showing the strength of his non-front-runner candidacy and the weakness of Nixon in the general election. The objective here was to play on the delegates' desire to nominate a winner. A second tactic is to create an issue before the presidential balloting and win on it. If the issue affects the rules that affect the vote, so much the better. Reagan in 1976 and Kennedy in 1980 tried this ploy but without success. Their defeats on key votes confirmed their status as also-rans and forced them to focus on the platform to influence the party and its nominee, to save face, and to position themselves for the next battle in four years.

The Mediated Convention: Theater and News

Radio began covering national conventions in 1924. Television broadcasting commenced in 1956. Because conventions in the 1950s were interesting and unpredictable events in which important political decisions were made, they attracted a large audience, one that increased rapidly as the number of households having television sets expanded. During the 1950s and 1960s, about 25 percent of the potential viewers watched the conventions, with the numbers swelling to 50 percent during the most significant part of the meetings. The sizable audience made conventions important for fledgling television news organizations, which were beginning to rival newspapers for news coverage during this period.

Initially, the three major networks provided almost gavel-to-gavel coverage. They focused on the official events, that is, what went on at the podium. Commentary was kept to a minimum.

The changes in the delegate selection process that occurred in the 1970s and 1980s had a major impact on the amount and type of television coverage as well as the size of the viewing audience. As the decision-making capabilities of conventions declined, their newsworthiness decreased, as did the proportion of households that tuned in and the amount of time spent watching them.

The major networks subsequently reduced their coverage substantially. In 1992, they covered each of the conventions for a total of fifteen hours; in 1996, reduced that coverage to twelve hours, and to eight and a half hours in 2000.[18]

Although cable and public television have extended their coverage, and the American public still feel that conventions serve a useful purpose,[19] the overall audience watching the conventions has declined. Surveys conducted by the Annenberg Public Policy Center and the Shorenstein Center for the Press, Politics, and Public Policy found about half the television audience indicating that they did not see any of the conventions.[20] Of those who did watch some portion of them, the majority were characterized as "inadvertent" viewers, people who came upon the conventions while channel surfing and for the most part watched for only a few minutes.[21]

Convention watching varied with age. Those over fifty were four times as likely to tune in for an hour or more than those twenty-nine and under.[22] Partisans watched their own convention more than the opposition's convention.[23]

Party officials, concerned with the declining participation and interest of young people in partisan national politics, created Web sites to attract this generation of voters. They trumpeted the interactive character of their convention sites. In addition, thirty-five other Internet sites, dominated by news organizations, covered the convention live. But "hits" on these news sites were down as well. PC Data Online, a firm that monitors traffic on news sites, reported a 14 percent drop in the number of people who accessed these sites during the convention.[24]

In short, the big news of the 2000 nominating conventions was that despite the increasing number of ways in which the electorate could follow them, despite each party's hype and public appeal, despite the news coverage of the conventions, more people did not watch them than did. The conventions were billed as major events in the presidential selection process by the parties, and to a much lesser extent the news media, but not by the public.

The decline in the viewing audience has produced two opposite effects. It has caused the parties to increase their scripting and orchestration of their conventions in an attempt to create more compelling theater; it has also encouraged the press to hunt for news and engage in endless analysis to make the conventions more newsworthy. The result has been to create two simultaneous conventions: the one staged by the parties and the other reported by the press.

Theater. The choice of a site; the selection of speakers; and the timing, length, and content of their talks are all made with television in mind. Conventions have become highly scripted and staged by armies of professionals from the decorations of the hall, to the entertainment package, to the speeches of the candidates and the order in which they are presented and the timing of the presentations.

One aspect of this theatrical orientation has been the use of a variety of entertainment formats to hold the delegates' and, especially, television viewers' interests: short speeches, film clips, and video biographies in addition to the pageantry, banners, and orchestrated cheers of the assembled throng. Another has been timing and sequencing events to occur during prime time and building up to the grand finale — the nominees' acceptance speeches.

A third feature of recent conventions has been the thematic content woven into the official proceedings. The Republicans scripted their 2000 convention to highlight certain policies and principles. Each day had a message and messengers,

Al Gore kisses his wife, Tipper, after officially receiving the 2000 Democratic nomination. In that brief moment, Gore demonstrated his spontaneity, passion, and fidelity — personal virtues he wished to emphasize as he launched his presidential candidacy before millions of American viewers. *(Photo Source: AP Photo/Charles Krupa)*

supplemented by a package of press releases, speeches, and other convention news available to anyone on the convention's Web site. On day one the message was that the Republican Party favored expanded opportunities for all Americans; no child was to be left behind. Improving education and extending health care were the primary vehicles by which this goal was to be accomplished. The candidate's wife, Laura Bush, a school librarian, and General Colin Powell, Chairman of the Joint Chiefs of Staff during the Gulf War and a proponent of volunteerism, especially mentoring needy children, served as symbols and speakers. On the second day, strength and security was the theme with addresses from John McCain, a Vietnam hero, Elizabeth Dole, initially a candidate herself for the 2000 nomination, and Dr. Condeleezza Rice, Bush's chief national security adviser. Keeping America prosperous and preserving the Social Security and Medicare systems was the focus of day three featuring speeches by a variety of small business entrepreneurs and vice presidential nominee, Dick Cheney. On the fourth day, the nominee, George W. Bush, was center stage with his acceptance speech as the main event.

The Democrats also orchestrated their convention although not as tightly as the Republicans. For the first two days, the Democrats focused on their presidential heros and what they had done for the country. Day one was devoted to the accomplishments of the Clinton administration with both the first lady, who was running for the Senate from New York, and the president as major speakers. The

Clintons then left the convention so as not to distract attention from the new nominees and their policies. The Kennedy legacy was featured on the second day of the Los Angeles convention. Forty years earlier, the last time the Democrats met in that city, John F. Kennedy had been nominated for president. Members of the Kennedy family including Senator Ted Kennedy and Caroline Kennedy Schlossberg, the former president's daughter, spoke about the Kennedy legacy. The keynote address was also given that night by an African-American congressman from Tennessee, Harold Ford, Jr. On the third day, the party featured women members of the House of Representatives, along with Dick Gephardt, the House minority leader, and an address by vice presidential nominee, Joseph Lieberman. The final day was reserved for Al Gore, who was introduced by his wife, Tipper, with his convention speech highlighting and ending the meeting.

Conventions have become faster paced and more varied than in the past, primarily to keep their viewing audience. From the standpoint of the parties, the more cogent the message and the more entertaining the proceedings, the more likely the convention will have a positive impact on the voters. Obviously, the press have a different objective and perspective.

News. Conventions may be entertaining, but from the perspective of the press, most of what goes on is public relations not news. As a consequence the thousands of correspondents covering the event must hunt for news beyond the official proceedings. Television cameras constantly scan the floor for dramatic events and human interest stories. Delegates are pictured talking, eating, sleeping, parading, even watching the convention on television. Interviews with prominent individuals, rank-and-file delegates, and family and friends of the prospective nominee are conducted. To provide a balanced presentation, supporters and opponents are frequently juxtaposed. To maintain the audience's attention, the interviews are kept short, usually focusing on reactions to actual or potential political problems. There are also endless commentary, prognostications, and forecasts of how the convention is likely to affect voters. Once the conventions are over, however, they are rarely mentioned in the reporting of the campaign although clips from convention highlights, especially from the acceptance speeches of the nominees will reappear in their advertising.

Coverage inside the convention is supplemented by coverage outside the hall. Knowing this, groups come to the convention city and arena to air grievances and to protest. The most violent of these political demonstrations occurred in 1968 in Chicago, where the Democratic Party was meeting. Thousands of people, many of them students, marched through the streets and parks protesting U.S. involvement in the Vietnam War. Police set up barricades, blocking, beating, and arresting many of the protestors. Claiming that the events were newsworthy, the broadcast networks broke away from their convention coverage to report on these activities and show tapes of the bloody confrontation between police and protestors. Critics charged that the presence of television cameras incited the demonstrators and that coverage was disproportional and distracted from the proceedings. In response, CBS News reported that it had devoted only thirty-two minutes to these events out of its thirty-eight hours of convention coverage.[25]

At subsequent conventions, protests have occurred but have not received as much attention by the mainstream press. Demonstrations in Philadelphia and Los Angeles during the 2000 conventions were noted but not emphasized, nor did they seem to distract from the proceedings of either convention.

The networks' orientation, which highlights conflict, drama, and human interest, often clashes with the parties' desire to present a united and enthusiastic front to launch their presidential campaigns. The clash between these two conflicting goals has resulted in a classic struggle for control between the news media and politicians. The more convention managers are successful in orchestrating their meetings to achieve their objectives, the less newsworthy the news media find the conventions to be. In contrast, the more the press report on division, dissension, and turmoil, the less the conventions meets the parties' and their nominees' principal goals. The same conflict is evident in news coverage of minor party conventions although, from the perspective of the planners of these events, a principal goal is just to obtain live coverage at all. (See Box 5–3, "Minor Party Conventions.")

Assessing the Convention's Impact

Do national nominating conventions have an impact on the election? Most observers believe that they do. Why else would the major parties devote so much time, money, and effort to these events? Why else would party leaders and academics concerned with civic education bemoan the reduction of convention coverage by the broadcast networks? Why else would the parties conduct focus groups, consult poll data, and even tally "hits" on their convention Web sites and monitor e-mail responses?

Political scientists also believe that conventions matter. They have hypothesized that there is a relationship between convention unity and electoral success. Since 1968, the party that appears to have had the most harmonious convention has emerged victorious. It is difficult, however, to say how much or even whether the unity contributed to the result or simply reflected the partisan environment that fostered the particular outcome.

In the short run, conventions almost always boost the popularity of their nominees and decrease that of their opponents. This boost is referred to as the convention "bounce" which tends to average about a six percent gain in the public opinion polls. The only recent nominee who did not get a bounce was George McGovern in 1972. Table 5–3 indicates the bounces which nominating conventions since 1960 have given their party's nominees. Bounces, however, can be short-lived as President Bush discovered in 1992, Robert Dole in 1996, and George W. Bush in 2000. Al Gore's bounce seemed to wipe away the gains which his Republican opponent made following the GOP convention.

The long-term impact is more difficult to measure. Nonetheless, political scientists have suggested three major effects of conventions on voters: (1) they heighten interest, thereby increasing turnout; (2) they arouse latent feelings, thereby raising partisan awareness; (3) they color perceptions, thereby affecting personal judgments of the candidates and their issue stands.[26]

BOX 5–3 ★

Minor Party Conventions

Minor parties also hold political conventions for the purpose of nominating candidates and promulgating their platform. In most cases these conventions are held with little fanfare and even less national media coverage. The absence of competition within the party combined with the improbability of winning the presidential election or even affecting its outcome explain the low visibility given to most of these events.

The Reform Party's conventions in 1996 and 2000 have been exceptions. Although they did not receive live coverage from the broadcast networks, they did from cable news and public affairs networks, such as CNN and C-SPAN, which covered some of their proceedings including the acceptance speeches of the presidential nominees. The broadcast networks covered them as items on the evening news. H. Ross Perot, the party's founder and financial backer, had much to do with the coverage the Reform Party's nomination process got in 1996 while the attraction in 2000 was the battle between supporters and opponents of Pat Buchanan, the former Republican who left that party to run as the Reform candidate.

In 1996, the party held a two-stage convention. At the first stage of the nomination process, Perot and his opponent, former Governor Richard D. Lamm of Colorado, were given an opportunity to address the assembled delegates. During the next week, partisans voted by regular or e-mail with the results announced at the second convention which also provided another opportunity for the winning candidate, Perot, to announce his vice presidential selection and make his acceptance speech.

In 2000, there was also a mail ballot as well as a convention vote, but it was the organizational battle over Buchanan's candidacy in the months leading up to the convention that attracted media attention. The hard-ball tactics that Buchanan's supporters employed to oust state party officials who opposed his candidacy created deep divisions within the party and ultimately led to a walkout by delegates hostile to Buchanan. These angry delegates proceeded to hold their own convention, nominate their own candidates, and claim the Reform Party label as theirs while Buchanan's backers nominated him as their Reform Party candidate. The dispute ended up in the courts which had to decide which of these two sets of candidates should be listed as the Reform nominees for 2000. Similarly, the Federal Election Commission had to determine which of them was entitled to the $12.6 million the party was to receive on the basis of Perot's 1996 vote. The commission chose Buchanan.

The other minor party that received some national coverage in 2000 was the Green Party which nominated consumer advocate and anticorporate crusader, Ralph Nader. Holding their convention in June before those of the Republicans and Democrats, the Green Party gained coverage by virtue of Nader's reputation as an outspoken critic of corporate America and its special interest politics as well as early polls which indicated that his candidacy could make a difference in the outcome of the Bush-Gore contest. In other words, Nader provided the party with visibility and the party gave him a pulpit from which to articulate his beliefs.

TABLE 5–3 ✯

Convention Bounces, 1968–2000

	Candidates (winner)	Last Poll before First Convention	Poll after First Convention (challenger/party)	Bounce for Challenger	Last Poll before Second Convention	Poll after Second Convention (incumbent/party)	Bounce for Incumbent
1968	Nixon (R)	40	45	+5	na	43	—
	Humphrey (D)	38	29	—	na	31	-7
	Wallace (AI)	16	18	—	na	19	—
1972	Nixon (R)	53	56	0	57	64	+7
	McGovern (D)	37	37	—	31	30	—
1976	Carter (D)	53	62	+9	57	50	+5
	Ford (R)	36	29	—	32	37	—
1980	Reagan (R)	37	45	+8	45	38	+10
	Carter (D)	34	29	—	29	39	—
	Anderson (I)	21	14	—	14	13	—
1984	Reagan (R)	53	46	—	52	56	+4
	Mondale (D)	39	48	+9	41	37	—
1988	Bush (R)	41	37	—	42	48	+6
	Dukakis (D)	47	54	+7	49	44	—
1992	Clinton (D)	40	56	+16	56	52	+5
	Bush (R)	48	34	—	37	42	—
1996	Clinton (D)	52	48	—	50	55	+5
	Dole (R)	30	41	+11	38	34	—
	Perot (Ref.)	12	7	—	7	6	—
2000*	Gore (D)	39	37	+4	39	47	+8
	Bush (R)	50	54	—	55	46	—
	Others	6	5	—	2	5	—
	No opinion	5	4	—	4	2	—

*Likely voters.

Source: Karlyn Bowman, American Enterprise Institute; updated by author from Gallup Poll, "Gore Gains in Race for President as a Result of Democratic Convention," August 21, 2000; <http://www.Gallup.com/poll/release/pr0082.asp>.

Each of these effects is supported by survey data taken before, during, and after recent conventions. The Vanishing Voter and Annenberg surveys found a substantial rise in public interest in the campaign immediately before, during, and after the Republican and Democratic conventions of 2000 as well as more positive feelings toward the parties and their nominees.[27] As expected, partisans of each party responded more favorably during the week of their party's nominating convention.[28] The reactions of partisans shored up support for their party's nominees which was reflected in election polls conducted after the conventions.[29] They also provided viewers with information; for those who watched, the conventions helped to clarify candidate images and policy positions.[30] In this way, they contributed to the knowledge necessary to making a more informed judgment. The Annenberg study on the 2000 conventions concluded:

> The number of voters feeling they have learned enough about the candidates to make an informed choice continues to climb, albeit slowly. Whereas at the beginning of the year only 20 percent felt they had learned enough, that number now stands at approximately 50 percent. The period of the conventions saw an increase of 10 percent in this figure.[31]

That Gore seemed to benefit more is indicated in Table 5–4 which notes the public's perceptions of the candidates' qualities and issue stands before, during, and after their political conventions.

In short, conventions can have a powerful psychological impact on their viewers, making them more inclined to follow the campaign and vote for a party's candidates. They can energize participants. They can also have an organizational effect, fostering cooperation among the different and frequently competing groups within the party, encouraging them to submerge their differences and work toward a common goal.

Studies have also shown that convention watchers tend to make their voting decisions earlier in the campaign.[32] Whether they make those decisions because they watch the convention or whether they watch the convention because they are more partisan and politically aware, and have made their voting decisions, is unclear, however. Nonetheless, about one-fifth of the electorate claim that they decide for whom they will vote at the time of the convention.

CHARACTERISTICS OF THE NOMINEES

The nominations of relatively obscure governors by the Democrats in 1976, 1988, and 1992 and a former movie actor and California governor by the Republicans in 1980 indicate that changes in the preconvention process have affected the kind of people chosen by their parties. In theory, many are qualified. The Constitution prescribes only three formal criteria for the presidency: a minimum age of thirty-five, a fourteen-year residence in the United States, and native-born status. Naturalized citizens are not eligible for the office.

In practice, a number of informal qualifications have limited the pool of potential nominees. Successful candidates have usually been well known and active in politics, and have held high government positions. Of all the positions from

TABLE 5–4 ★

SHIFTING PERCEPTIONS OF THE CANDIDATES: SHORT-TERM IMPACT OF THE CONVENTIONS (IN PERCENTAGES)

Question: Thinking about the following characteristics and qualities, please say whether you think each one applies more to Al Gore or more to George W. Bush.

	Before GOP Convention		After GOP Convention		After Democratic Convention	
	Bush	**Gore**	**Bush**	**Gore**	**Bush**	**Gore**
Qualities						
Cares about people like you	43	43	49	39	35	51
Understands complex issues	43	41	47	37	36	47
Generally agrees with you on issues you care about	45	42	49	40	40	50
Shares your values	46	41	51	38	40	48
Is someone you would be proud to have as president	46	39	52	34	38	46
Has a vision for the country's future	45	38	53	32	37	46
Is honest and trustworthy	44	37	48	32	35	45
Can manage the government effectively	49	37	53	33	40	45
Is a strong and decisive leader	54	32	60	28	46	42

Question: Regardless of which presidential candidate you support, please tell me if you think Al Gore or George W. Bush would better handle each of the following issues.

	Bush	**Gore**	**Bush**	**Gore**	**Bush**	**Gore**
Issues						
National defense	58	31	62	29	54	38
Taxes	51	36	54	35	43	47
Foreign affairs	50	36	—	—	43	47
Handling budget surplus	49	38	51	38	41	48
Guns	46	37	50	39	42	45
The economy	47	40	52	39	40	50
Education	43	45	50	41	39	51
Social Security	43	45	52	38	38	53
Abortion	38	44	43	43	36	48
Healthcare	41	47	46	43	33	57
Medicare	39	49	47	42	34	56

Source: "Gore 'Bounce' in Presidential Race Due to Overall Positive Reassessment of Vice President," *Gallup Poll,* August 23, 2000. <http://www.gallup.com/poll/releases/pr00823.asp>.

which to seek the presidential nomination, the presidency is clearly the best. Only five incumbent presidents (three of whom were vice presidents who had succeeded to the office) have failed in their quest for the nomination. It should be noted, however, that several others were persuaded to retire rather than face tough challenges.

Over the years, there has been a variety of paths to the White House. When the congressional caucus system was in operation, the position of secretary of state within the administration was regarded as a stepping-stone to the nomination if the incumbent chose not to seek another term. When national conventions replaced the congressional caucus, the Senate became the incubator for most successful presidential candidates. After the Civil War, governors emerged as the most likely contenders, particularly for the party that did not control the White House. Governors of large states in particular possessed a political base, a prestigious executive position, and leverage by virtue of their control over their delegations.[33] Today, the vice presidency is seen as a stepping-stone to the presidential nomination.

There are other informal criteria, although they have less to do with qualifications for office than with public prejudices. Only white males have ever been nominated by either of the major parties although African Americans have sought the Democratic nomination. Until John F. Kennedy's election in 1960, no Catholic had been elected, although Governor Alfred E. Smith of New York was chosen by the Democrats in 1928. Joseph Lieberman's selection as Al Gore's running mate is the first time a Jewish American has been nominated for that position. Michael Dukakis was the first candidate whose ancestry could not be traced to northern Europe, a surprising commentary on a country that has prided itself for many years on being a melting pot. The selection of a woman, Geraldine Ferraro, by the Democrats in 1984 for their vice presidential nomination, the candidacy of Elizabeth Dole for her party's 2000 presidential nomination, and the appeal of General Colin Powell in 1996 as a potential Republican candidate, however, have made gender and race seem less of a barrier today than they were in the past.

Public attitudes are changing. A poll taken after Lieberman's selection found an overwhelming percentage of those surveyed (88 percent) indicated that Lieberman's Jewish religion made no difference to them.[34] Gallup polls reveal a growing public tolerance toward electing people of various racial and religious backgrounds to the nation's highest office. A 1999 survey indicated that being a woman, an African American, or a Jew no longer automatically disqualifies an individual in the minds of most Americans. However, a significant proportion of the population would still not vote for an atheist or a homosexual for president. Table 5–5 presents the findings of Gallup polls over a sixty-year period.

Personal matters, such as health and family life, can also be factors. After Alabama governor, George Wallace, was crippled by a would-be assassin's bullet, even his own supporters began to question his ability to withstand the rigors of the office. Senator Thomas Eagleton was forced to withdraw as the Democratic vice presidential nominee in 1972 when his past psychological illness became public. Before George W. Bush announced Dick Cheney's selection as his running mate, he had his father, former President George Bush, inquire about Cheney's medical condition. Cheney, who had suffered three heart attacks in the 1980s, was described by his Houston doctors as in excellent health. Today, presidential and

TABLE 5–5 ★

TOLERANCE IN VOTING FOR WOMEN AND MINORITIES
FOR PRESIDENT (PERCENTAGE WHO WOULD *NOT* VOTE
FOR A PERSON WITH CERTAIN CHARACTERISTICS)

	Year			
Characteristic	**1937**	**1958**	**1978**	**1999**
Women	64%	41%	19%	07%
African American	—	53	18	04
Jew	47	28	12	06
Catholic	30	24	04	04
Atheist	—	75	53	48
Homosexual	—	—	66	37

Source: Frank Newport, "Americans Today Much More Accepting of a Woman, Black, Catholic, or Jew as President," Gallup Organization, <http://www.gallup.com/poll/releases/pr990329.asp>, April 1, 1999.

vice presidential candidates are expected to release detailed medical reports on themselves. Senator Dole released his early in the nomination process to demonstrate that he was healthy and fit despite his age of seventy-three.

Family ties have also affected nominations and elections, as the father-son relationship between the Bushes demonstrates. There have been only two bachelors elected president, James Buchanan and Grover Cleveland.[35] During the 1884 campaign, Cleveland was accused of fathering an illegitimate child and was taunted by his opponents with "Ma, Ma, Where's my Pa? Gone to the White House, Ha! Ha! Ha!" Cleveland admitted responsibility for the child, even though he was not certain he was the father.

Until 1980, no person who was divorced had ever been elected. Andrew Jackson, however, married a divorced woman, or at least a woman he thought was divorced. As it turned out, she had not been granted the final court papers legally dissolving her previous marriage. When this information was became public during the 1828 campaign, Jackson's opponents asked rhetorically, "Do we want a whore in the White House?"[36] Jackson and Cleveland both won. That a candidate has been divorced and remarried seems to have little impact or even gain much notoriety today.

Adultery is another matter. Senator Edward Kennedy's marital problems and his driving accident on Chappaquiddick Island, off the coast of Massachusetts, in which a young woman riding with the senator was drowned, were serious impediments to his presidential candidacy in 1980. Similarly, Gary Hart's alleged "womanizing" forced his withdrawal in 1988, whereas the length of the period between Pat Robertson's marriage and the birth of his first son raised some eyebrows and was a topic of conversation and concern among some of his religious followers. Bill Clinton's nomination in 1992, despite the allegations of marital infidelity, marijuana smoking, and draft dodging, and in 1996, despite a pending sexual harassment suit by an Arkansas employee and the ongoing Whitewater investigation, as well as George W. Bush's self-admitted binge drinking as a younger man suggest that the electorate is more concerned about contemporary conditions and behavior than they are with relationships and behavior that have occurred in previous years, especially in the distant past.[37]

The informal qualifications of the presidential nominee have in general been matched by those of the vice presidential candidate as well. The vice presidential search has traditionally been affected by the perceived need for geographic and ideological balance. Presidential aspirants have tended to choose vice presidential candidates primarily as running mates and only secondarily as governing mates. In 2000, however, more attention was given to the governing qualifications of the vice presidential selections by the presidential nominees.

Bill Clinton chose Al Gore in 1992 not so much to create a balance as to emphasize his centrist policy positions, southern roots, and generational appeal to the baby boomers. Both Bush and Gore indicated that their primary criteria for choosing their running mates in 2000 were the government experience, judgment and maturity, and exemplary personal qualities that each of them possessed, not the geographic or ideological balance they added to the ticket. (For lists of Republican and Democratic Party conventions and nominees, see Appendix F.)

SUMMARY

With the end of the competitive stage of the caucuses and primaries coming earlier and earlier, candidates who emerge victorious have to continue campaigning right up until their national convention even though their nomination may be secure. During this interregnum, which in 2000 lasted more than four months, the winners had to consolidate their base, unify their party, gain the support and endorsements of their nomination opponents, and overcome any negative perceptions left over from the race for delegates. In addition, they have to raise money for the party, and if they did not accept federal funds, they also need to raise it for themselves. They have to plan their general election strategy, developing and testing the themes they wish to articulate and the personal images they want to project. Moreover, they have to stay in the news, avoid mistakes, and build their campaign organization. There is little rest for the weary.

As the nomination process now preordains the party's presidential candidate who controls the committees that set the rules, review the credentials, and draft the platform, the national nominating conventions have become more entertainment than news. Great effort goes into scripting and orchestrating the meetings to present a good show, one that will attract viewers, emphasize mainstream policy positions, and create or reinforce leadership images.

The parties still see their conventions as important events that provide a favorable environment for launching their fall campaigns. From the perspective of convention planners, the goals are to convey a unified party which enthusiastically and confidently supports its nominees. From the perspective of the party, the goals are to raise the spirits and hopes of its workers, both delegates and the partisans at home, obtain even more soft-money donations, and mobilize the faithful for the fall campaign. From the perspective of the nominees, the goals are to demonstrate their broad-based policy appeal and strong leadership images.

The press covering the convention have different goals. Not oblivious to their public service function, they still need to maximize their viewing audience by reporting the convention as news, as well as presenting it as the party's public relations spectacular. To do this, they must find and report newsworthy events, those that are dramatic, divisive, and unexpected, provide analysis, and engage in endless prognosis about what it all means for the election and for the next government.

These differing goals can create tension between and among successful and unsuccessful candidates, party factions, campaign organizers and party regulars, and convention planners and the news media. These tensions often become the focus of the news media.

Although contemporary conventions are highly theatrical events, they do attract public attention, increase electoral awareness, and help shape perceptions of the candidates, parties, and their respective issue positions. Their impact varies with the attitudes and predispositions of those who watch or read about them. For partisans, conventions reinforce allegiances making party identifiers more likely to vote and work for their party's nominees. For those less oriented toward a particular party, conventions deepen interest in the campaign; in 2000, they also contributed to a more positive outlook about the candidates and their parties. In general, conventions provide the electorate with information with which to make a more informed voting decision; they also hasten that decision for a certain percentage of voters.

The changes in the nominating process have also affected the characteristics, qualities, and background of those gaining their party's nomination. They have enlarged the selection zone for potential standard-bearers. It is unlikely that a Democratic convention before 1972 would have chosen a McGovern, Carter, Dukakis, or even Clinton, or that a former movie actor and governor would have come as close as Reagan did to defeating President Gerald Ford for the Republican nomination in 1976. Moreover, the selection of a woman by the Democrats in 1984 and a Jew in 2000 as vice presidential nominees combined with the boomlet for General Colin Powell in 1996 and Elizabeth Dole's own candidacy four years later suggests that gender, religion, and race may no longer be the critical criteria they once were for presidential and vice presidential nominees. Times have changed; the electorate, reflecting the mores of the society, has become more tolerant. The selection zone has gotten larger.

WHERE ON THE WEB?

The political parties are obviously a good source of information about their nominating conventions. Here are the sites for the major parties and the Green and Reform Parties.

- **Democratic National Committee**
  http://www.democrats.org
- **Green Party**
  http://www.greenparty.org

- **Reform Party**
  http://www.reformparty.org
- **Republican National Committee**
  http://www.rnc.org
For other parties see:
- **Democracy Network**
  http://www.dnet.org

EXERCISES

1. Compare the Democratic and Republican conventions on the basis of their schedule, the tenor of the televised speeches, and the video presentations. Which did you find more interesting and why?
2. Compare the acceptance speeches of the major party candidates for the presidential and vice presidential nominations. On the basis of your comparison, indicate to what extent these speeches augured the principal appeals of the candidates in the general election. Compare these appeals to that of the Reform and Green Party candidates.
3. Contrast the major party platforms with those of two third parties, one on the left of the political spectrum and one on the right. Are the major parties both centrist with most of their positions within the mainstream of American public opinion?
4. Looking back over the last presidential campaign, particularly the issue debate, indicate which of the Republican and Democratic Parties' platform positions were emphasized by the candidates and which were not. Which of the major party candidates seemed more loyal to his party in speeches, advertising, or debate responses? (You can obtain information about the candidates from their Web sites <http://www.georgebush.com>; <http://www.algore2000.com> if they are still operative; from their party's sites <http://www.rnc.org>; <http://www.democrats.org>; and from the national media such as the *New York Times* <http://www.nytimes.com> or the Associated Press <http://www.ap.org>.
5. Examine the inauguration address of the newly elected president and any other major addresses made within his first 100 days in office to see which of his party's platform positions are highlighted and which are not. On the basis of your analysis, do you think that platforms are important agenda setters for the new administration?

SELECTED READING

Adler, Wendy Zeligson. "The Conventions on Prime Time." In *The Homestretch: New Politics,* edited by Martha FitzSimon and Edward C. Pease, 55–57. New York: The Freedom Forum Media Studies Center, 1992.

Cammarano, Joseph, and Jim Josefson, "Putting it in Writing: An Examination of Presidential Candidate Platforms in the 1992 Election." *Southeastern Political Review* 23 (June 1995): 187–204.

Davis, James W. *National Conventions in an Age of Party Reform.* Westport, Conn.: Greenwood Press, 1983.

Maisel, L. Sandy. "The Platform-Writing Process." *Political Science Quarterly* 108 (Winter 1993–1994): 671–698.

Pavlik, John V. "Insider's Guide to Coverage of the Conventions and the Fall Campaign." In *The Homestretch,* 40–54.

Shafer, Byron E. *Bifurcated Politics: Evolution and Reform in the National Party Convention.* Cambridge, Mass.: Harvard University Press, 1988.

Smith, Larry David, and Dan Nimmo. *Cordial Concurrence: Orchestrating National Party Conventions in the Telepolitical Age.* New York: Praeger, 1991.

NOTES

1. Gore had less money available than Bush (Gore had $5.7 million and Bush $6 million), but Gore expected to receive an additional $4.5 million in matching funds from the Federal Election Commission.

2. "Excerpts from Interview with Bush on Campaign Issues and Election Strategy," *New York Times,* March 16, 2000, A16.

3. Alison Mitchell, "Bush Strategy Recalls Clinton on the Trail in '96." *New York Times,* April 18, 2000, A18.

4. Terry M. Neal and Ceci Connolly, "Bush, Gore Both Grab for Reform Mantle," *Washington Post,* March 13, 2000, A4.

5. Alison Mitchell, "Bush's Strategy Evokes Images of Rose Garden," *New York Times,* July 17, 2000, <http://www.nytimes.com>.

6. In August, following the Republican convention, Bush criticized Democratic candidate Michael Dukakis for his softness on crime, his weak defense posture, his environmental record in Massachusetts, and his association with liberal policy and liberal groups.

7. Dan Balz and Terry M. Neal, "Suddenly Sunny Gore Lets Allies Rain on Bush," *Washington Post,* June 1, 2000, A4.

8. CNN network, "GOP Convention at a Glance," July 31, 2000, and "Democratic Convention at a Glance," August 14, 2000, <http://www.cnn.com/ELECTIONS>.

9. Perhaps the most famous of all keynote addresses was William Jennings Bryan's. A relatively unknown political figure, Bryan, at the age of thirty-six, electrified the Democratic convention of 1896 with his famous "Cross of Gold" speech. His remarks generated so much enthusiasm that the delegates turned to him to lead them as their standard-bearer. He did, and lost.

10. Ann Richards, "Address to the Democratic Convention in Atlanta, Georgia on July 19, 1988," as quoted in *Congressional Quarterly* 46 (July 23, 1988): 2024. George W. Bush was so incensed by this characterization, as well as by other comments Governor Richards made about his father, that he determined he would challenge the governor in her next election. He did; he won; and thus began his campaign on the road to the White House.

11. Buchanan had agreed to submit a copy of his speech to Bush's managers twenty-four hours in advance of delivery to ensure that it was consistent with the campaign's themes and did not preempt former President Ronald Reagan who was to follow Buchanan. Fearful that the campaign organization would leak the speech, however, Buchanan decided to give another address, one of his stump speeches which was shown only to convention coordinator, Craig Fuller and faxed to Bob Teeter, Bush's pollster and strategist. Bay Buchanan, quoted in Charles T. Royer, ed. *Campaign for President: The Managers Look at '92* (Hollis, N.H.: Hollis Publishing, 1994), 208.

12. Quoted in Malcom Moos and Stephen Hess, *Hats in the Ring* (New York: Random House, 1960), 157–158.

13. "Transcript of Gore's Speech," Associated Press, <http:wire.ap.org>; August 17, 2000.

14. In both cases, grassroots challenges to old-line party leaders generated competing delegate claims. The convention in 1912 rejected these challengers and seated the regular party delegates, producing a walkout by Roosevelt's supporters and giving the nomination to Taft. Forty years later, the delegates denied the nomination to Taft's son by recognizing the credential of delegates pledged to Eisenhower and rejecting those supporting Senator Taft.

15. The California challenge at the 1972 Democratic convention illustrates the last of these complaints. George McGovern had won the primary and, according to California law at the time, was entitled to all the delegates. The party's credentials committee, however, decided that the state's delegates should be divided in proportion to the popular vote because the commission that had revised the Democratic rules for 1972 (a commission McGovern initially chaired) had affirmed the principle of proportional voting, although it did not require states to change their law to conform to this principle until 1976. McGovern challenged the credentials committee ruling and won on the convention floor, thereby making his nomination all but certain.

16. Gerald M. Pomper, "Control and Influence in American Politics," *American Behavioral Scientist* 13 (November/December 1969): 223–228; Gerald M. Pomper with Susan S. Lederman, *Elections in America* (New York: Longman, 1980), 161.

17. Ibid., 161. One reason that platform promises have been acted on is that elected officials participate in the drafting; in fact, they hold many of the key committee positions. For the party in power, the incumbent president seeking reelection usually takes the lead, exercising the most influence over the composition of the platform committee and the product it produces. For the party out of power, the chair of the national committee usually selects the leadership of the platform committee, and the successful nominee usually controls a majority of the delegates.

18. Thomas E. Patterson, "Lessons from the Last Convention," *Vanishing Voter*, Joan Shorenstein Center on the Press, Politics, and Public Policy, August 13, 2000, <http://www.vanishingvoter.org/releases/08-13-00conv-1.shtml>.

19. Gallup Poll, "Most Americans Think Conventions Serve a Useful Purpose," July 20, 2000; <http://www.gallup.com/poll/072100.asp>.

20. Kathleen Hall Jamison, et al. "The Public Learned about Bush and Gore from Conventions; Half Ready to Make an Informed Choice," Annenberg Public Policy Center, August 25, 2000, 2; "GOP Convention Struggles for Audience," *Vanishing Voter*, August 11, 2000, <http://www.vanishingvoter.org/releases/08-25-00conv.shtml>.

21. Patterson, "Lessons from the Last Convention."

22. "GOP Convention Struggles."

23. Jamison et al., "The Public Learned about Bush and Gore from Conventions," 2.

24. Howard Kurtz, "Web Coverage Does Not Spark Convention Interest," *Washington Post*, August 14, 2000, <http://www.washingtonpost.com/wp-dyn/articles/A24614-2000Aug14.html>.

25. "Republicans Orchestrate a Three-Night TV Special," *Broadcasting*, August 28, 1972, 12.

26. Thomas E. Patterson, *The Mass Media Election* (New York: Praeger, 1980), 72–74.

27. Jamison et al., "The Public Learned about Bush and Gore from Conventions," 2; "Voter Involvement Index," *Vanishing Voter*, August 20, 2000, <http://www.vanishingvoter.org/graphs/vi08-20-00.shtml>.

28. Jamison et al., "The Public Learned about Bush and Gore from Conventions," 2.

29. Gallup Poll, "Bush Up 54% to 37% over Gore after GOP Convention," August 7, 2000, <http://www.gallup.com/poll/releases/pr000807.asp>; "Gore Gains in Race for President as Result of Democratic Convention," August 21, 2000, <http://www.gallup.com/poll/releases/pr000821.asp>.

30. Jamison et al., "The Public Learned about Bush and Gore from Conventions," 3–5; "Conventions Boost Americans' Issue Awareness," *Vanishing Voter,* August 30, 2000.

31. Ibid.

32. Patterson, *Mass Media Election,* 103.

33. The House of Representatives has not been a primary source of nominees. Only one sitting member of the House, James A. Garfield, has ever been elected president, and he was chosen on the thirty-fifth ballot. In recent nomination contests, however, a number of representatives have sought their party's nomination. Representative Morris Udall finished second to Jimmy Carter in 1976; Representative John Anderson competed for the Republican nomination in 1980 before running as an independent candidate in the general election. In 1988, Representatives Jack Kemp and Richard Gephardt were candidates for their party's nomination. There were no serious House candidates for either party in 1992. In 1996, Representative Robert Dornan sought the Republican nomination while Speaker Newt Gingrich did not close the door on a potential draft movement for his nomination. The only House candidate in 2000 was Republican John Kasich of Ohio.

34. Gallup Poll, "Positive Public Reaction to Gore's Choice of Lieberman as VP," August 8, 2000, <http://www.gallup.com/poll/releases/pr000808.asp>.

35. Historian Thomas A. Bailey reports that in his quest for the presidency, Buchanan was greeted by a banner carried by a group of women that read, "Opposition to Old Bachelors." *Presidential Greatness* (New York: Appleton-Century Crofts, 1966), 74.

36. Ibid.

37. Clinton feared that he would not have been renominated and reelected if the Monica Lewinsky affair had become public before the convention and general election campaign.

PART III

THE
CAMPAIGN

ORGANIZATION, STRATEGY, AND TACTICS

6

INTRODUCTION

Elections have been held in the United States since 1789; campaigning by parties for their nominees began soon thereafter. It was not until the end of the nineteenth century, however, that presidential candidates actively participated in the campaigns. Personal solicitation was viewed as demeaning and unbecoming of the dignity and status of the presidency.

Election paraphernalia, distributed by the parties, first appeared in the 1820s; by 1828, there was extensive public debate about the candidates. Andrew Jackson, and to a lesser extent, John Quincy Adams, generated considerable commentary and controversy. Jackson's supporters lauded him as a hero, a man of the people, "a new or second Washington"; his critics referred to him as "King Andrew the first," alleging that he was immoral, tyrannical, and brutal.[1] Adams was also subjected to personal attack. Much of this heated rhetoric appeared in the highly partisan press of the times.

The use of the campaign to reach, entertain, inform, and mobilize the general electorate began on a large scale in 1840. Festivals, parades, slogans, jingles, and testimonials were employed to energize voters. The campaign of 1840 is best remembered for the slogan, "Tippecanoe and Tyler too," promoting Whig candidates General William Henry Harrison, hero of the battle of Tippecanoe in the War of 1812, and John Tyler, and for its great jingles:

WHAT HAS CAUSED THIS GREAT COMMOTION?
(SUNG TO THE TUNE OF "LITTLE PIG'S TAIL")

What has caused this great commotion, motion, motion,
Our country through?
It is the ball a rolling on, on.

Chorus
For Tippecanoe and Tyler too — Tippecanoe and Tyler too,
And with them we'll beat little Van, Van, Van, [Martin Van Buren]
Van is a used up man,
And with them we'll beat little Van.[2]

The successful Whig campaign made it a prototype for subsequent presidential contests.

The election of 1840 was also the first in which a party nominee actually campaigned for himself. General William Henry Harrison made twenty-three speeches in his home state of Ohio.[3] He did not set a precedent that was quickly followed, however. It was twenty years before another presidential candidate took to the stump and then under the extraordinary conditions of the onset of the Civil War and the breakup of the Democratic Party.

Senator Stephen A. Douglas, Democratic candidate for president, spoke out on the slavery issue to try to heal the split that it had engendered within his party. When doing so, however, he denied his own personal ambitions. "I did not come here to solicit your votes," he told a Raleigh, North Carolina, audience. "I have nothing to say for myself or my claims personally. I am one of those who think it would not be a favor to me to be made President at this time."[4] Abraham Lincoln, Douglas's Republican opponent, refused to reply, even though he had debated Douglas two years earlier in their contest for the Senate seat from Illinois, a contest Douglas won. Lincoln, who almost dropped out of public view when the campaign was under way, felt that it was not even proper for him to vote for himself.[5] He cut his own name from the Republican ballot before he cast it for others in the election.[6] For their part, the Republicans mounted a massive campaign on Lincoln's behalf. They held what were called "Wide Awake" celebrations in which large numbers of people were mobilized. An account of one of these celebrations reported that

> the Wide-Awake torch-light procession is undoubtedly the largest and most imposing thing of the kind ever witnessed in Chicago. Unprejudiced spectators estimate the number at 10,000. Throughout the whole length of the procession were scattered portraits of Abraham Lincoln. Banners and transparencies bearing Republican mottoes, and pictures of rail splitters, were also plentifully distributed. Forty-three bands of music were also in the procession.[7]

Presidential candidates remained on the sidelines until the 1880s. Republican James Garfield broke the tradition by receiving visitors at his Ohio home. Four years later in 1884, Republican James Blaine made hundreds of campaign speeches in an unsuccessful effort to offset public accusations that he profited from a fraudulent railroad deal. Benjamin Harrison, the Republican candidate in 1888, resumed the practice of seeing people at his home, a practice that has been referred to as front-porch campaigning. Historian Keith Melder writes that Harrison met with 110 delegations consisting of almost two hundred thousand people in the course of the campaign.[8] William McKinley saw even more visitors over the course of his front-porch campaign in 1896. He spoke to approximately 750,000 people who were recruited and in some cases transported to his Canton, Ohio, home by the Republican Party.[9]

McKinley's opponent, William Jennings Bryan, actually traveled around the country making speeches. By his own account, he logged more than eighteen thousand miles and made more than six hundred speeches, and, according to press estimates, he spoke to almost 5 million people, nearly collapsing from exhaustion at the end of the campaign.[10]

In 1900, Republican vice presidential candidate Theodore Roosevelt took on Bryan, "making 673 speeches, visiting 567 towns in twenty-four states, and traveling 21,209 miles."[11] Twelve years later, ex-president Theodore Roosevelt, once again took to the hustings, only this time he was trying to defeat a fellow Republican president, William Howard Taft, for his party's nomination. Roosevelt won nine primaries, including one in Ohio, Taft's home state, but was denied the nomination by party leaders. He then launched an independent candidacy in the general election, campaigning on the Progressive, or "Bull Moose," ticket. His Democratic opponent, Woodrow Wilson, was also an active campaigner. The Roosevelt and Wilson efforts ended the era of passive presidential campaigning. The last front-porch campaign was waged by Warren G. Harding in 1920.

Harding's campaign was distinguished in another way; he was the first to use radio to speak directly to voters. This new electronic medium and television, which followed it, radically changed presidential campaigns. Initially, candidates were slow to adjust their campaign style to these new techniques.[12] It was not until Franklin Delano Roosevelt that radio was employed skillfully in political campaigns. Roosevelt also pioneered the "whistle-stop" campaign train, which stopped at railroad stations along the route to allow the candidate to address the crowds that came to see and hear him. In 1932, Roosevelt, who personally took a train to Chicago to accept his nomination, visited thirty-six states, traveling some thirteen thousand miles in his presidential campaign. His extensive travels, undertaken in part to dispel a whispering campaign about his health — he had polio as a young man, which left him unable to walk or even stand up unaided — forced President Herbert Hoover onto the campaign trail.[13]

Instead of giving the small number of speeches he had originally planned, Hoover logged more than ten thousand miles, traveling across much of the country. He was the first incumbent president to campaign actively for reelection. Thereafter, with the exception of Franklin Roosevelt during World War II, personal campaigning became standard for incumbents and nonincumbents alike.

Harry Truman took incumbent campaigning a step further. Perceived as the underdog in the 1948 election, Truman whistle-stopped the length and breadth of the United States, traveling thirty-two thousand miles and averaging ten speeches a day. In eight weeks, he spoke to an estimated 6 million people.[14] While Truman was rousing the faithful by his down-home comments and hard-hitting criticisms of the Republican-controlled Congress, his opponent, Thomas E. Dewey, was promising new leadership but providing few particulars. His sonorous speeches contrasted sharply and unfavorably with Truman's straightforward attacks.

The end of an era in presidential campaigning occurred in 1948. Within the next four years television came into its own as a communications medium. The number of television viewers grew from less than half a million in 1948 to approximately 19 million in 1952, a figure that was deemed sufficient in the minds of campaign planners to launch a major television effort. The Eisenhower presidential organization budgeted almost $2 million for television, and the Democrats promised to use both radio and television "in an exciting, dramatic way" in that election.[15]

The potential of television was evident at the outset. Republican vice presidential candidate, Richard Nixon, took to the airwaves in 1952 to reply to accusations that he had appropriated campaign funds for his personal use and had received money and other gifts from wealthy supporters, including a black-and-white cocker spaniel named Checkers. Nixon denied the charges but said that under no circumstances would he and his family give up the dog, which his children dearly loved. A huge outpouring of public sympathy for Nixon followed, effectively ending the issue, keeping him on the ticket, and demonstrating the impact television could have on a political career and a presidential campaign.

Television made a mass appeal easier, but it also created new obstacles for the nominees. Physical appearance became more important as did oratory style. Instead of just rousing a crowd, presidential aspirants had to convey a personal message and image to television viewers.

Television had other effects as well. It eventually replaced the party as the principal link between the nominees and the voters. It decreased the incentive for holding so many election events — rallies, parades, speeches — since many more people could be reached through this mass medium. Finally, it required that campaign activities and events be carefully orchestrated and scripted, keeping in mind how they would appear on the screen and what images they would convey to voters. Off-handed comments and quips were discouraged because they often got candidates into trouble.

The people who organized and ran campaigns were also affected. Public relations experts were called on to apply mass marketing techniques. Pollsters and media consultants supplemented and to some extent replaced old style politicians in designing and executing strategies. Even the candidates seemed a little different. With the possible exception of Lyndon Johnson and Gerald Ford, both of whom succeeded to the presidency through the death or resignation of their predecessors, incumbents and challengers alike reflected the grooming and schooling of the age of mass communications. And where they did not, as in the cases of Walter Mondale, Michael Dukakis, and Robert Dole, they fared poorly.

This chapter and the one that follows discuss these aspects of modern presidential campaigns. Organization, strategy, and tactics serve as the principal focal points of this chapter, whereas news coverage, image, and issue projection, and the impact of the media on campaigns are addressed in the next one.

The next section of this chapter describes the structures of modern presidential campaigns and the functions they perform. It examines attempts to create hierarchical campaign organizations but also notes the decentralizing pressures. The tensions between candidate organizations and the regular party structure are discussed as well.

The basic objectives that every strategy must address are explored in the section that follows. These include designing a basic appeal, creating a leadership image, sometimes coping with the incumbency factor, and building a winning geographic coalition. The last section of the chapter deals with tactics, describing the techniques for communicating the message, orchestrating the campaign, targeting and timing appeals, and finally, turning out the voters on election day.

ORGANIZATION

Running a campaign is a complex, time-consuming, nerve-racking venture. It involves coordinating a variety of functions and activities, including advance work, scheduling, press arrangements, issue research, speech writing, polling and focus groups, media advertising and orchestration, finances and legal issues, and party and interest group activities. To accomplish these varied tasks, a large, specialized campaign organization is necessary.

All recent presidential campaigns have had such organizations with similar features. There is a person, usually titled chairman, who presides over the organization and acts as a liaison among the candidate, the party, and the public; a hands-on manager who orchestrates the operation; a political director and several deputies charged with supervising day-to-day activities; usually an administrative head of the national headquarters; division chiefs for special operations; and a geographic hierarchy that reaches to the state and local levels. Every campaign also has pollsters, media consultants, strategists, and grassroots organizers, plus an array of technical experts, including accountants and lawyers.

Within this basic structure, organizations have varied somewhat in style and operation. Most have been centralized, with a few individuals making the key strategic and tactical decisions; a few have been decentralized. Some have worked through or in conjunction with national and state party organizations; others have disregarded these groups and created their own field organizations. Some have operated from a comprehensive game plan; others have adopted a more incremental, design-it-as-you-go approach. In some, the nominee has assumed an active decision-making role; in others, the candidate defers to the principal campaign advisers who collectively make major strategic and tactical decisions.

The Goldwater (1964), Nixon (1972), Reagan (1984), Bush (1988), Clinton (1992 and 1996) and George W. Bush (2000) campaigns all exemplify the tight, hierarchical structure in which a few individuals control decision making and access to the candidate. In Goldwater's case, his chief advisers were suspicious of top party regulars, most of whom did not support the senator's candidacy. They opted for an organization of believers, one that would operate in an efficient fashion.[16]

The same desire for control and for circumventing the party was evident in Richard Nixon's reelection campaign in 1972. Completely separated from the national party, even in title, the Committee to Reelect the President (known as CREEP by its critics) raised its own money, conducted its own public relations (including polling and campaign advertising), scheduled its own events, and even had its own security division. It was this division, which operated independently from the Republican Party, that harassed the Democratic campaign of George McGovern by heckling his speeches, spreading dishonest rumors, and perpetrating other illegal acts, including the attempted wiretapping of the Democratic National Committee headquarters at the Watergate Office Building.

The excesses perpetuated by individuals in the Nixon campaign illustrate both the difficulty of overseeing all the aspects of a large presidential campaign and the risk of placing nonprofessionals in key positions of responsibility. Had the more experienced Republican National Committee exercised greater influence over the presidential campaign, there might have been less deviation from accepted standards of behavior.

The Reagan and Bush (1988) efforts operated more closely with state Republican Party organizations than had either Goldwater's or Nixon's. Directed by separate campaign organizations, each was linked to the party at both the national and the state levels. Fund-raising efforts and grassroots activities were primarily party affairs, whereas the presidential campaign organization exercised most of the control over the basic strategy, thematic content of the campaign, relations with the media, resource allocation, and the scheduling and appearances of the presidential and vice presidential candidates.

Bush's organization in 1988 has received considerable praise for its tight-knit structure and efficient operating style. A small circle of advisers, each with designated areas of responsibility, ran the campaign and interacted with the nominee. By contrast, his 1992 organization was disjointed, uncoordinated, and internally competitive, with three separate groups, the White House, the reelection committee, and the campaign's media operation, vying for power. The Dole organization in 1996 was also not as tightly organized nor as efficiently run as the Reagan-Bush campaigns of the 1980s.

The George W. Bush campaign in 2000 was a model of the well-run, well-coordinated effort. Four of Bush's closest friends and political advisors in his race for governor oversaw the campaign from its inception to its conclusion. Donald L. Evans functioned as the national finance chairman. After the money phase of the campaign was concluded, Evans was given the title of campaign chairman. Karl Rove, who had planned Bush's challenge to Governor Ann Richards, was the campaign's principal political strategist, Joe Allbaugh, the day-to-day campaign manager, and Karen P. Hughes, director of communications and principal link to the press (see Figure 6–1).

Democratic campaign organizations have tended to be looser in structure and more decentralized in operation than have the Republicans'. Until the 1970s, the Democrats had stronger state parties and a weaker national base. As a consequence, their presidential candidates tended to rely more heavily on state party organizations than did the Republicans.

In recent years Democratic presidential campaigns have designated regional and state coordinators to oversee state party efforts on their behalf. These coordinators, placed on the payroll of the state parties to reduce administrative overhead, also have served as intermediaries between the official party organizations and the campaign.

Although the organizations of Walter Mondale and Michael Dukakis had difficulty carrying out coordinated campaign efforts, the Clinton campaigns did not. They were tightly run operations, with carefully designed strategic plans, and a "war room" for tactical operations. Both Clinton campaigns were highly

FIGURE 6–1 ★

THE GEORGE W. BUSH CAMPAIGN ORGANIZATION IN 2000

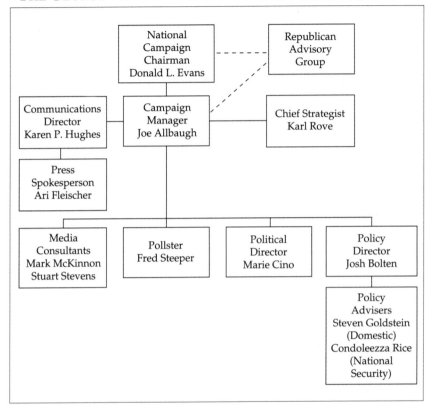

centralized, both relied heavily on pollsters to monitor the public mood, and both depended on a media team to design and target advertising. Clinton himself was heavily involved in these efforts, particularly in the early phases of both campaigns.

There was, however, a clash of personalities at the outset of the 1996 Clinton organization during the early phases of the campaign. The principal antagonists were chief strategist Dick Morris along with the campaign operatives he brought on board and senior White House staffers who saw their roles as advisers and felt their access to the president threatened by the Morris group. However, these differences were muted by the apparent success of the Clinton campaign, the president's steady rise in the polls, and the joint Wednesday evening strategy sessions, run by the president, in which major campaign and tactical issues were addressed. The friction ended with Morris's resignation from the campaign after allegations of his weekly liaison with a Washington "call girl" became public. However, the strategic plan, which Morris had developed, continued to guide the campaign.

The Gore 2000 campaign was also plagued by internal tension that surfaced during periods in which Gore seemed to be losing ground to his political opponents, first Bill Bradley and later George W. Bush. Those tensions, the inevitable consequence of ambitious people working long hours under constant pressure, often within severe time constraints, and above all, the target of external and internal criticism, resulted in press leaks, competing strategies, and internal backbiting.

Tony Coelho, former member of Congress and Democratic House whip, managed the campaign from October 1999 through the primaries until June 15, 2000 when he resigned for reasons of health. Coelho's resignation, however, came after a period of drift in which Gore had fallen behind Republican challenger, George W. Bush, in the polls. William M. Daley, commerce secretary and architect of the Clinton administration's public relations campaign for the North American Free Trade Agreement (NAFTA), was immediately chosen for the top position. Daley imposed discipline on the campaign and helped his candidate gain the initiative by the end of the Democratic convention, until the presidential debates when Gore fell behind once again. Working closely with Coelho and Daley were the vice president's college friend and major media advisor, Carter Eskew; political consultants, Robert Strum, Tad Devine, and Michael Donilon; and campaign manager, Donna Brazile. Figure 6–2 shows the principals of the Gore organization.

FIGURE 6–2 ★

THE GORE CAMPAIGN ORGANIZATION IN 2000

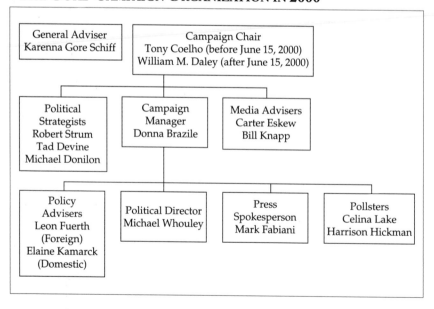

How presidential campaigns are organized, who holds the key positions, and what is the organization's relationship to the party all have important implications for government. A campaign organization reflects a candidate's management style: his or her willingness to take advice; to delegate to others; to make decisions and adhere to them or adjust them if the situation changes. Reagan's reliance on his campaign organization, his reluctance to second-guess his advisers, augured his White House staffing arrangement and his passive administrative style. In contrast, Clinton's penchant for details, his involvement in campaign strategic and tactical decisions, and his constant desire to assess the public mood before, during, and after he voiced his policy preferences were also reflected in the way in which he did business as president. Similarly, Bush's hands-off style and Gore's hands-on mode of operation suggest the management approach each would pursue as president.

A second way in which campaigns affect governance is through the personnel who are recruited for key administration positions, particularly for those in the White House. Many of the senior aides in the White House have also served in the inner circles of presidential campaigns, as have many junior aides. However, the success with which these campaign personnel have made the adjustment to White House staff has been mixed at best.

The relationship between the candidate's organization and the party's organization also impacts on governance. Candidates who circumvent their party and its elected officials in the planning and conduct of their presidential campaigns, as Richard Nixon did in 1972, Jimmy Carter did in 1976, and, to a lesser extent, Bill Clinton did in 1992, find it more difficult to mobilize the partisan support needed to bridge the separation of powers and govern effectively. They have less inclination to build a strong national organization and more incentive to convert it into a personal following, responsive to their needs, particularly reelection. When the president leaves office, however, these supporters lose their patron and ultimately their position, although they may reappear in other campaigns or other administrations. When the party loses a presidential campaign, the candidate's organization disintegrates, and the party, blamed in part for the defeat, must try to rebuild itself. Not only does this situation contribute to frequent turnover among national party leaders, but it weakens the party.

STRATEGIC OBJECTIVES

Strategies are game plans, blueprints, calculated efforts to convince the electorate to vote for a particular candidate. They include a basic appeal as well as a plan for implementing it.

Certain decisions cannot be avoided when developing an electoral strategy. These decisions stem from the rules of the system, the costs of the campaign, the character of the electorate, and the environment in which the election occurs. Each of them involves identifying objectives, allocating resources, and monitoring and adjusting that allocation over the course of the campaign. That is what a strategy is all about: it is a plan for developing, targeting, and tracking campaign resources.

Most strategies are articulated before the race begins; others are forged during the election itself. In 1984, Reagan strategists designed an elaborate plan well before the Republican convention. The Bush plan in 1988 and the Clinton plans in 1992 and 1996 were also designed before their respective conventions met to nominate them. In the words of James Carville, principal Clinton strategist in 1992:

> By the time the convention had come, we had spent a lot of time, a lot of money, a lot of research on determining what it was that we wanted to do. By mid-June, . . . we had a pretty good idea of the things that we needed to accomplish, of the nature and depth of our problems and how we wanted to solve them and accomplish our objectives. . . . Strategically, we knew 85 percent of what we wanted to do by late June.[17]

Four years later, the strategic plan was in place before the nomination process began. It worked so well that the campaign did not deviate from it.

In contrast, Humphrey's 1968 strategy, Dukakis's in 1988, and Bush's in 1992 emerged after their nominations and in the midst of their presidential campaigns. Although Dole's plan was designed before his nomination in August, his aides constantly adjusted it over the course of the campaign, with little apparent success.

Designing a Basic Appeal

The first step in constructing a campaign strategy is designing a basic appeal. This appeal has two principal components: one consists of the emphasis placed on party images and the other on key policy issues. The objective is to frame the electoral choice in as advantageous a manner as possible to the candidate and party.

Partisan Images. All things being equal, the candidates of the dominant party have an advantage which they try to maximize by emphasizing their partisan affiliation, lauding their partisan heroes, and making a blatant partisan appeal. When the Democrats were the majority, their candidates traditionally clothed themselves in the garb of their party. During the same period, the Republicans did not. Eisenhower, Nixon, and Ford downplayed partisan references, pointing instead to their personal qualifications and positions on certain types of issues. As the gap between the two parties narrowed, however, Republican candidates became more willing to wear a partisan label. Today both major party candidates wear that label proudly.

Identifying with the party is only one way in which the partisan orientations of the electorate are activated and reinforced. Recalling the popular images of the party is another. For the Democrats, common economic interests are still the most compelling link that unites their electoral coalition. Perceived as the party of the average person, the party that got the country out of the Great Depression, the party of labor and minority groups, Democrats have tended to do better when economic issues are salient as they were in 1992 and 1996.

Democratic candidates emphasize "bread-and-butter" issues, such as jobs, wages, education, and other benefits for the working and middle class. They contrast their concern for the plight of the average American with Republicans' "mean-spirited" approach and with that party's ties to the rich and especially to business. The Democrats' sympathy for the less fortunate, however, has been a mixed blessing in recent years. Beginning in the 1970s and continuing into the

1990s, this sympathy has been perceived by much of the electorate as antithetical to the interests of the middle class. Exploiting this perception, Republicans have repeatedly criticized their liberal "tax-and-spend," big government opponents.

Bill Clinton sought to reassert his party's middle-class appeal in his presidential campaigns. Calling himself a "New Democrat," Clinton took pains to distinguish his own moderate policy orientation from the more liberal views of his Democratic predecessors and the more conservative positions of his Republican opponents. He projected himself as a change-oriented candidate in 1992 and as a builder of progress in 1996. In contrast, Al Gore took a more populist approach in 2000, initially emphasizing his desire to help working families and later pitching his appeal to middle-class voters.

Whereas economic issues have tended to unite the Democrats, social issues have been more divisive. Since the 1970s, Republican presidential candidates have taken advantage of these differences by focusing on those issues that divide Democrats: public school vouchers, private investment of Social Security funds, and programs that establish preferences on the basis of race (such as affirmative action) or that mandate benefits regardless of sexual orientation. In doing so, they have not only appealed to the fears and frustrations of moderate and conservative Democrats but have reaffirmed their own support for the traditional American values of individual initiative, family responsibility, and local autonomy.

In 1992, and again in 1996, the Clinton campaign effectively countered this Republican imagery by taking policy positions that promoted family and community values, personal safety, and a less intrusive role for government. In 2000, it was the Republican candidate, George W. Bush, who occupied the political center, thereby muting the more conservative social policy views of the congressional Republican majority. The issue of abortion, however, is one that continues to offer clear-cut alternatives between the parties and their nominees.

When foreign and national security issues have been salient, Republican candidates have traditionally done better. This is why they tend to stress these issues in their campaigns. Not only does the more favorable perception Republicans have enjoyed in this area help their candidates, it also reduces the impact of partisanship on voting since international concerns have usually not engendered the same degree of partisanship that domestic issues have.

In 1952, Eisenhower campaigned on the theme "Communism, Corruption, and Korea," projecting himself as the candidate most qualified to end the war. Nixon took a similar tack in 1968, linking Humphrey to the Johnson administration and the war in Vietnam. Four years later, Nixon varied his message, painting George McGovern as the "peace at any price" candidate and himself as the experienced leader who could achieve peace with honor. Gerald Ford, though, was not nearly as successful in conveying his abilities in foreign affairs, in part because he was overshadowed by the expertise and statesmanship of his secretary of state and national security adviser, Henry Kissinger. Reagan, despite his own lack of experience in foreign affairs, pointed to the Soviet invasion of Afghanistan and to the Iranian hostage situation to criticize the foreign policy of the Carter administration in 1980 as well as urge greater expenditures for defense; in 1984, he pointed to the increased defense capacity of the United States and to its success in containing the expansion of communism. Similarly, George Bush cited his experience in foreign affairs and his personal acquaintance with many world leaders in 1988. He was unable to "sell" his foreign policy prowess four year later, however. With the Cold War over, the Persian Gulf war concluded, and the public preoccupied with domestic issues, Bush's emphasis on his foreign policy presidency became a liability not an asset. Bush's son, George W. Bush, lacked his father's expertise in foreign affairs and thus did not stress foreign policy in his 2000 campaign although he, along with his vice presidential running mate, Dick Cheney, frequently supported their party's strong military posture.

The general perception that the Democrats are weaker in foreign and military affairs has prompted some of their recent standard-bearers to talk even tougher than their opponents. In his 1976 campaign, Carter vowed that an Arab oil embargo would be seen by his administration as an economic declaration of war. In 1984, Walter Mondale supported the buildup of U.S. defenses, including Reagan's strategic defense initiative. In 1988, Dukakis spoke about the need for the United States to be more competitive within the international economic arena as did Clinton in 1992. In 1996, Clinton pointed to the success of U.S. military interventions in establishing peace and permitting democratic elections to be held in Bosnia and Haiti. Gore reiterated Clinton's theme and emphasized his own foreign policy experience in the House, Senate, and as vice president. He also pointed to his vote in favor of the Persian Gulf resolution in 1991 that authorized the use of armed forces and his support for increased military spending.

Salient Issue Positions. The electoral environment affects the priorities and substance of a candidate's policy appeal. In 1992, the electorate was concerned mostly about the economy, particularly jobs and the federal budget deficit. In 1996, with the economy growing, unemployment low, inflation in check, and the stock market at a record high, the electorate in general expressed satisfaction with the country's economic condition, a situation that favors the incumbent. The salient issues in 2000 were how to extend the prosperity and spend the budget surplus. Gore proposed new federal programs in education, health care, and the environment, with a locked box to conserve the surplus from the Social Security trust fund. Bush emphasized his plan to reduce income tax rates, eliminate other taxes, and build a stronger defense.

In general, economic issues tend to be the most recurrent concerns in American elections. They "hit home" in a way that social and national security issues may not. A poor economy helps the party that is out of power and hurts an incumbent running for reelection. Ronald Reagan drove the economic problem home in 1980 with the question he posed at the end of his debate with President Jimmy Carter, a question directed at the American people: "Are you better off now than you were four years ago?" Similarly, James Carville, chief strategist of the 1992 Clinton campaign, kept a sign over his desk that read, "It's the economy, stupid." He did not want anyone in the Clinton organization to forget the campaign's primary issue. Having a weak economy was a particularly severe problem for President George Bush in 1992 because he faced not one but two challengers who echoed the same theme — economic conditions were poor and the Bush administration was to blame for them.

A strong economy helps the party in power. The economic progress that occurred during the Clinton administration muted Dole's criticism that the economy could do better and would if he were elected. Thus, it is surprising that Gore did not focus more attention on the economic progress that had been made during the previous eight years. In his desire to distance himself from President Clinton, Gore chose instead to emphasize his policy differences with Bush rather than his policy agreements with Clinton. Only in the final weeks of the campaign did he return to the "prosperity now" theme as a reason for keeping him in office.

Creating a Leadership Image

Regardless of the partisan imagery and thematic emphases, candidates for the presidency must stress their own qualifications for the job and cast doubt on their opponents'. They must appear presidential, demonstrating those personal characteristics and leadership qualities the voters consider essential.[18]

Accentuating the Positive. A favorable image, of course, cannot be taken for granted. It has to be created, or at least polished. Contemporary presidents are expected to be strong, assertive, and dominant. During times of crisis or periods of social anxiety, these leadership characteristics are considered absolutely essential. The strength that Franklin Roosevelt was able to convey by virtue of his successful bout with polio, Dwight Eisenhower by his military command in World War II, and Ronald Reagan by his tough talk, clear-cut solutions, and consistent policy goals contrast sharply with the perceptions of Adlai Stevenson in 1956, George McGovern in 1972, Jimmy Carter in 1980, and Walter Mondale in 1984 as weak, indecisive, and vacillating.[19]

When Gerald Ford and Jimmy Carter were criticized for their failure to provide strong leadership, their campaign organizations countered by focusing on their actions as president, emphasizing those situations in which they were in charge — giving orders, making decisions, announcing policies, negotiating agreements. George Bush tried to use the same strategy to overcome the perception that he equivocated on the issue of raising taxes and failed to design a program to deal with the economic recession. Bill Clinton's reelection campaign also presented him as similarly assertive in his official capacity as president.

For challengers, the task of seeming to be powerful, confident, and independent (one's own person) can best be imparted by a no-nonsense approach, a show of optimism, and a conviction that success is attainable. John Kennedy's rhetorical emphasis on activity in 1960 and Richard Nixon's tough talk in 1968 about the turmoil and divisiveness of the late 1960s helped to generate the impression of a take-charge personality. Kennedy and Nixon were seen as leaders who knew what had to be done and would do it. George W. Bush took another tack. He talked quietly in moderate tones to distinguish himself from the strident rhetoric of Washington politicians and to give added credibility to his pledge to pursue a bipartisan approach if elected. Gore was more aggressive, more partisan, more passionate, and more issue-oriented. He tried to present himself as the more knowledgeable and experienced candidate.

In addition to seeming tough enough to be president, it is also important to exhibit sufficient knowledge and skills for the job. In the public's mind, personal experience testifies to the ability to perform. In 1992, Bush was able to contrast his governing experience with that of his opponents, leaving Perot to emphasize his can-do qualities as a successful businessman and Clinton to emphasize his experience as governor. There was no such contrast between the major party candidates in 1996 but in 2000 there was. Gore emphasized his twenty-four years in government compared to Bush's six years as governor of Texas. Bush, however, used the presidential debates to overcome Gore's experiential advantage. By providing substantive answers to questions about his policy proposals and how he would deal with potential foreign policy issues, Bush tried to demonstrate that he had a sufficient understanding of contemporary problems and the cognitive skills to govern effectively.

Empathy is also an important attribute for presidential candidates. People want a president who can respond to their emotional needs, one who understands what and how they feel. As the government has become larger, more powerful, and more distant, empathy has become more important. Roosevelt and Eisenhower radiated warmth. Carter, Clinton, and George W. Bush were particularly effective in generating the impression that they cared, whereas Al Gore expressed his concern on the basis of the issue positions he took. By comparison, McGovern, Nixon, Dukakis, and Dole appeared cold, distant, and impersonal.

Candor, integrity, and trust emerge periodically as important attributes in presidential image building. Most of the time these traits are taken for granted. Occasionally, however, a crisis of confidence, such as Watergate or the Clinton impeachment, dictates that political skills be downplayed and these qualities stressed. Such crises preceded the elections of 1952, 1976, and 2000. In the first two of these elections, Dwight Eisenhower, a war hero, and Jimmy Carter, who promised never to tell a lie, both benefited from the perception that they were honest, decent men not connected with the "mess" in Washington. George W. Bush made much of the scandalous behavior in the Clinton administration during his nomination campaign, but much less during the general election campaign. However, he often repeated the line that brought him the most accolades before Republican audiences: "When I put my hand on the Bible, I will swear to not only uphold the laws of our land, I will swear to uphold the honor and dignity of the office to which I have been elected, so help me God."[20] In contrast, Gore pledged emphatically not to let the American people down.

Character is important in elections when character issues have preoccupied past administrations. It also tends to be more impotant when less is known about the candidates — at the beginning of their presidential quest. It is less important for reelection because the electorate by then has a basis for evaluating the kind of president that person has made.

Highlighting the Negative. Naturally, candidates can be expected to raise questions about their opponents. These questions assume particular importance if the public's initial impression of the candidates is fuzzy, as it may be with outsiders who win their party's nomination. When Republican polls and focus groups revealed Dukakis's imprecise image in 1988, senior Bush advisers devised a strategy to take advantage of this situation and define Dukakis in ways that would discredit him. The strategy was based on the premise that the higher the negative perceptions of a candidate, the less likely that candidate would be to win.[21] Lee Atwater, architect of this strategy, put it this way: "When I first got into politics, I just stumbled across the fact that candidates who went into an election with negatives higher than 30 or 40 points just inevitably lost."[22]

In 1992, Bush also challenged the qualifications of his opponents. With Clinton's moderate policy positions making it difficult for Bush to paint him as liberal as he had done to Dukakis, Bush chose to emphasize the issues of trustworthiness and candor. But here his campaign ran into a public reactions problem generated by adverse reactions to his negative Dukakis campaign four years earlier and to the allegations about Ross Perot that were leaked to the media by supporters of Bush. Fearing that his first negative commercials would be greeted by a "there he goes again" refrain by the press, the Bush campaign delayed their airing and then introduced them with a touch of humor to soften their effect.[23] Still, voters were leery.[24]

Unlike Dukakis, who chose initially not to dignify Bush's attacks by replying to them, Clinton helped defuse the attacks against him by reacting quickly and directly. This rapid reaction not only deflected criticism, but it enabled the Clinton campaign to keep the media focus on their issue — the economy, not Bush's — the character debate.

Negativity continued in 1996. Prior to the first presidential debate, the Clinton campaign unleashed a barrage of press releases, advertisements, and oppositional research in which Dole's extensive voting record in the Senate was criticized. The senator's votes against such popular issues as Medicare, family leave, and education were highlighted. Subsequently, the Dole campaign countered with accusations of their own against Clinton, noting the discrepancies between his words and deeds.

Negative campaigning persisted in 2000, although for most of the campaign the candidates and parties were careful not to go overboard on character criticism. Gore's credibility, particularly his tendency to exaggerate his own importance and embellish stories he told, became the focus of Republican attacks after the first and second presidential debates in which the Democratic candidate misspoke several times. In contrast, the Democratic criticism of Bush was based on his competence, not his character. Democrats alleged that confusion over details and factual errors indicated that Bush lacked a deep understanding of the issues. In the words of ABC television correspondent Cokie Roberts, "The story line is Bush isn't smart enough and Gore isn't straight enough."[25] The most striking negative attacks came from party and nonparty groups in the final weeks of the campaign.

In summary, candidates try to project images of themselves that are consistent with public expectations of the office and its occupant. Traits such as inner strength, decisiveness, competence, and experience are considered essential for the office, and others such as empathy, sincerity, credibility, and integrity are viewed as necessary for the individual. Which traits are considered most important varies to some extent with the assessment of the strengths and weaknesses of the incumbent. The negative attributes of a sitting president become the essential traits for the next one.

Dealing with Incumbency

Claiming an image of leadership requires a different script for an incumbent than for a challenger. Until the mid-1970s when the media became more critical of presidential performance, incumbents were thought to have an advantage. (See Box 6–1, "An Incumbency Balance Sheet.") Between 1900 and 1972, thirteen incumbents sought reelection and eleven won; and the two who lost, Taft in 1912 and Hoover in 1932, faced highly unusual circumstances. In Taft's case he was challenged by the independent candidacy of former Republican president, Theodore Roosevelt. Together, Taft and Roosevelt split the Republican vote, enabling Democrat Woodrow Wilson to win with only 42 percent of the total vote. Hoover ran during the Great Depression, for which he received much of the blame.

Following the 1972 election, however, incumbents have not fared as well. All have sought reelection, but only Reagan and Clinton have succeeded. Adverse political and economic factors help explain the more recent defeats. The worst political scandal in the nation's history and the worst economic recession in forty years hurt Ford's chances, as did his pardon of the person who had nominated him for the vice presidency, Richard Nixon. In 1980 and 1992, a weak economy, a loss of confidence in the president's leadership abilities, and an anti-Washington mood among the electorate contributed to Carter's and Bush's losses.

Today incumbents are advantaged or disadvantaged based on their perceived performance in office. Having a good record contributes to a president's reelection potential just as a poor record detracts from it. Bad times almost always hurt an incumbent. Rightly or wrongly, the public places most responsibility for economic conditions, social relations, and foreign affairs on the president. That a president may actually exercise little control over some of these external factors seems less relevant to the electorate than do negative conditions themselves, the desire that they be improved, and the expectation that *the president* do something about them.

Building a Winning Geographic Coalition

In addition to designing a general appeal and addressing the leadership-incumbency issues, a winning geographic coalition must be assembled. Since the election is decided by the Electoral College, the primary objective must always be to win a majority of the college, not necessarily a majority of the popular vote.

Electoral College strategies almost always require candidates to campaign in the large states with the most electoral votes. Failure to win a majority of these states makes it extremely difficult to put together a winning coalition. The basic strategic consideration is how many resources should be expended in these states. The answer usually is a lot, probably even more than the proportional share of the vote these states have in the Electoral College.[26]

Critical to designing an Electoral College strategy is determining the most competitive states. These states assume added importance because of the winner-take-all method by which most states allocate their electoral vote. Polling is used

BOX 6–1 ★

AN INCUMBENCY BALANCE SHEET

Incumbency can be a two-edged sword, strengthening or weakening a claim to leadership. Incumbents ritually point to their accomplishments, noting the work that remains, and sounding a "stay-the-course" theme; challengers argue that it is time for a change and that they can do better.

ADVANTAGES OF INCUMBENCY

Being president is thought to help an incumbent in the quest for reelection more often than not. The advantages stem from the visibility of the office, the esteem it engenders, and the influence it provides. The president is almost always well known. A portion of the population may even have difficulty at the outset in identifying challengers although the primaries have now contributed to the name recognition of all the candidates.

Moreover, incumbents are generally seen as experienced and knowledgeable, as leaders who have stood the tests of office in the office. From the public's perspective, this quality creates a climate of expectations that works to the incumbent's benefit more often than not. Since security is one of the major psychological needs that the presidency serves, the certainty of four more years with a known quality is likely to be more appealing than the uncertainty of the next four years with an unknown one provided the performance in office for the past four years has been viewed as generally acceptable.

Translated into strategic terms generally, the public's familiarity and comfort with incumbents permits them to highlight their opponent's lack of experience, and contrast it with their own and their record in office. Carter used a variation of this tactic in 1980. He emphasized the arduousness of the job in order to contrast his energy, knowledge, and intelligence with Reagan's. Clinton contrasted himself with his opponent in another way in 1996. He portrayed himself as the candidate for the future and his seventy-three-year-old opponent as the link to the past.

The ability of presidents to make news, to affect events, and to dispense the "spoils" of government can also work to their advantage. Presidents are in the limelight and can maneuver to remain there. The media focus is always on them. Clinton has emphasized these presidential activities, giving rise to the term *constant campaign*. He all but obliterated the line between governing and campaigning.

All recent presidents who have campaigned for reelection have tried to utilize the symbolic and ceremonial presidency, signing legislation into law in the Rose Garden of the White House, meeting heads of state in Washington or their own capitals, making speeches and announcements, holding press conferences, honoring military and civilians—all behind the presidential seal.

Presidents have another trump card. Presumably, their actions can influence events. They try to gear economic recoveries to election years. They also use their discretionary authority to distribute the resources at their disposal, such as grants, contracts, and emergency aid. They must be careful, however, not to seem overtly partisan. Actions that appear to be solely or primarily for political purposes, such as Ford's pardon of Nixon in 1974 or announcements of juicy federal government contracts can backfire.

The incumbency advantages extend to vice presidents seeking their party's presidential nomination but not as much to their general election campaign. Of the three incumbent vice presidents who tried to succeed to the presidency directly from the vice presidency, only one was successful — George Bush in 1988. Although Nixon lost in 1960, he won in 1968. Gore lost in 2000.

The difficulty that incumbent vice presidents face is that they cannot exert leadership skills from a position of followership. To establish their leadership credentials, vice presidents need to get out of the president's shadow; they have to separate themselves from the president. If they do so on the basis of their policy differences with the administration, it becomes that much more difficult to embrace the successes of that administration. George Bush dealt with this problem by stating that he would pursue Reagan's agenda but would do so in a kinder and gentler way. Moreover, he refused to indicate positions he had taken or advice he had given to Reagan, thereby casting his fate with his popular predecessor and forcing the electorate to judge him in 1988 on the basis of the performance of the administration in which he served. Gore, on the other hand, articulated a populist policy in contrast to the Clinton administration's more incremental, mainstream approach. Moreover, in his acceptance speech at the Democratic convention, Gore made a point of asking voters to support him on the basis of his policy goals and priorities and not primarily for the prosperity of the Clinton years. "This election is not an award for past performance. I'm not asking you to vote for me on the basis of the economy we have. Tonight I ask for your support on the basis of the better, fairer, more prosperous America we can build together."[27] It was not until the closing weeks of the campaign that he began to emphasize the current economic conditions as a reason for supporting his candidacy.

DISADVANTAGES OF INCUMBENCY

Today these incumbency advantages can be offset by equally strong disadvantages. They stem from the dilemmas of contemporary presidents, the persistent media criticism, and the anti-Washington, antipolitician mood of the contemporary electorate.

In their campaigns for office, presidential candidates hype themselves, make promises, and create great expectations. Once in office, however, they find those expectations difficult to meet. With the constitutional system dividing authority; the political system decentralizing power; and public opinion fluid, ambiguous, often inconsistent, and compartmentalized, it is difficult for presidents to build and maintain a governing consensus. Yet their leadership role demands that they do so — hence the gap between expectations and performance.

Persistent media criticism has contributed to the president's problems. With radio and television talk-show hosts railing against presidents, their policies, and their behavior in office, with television and newspaper investigative reporters heightening public awareness of policy problems and inadequate governmental responses to them, with network news coverage generally more critical of incumbents, particularly during presidential campaigns, it has become increasingly difficult for presidents to project a favorable leadership image although Reagan was able to do so and Clinton gained high job approval ratings during his last five years in office.

to monitor a candidate's strength in these states as well as the nation as a whole. As polls reveal preference shifts among registered and likely voters, candidates reschedule their campaign appearances and move their resources from state to state, shoring up support in some and building it in others. Resource calculations are made on the basis of polling data and the relative strength or weakness of the party organization in the state.

In building their Electoral College coalitions, candidates start with their base — areas that have been traditionally favorable to their party's nominees. Following the Civil War, the Democrats could depend on the "Solid South" while Republicans were stronger in the Northeast. Beginning in the 1960s, these areas began to shift their partisan orientation. Conservative, white southerners, reacting negatively to the civil rights revolution, moved into the Republican camp in large numbers. Since 1960, the only Democratic presidential candidates who have been able to win in the South were southerners such as Jimmy Carter (Georgia) who carried much of the South in 1976 but not in 1980 and Bill Clinton (Arkansas) who won approximately half the southern states in 1992 and 1996. Although the increasing social conservatism of the Republican Party has helped that party establish a base in the South, it has also eroded Republican strength in the Northeast, a region that has become more Democratic. With the Rocky Mountain region strongly Republican and the Pacific Coast states leaning Democratic, the focus of recent campaigns has been the Midwest, America's so called "weather vane," a region that tends to reflect the country's mood.

In 1968, Nixon strategists set their sights on ten battleground states, including the big seven — California, Illinois, Michigan, New York, Ohio, Pennsylvania, and Texas — plus New Jersey, Wisconsin, and Missouri, where Humphrey provided the main opposition, and on five peripheral southern states, where George Wallace was the principal foe. In 1976, however, Ford found himself in a situation that required a broad-based national effort because the Democrats had nominated a southerner whose candidacy threatened to retain the traditional Democratic states and regain the South. Carter achieved his goal in 1976, but by 1980 his coalition had disintegrated to the Republicans' advantage.

Reagan's strategy in both 1980 and 1984 was to rely on Republican support in the South and West and concentrate his campaign on the industrial heartland, specifically Michigan, Illinois, and Ohio. By saturating several key midwestern states with money, media, and appearances by the candidates and well-known boosters, Reagan's campaign advisers hoped to make it impossible for the Democratic ticket to obtain a majority in the Electoral College. The Reagan strategies in 1980 and 1984 provided the operational model for Bush in 1988.

Bush's task in 1992 and Dole's in 1996 were more difficult. Trailing in California, New York, and the battleground states of the Midwest, their strategists had to identify those states that they were likely to win and then others in which they could conceivably catch up. Only a handful of the larger states were thought to be Republican or leaning that way at the beginning of each of these campaigns. Adding to this group those states in which the Republicans had a reasonable chance still totaled less than the majority needed to win. The question was, how to make up the difference. Bush chose to concentrate on almost all the battleground states in the Midwest, but he ended up winning only Indiana. Dole kept shifting his focus. Initially, he planned to concentrate on the Midwest. When polls indicated that he was far behind in such key states as Illinois and Michigan, he turned his efforts to New Jersey, Pennsylvania, and Connecticut, in addition to Ohio which remained a principal objective throughout the campaign. Within the last three weeks, the Electoral College strategy shifted once again, this time to California, a state that Dole's strategists had previously written off because of Clinton's large lead. Dole went back to California because his polls indicated that he was making little progress in the mid-Atlantic area and Ohio, and it was the only option that would give him the necessary electoral votes to win.

In contrast, Clinton had the luxury of leading in five of the seven largest states at the beginning of both campaigns and was competitive in at least one other, Florida. Prior to the Democratic conventions in 1992 and 1996, his campaign targeted the five large states in which he was ahead plus fifteen others. Together these states had well over the number of votes needed to win. Clinton's targeting effort proved extremely accurate, winning almost all the states he targeted in 1992 and 1996.

Carter's and Clinton's successful geographic strategies in 1976, 1992, and 1996 seem to offer the Democrats their best hopes of winning an Electoral College majority. Key to any Democratic success is narrowing the Republican's geographic base in the South. By competing in the South, the Democrats force the Republicans to devote resources to these areas. By spreading Republican resources, the Democrats maximize their own flexibility in deciding where to campaign and how much time, money, and effort to devote to a state or region. Key to any Republican victory is maintaining the party's southern vote and cutting into Democratic support in the Northeast and Pacific Coast regions. The Midwest remains a highly competitive area for both parties.

Campaigning in the most competitive states became a real challenge in 2000 because the race was so close in so many states. At one time or another, eighteen states were in contention. The Bush camp devoted its attention and financial resources to five toss-up states: Pennsylvania, Ohio, Michigan, Wisconsin, and Florida. All had Republican governors who had endorsed Bush. All were key to Bush's obtaining an electoral majority. Conceding California, Illinois, and New York to the Democratic opponent, Bush's strategists believed that they needed to win at least three and perhaps four of these states to gain an Electoral College majority. Later other competitive states such as Missouri, Oregon, and Washington were added to Bush's list. In the end, the GOP won two of its five major target states.

The concentration of efforts in these states can be seen by the advertising buys of the candidates and their parties. The Brennan Center of Justice, in conjunction with faculty at the University of Wisconsin, calculated overall and individual state advertising during the presidential campaign beginning June 1, 2000. According to the center, the candidates, parties, and outside groups ran 62,210 ads (through October 8, 2000) in the major media markets of these five toss-up states.[28]

That so many states were in contention throughout the campaign may suggest that a growing national trend is emerging in presidential electoral politics.

The distinctiveness of regions and the old patterns of state voting seem to be weakening while national issues that cross state boundaries are becoming more important. The near parity of the two major parties also contributes to the tightness of the contest. A third factor in 2000 was the third-party campaign of Ralph Nader. Democrats were so concerned about Nader's incursions into their liberal constituency that they launched a major campaign in the final two weeks of the campaign, arguing that a vote for Nader in toss-up states was in reality a vote for Bush. As part of this effort, an e-mail petition, circulated by some of Nader's past and current supporters, urged him to instruct his backers in the key, competitive states to vote for Gore. To counter the Democrat's anti-Nader push, a pro-Bush group, the Republican Leadership Council, ran $100,000 worth of ads quoting Nader's criticism of Gore in Oregon, Minnesota, and Wisconsin.[29]

TACTICAL CONSIDERATIONS

Whereas the basic objectives set the contours of the campaign strategy, tactical considerations influence day-to-day decisions and activities. Tactics are the specific ways by which strategic objectives are achieved. They involve techniques to communicate, target, and time the message so that it has maximum impact. Unlike strategy, which can be planned well in advance, tactics change with the environment and events. The circumstances, in short, dictate different tactical responses.

Sometimes candidates are criticized for overemphasizing tactics at the expense of strategy. This accusation was directed at Bob Dole in 1996.[30] During the Republican primaries and caucuses, Dole emphasized his Senate leadership role in contrast to the less impressive resumes of his challengers; after he had effectively sewn up the nomination and the Senate got mired in controversy, Dole changed his tactical focus and resigned from the Senate to become "Citizen Dole." When the citizenship role did not close the gap with an incumbent president, Dole turned to substantive issues, specifically, his proposal to cut income taxes by 15 percent. When the tax issue failed to generate the desired response, the Dole campaign changed its focus to other policy issues. Failing again to gain much leverage from these issues, Dole turned his attention to the president, first emphasizing Clinton's liberalism and, then, his "character issue." Al Gore also kept changing his tactics when debating George W. Bush. He was confrontational and impolite during their first debate, placid during their second, and physically aggressive during their third, at one point walking toward Bush and confronting him directly.[31]

Reaching Voters

There are a variety of ways to convey a political message, including door-to-door canvassing, direct mail, and mass media. At the local level especially, door-to-door campaigning may be a viable option.

Personal contact is generally considered to have a greater influence on voters than any other kind of campaign activity. It is most effective in stimulating voting. To a lesser extent, it may also influence the decision on how to vote. The problem with personal contact is that it is time-consuming, volunteer-intensive, and reaches a limited number of people. Once candidates get by the early, small-state caucuses and primaries, it becomes more difficult and less cost-effective.

The Kennedy organization in 1960 was one of the first to mount a campaign on the local level. Using the canvass as a device to identify supporters and solicit workers, Kennedy's aides built precinct organizations with the newly recruited volunteers. The volunteers, in turn, distributed literature, turned out the voters, and monitored the polls on election day. They were instrumental in Kennedy's narrow victory in several states. Organized labor and the Christian Coalition are two groups that regularly use grassroots methods to get their supporters out to vote.

In making contacts, candidate organizations usually rely on telephone banks and computerized mailing lists to identify likely supporters. The Perot campaign was particularly successful in using the telephone, specifically its toll-free number, to organize potential voters. Unable to turn to lists of registered voters or past supporters as the major parties could, Perot publicized his 800 number, and his organization recorded the telephone number of all callers, used their names and addresses to compile a geographic map of areas of potential strength, and then proceeded to direct advertising to these areas.

Direct mail, a technique frequently used in fund-raising, has also been employed to distribute information about the candidate and the party and mobilize voters. For conveying a substantive message to a specific audience, direct mail can be extremely efficient, although its effectiveness varies with the level of education of the group to which it is directed. It tends to have greater impact on those who are less educated, particularly those who do not receive a lot of other mail.

Another option is the electronic media: radio, television, and the Internet. More costly than the telephone, radio and television have the advantage of reaching large numbers of people. Although messages cannot be personalized, they can be targeted on radio, cable, and local television to specific audiences, regionally and, on non-English language cable stations, ethnically. (Media advertising is discussed in Chapter 7.)

The reach of radio and television, the size of their potential audiences, and their ability to direct messages to sympathetic listeners or viewers explain why an increasing proportion of expenditures by the campaigns of the presidential candidates are spent on the production and airing of this form of advertising. In 1976, total expenditures on all forms of media accounted for approximately half the campaign budget; by 1992 it was about two-thirds, with television advertising being the largest single expenditure; in 1996 and again in 2000, candidate advertising was supplemented by the parties' generic ads for an even larger expenditure of funds.

Developments in the communications media, specifically satellite technology, have also enabled candidates to design and project their messages to local audiences. They can remain in their studios and be interviewed by local anchors around the country. Electronic town meetings and press conferences have now become standard fare, as has the use of the Internet to raise money, enlist volunteers, provide information, and to the extent possible, mobilize the vote.

No matter how extensive a candidate's use of mass media may be, a certain amount of personal campaigning is still necessary. Appearances by presidential hopefuls create news and generate excitement among partisans. The problem with personal appearances is that they are wearing, have questionable impact, and are not completely controlled even though extensive preparation goes into them.

Orchestrating the Campaign

Whether appearing in person or on television, much advance work is necessary. Nothing is left to chance. Jerry Bruno, who advanced Democratic presidential campaigns in the 1960s, described his tasks as an advance man, tasks that have not changed all that much over the years:

> It's my job in a campaign to decide where a rally should be held, how a candidate can best use his time getting from an airport to that rally, who should sit next to him and chat with him quietly in his hotel room before or after a political speech, and who should be kept as far away from him as possible.
>
> It's also my job to make sure that a public appearance goes well — a big crowd, an enthusiastic crowd, with bands and signs, a motorcade that is mobbed by enthusiastic supporters, a day in which a candidate sees and is seen by as many people as possible — and at the same time have it all properly recorded by the press and their cameras.[32]

Bruno's efforts are indicative of the great lengths to which modern campaigns go to prevent uncontrolled and unanticipated events from marring a presidential candidate's appearance.

Even with all the advance preparations, however, things can go wrong. If the crowds are thin, if the candidate is heckled, if a prominent public figure refuses to be on the platform with the candidate or a controversial one appears, or if the candidate makes a verbal slip, then the event may do more harm than good. Walter Mondale got off to an embarrassing start in 1984 when an early hour Labor Day parade in which he was to appear drew relatively few onlookers. The news was not Mondale but the absence of spectators. Television cameras pictured Mondale walking down nearly-empty streets in New York City. The message was clear — his candidacy sparked little enthusiasm.

Dole was plagued by poor advance work in 1996. Here's how *New York Times* reporter Adam Nagourney described some of the problems the campaign encountered in its closing days as it tried to generate momentum:

> The Republican candidate, an awkward public figure to begin with, these days often finds himself standing in front of small crowds, or shouting over a screechy or failing sound system, or watching as balloons drop or confetti shoots off in the middle of a speech, or taking the stage to such metaphorically challenging music as the "Mission Impossible" theme, or driving off in his limousine and leaving part [of] his motorcade behind.
>
> Sometimes the results are amusing: In Jacksonville, Fla., . . . Mr. Dole found himself speaking at a festive waterfront rally — a classic "photo op" backdrop indeed, except for one thing: just to one side, about fifteen scantily dressed women hung over a railing, taking in the action. Mr. Dole's aides had arranged to have their candidate speak outside a branch of the franchise Hooters.[33]

The arduous and exhausting schedules of modern campaigns have contributed to displays of emotion by candidates that have embarrassed them and damaged their public image, such as when Senator Edmund Muskie seemed to break into tears during a speech in New Hampshire when defending his wife from the attacks of William Loeb, publisher of the state's *Manchester Union Leader*. In the minds of some, the incident made Muskie look weak and not presidential.

Candidates have also made off-color or inappropriate remarks that have caused controversy. When addressing a group of supporters following his 1984 campaign debate with Democratic vice presidential candidate, Geraldine Ferraro, Vice President George Bush stated that he had intended "to kick ass" during the debate. The comment, designed to show a macho George Bush, was greeted with enthusiasm by his supporters but not by his opponents.[34] Sixteen years later, George W. Bush was overheard using an epithet to describe a *New York Times* reporter he apparently did not like.

Some one-liners have worked to the candidate's advantage, at least in the short run. When Republican vice presidential nominee Dan Quayle compared his Senate experience with John F. Kennedy's in his debate with Lloyd Bentsen, the Democratic candidate shot back, "I served with Jack Kennedy; I knew Jack Kennedy; Jack Kennedy was a friend of mine. Senator, you are no Jack Kennedy."[35] Quayle, shaken by Bentsen's blunt reply, remained on the defensive for the remainder of the debate. Bush's "Read my lips" pledge not to raise taxes enhanced his popularity during the 1988 campaign but made it more difficult for him to find an acceptable solution to the problem of the budget deficit once in office and came back to haunt him during the 1992 campaign.

Targeting Messages

Candidates are normally very careful about their public utterances. Knowing that the press focuses on inconsistencies and highlights controversies, presidential candidates tend to stick to a prepared script that coordinates themes, positions, pictures, and words. Reagan did this successfully in 1984. His campaign introduced a new theme every ten days to two weeks and keyed the president's speeches to it. Situations that might have distracted public attention or confused it were carefully controlled. Both major party candidates in 2000 adhered to this practice as well.

Speeches and policy statements are carefully constructed on the basis of survey research and focus group testing. They are targeted to specific groups and put in language that the group understands; frequently code words are used to generate a particular response. The message is often compartmentalized. Groups get only those positions and priorities which the campaign has determined to be most in accord with their interests and beliefs. Other candidate stands and beliefs are not conveyed in these types of targeted messages. The specialized, targeted message can lead to unrealistic expectations and even perceptions of deception if the promises are not realized.

The new technology has facilitated computerized mailings, including e-mailings. Parties and interest groups purchase and maintain lists of their donors and others whose characteristics suggest that they would be sympathetic to the party or group's appeal. In its voter files, for example, the Republican National Committee has collected names, addresses, and relevant political and demographic data on 165 million voters.[36] The GOP lists, broken down by states, are distributed to state parties to raise money, as well as to target and turn out the vote on election day.

The use of the Internet has facilitated a new "activist" approach by parties and groups in which a steady stream of electronic messages are directed toward potential supporters with minimal cost. The danger with mass mailings on the Internet is that recipients may become irritated by all the unsolicited e-mail, often referred to as "spam." To counter this problem, the Republican Web site and others that request e-mail addresses of those who access sites often attach a clause which indicates that messages will be sent to those who supply their address.[37]

Timing Appeals

In addition to the problem of to whom to appeal, what to say, and how to say it, decisions about when to make an appeal are important. Candidates naturally desire to build momentum as their campaigns progress. This goal usually dictates a phased effort, especially for the underdog.

Goldwater's campaign of 1964 illustrates the plight of the challenger. Having won the Republican nomination after heated primary contests against Nelson Rockefeller, the senator initially had to reunite the party. The first month of his campaign was directed toward this end. Endorsements were obtained; the party was reorganized; traditional Republican positions were articulated. Phase two was designed to broaden Goldwater's electoral support. Appeals to conservative Democratic and independent voters were made on the basis of ideology. The third phase was the attack. Goldwater severely criticized President Johnson, his Great Society programs, and his liberal Democratic policies. In phase four, the Republican candidate enunciated his own hopes, goals, and programs for America's future. Finally, at the end of the campaign, perceiving that he had lost, Goldwater adhered to his views and became increasingly uncompromising in presenting his conservative beliefs.

In 1988, George Bush's strategy was also phased. The first stage of his campaign during the Republican convention was to establish his own qualifications for the office as an experienced national leader and a loyal vice president but also a person with his own ideas. Cutting Dukakis down to size was the focus of stage two. In the third part of his campaign, Bush sought to accentuate the positive. The theme of his ads, "peace and prosperity," was designed to generate and maintain a positive feeling in the last month of the campaign. The staging of the Bush campaign was less distinctive and less successful in 1992, as was Dole's in 1996.

The 1996 Clinton campaign was one of the most successful in adhering to a timed plan for communicating various messages to the voters. In the year before the election, the president emphasized his centrist and moderate positions, co-opting many of the Republicans' policy stands in the process. As the nomination campaign got under way, the president talked about family values and showcased himself in various presidential roles, in stark contrast with the Republican candidates who were criticizing one another's credentials for the presidency. During the general election campaign, Clinton remained on his presidential pedestal, emphasizing the accomplishments of his administration and his desire to build a "bridge to the future."

In the 2000 election, both candidates focused on the most competitive states. Bush allocated his resources evenly over the course of the campaign, although he was criticized for being overconfident, failing to campaign energetically, and spending time and money in states where he had little chance of winning in the final week of the campaign.[38] Gore spent more heavily in the final weeks although the Republican National Committee, which had more money on hand than its Democratic counterpart, made up the difference by running advertising on Bush's behalf.

Turning Out Voters

When all is said and done, it is the electorate that makes the final judgment. Who comes out to vote can be the critical factor in determining the winner in a close election. Although turnout is influenced by a number of variables, including the demographic characteristics and political attitudes of the population, registration laws and procedures, the kind of election and its competitiveness, and even the weather (see Chapter 3), it is also affected by the campaign itself.

On balance, lower turnout has hurt the Democrats more than the Republicans, because a larger proportion of Democratic party identifiers have been less likely to vote. Thus, a key element in the strategy of most Democratic candidates since Franklin Roosevelt has been to maximize the number of voters by organizing get-out-the-vote drives, particularly among core Democratic groups.

Traditionally, the party organizations at the state and local levels, not the candidate's central headquarters, mount these drives. A party divided at the time of its convention can seriously damage its chances in the general election. A case in point was the Humphrey campaign of 1968. Humphrey received the nomination of a party that took until late October to coalesce behind his candidacy, too late to register a large number of voters for the November election. Had it not been for organized labor's efforts in registering approximately 4.6 million voters, Humphrey probably would not have come as close as he did.

Whereas Humphrey's loss in 1968 can be attributed in part to a weak voter registration drive, Carter's victory in 1976 resulted from a successful one. The Democratic National Committee coordinated and financed the drive. With the support of organized labor, Democrats outregistered Republicans. Labor's efforts in Ohio and Texas contributed to Carter's narrow victory in both states. A successful program to attract African-American voters also helped increase Carter's margin of victory.

Both sides engaged in a massive grassroots effort to get out the vote in 2000. Like much of the campaign this effort was concentrated in the battleground states. The Republicans claimed to have made 62 million telephone calls, mailed 110 million letters (50 million in Pennsylvania, Michigan, Wisconsin, Florida, and California alone), placed 1.2 million signs in yards across the country, and distributed 1.5 million bumper stickers by election day.[39] Not to be outdone, the Democrats fielded an army of forty thousand volunteers to make personal contacts with potential Democratic voters and mailed an estimated 50 million letters.[40]

Interest groups played a large role in these efforts. The NAACP spent $9 million to raise the level of African-American turnout in the key battleground states, such as Florida where 952,000 African Americans voted in 2000 compared to 527,000 in 1996.[41] The group launched a targeted advertising campaign on television's Black Entertainment Network (BET) and in newspapers and radio, catering to the African-American community. A telephone campaign featuring recorded announcements from President Clinton and African-American leaders and a ministerial effort from the pulpits of black churches also urged members of this racial group to vote. The NAACP went so far as to register over eleven thousand prisoners incarcerated at county jails in the South in the hopes of increasing turnout.[42]

The NAACP was not alone. The National Rifle Association and other gun control advocates, pro-life and pro-choice groups on the abortion issue, business associations, labor unions, environmental organizations, and a host of other groups attempted to mobilize their supporters to vote. However, these efforts had the effect of only increasing turnout by about 2 percent compared to the previous presidential election.

SUMMARY

Throughout much of the nineteenth century, presidential campaigns were run by the parties on behalf of their nominees. The goal was to energize and educate the electorate with a series of public activities and events. Beginning in the 1840s, but accelerating in the 1880s, presidential candidates became increasingly involved in the campaign. By the 1920s, they had become active participants, using radio, later television, and now the Internet, to reach as many voters as possible. To some extent, the electronic media has replaced the parties as the critical link between candidates and voters.

Advances in transportation and communications have made campaigning more complex, more expensive, and more sophisticated. These advances require considerable activity by the candidates and their staffs. Campaign strategy and tactics are now more closely geared to the technology of contemporary politics and run by the professionals of the new technology: pollsters, media consultants, direct mailers, grassroots organizers, lawyers, accountants, and a host of other specialists. Their inclusion in the candidate's organization has made the coordination of centralized decision making more difficult but more necessary. It has also produced at least two separate organizations, one very loosely coordinated by the party's national committee and the other more tightly controlled by the candidates and their campaign staffs.

The job of campaign organizations is to produce a unified and coordinated effort. Most presidential campaigns follow a general strategy based on the prevailing political attitudes and perceptions of the electorate, the reputations and images of the nominees and their parties, and the geography of the Electoral College. The strategy includes designing a basic appeal, creating a leadership image, dealing with incumbency (if appropriate), and allocating campaign resources in the light of Electoral College politics.

In designing a basic appeal, Democratic candidates have emphasized their party label and those "bread-and-butter" issues that have held their coalition together since the 1930s. Republican candidates, on the other hand, did not emphasize partisanship until the 1980s. Instead, they stressed foreign policy and national security concerns, and in the 1990s and 2000, character issues. They also used economic issues to their advantage by contrasting domestic conditions during the Carter and Reagan administrations.

Part of the strategy of every presidential campaign is to project an image of leadership. Candidates do this by trumpeting their own strengths and exploiting their opponent's weaknesses. They try to project a litany of traits that the public desires in their president, traits which are emblematic of the office and resonate with the public mood of the election period.

An established record, particularly by presidents seeking reelection, shapes much of that leadership imagery. Depending on the times, that record may contribute to or detract from the candidates' reelection potential. In good times, incumbents have an advantage; in bad times, they do not. Being president — making critical decisions, exercising the powers of the office — is viewed as evidence of the leadership skills that presidential candidates have to demonstrate.

When allocating resources, the geography of the Electoral College must be considered. Each party begins with a base of safe states. In the 1980s, that base was thought to be larger for the Republicans than for the Democrats. Population movements to the South and the West resulted in a regional advantage for the Republicans, one that allowed them greater flexibility in designing their geographic strategy. In the 1990s, however, the Democrats seemed to have gained an advantage in the Northeast and Pacific coast. Nevertheless, much of the country has remained competitive for the major parties, thereby denying either one a lock on the Electoral College.

The candidates' strategies influence the conduct of their campaigns, but their tactics tend to have greater and more direct effect on day-to-day events. Key tactical decisions include what communication techniques are to be used, when, and by whom. They also include what appeals are to be made, how, when, and to whom.

Other than the belief that flexibility and rapid responses are essential, it is difficult to generalize about tactics. Much depends on the basic strategic plan, the momentum of the campaign, external conditions, and the unfolding of events. In the end, the methods that mobilize the electorate by getting people excited about a candidate are likely to be of the greatest benefit in turning out and influencing the vote. Much of the campaign is filtered through the news media. The next chapter explores this mediation and its impact on the election.

WHERE ON THE WEB?

Many of the *Where on the Web* sites listed in the previous chapters will be useful for the general election as well. Here are some additional sites you may find interesting and useful.

- **CNN/ All Politics: Elections 2000**
  http://CNN.com/ALLPOLITICS
  A combined site for CNN and *Time* magazine, this site contains articles and information on the presidential campaign.

- **C-SPAN**
  http://www.cspan.org
  This site has C-SPAN programming on the campaign as well as candidate appearances, speeches, student surveys, and political debates.
- **PBS Online — Democracy Project**
  http://www.pbs.org/election
  Allows you to participate in polls on the election and discuss current issues; also provides analyses of the campaign.
- **Web White and Blue**
  http://www.webwhiteblue.org
  Internet-oriented site sponsored by the Markle Foundation and featuring a rolling cyber debate on questions submitted by the public, as well as an on-line campaign trail.

EXERCISES

1. Assess how the candidates targeted their appeals. What appeals did they direct toward their partisans, especially to the principal groups in their party's traditional electoral coalition and how did they deal with independents and other party partisans, including those who supported third-party candidates?
2. Indicate the initial geographic strategies of the major party candidates and then how those strategies changed over the course of the campaign. Did these strategies make sense given the strengths and weaknesses of the candidates and their principal opponents?
3. What were the principal differences in the tactics which the major candidates employed in the 2000 election? Which of these tactics were most successful and which seemed to backfire? What do these tactics suggest about the mood of the electorate in 2000?

SELECTED READING

Harvard University Institute of Politics. *Campaign for President: The Managers Look at '96.* Hollis, N.H.: Hollis Publishing, 1997.

McCubbins, Mathew D., ed. *Under the Watchful Eye: Managing Presidential Campaigns in the Television Era.* Washington, D.C.: Congressional Quarterly Press, 1992.

Melder, Keith. *Hail to the Candidate: Presidential Campaigns from Banners to Broadcasts.* Washington, D.C.: Smithsonian Institution Press, 1992.

Morris, Dick. *Behind the Oval Office.* New York: Random House, 1997.

Tenpas, Kathryn Dunn, *Presidents as Candidates.* New York: Garland, 1997.

Thomas, Evan, et al. *Back from the Dead.* New York: Atlantic Monthly Press, 1997.

Troy, Gil. *See How They Ran: The Changing Role of the Presidential Candidate.* New York: Free Press, 1991.

White, Theodore H. *The Making of the President: 1960.* New York: Atheneum, 1988.

———. *The Making of the President, 1964.* New York: Atheneum, 1965.

————. *The Making of the President, 1968.* New York: Atheneum, 1969.

————. *The Making of the President, 1972.* New York: Atheneum, 1973.

————. *America in Search of Itself: The Making of the President, 1956–1980.* New York: Harper and Row, 1982.

Woodward, Bob. *The Choice.* New York: Simon & Schuster, 1997.

NOTES

1. Keith Melder, *Hail to the Candidate: Presidential Campaigns from Banners to Broadcasts* (Washington D.C.: Smithsonian Institution Press, 1992), 70–74.
2. Ibid., 87.
3. Ibid., 88.
4. Quoted in Marvin R. Weisbord, *Campaigning for President* (New York: Washington Square Press, 1966), 45.
5. Historian Gil Troy writes that Lincoln's avoidance of anything that smacked of political involvement was in fact a political tactic that he used throughout the campaign, emphasizing passivity and partisanship. Gil Troy, *See How They Ran: The Changing Role of the Presidential Candidate* (New York: Free Press, 1991), 66.
6. Weisbord, *Campaigning for President,* 5.
7. Quoted in Melder, *Hail to the Candidate,* 104.
8. Ibid., 125.
9. Keith Melder, "The Whistlestop: Origins of the Personal Campaign," *Campaign and Elections* 7 (May/June 1986): 49.
10. William Jennings Bryan, *The First Battle* (1896; reprint, Port Washington, N.Y.: Kennikat Press, 1971), 618.
11. Melder, *Hail to the Candidate,* 129.
12. Weisbord, *Campaigning for President,* 116.
13. Franklin Roosevelt had been crippled by polio in 1921. He wore heavy leg braces and could stand only with difficulty. Nonetheless, he made a remarkable physical and political recovery. In his campaign, he went to great lengths to hide the fact that he could not walk and could barely stand. The press generally did not report on his disability. They refrained from photographing, filming, or describing him struggling to stand with braces.
14. Cabell Phillips, *The Truman Presidency* (New York: Macmillan, 1966), 237.
15. Stanley Kelley, *Professional Public Relations and Political Power* (Baltimore: Johns Hopkins Press, 1956), 161–162.
16. Karl A. Lamb and Paul A. Smith, *Campaign Decision Making: The Presidential Election of 1964* (Belmont, Calif.: Wadsworth, 1968), 59–63.
17. James Carville, quoted in Charles T. Royer, ed. *Campaign for President: The Managers Look at '92* (Hollis, N.H.: Hollis Publishing, 1994), 194.
18. An excellent examination of presidential traits appears in Benjamin I. Page, *Choices and Echoes in Presidential Elections* (Chicago, Ill.: University of Chicago Press, 1978), 232–265. The discussion that follows in the text draws liberally from Professor Page's description and analysis.
19. Dole also pointed to his recovery from a near-fatal injury suffered during World War II that left him without the use of his right arm and hand as proof that he could overcome adversity and was tough enough for the job.
20. George W. Bush, "Acceptance Speech at the Republican National Convention," <http://www.georgebush.com>, August 3, 2000.

21. Following the Republican convention in August, when the public was just beginning to compare the candidates and form their initial impression of the nominees, Bush unleashed his anti-Dukakis campaign, painting his opponent as a free-spending liberal, soft on crime, weak on defense, and short on experience — a Democrat in the tradition of such unsuccessful and discredited Democratic candidates as George McGovern, Jimmy Carter, and Walter Mondale. Dukakis chose initially not to reply to Bush's attacks. His failure to do so compounded his problem, allowing the Republicans to shape early public perceptions of the Democratic nominee. By the time Dukakis did respond, his negative image had been established in the minds of the voters. The Dukakis experience served as a lesson to the Clinton campaign.

22. Quoted in Thomas B. Edsall, "Why Bush Accentuates the Negative," *Washington Post*, October 2, 1988, C4.

23. Fred Steeper, in Royer, *Campaign for President*, 192.

24. A survey conducted by the Times Mirror Center for The People & The Press in early October 1992 found that 50 percent of those who saw the Bush advertisements felt that they were not truthful compared with 35 percent for the viewers of Clinton's ads. Times Mirror Center for The People & The Press, "Campaign '92: Air Wars," October 8, 1992, 2.

25. Cokie Roberts as quoted in Howard Kurtz and Terry M. Neal, "Bush Team Devised Truth Trap That's Tripping Gore," *Washington Post*, October 15, 2000, A11.

26. A political scientist, Steven J. Brams, and a mathematician, Morton D. Davis, devised a formula for the most rational way to allocate campaign resources. They calculated that resources should be spent in proportion to the "3/2's power" of the electoral votes of each state. To calculate the 3/2's power, take the square root of the number of electoral votes and cube the result. They offer the following example: "If one state has four electoral votes and another state has sixteen electoral votes, even though they differ in size only by a factor of four, the candidates should allocate eight times as much in resources to the larger state." In examining actual patterns of allocation between 1960 and 1972, Brams and Davis found that campaigns generally conformed to this rational allocation rule. "The 3/2's Rule in Presidential Campaigning," *American Political Science Review* 68 (1974): 113.

27. Al Gore, "Acceptance Speech to the Democratic National Convention," <http://www.algore2000.com>, August 17, 2000.

28. Brennan Center for Justice, <http://www.brennancenter.org/tvads2000.html>.

29. Laura Meckler, "GOP Group to Air Pro-Nader TV Ads," Associated Press, <http://www.ap/20001028>, October 28, 2000.

30. Dan Balz, "In Challenger's Quest, Tactics More Prominent Than Strategy," *Washington Post*, October 25, 1996, A1, 18.

31. Clinton had used a similar tactic against Dole, moving toward him in their debate when he sensed that Dole was about to unleash a character attack against him.

32. Jerry Bruno and Jeff Greenfield, *The Advance Man* (New York: Morrow, 1971), 299.

33. Adam Nagourney, "Disorders of All Kinds Plague Dole Campaign," *New York Times*, October 25, 1996, A1, 29. It was reports such as Nagourney's that prompted Dole to lash out at the *New York Times* for its liberal bias against him.

34. Another well-reported incident, this one involving Vice President Nelson Rockefeller, occurred in 1976. It too was precipitated by heckling. The Republican vice presidential candidate of that year, Senator Robert Dole, accompanied by Rockefeller, was trying to address a rally in Binghamton, New York. Constantly interrupted by the hecklers, Dole and then Rockefeller tried to restore order by addressing their critics directly. When this approach failed, Rockefeller grinned and made an obscene gesture,

extending the middle fingers of each of his hands to the group. The vice president's response was captured in a picture that appeared in newspapers and magazines across the country, much to the embarrassment of the Republican ticket.

35. Quoted in "Transcript of the Vice Presidential Debate," *Washington Post,* October 6, 1988), A30.
36. John Mintz and Robert O'Harrow Jr., "Software Digs Deep Into Lives of Voters," *Washington Post,* October 20, 2000, A6.
37. John Mintz, "Political Groups Scramble to Find E-Mail Addresses of Likely Backers," *Washington Post,* October 22, 2000, A21.
38. Richard L. Berke, "GOP Question Bush's Campaign," *New York Times,* November 13, 2000, A1.
39. Frank Bruni, "Push to Portray an Aura of Strength for Bush," *New York Times,* October 30, 2000, A15; Thomas B. Edsall, "Parties Use 'Ground War' as Close Race Nears End," *Washington Post,* October 30, 2000, A1, 16.
40. Edsall, "Parties Use Ground War," A16.
41. Susan Schmidt and Joan Mintz, "Voter Turnout Up Only Slightly Despite Big Drive," *Washington Post,* November 9, 2000, A35.
42. David Firestone, "Drive Under Way to Raise Turnout of Black Voters," *New York Times,* October 29, 2000, A1, 22.

MEDIA POLITICS

7

INTRODUCTION

Media and politics go hand-in-hand. The press has served as an outlet for divergent political views from the founding of the Republic. When political parties developed at the end of the eighteenth century, newspapers became a primary means for disseminating their policy positions and promoting their candidates.

This early press was contentious and highly adversarial, but it was not aimed at the masses. Written for the upper, educated class, newspapers contained essays, editorials, and letters that debated economic and political issues. It was not until the 1830s that the elitist orientation of the press began to change. Technological improvements, the growth in literacy, and the movement toward greater public involvement in the democratic process all contributed to the development of the so-called "penny press," newspapers that sold for a penny and were directed at the general public.

The penny press revolutionized American journalism. Newspapers began to rely on advertising rather than subscriptions as their primary source of income. To attract advertisers, they had to reach a large number of readers. To do so, newspapers had to alter what they reported and how they reported it.

Prior to the development of the penny press, news was rarely "new"; stories were often weeks old before they appeared and were rewritten or reprinted from other sources. With more newspapers aimed at the general public, a higher premium was placed on gathering news quickly and reporting it in an exciting, easy-to-read manner.

The invention of the telegraph helped in this regard, making it possible for an emerging Washington press corps to communicate information to the entire country. What was considered news also changed. Events replaced ideas, human interest stories supplemented the official proceedings of government, drama and conflict were featured.

Stories of crime, sex, and violence captured the headlines and sold papers, not essays and letters on public policy. Joseph Pulitzer's *New York World* and William Randolph Hearst's *New York Journal* set the standard for this era of highly competitive "yellow journalism."[1]

Not all newspapers featured sensational news. In 1841, Horace Greeley founded the *New York Tribune* and ten years later, Henry Raymond began the *New York Times*. Both papers appealed to a more-educated audience interested in the political issues of the day. After a change in ownership, the *New York Times* became a paper of record. Operating on the principle that news is not simply entertainment but valuable public information, the *Times* adopted the motto, "All the news that's fit to print." It published entire texts of important speeches and documents and detailed national and foreign news.

Toward the middle of the nineteenth century, newspapers began to shed their advocacy role in favor of more neutral reporting. The growth of news wire services, such as the Associated Press and United Press, and of newspapers that were not tied to political parties, contributed to these developments.

As candidates became more personally involved in the campaign, they too became the subject of press attention. By the beginning of the twentieth century, the focus had shifted to the nominees, so much so that at least one candidate, Alton Parker, Democratic presidential nominee for 1904, angrily criticized photographers for their unyielding efforts to take pictures of him while he was swimming in the nude in the Hudson River.[2] Despite the intrusion into their personal lives, candidates began taking advantage of the press's interest in them, using "photo opportunities" and news coverage to project their image and extend their partisan appeal.

With the advent of radio in the 1920s and television in the 1950s, news media coverage of campaigns changed once again. Radio supplemented the print media. Although it did not provide regular news coverage, radio excelled at covering special events as they were happening. The 1924 presidential election was the first to be reported on radio; the conventions, major speeches, and election returns were broadcast live that year. During the 1928 election, both presidential candidates, Herbert Hoover and Alfred E. Smith, spent campaign funds on radio advertising.

Radio lost its national audience to television in the 1950s, but remained a favorite communications medium of candidates seeking to target their messages to specific groups in specific locations. A cheap and accessible electronic medium, radio continues to be used extensively, particularly during the nomination phase of the electoral process.

The influence of television on presidential elections was first felt in 1952. The most important news event of that presidential campaign was a speech by General Dwight Eisenhower's running mate, Richard Nixon. Accused of obtaining secret campaign funds in exchange for political favors, Nixon defended himself in a television address. He denied accepting contributions for personal use, accused the Democratic administration of being soft on communism, criticized his campaign opponents, and vowed that he would never force his children to give up their dog, Checkers, who had been given to the Nixon family by political supporters. The emotion of the speech, and particularly the reference to Checkers, generated a

President Coolidge Poses with Native Americans   President Coolidge used "photo ops" to attract attention in an otherwise dull campaign in 1924. *(Photo Source: AP/Wide World Photos)*

favorable public reaction, ended discussion of the campaign funds, kept Nixon on the Republican ticket, and demonstrated the power of television for candidates in their campaigns.

Paid television advertising by the political parties also first appeared in the 1952 presidential campaign. The marketing of candidates as if they were commercial products revolutionized the electoral process, particularly the strategy and tactics of the campaign. It enabled those seeking office to craft and project their image as well as attack their opponents' and to do so before a large viewing audience.

Campaigns have now become made-for-TV productions. Rallies and speeches are staged as media events, and on-air interviews are also part and parcel of the electoral process. Political advertising, designed to reinforce positive and negative candidate and party images, regularly consume more than half of the candidates' campaign budgets.

Nor has television broadcasting become the last word. Communication satellites, laser fiber optics, integrated circuits for high-speed transmission of digital images and data, and the Internet have opened additional channels for communicating during campaigns, and candidates are now beginning to take advantage of them. All the presidential campaigns in 2000 had Internet addresses that provided information about the candidates, their positions, and their campaigns.

This chapter examines these developments and their impact on presidential electoral politics. The first section discusses traditional "hard" news coverage of campaigns. It examines how network news organizations interpret political events and how candidates react to that interpretation. The "soft" news-entertainment format is explored in the second section. Here the chapter describes the techniques that candidates have used in recent campaigns to circumvent the national press corps. The third section turns to another news-entertainment feature — presidential debates. It describes their history, structure, staging, and impact on the public. Political advertising is the subject of the fourth section, in which some of the most successful advertisements are presented, the increasing emphasis on negativity examined, and the effect of advertising on the electorate's perceptions of the candidates assessed. The final section looks at the media's cumulative impact on voting choice.

TRADITIONAL COVERAGE: HARD NEWS

The modus operandi of news reporting is to inform and interest the public. But the press does so with its own professional orientation — one that affects what is covered and how it is covered. Political scientist Thomas E. Patterson argues that the dominant conceptual framework in which the election is reported is that of a game. The candidates are the players and their moves (words, activities, images) are seen as strategic and tactical devices to achieve their principal goal — to win. Even their policy positions are frequently evaluated within this gaming aspect of electoral politics, described as calculated attempts to appeal to certain political constituencies. Although Patterson argues that the gaming aspect of electoral politics is most pronounced at the beginning of the presidential selection process, he sees it as an organizing principle for the news media throughout the entire election cycle.[3]

Why do media use the game, often referred to as a "horse race," as a primary focus? The answer is that they are in the entertainment business. Viewing elections as a game heightens viewers' interest. Heightened interest, in turn, increases the size of the audience and, of course, the profits, since advertising revenue is based on the estimated number of people watching, hearing, or reading a particular program or paper.

There is another reason. The game format lends an aura of objectivity to reporting. Rather than presenting subjective accounts of the candidates' positions and their consequences for the country, this format encourages the news media to present quantitative data on the public's reaction to the campaign. Public opinion surveys reported as news are frequently the dominant story during the primaries and caucuses and share the spotlight with other campaign issues, such as the candidates' character, strategies, and tactics, during the general election.

Covering campaigns as if they were sporting events is not a new phenomenon. In 1976, Thomas Patterson found about 60 percent of television election coverage and 55 percent of newspaper coverage was devoted to the campaign as a contest.[4] Michael J. Robinson's and Margaret Sheehan's analysis of the *CBS Evening News* during the 1980 election revealed that five out of six stories emphasized the competition.[5]

What seems to be different today is the increasing emphasis placed on the game and the decreasing attention given to policy debate. Robinson and Sheehan found that the CBS evening news devoted an average of only ninety seconds per program in 1980 to issues of policy, approximately 20 to 25 percent of the total election coverage.[6] In 1984, no policy question received more attention than did Geraldine Ferraro's finances or Ronald Reagan's age.[7] Although policy issues received more coverage in 1988, the focus on policy declined four years later, a surprising finding in the light of the economic recession and concern about budget deficits, business competitiveness, and health care in that election.[8] In 1996, the networks devoted less than one-third of campaign coverage on their evening news shows to policy issues during the Republican primaries but almost half of it to policy thereafter. The horse race aspect which dominated coverage during the primary period declined after that — undoubtedly a product of Clinton's large lead in the polls.[9] The absence of a close race discouraged the press from giving as much coverage to the 1996 election as it did in 1992.

Although there was a close contest in 2000, the amount of election coverage on the evening news shows declined. Less time was given to the presidential campaign by the major television broadcast networks on these news programs than in previous elections, 12 percent less than in 1996 and 53 percent less than in 1992. In contrast, the morning talk and news-entertainment shows provided greater coverage.[10] The focus on the horse race aspect of the election continued to dominate coverage. (See Figure 7–1).

FIGURE 7–1 ★

FOCUS OF CAMPAIGN COVERAGE, 1992–2000

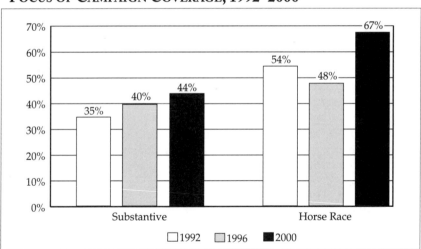

Note: Substantive stories provide extensive discussion of policy issues or the candidates' qualifications or professional background, or both. Horse race stories focus on who's ahead, who's behind, and candidate election strategies. Both substantive policy issues and election strategies/horse race topics may be found within the same story. Based on 622 stories from August 31, 1992 to October 25, 1992; 391 stories from September 2, 1996 to October 27, 1996; and 340 stories from September 4, 2000 to October 29, 2000 from the ABC, CBS, and NBC evening news.

Source: Stephen Hess, "Hess Report on Campaign Coverage in Nightly Network News," Brookings Institution, <http://www.brookings.edu/gs/projects/hessreport/week9.htm>.

The Bad News Syndrome

Once the campaign begins, the principal candidates get approximately the same amount of coverage.[11] Contrary to popular belief, incumbents seeking reelection do not usually dominate the election news.[12] In 1996, however, Clinton did.

Incumbents tend to receive more negative coverage than challengers. In 1980, Jimmy Carter was treated more harshly than Ronald Reagan, and in 1984, Reagan was treated more harshly than Walter Mondale. Vice President George Bush running for president in 1988 fared poorly as well, as did his Democratic opponent, Michael Dukakis. Each received two negative comments for every positive one.

Much the same pattern emerged in 1992. In their analysis of network evening news coverage in 1992, S. Robert Lichter and his associates at the Center for Media and Public Affairs found that 69 percent of the evaluations of Bush — his campaign, his positions, his performance, his general desirability — were negative. Bad news, however, was not restricted to Bush in 1992. Sixty-three percent of all the comments about Clinton were negative compared with 54 percent for Perot.[13]

Bill Clinton got better television coverage on the evening news in 1996. In fact, it was the best coverage he received during his first term as president with positive assessments outnumbering negative ones. Dole, on the other hand, got more negative coverage, contributing to his accusation and the Republicans' perception that the press has a liberal, Democratic bias.

The bad news syndrome continued in 2000 although it wasn't quite as bad as in previous elections. In September, two out of three evaluations of George W. Bush were negative compared to more balanced coverage for Gore. After September, however, Gore received about as much negative coverage as Bush did. Overall, 65 percent of the comments about Bush were negative compared to 62 percent for Gore.[14] (See Figure 7–2.)

What is the reason for the generally bad press that candidates receive? Does it really indicate an ideological bias? Most academic experts do not believe that it does, pointing out that conservatives have been treated no better or worse than liberals. There does, however, appear to be a journalistic orientation that shapes election news coverage and may help explain this bad news syndrome.

That orientation relates to the question, what is news? A fresh face winning and an experienced candidate losing are news; an experienced one winning and a new one losing are not. Similarly, the first time a candidate states a position, it is news; the second time it is not. Since candidates cannot give new speeches every time they make an address, the news media that cover the candidates look for other things to report.

Verbal slips, inconsistent statements, and mistakes often become the focus of attention. Kiku Adatto found, "only once in 1968 did a network even take note of a minor incident unrelated to the content of the campaign."[15] In recent elections there is much more frequent reporting of trivial slips. Roger Ailes, Bush's 1988 media director, explained this phenomenon in the following manner:

> Let's face it, there are three things that the media are interested in: pictures, mistakes, and attacks. That's the one sure way of getting coverage. You try to avoid as many mistakes as you can. You try to give them as many pictures as you can. And if you need coverage, you attack, and you will get coverage.

FIGURE 7–2 ★

GOOD NEWS VERSUS BAD NEWS IN CAMPAIGN 2000

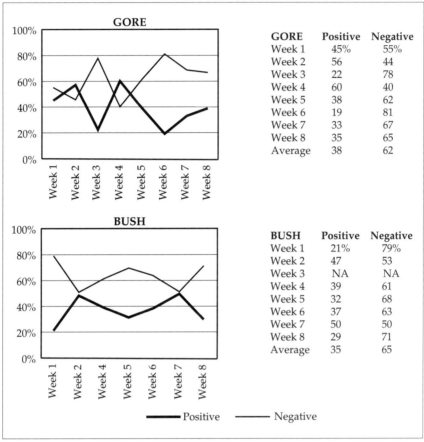

GORE	Positive	Negative
Week 1	45%	55%
Week 2	56	44
Week 3	22	78
Week 4	60	40
Week 5	38	62
Week 6	19	81
Week 7	33	67
Week 8	35	65
Average	38	62

BUSH	Positive	Negative
Week 1	21%	79%
Week 2	47	53
Week 3	NA	NA
Week 4	39	61
Week 5	32	68
Week 6	37	63
Week 7	50	50
Week 8	29	71
Average	35	65

━━━ Positive ──── Negative

Note: Statistics on the percent of positive and negative evaluations based on total number of evaluations in the stories. Explicitly negative and positive statements by nonpartisan sources were considered when judging whether coverage was negative or positive. Based on 340 stories from September 4, 2000 to October 29, 2000 from the ABC, CBS, and NBC evening news. During Week 3 there were too few evaluations in the TV networks evening news for George W. Bush to report meaningful results. Between September 4 and October 27, 2000, PBS's *NewsHour with Jim Lehrer* had 57 percent positive and 43 percent negative evaluations of Bush, and 56 percent positive and 44 percent negative evaluations of Gore (based on evaluations in 177 stories).

Source: Stephen Hess, "Hess Report on Campaign Coverage in Nightly Network News," Brookings Institution, <http://www.brookings.edu/gs/projects/hessreport/week9.htm>.

It's my orchestra pit theory of politics. If you have two guys on stage and one says, "I have a solution to the Middle East problem," and the other guy falls in the orchestra pit, who do you think is going to be on the evening news?[16]

The news media's penchant for reporting embarrassing misstatements encourages the candidates not to be spontaneous, not to be candid, not to make mistakes.

But it also forces candidates to acknowledge their errors, misstatements, and unbecoming episodes in their past to try to minimize any negative fallout. In 2000, Al Gore admitted making factual errors during the first presidential debate; George W. Bush conceded that he had once been arrested for drunk driving many years earlier.

A candidate's failure to provide the news media with information, pictures, or even the pose they need can be a source of admonishment. Take the comment that ABC correspondent Sam Donaldson made to Michael Dukakis, who was playing a trumpet with a local marching band in the midst of his 1988 presidential campaign. Donaldson reported, "He played the trumpet with his back to the camera." As Dukakis played the Democratic victory tune, "Happy Days Are Here Again," Donaldson could be heard saying off-camera, "We're over here governor."[17]

Television news has an additional bias. As an action-oriented, visual medium, its content must move quickly and be capable of projecting as an image on a screen. Television emphasizes pictures and deemphasizes words; less attention is devoted to what candidates say and more to how people react to their words and images. That is why campaign speeches are laden with sound bites and catch phrases, such as "Where's the beef?" "It is morning in America," "Read my lips — No new taxes," "a bridge to the twenty-first century," and "compassionate conservatism."

From the candidates' perspective, the bad news is magnified by the fact that they do not get the opportunity to tell their own story in their own words on the news that is broadcast by the major networks. The average length of a quotation from candidates on the evening news in 1968 was 42.3 seconds. In 1988, it was 9.8 seconds; in 1992, it was 8.3 seconds. During the 1996 Republican primaries and caucuses, it dropped even further, averaging only 7.2 seconds. There was a slight increase during the general election to 8.2 seconds, but still, according to Lichter and associates, journalists were on the air six times longer than were the candidates.[18] The same pattern was evident in 2000. The average sound bite on the evening news was 7 seconds for the major party candidates with Gore averaging a second more than Bush. In the average news story, correspondents were on camera seven times longer than were the candidates.[19] The bottom line is that it is the networks' anchors and correspondents, not the candidates, who present the election to the voters.

The Story Line

In addition to the presumption about the nature of news and the format in which it is portrayed, there is also a framework into which that news is fitted. According to Patterson, a dominant story line emerges and much of the campaign is explained in terms of it. In 1992, it was Pat Buchanan's surprising showing against Bush that was news, not Bush's easy wins over his Republican rival; it was the conservative-controlled Republican convention and platform that garnered the headlines, not the adulation that greeted Bush and his running mate, Dan Quayle; it was the president's inability to turn the election around, to "hit a home run" during his debates with Clinton and Perot that was news rather than Bush's plans for the future or even the character issues he raised about his opponents. In Patterson's words:

> Bush's bad press was mainly a function of journalistic values. The news form itself affected both the content and the slant of most of his coverage. Bush's story was that of a reelection campaign in deep trouble — much like the story of a baseball team that was favored to win the pennant but stumbled early and never regained its stride.[20]

Patterson describes this story line as the likely-loser scenario.[21] It was the story of the Dole campaign in 1996. Portrayed as a weak opponent, hopelessly trailing the incumbent president, Dole's position in the race was used as the basis for evaluating and assessing the status of his campaign and how his strategy and tactics were or were not working. Unfortunately for Dole, that evaluation was harsh. The news media repeatedly referred to his struggling campaign and his attempts to "jumpstart" it. Thus, the horse race metaphor contributed to the likely-loser scenario into which the press fit the story of the Dole campaign.

For Clinton, the story line was just the opposite. It was that of the front runner who had a large lead and who had skillfully maneuvered to keep it. In this particular story, the press attributed Clinton's lead and inevitable success to a beneficial economic environment, superior resources, especially the perquisites of the presidency, and an extremely well-organized and well-run campaign. The news media's depiction of Ronald Reagan's 1984 presidential campaign was presented in a similar manner and provides another illustration of the press's use of the front-runner script.

Two other narratives, according to Patterson, are the bandwagon in which one candidate builds a larger and larger lead over the course of the campaign as people join the bandwagon and the opposite scenario in which the front-runner loses ground. In the first scenario, an image of strong and decisive leadership generates support; in the second, the image of a weak and vacillating leadership contributes to the erosion. Jimmy Carter's primary spurt in 1976 provides an illustration of the bandwagon; his decline in the general election exemplifies the losing-ground story.[22]

The story line in 2000 focused on the closeness of the race, attributed in part to the weaknesses of both candidates: Gore's personal shortcomings and Bush's lack of depth on the issues. A variant on the competition theme toward the end of the campaign was Ralph Nader as a spoiler for Gore.

Patterson's point is that the press fits the news of the campaign into the principal story rather than creates a new story from the changing events of the campaign. Naturally, the perceptions of the news media affect the electorate's understanding of what is happening.

Impact of the News Media

What impact does the style and substance of election news coverage have on the voters? Studies of campaigning in the 1940s indicated that the principal effect of the print media was to activate predispositions and reinforce attitudes rather than to convert voters. Newspapers and magazines provided information, but primarily to those who were most committed. The most committed, in turn, used the information to support their beliefs. Weeding out opposing views, they insulated themselves from unfavorable news and from opinions that conflicted with their own.[23]

With the bulk of campaign information coming from print press in the 1940s, voters, especially partisan voters, tended to minimize cross-pressures and to strengthen their own preexisting judgments. In contrast, the less committed also had less incentive to become informed. They maintained their ignorance by avoiding information about the campaign. The format of newspapers and magazines facilitated this kind of selective perception and retention.

Television might have been expected to change this because it exposed the less committed to more information and the more committed to other points of view. Avoidance became more difficult, although the use of remote control devices has rendered viewers less captive to the picture on a particular channel than they were when television first began to cover presidential campaigns.

Television news also compartmentalizes more than the print press. The evening news fits a large number of stories into a thirty-minute broadcast (which includes only twenty-three minutes of news). Of necessity, this time frame restricts the coverage that can be given to each item. Campaign stories average ninety seconds or less on the evening news, the equivalent of only a few paragraphs of a printed account. Their brevity helps explain why viewers do not retain much information from television coverage of them.

Nonetheless, television news coverage is still influential if only because more people follow presidential campaigns on television than through any other medium. It is the prime source of news for approximately two-thirds of the population. Newspapers are a distant second, with only 20 percent of the population, but the most informed voters, listing them as their principal source of news.[24] Radio and magazines trail far behind.

Television news helps set the agenda for the campaign. Its emphasis or lack of emphasis on certain issues affects the content of the debate, the attention that the candidates must give to specific policy and character issues, and to some extent, the kinds of responses they have to provide. Media expert Michael J. Robinson believes that this agenda-shaping function directly affects the political elites. He argues that the press influences how political elites "relate" to the mass public and how those elites communicate political options.[25] In this way the news media affect the conduct of the campaign, which in turn influences the decisions of the electorate.

The news media may have a direct influence on voters as well. They provide information that colors public perceptions of the candidates and parties, particularly the candidates' qualifications for leadership. From the perspective of those running for office, this coverage is harsh and the reporters and commentators are adversarial. The candidates' motives are questioned, their speeches are summarized into a very few points or sound bites, their misstatements are highlighted, their character frailties emphasized, and their policy positions criticized and often portrayed as inconsistent, even hypocritical.

Yet even with all the negative coverage, most candidates conclude that critical coverage is better than no coverage at all. Media attention conveys legitimacy; it is an indication that the press takes a candidate seriously. That is why candidates try their utmost to get coverage and to try to shape it in a favorable way.

But they also try to reach around the national press corps to appeal to their audiences directly. One of the newer methods for circumventing critical press coverage involves appearances on talk-entertainment shows, the nontraditional news media.

NONTRADITIONAL COVERAGE: SOFT NEWS

A major change in media politics in the 1990s has been the use of a soft news format by the major party candidates. Pioneered by Ross Perot on television and Jerry Brown on radio in 1992, this new format provides a candidate-friendly environment in which to engage the electorate. Appearances on the morning and evening television news-talk shows (such as CBS's *The Early Show*, ABC's *Good Morning America*, NBC's *Today*, CNN's *Larry King Live*) and syndicated programs on these and other networks including MTV have now become commonplace.

Even incumbent presidents are expected to use this medium in their quest for reelection. Bush initially resisted in 1992, and when he finally consented to talk show interviews, he appeared ill at ease, especially on MTV. Bill Clinton was just the opposite. His appearance on the *Arsenio Hall Show* before the Democratic convention in 1992, wearing sun glasses and playing his saxophone, portrayed him as a "real guy," someone with whom the audience could identify. For Perot, talk show appearances constituted much of his "live" campaign, beginning with his announcement that he might run for president on the *Larry King Live* show in 1992 and again in 1996.

The candidates made the rounds in 2000. George W. Bush did much to strengthen his appeal among women with an appearance on *Oprah*; Al Gore had previously appeared on Oprah Winfrey's popular talk show. Both candidates taped parodies of themselves for a special election edition of *Saturday Night Live* as well as joked with the late-night comedians. Joseph Lieberman also went on the talk-entertainment circuit, but his counterpart, Dick Cheney, did not. Cheney limited his appearances to shows with a news discussion format.[26]

The use of the talk-entertainment format has several advantages for candidates. They are treated more like celebrities than politicians. Their hosts tend to be more cordial and less adversarial than news commentators and reporters. Moreover, their audience is different. People who watch these shows tend to be less oriented toward partisan politics, and thus may be more amenable to influence by the candidates who appear on these programs.

Variations of talk-entertainment format are town meetings and call-in programs in which candidates answer questions posed by average citizens. By interacting with ordinary people, presidential candidates can demonstrate their responsiveness, sincerity, and empathy with the problems people face. Bill Clinton was particularly effective in such a setting during his two presidential campaigns.

There are other benefits of the soft news format. For one thing, it distances candidates from the aggressive "gotcha" style of reporting in which national correspondents frequently engage. Instead of being asked very specific, often tricky, "hardball" questions, that focus on personality, image, horse race issues, and contradictions and ambiguities in the candidates' policy positions, interviewers,

Clinton on the *Arsenio Hall Show* To reach larger, less politically involved audiences in 1992, presidential candidates appeared on entertainment shows. Here Bill Clinton plays his saxophone for Arsenio Hall. This appearance, like one on MTV, contrasted the younger, "swinging" Clinton with George Bush—a contrast that worked to Clinton's advantage. *(Photo Source: AP/Wide World Photos)*

audience, or call-in participants tend to ask "softer" questions that are more straightforward, issue-oriented, and easier to answer, questions which may even have been screened in advance by program producers. And the candidates can give longer answers that are broadcast in their entirety rather than in one or two sound bites. George W. Bush spoke for thirteen minutes on a single appearance on the *Late Show with David Letterman* in October—longer than the total time he appeared on the evening news of three television broadcast networks during the *entire* month of October. Similarly, Gore appeared on Letterman's show in September for more time than he appeared on the three evening news shows during that whole month.[27] Another advantage of doing the talk-entertainment circuit is that the candidates' appearances themselves may be newsworthy, thereby generating an even larger impact for the candidates when clips of their comments are rebroadcast or summarized on the news. Nor are the expenses associated with appearances on these shows comparable to the costs of staging a major media event.

The larger audience, the higher comfort level, and the greater ability of candidates to project their desired images and present seemingly spontaneous but often carefully crafted answers suggest that this soft news format will continue to be used by presidential campaigns to circumvent the national press corps and reach a portion of the general public directly.

PRESIDENTIAL DEBATES

Debates represent another "entertainment" component of presidential campaigns, one which candidates, particularly those who are behind, find useful. They see them as an opportunity to improve their own images and damage their opponents'. Unlike most of their campaign rhetoric — speeches, statements, and responses to questions — debates are live and unedited although the formats limit the time for responses, and the candidates' answers are usually carefully rehearsed. Nonetheless, debates give candidates greater latitude to present their thoughts as they wish them presented. That is why candidates like them. The news media also like the debate format because it generates interest and facilitates comparison among the candidates. It is a newsworthy event that fits within the game motif.

The first series of televised debates occurred in 1960. John Kennedy used them to counter the impression that he was too young and inexperienced. Richard Nixon, on the other hand, sought to maintain his stature as Dwight Eisenhower's knowledgeable and competent vice president and the obvious person to succeed his "boss" in office.

In the three elections that followed, Lyndon Johnson and then Nixon, both ahead in the polls, saw no advantage in debating their opponents and refused to do so. Gerald Ford, however, trailing Jimmy Carter in preelection polls in autumn 1976, saw debates as his best opportunity to win in November. The Carter camp, on the other hand, saw them as a means of shoring up their support. In 1980, the rationale was similar. From Reagan's perspective, it was a way to reassure the electorate about himself and his qualifications for office. For Carter, it was another chance to emphasize the differences between himself and Reagan, between their parties, and between their issue and ideological positions.

By 1984, presidential debates had become so much a part of presidential campaigns that even incumbents could not avoid them without making their avoidance a major campaign issue. Thus, Ronald Reagan was forced by the pressures of public opinion to debate Walter Mondale, even though he stood to gain little and could have lost much from their face-to-face encounter. And in the 1992 election, George Bush's initial refusal to accept a plan for a series of campaign debates put forth by the Commission on Presidential Debates, a nonpartisan group that had organized the 1988 presidential and vice presidential debates, hurt him politically. Bill Clinton chided the president repeatedly for his refusal to debate. Democrats dressed as chickens appeared at Bush's campaign rallies. President Bush finally relented, telling his handlers, "I am tired of looking like a wimp."[28]

The issue in 1996 and again in 2000 was not whether to debate but whom to include. In 1992, Ross Perot and his running mate, Admiral James Stockdale, were invited to participate, and they did, to Perot's advantage but not to Stockdale's. In 1996, Perot and his running mate, Pat Choate, were not asked. The Bipartisan Commission on Presidential Debates, comprising five Democrats and five Republicans, concluded that Perot's candidacy was not viable, that he had no chance to win the election even though his name appeared on the ballot in all fifty states and the District of Columbia. The commission based its decision on Perot's standing in the polls, which was about 5 percent at that time, and on the judgment of a small number of political scientists and journalists, surveyed by the commission's staff and advisory council, who unanimously concluded that Perot not only could not win the election but would not carry a single state.[29]

The commission employed similar reasoning in 2000. It established three criteria for inclusion in the debates: a candidate had to meet the test of constitutional eligibility (be a natural born citizen, thirty-five years of age or older, and a resident of the United States for at least fourteen years), be on the ballot in enough states to have a chance of winning a majority of the electoral votes, and demonstrate a sufficient level of electoral support by receiving an average of 15 percent or more in public opinion polls. Neither Nader or Buchanan came close to reaching the minimum level of support in the polls. As a consequence they were excluded.[30]

By bringing the candidates together on the same stage at the same time, the debates become major campaign stories, routinely covered by the news media — stories that attract many viewers, more than any other single event of the entire campaign. (See Table 7–1.) Moreover, they tend to freeze the rest of the campaign until they are concluded.

Although presidential debates have now become part of the American political tradition, their number, scheduling, and format are still subject to arduous

TABLE 7–1 ★

PRESIDENTIAL DEBATES, 1960–2000

Year		Number of Debates	Average Estimated Size of the Television Audience (in millions)
1960	John Kennedy v. Richard Nixon	4	77
1976	Jimmy Carter v. Gerald Ford	4*	65
1980	Jimmy Carter v. Ronald Reagan	1	81
1984	Walter Mondale v. Ronald Reagan	3*	66
1988	Michael Dukakis v. George Bush	3*	66
1992	George Bush v. Bill Clinton v. Ross Perot	4*	66
1996	Bill Clinton v. Bob Dole	3*	40
2000	Al Gore v. George W. Bush	4*	38†

*Includes one vice presidential debate.

†The average for just the three presidential debates in 2000 was 40.6 million.

Sources: Estimates of audience sizes from 1960–1992, "How Many Watched," *New York Times,* October 6, 1996, A25. Estimates for 1996, "Debate Ratings Beat Baseball," Associated Press, October 17, 1996. Estimates for 2000 based on ratings by Nielsen Media Research as reported in the *New York Times,* October 19, 2000, A22.

negotiation between the principal contenders and their staffs. In these negotiations each side naturally wishes to maximize its advantages. Candidates who are ahead in the polls when these negotiations occur, usually the incumbent, call the shots. Thus, President Carter refused to include independent John Anderson in the 1980 debate; in 1984, President Reagan set the parameters for the debates with Mondale, as did Vice President Bush for Dukakis in 1988. It was a different story, however, in 1992. With President Bush trailing in the polls, the campaign moving into the late-September–early-October period, and Clinton making an issue of Bush's refusal to debate, the president could not dictate the terms and had to accept a compromise that included formats that he and his advisers initially opposed.

Similarly, in 1996 with Clinton well ahead in the polls and sitting in the driver's seat, the Dole campaign had little choice but to accept the schedule, format, number, and length of the debates that Clinton's handlers proposed. The most important consideration for Dole was that Perot not be included. Dole wanted to present himself as the sole alternative to Clinton. He also wanted to extend the debates as long as possible. The reason was simple. Once the last debate was concluded, he did not want the press to write that the election was effectively over.[31]

The Commission on Presidential Debates proposed four ninety-minute debates in 2000, three involving the presidential candidates and one, the vice presidential nominees. Al Gore accepted immediately, but George W. Bush did not. Instead, Bush proposed debates on two network talk shows, *Meet the Press* and *Larry King Live*, and wanted only to participate in one of the commission's debates. With Gore enjoying a better reputation as a skilled and knowledgeable debater than Bush, the press interpreted the Republican candidate's counterproposal as an attempt to make the debates less formal, have them seen by fewer people, and reduce their impact on the electorate.[32] Although the vice president had stated that he would debate his opponent in any venue, including news shows, he refused to accept Bush's invitation unless and until the governor agreed to accept the bipartisan commission's entire debate proposal, which Bush eventually did.

Preparation

To get ready for the debates candidates take time out of their busy campaign schedules to go over briefing books that their aides compile, view videotapes of their opponents, and engage in mock debates with stand-ins playing their opposite number. This extensive preparation is designed to ensure that there are no surprises, that the candidates anticipate the questions and provide thoughtful answers that are consistent with their previous statements and advertising, and that they make no gaffes or misstatements that can be used against them by the press or by their opponent.

In addition to the concern about substance and rhetoric, campaign media consultants are also concerned about style — how candidates look, how they speak, and how they interact with the questioners and with their opponents. Kennedy and Carter talked faster than their opponents to create an action-oriented psychology in the minds of the viewers. Both tried to demonstrate their knowledge by citing many facts and statistics in their answers. Ford and Reagan spoke in more general terms, expressing particular concern about the size and structure of government. Reagan's wit and anecdotes in 1980, Bush's manner in 1988, and Perot's down-to-earth language and self-deprecating humor in 1992 conveyed a human dimension with which viewers could identify in contrast to their opponents' less "identifiable" responses. Dukakis was particularly hurt by his reply to the question of whether he would favor an irrevocable death penalty for a person who raped and killed his wife. His matter-of-fact, rambling response sealed his technocratic, iceman image.

When George W. Bush was asked about capital punishment in the first debate of the 2000 campaign, he appeared to relish Texas's record as number one in executions. The governor's manner, noted by the press, prompted a question in the third debate about whether Bush was proud of Texas's executions. Sounding much more contrite, Bush answered "no" but defended his decisions on individual death penalty appeals. Similarly, Gore's sighs and expressions of dismay during Bush's responses in their first debate produced a negative public reaction to behavior deemed inappropriate, even unpresidential. Gore was careful not to make the same mistake again. In the second debate he was on his best behavior, so much so that his placid and nonconfrontational style seemed ingenuine to those accustomed to his more aggressive debate posture.

Despite the appearance of spontaneity, debates are highly scripted, carefully orchestrated events. The candidates are coached and rehearsed. They often sound like their stump speeches and ads. Over the course of the debates, there are times when candidates sound like a tape or CD repeating itself. Although most debate participants prepare extensively for them, Richard Nixon in his first debate with Kennedy, and James Stockdale in the 1992 vice presidential debate did not and suffered by comparison with their more polished opponent.[33]

Strategy and Tactics

Much calculation goes into debate strategy and tactics. Candidates need to decide what issues to stress and how to stress them; how to catch their opponents off guard or goad them into an error; whether and how to respond to a personal attack and to criticism of their policy positions. In 1992, Clinton emphasized the need to change policy. In 1996, he took credit for his policies and the good times that followed from them. In 1992, he was critical of Bush on the issues, especially the economy; in 1996, he took the high road as president.

Clinton had three broad objectives in 1992: stay focused on the economy, respond to any personal attack, and ignore Perot. Since he was in the lead, Clinton wanted to avoid making a big mistake. To present a knowledgeable, presidential image, he cited statistics and specific policy proposals and swiftly responded to any personal attacks against him. In one particularly effective response to Bush's imputation about his patriotism for protesting against the Vietnam War as a Rhodes scholar at Oxford University in Great Britain, Clinton said:

When [Senator] Joe McCarthy went around this country attacking people's patriotism, he was wrong. . . . And a senator from Connecticut stood up to him named Prescott Bush. Your father was right to stand up to Joe McCarthy; you were wrong to attack my patriotism. I was opposed to the war, but I love my country.[34]

Bush looked away from his Democratic opponent and down at the podium as Clinton uttered these words about his father, indicating that Clinton's response hit home. Clinton was extremely persuasive in their second town meeting–style debate as well, empathizing with questioners and directing his responses to them. Bush, however, seemed ill at ease in this format. Beginning his answers with such phrases as "I'm a little confused here, . . . I'm not sure that, . . . I'm not sure that I get it. Help me with the question and I will try to answer it," he seemed uncertain of himself and on the defensive. His hesitation, especially in response to a question on how the national debt affected him personally, reinforced the image that Democrats were trying to project that the president "just didn't get it." At one point near the end of the debate, television cameras caught him looking at his watch, thereby conveying the impression that he was uncomfortable and just wanted out. Only in the last debate did Bush seem animated, taking the offensive against Clinton.

In 1996, Clinton took a very different tack from the one he assumed four years earlier. His objective was to look, sound, and act presidential. Stating that he would not engage in personal criticism about his opponent, but instead would stick to the issues, his issues — education, family leave, tobacco, Clinton appealed to his core constituency, particularly women voters. He ignored the trust and ethical issues that Dole raised but moved closer to his opponent and looked directly at him when he raised them.

Dole was in a far more difficult position. Trailing the president in the polls, he had to make the case for change and for himself. To make matters worse, he had to overcome a reputation for being mean-spirited while doing so. In the first debate, Dole tried to achieve his objective by focusing on the substantive policy issues, reiterating the arguments and policy appeals he had made on the campaign trail. In the second debate, still far behind in the polls, he raised the issue of trust and character, presenting himself as a person who keeps his word and suggesting that the president did not keep his. He repeated much the same refrain later in the debate. The president did not take the bait. He did not respond. The debate ended. There was little more Dole could do.

A strategic goal of most candidates during debates is to overcome any negative perceptions that have developed about them and, at the same time, magnify their positive attributes. For George W. Bush in 2000, this meant demonstrating his command of the issues, communication skills, and leadership potential for a government divided by institutions and partisanship. For Al Gore, the task was to contrast his knowledge and experience with his opponent's, distinguish his brand of Democratic populism from Bush's more conservative posture, and convey that he had the strength of character, passion, and people skills to govern effectively.

Bush achieved his strategic goals; Gore did not. Going into the debates with low public and media performance expectations, Bush countered the gravitas issue by presenting his policies in greater detail than he had in his stump speeches; he overcame allegations that he was prone to verbal slips and incoherency by employing well-tested words and phrases memorized from his speeches and ads, and he helped himself on the governing issue by reiterating his desire to soften the strident Washington rhetoric and overcome the partisan divide with a new spirit of bipartisanship and cooperation. Although Gore did well in differentiating his policy positions from those of his Republican opponent, the aggressive manner in which he did so, served to undermine his "I do care, I will help you" appeal.

Normally, the vice presidential debate is not nearly as consequential as the presidential one. Fewer people watch it since it involves the number two players on the team. But the debate can raise or allay doubts about the vice president's capacity to fill in, if something were to happen to the president. In 1988, the vice presidential debate worked to Dan Quayle's disadvantage when his performance confirmed rather than challenged the impression that he was not up to the job. In 1992, Admiral James Stockdale, Perot's running mate, seemed unprepared which left doubts in voters' minds whether he (and by implication, Perot) were qualified for the country's top two jobs. No such concerns were evident about either vice presidential nominee during their one debate in 2000.

Evaluation and Impact

Once the candidates finish debating, the news media evaluate their performance. They use the winner-loser scenario when doing so. Knowing that the press will assess the debates in this manner, the campaigns try to affect the press's evaluation through the use of "spin doctors," luminaries who are made available to the media following the debate. Here's how *New York Times* reporter James Bennet described the Clinton "spin" operation following the first presidential debate in 1996:

> It was not the grove of little red signs, perched at the ends of sticks to make and identify each Clinton spokesman for reporters swarming for comment when the Presidential debate ended here Sunday night.
>
> It was not that the entire Administration seemed to materialize in the basement of the Hartford Civic Center, . . . not to mention Anne Richards and Jesse Jackson.
>
> And it was not that the campaign's five-and-a-half-page, single-spaced critique of Bob Dole's facts rattled over the ABC fax machine four minutes after the debate ended.
>
> No, . . . Mr. Clinton's aides have become so relentless, even zealous, in trying to keep the Dole campaign pressed to the mat that by Sunday night they were spinning even in Spanish.[36]

Dole's spin doctors were on the scene as well but not in the numbers of the Clinton entourage.

Does spin make a difference? With the exception of Perot in 1992 and to a lesser extent Bush in 2000, the numbers do not reveal significant shifts in public opinion following the debate. (See Table 7–2.) In 1976, there was a perceptible

TABLE 7–2 ★

THE IMPACT OF PRESIDENTIAL DEBATES ON ELECTORAL SUPPORT, 1992–2000

1992

Dates	Bush	Clinton	Perot	Other/Undecided
September 28–30	35%	52%	7%	6%
October 8–10	33	51	10	6
October 13–15	34	47	13	6
October 21–22	31	43	18	8
October 24–25	34	43	17	6

Debate dates: October 11, 13 (vice presidential), 15, and 19.

1996

Dates	Clinton	Dole	Perot
September 29	52%	37%	5%
October 8	54	38	5
October 13	54	39	4
October 16	54	41	5
October 17	50	40	6
October 18	52	41	5

Debate dates: October 6, 9 (vice presidential), and 16.

2000

Dates	Gore	Bush	Nader	Buchanan
October 1–3	49%	41%	2%	1%
October 4–6	41	48	4	1
October 7–9	44	47	3	1
October 10–12	45	45	3	—
October 13–15	44	47	3	—
October 16–18	39	49	5	—
October 19–21	41	50	3	1

Debate dates: October 3, 5 (vice presidential), 11, and 17.

Sources: 1992 figures are based on the *Gallup Poll Monthly* (September and October, 1992); 1996 figures are based on ABC News tracking poll of likely voters; 2000 figures from Gallup Poll of likely voters, <http://www.gallup.com>, October 23, 2000.

shift, however, in which media analysts played a part. In the course of a foreign policy debate, President Ford stated that the Soviet Union did not dominate the communist countries of Eastern Europe when in fact it did. News analysts made much of this faux pas, and Ford did not recant his comments for three days. In the interim his image, which had been initially enhanced by the second debate, was seriously damaged.[37] The debate reinforced the impression of many that he was just not up to the job.

Today, instant polls and surveys of focus groups have shortened reactions to the debates and in the process reduced the ability of news media analysts and spin doctors to shape public opinion. In 1996 and again in 2000, the networks reported poll results of preselected groups minutes after the debates were concluded. Table 7–2 indicates public opinion before and after the last three presidential campaign debates.

The Clinton experience in the 1992 and 1996 presidential campaigns testifies to the conventional wisdom that debates tend to solidify partisan support. Those who are more involved are more likely to watch the debates; those who are more knowledgeable are more likely to learn from them; those who are more partisan are more apt to be convinced by them. People root for their own candidates. The debate reconfirms their initial perceptions and predilections.

For weaker partisans and independents, the debates can increase interest and can clarify, color, or even change opinions about the candidates. Before debating, Kennedy was thought by many to be less knowledgeable and less experienced than Nixon; Carter was seen as an enigma, as fuzzier than Ford; Reagan was perceived to be more doctrinaire and less informed than his first Democratic opponent, President Carter. Perot was seen as self-serving, autocratic, and arrogant while Democrats contended that Bush was not up to the task, not sufficiently knowledgeable and experienced to be president. The debates helped each of these candidates to overcome these negative perceptions. But they did not help Mondale, Dukakis, and Dole, at least not with a significant portion of the electorate, which apparently had already decided for whom to vote.

The 2000 debates benefited George W. Bush and hurt Al Gore. Trailing his Democratic opponent going into the debates, Bush led Gore coming out of them. Overall, the Gallup Poll estimated that Bush gained about 7 percent in the polls during and after the period in which the debates were held. According to Gallup, Gore led Bush by an average of 47 to 44 percent in the thirty days preceding the debates while Bush led Gore by an average of 47 to 43 in the fifteen days following them.[38] Bush's largest gain was among independents and women. Gore had sizable leads among both groups before the first debate, but following the last, he was behind among independents and barely ahead among women. Although partisans continued to stick with their nominees, men moved slightly more in Bush's direction.

CAMPAIGN ADVERTISING

Candidates are marketed much like any other commercial product. Advertising is used to gain attention, make a pitch, and leave an impression. The goal, of course, is to get the electorate to do something — vote for a specific candidate on election day.

Media consultants and professionals specializing in political advertising are hired to supplement regular campaign staff. Often referred to as "media gurus," this small group of savvy professionals designs, produces, and targets the advertisements as well as buys time on different stations to air them. Each campaign normally retains a political media consulting firm to coordinate its advertising program.

In 1992, the Bush campaign, unable to secure the return of its 1988 media whiz Roger Ailes, who had also run Richard Nixon's 1968 advertising campaign, turned to a team of Madison Avenue executives who had considerable experience in commercial advertising but not in political advertising. When tensions and differences emerged between the advertising team and senior officials of the Bush reelection committee, the president was forced to replace his media consultants in the middle of the campaign.

The same thing happened four years later to Robert Dole. A dispute between his campaign managers and media consultants over the theme and content of the advertising led to the latter's resignation at the beginning of the fall campaign, the period when the advertising plan usually is being developed, the ads designed, and the time purchased on various media outlets; in other words, it was the worst time for the Dole campaign. The resignations cost the campaign valuable time and thousands of dollars on ads which were designed but not used.

Clinton used established Washington political public relations firms in his two campaigns as did Gore in 2000. Perot employed executives from a Texas advertising firm to help develop, produce, and place the ads of his two presidential campaigns. George W. Bush relied on a New York filmmaker, Stuart Stevens, and a Texas media consultant, Mark McKinnon.

Techniques and Timing

Advertising allows candidates to say and do what they want. The trick is to make it look real. Candidate-sponsored programs are not unbiased, and the public knows it.

To be effective, advertising must be believable. That is why the most effective ads are those which reinforce the news. If ads become news, so much the better. Take the Democrats' 1964 ad suggesting that Barry Goldwater might get the country involved in a nuclear war. Designed to reinforce the impression that Goldwater was a trigger-happy zealot who would not hesitate to unleash nuclear weapons against a communist foe, the ad pictured a little girl in a meadow plucking petals from a daisy. She counted to herself softly. When she reached nine, the picture froze on her face, her voice faded, and a stern-sounding male voice counted down from ten. When he got to zero there was an explosion, the little girl disappeared, and a mushroom-shaped cloud covered the screen. Lyndon Johnson's voice was heard: "These are the stakes — to make a world in which all of God's children can live, or go into the dark. We must either love each other, or we must die." The ad ended with an announcer saying, "Vote for President Johnson on November 3. The stakes are too high for you to stay home."

The commercial was run only once. Goldwater supporters were outraged and protested vigorously, but their protestations actually kept the issue alive. In fact, the ad itself became a news item, and parts of it were shown on television newscasts. The Democrats had made the point, and the news media helped reinforce it.

A daisy girl look-alike advertisement was aired in several battleground states in 2000 by a nonprofit, Republican-oriented group from Texas. Like its famous

Campaign Advertising   The "daisy girl," from the infamous campaign commercial for Lyndon Johnson, just before she was seemingly annihilated by an atomic explosion. *(Photo Source: LBJ Library Collection)*

predecessor, the ad featured a young girl plucking the petals of a daisy, a count-down, and a nuclear explosion. The message was that the Clinton-Gore adminis-tration had jeopardized the nation's security by providing nuclear secrets to China in exchange for campaign contributions, giving China the capacity to unleash a nuclear attack against the United States. The ad ended with the words, "Don't take a chance, please vote Republican."[39]

A public outcry followed the airing of this advertisement. Democrats denounced it as outrageous and irresponsible. The Bush campaign, fearing a back-lash, disavowed responsibility and urged the group sponsoring the ad to pull it. They did, but not before it had become a news item, thereby heightening the attention it received from the press. Unlike the original daisy girl ad, however, the 2000 version did not reinforce campaign themes or messages, and thus had little discernible impact on the electorate.[40]

Not only must media presentations appear authentic; they must seem realis-tic. When candidates are placed in situations in which they do not fit, the visual media can do more damage than good. Such was the case when Michael Dukakis's staff created a photo opportunity in which their candidate wore an army helmet and rode in a combat-ready tank. The objective of the advertisement was to demonstrate Dukakis's support for the military and for a strong national defense policy. The situation, however, was so contrived and the candidate looked so silly that the Republicans countered with a commercial in which a scene from the Dukakis ad was featured along with information about the Democratic candidate's opposition to a long list of military programs and weapons systems.

Political commercials take many forms. Short spots are interspersed with other commercials in regular programming. Longer advertisements that preempt part of the standard broadcast fare and full-length productions, such as interviews, documentaries, and campaign rallies, have also been employed, perhaps less so in recent elections because of their expense. The primary benefits of the short spots are that they make a point, are cheaper to produce and air, and are usually viewed by a larger audience. Longer programs, which may go into greater detail about the candidate's career, qualifications, and beliefs, are generally seen by fewer people, although Ross Perot's novel media campaign in 1992 attracted and maintained a sizable audience even though most of his programs lasted thirty minutes or even longer. He did not have the same success in attracting as large an audience in 1996; it was only about one-third the size of the one he had in 1992.[41]

In addition to length, scheduling is also a critical consideration for campaign advertisers. For the candidate who appears to be ahead, the advertising should appear at a steady rate over the course of the campaign. Nixon in 1968 and 1972, Carter in 1976, Clinton in 1992 and 1996, and George W. Bush in 2000 followed this practice. Reagan in 1984, Bush in 1988 and 1992, and Gore in 2000 did not. Each decided to increase their advertising buys as the campaign progressed.

Most campaign advertising is sequenced as well. At the outset, it is necessary to provide biographical information about family, experience, and qualifications for the office. The Clinton biographical ads were particularly effective in 1992. His biography, entitled "The Man from Hope," presented the personal Clinton from his childhood in Hope, Arkansas, the town in which he was born and initially raised, to his governorship of that state. The film used the town's name to convey Clinton's optimism and his life story to demonstrate his ability to achieve his dreams and the country's.

Both Al Gore and George W. Bush, who had run biographical ads in their 2000 nomination campaign, continued and supplemented those ads at the beginning of the general election campaign. The Gore ads stressed their candidate's career as a journalist, his service during the Vietnam War, and his twenty-four years of public service as a representative, senator, and vice president. Bush's ads pointed to his popularity as governor of Texas and his ability to bring people together.

Once the personal dimension has been established, the policy orientations of the candidates and their priorities for the coming years are articulated. In this phase of advertising, themes are presented and policy positions noted. In the third stage, the candidate frequently goes on the offensive by running a series of ads in which the reasons not to vote for the opponent are stressed. Candidates who are behind may frequently use their earlier stages to "go negative" as well. Most candidates like to end their campaign on a positive note. In the final phase, "feel good" commercials are shown. Replete with catchy, upbeat jingles, smiling faces, happy families, and much Americana, they strive to make voters feel good about supporting the candidate.[42]

Targeting

Targeting is a very important component of political advertising. It enables campaigns to direct their messages to a particular group within the electorate and to do so in the most efficient manner.

Most presidential campaigns go to great lengths to place their advertising where it will do the most good, taking the Electoral College into account when doing so. Clinton targeted his 1996 ads toward twenty-four key states, very similar in composition to the group he targeted four years earlier. A little less than half the ads ran in five of the largest, most competitive states: California, Florida, Michigan, Pennsylvania, and Ohio. Since Clinton advertised early and often, his media consultants avoided the big and expensive news media markets in New York, Washington, D.C., and Los Angeles in the hope that this unusually early advertising campaign would not become a campaign issue. It didn't. Only two stories about Clinton's ads appeared in the mainstream press during this period.[43]

Dole also targeted his ads toward the key states. The problem was that the designation of key Dole states changed over the course of the campaign. At the outset, Dole focused on the Midwest and mid-Atlantic states. When his polls showed little gain from the advertising, he shifted about $4 million to his California budget, thereby wasting much of the effort and money that had been put into the earlier states. The advertising shifted in content as well as the campaign struggled to find wedge issues.

The targeting was even more concentrated in 2000 with both candidates and their parties dueling over the airways in the battleground states. There were, however, differences in their advertising strategies and tactics. Gore ran more ads than Bush by using the less expensive day spots which have a larger female audience. Outside groups—pro-choice, environmental, and gun control advocates—reinforced Gore's effort with millions of dollars of advertising in key states.[44] These groups also waged an advertising campaign against Nader on Gore's behalf. In contrast, groups sympathetic to Bush did not match the media efforts of their pro-Gore counterparts.

There was also a differential in advertising expenditures between the Republican and Democratic candidates in the battleground states with Gore spending more than Bush. That differential was a consequence of a strategic decision that the Bush campaign made to advertise extensively in the expensive media market of California, thereby leaving less money available for the battleground states. From June 1, 2000 onward, Bush and the Republicans spent more than $5.5 million in California whereas Gore and the Democrats were so confident about winning California that they did not advertise on the presidential level in that state.[45]

Both parties' national committees engaged in extensive soft-money advertising on behalf of their presidential nominees. For the first time since the campaign finance law took effect, the parties actually spent more on presidential commercials than their nominees' campaigns. Republicans, who enjoyed a significant soft-money advantage, unleashed a barrage of advertising in the final weeks to counter Gore's.

Images and Messages

The name of the game is image making. With the emphasis on leadership, three dimensions of presidential qualities are usually stressed: one has to do with character and persona; another with issue positions and basic values; and a third with essential leadership skills — vision, charisma, decisiveness, and the capacity for getting things done.

Positivity. Positive campaign advertisements emphasize the strengths of a candidate. For presidents seeking reelection, or even vice presidents running for the top office, one of those strengths is clearly experience in high office. Their advertising pictures them in a variety of presidential roles. One of Jimmy Carter's most effective 1980 commercials showed him in a whirl of presidential activities ending as darkness fell over the White House. A voice intoned, "The responsibility never ends. Even at the end of a long working day there is usually another cable addressed to the chief of state from the other side of the world where the sun is shining and something is happening." As a light came on in the president's living quarters, the voice concluded, "And he's not finished yet." Ronald Reagan in 1984 and George Bush in 1992 used a variation of the president-at-work ad.

Comparisons are also important. Although all candidates must demonstrate their presidential qualities, they also need to distinguish themselves from their opponents. In 1976, Carter emphasized his unusual leadership abilities. His slogan, "A leader, for a change," as well as his less formal appearance and even his decision to use green as the color of his literature in contrast to the traditional red, white, and blue, conveyed "freshness" and set him apart from old-style Washington politicians in general and the two Republican presidents who preceded him in particular. In 1980, Reagan stressed the different kinds of solutions to the nation's old and persistent policy problems, as did Perot in 1992. Perot's ads that year were among the most distinctive ever used in a presidential campaign. Their amateurish quality was purposely designed to set them apart from the slick, smooth, professional commercials of his Republican and Democratic opponents. It was precisely this contrast that Perot wished to convey to the American people. His ads in 1996 lacked the visual appeal and uniqueness of those he aired in 1992. In 2000, Bush's ads emphasized his likability and trustworthiness; Gore's stressed his knowledge, experience, and his caring and crusading spirit as a fighter for the working class. Both candidates' organizations ran mostly positive commercials until the final two weeks of the campaign, but their parties went negative earlier.

Negativity. Ads that exploit an opponent's weaknesses by focusing on character deficiencies, issue inconsistencies, or false leadership claims are referred to as confrontational, attack, or negative ads. This type of advertising has increased since the 1970s.

Negative campaigning, of course, is nothing new. In fact, it is as old as presidential electoral politics. George Washington was called a philanderer and a thief; Andrew Jackson was accused of marrying a prostitute; at the outset of the Civil War, Abraham Lincoln was charged with being illegitimate and black; Theodore

Roosevelt was said to be a drunkard; Herbert Hoover, a German sympathizer during World War I; and Franklin D. Roosevelt, a lecher, lunatic, and a closet Jew whose real name was Rosenfeldt.

What seems to be different today is the increasing emphasis placed on these negative ads by the candidates; the extent to which they seem to have affected the tenor, agenda, and issues of the campaign; and the widely held belief that they have had a major impact on the perceptions of the electorate.

Instead of playing to a candidate's strengths, negative advertising exploits the opposition's weaknesses, using ridicule and stereotyping to drive the point home. As early as 1952 when political advertising first appeared on television, negative commercials were used to highlight potentially vulnerable positions and images of the opposition. And they have continued to do so.

One of the most successful and repeated negative commercials, "the people-in-the-street ad," features interviews with ordinary citizens who are asked about the candidates. The comments usually are edited to highlight a message, and the ads sound like news. In Ford's 1976 ads, for example, most of people interviewed were from Carter's home state of Georgia. "He [Carter] didn't do anything," stated one man from Atlanta. "I've tried, and all my friends have tried, to remember exactly what Carter did as governor, and nobody really knows." The commercial concluded with an attractive woman, also from Georgia, saying, in a thick southern accent, "It would be nice to have a President from Georgia — but not Carter." She smiled. The ad ended.

Negative advertising has been used extensively in recent campaigns. In 1988, researchers estimated that anywhere from 40 to 60 percent of all the advertising broadcast was negative.[46] What has distinguished recent negative ads, particularly those of the 1988 presidential election, was that they played on the fears and anxieties of the American people.

One ad in particular evoked a strong, emotional response. Directed against Michael Dukakis, it featured a mug shot of Willie Horton, an African-American prisoner who had raped a white woman while on a weekend furlough from a Massachusetts jail. (See Box 7–1, "The Willie Horton Ad: 'Weekend Passes.'") Aimed at those who were fearful of crime, of African Americans, and of liberals and their "do-good" social policies, the ad placed Dukakis squarely in the liberal, do-gooder camp.

Sponsored by a political action committee supporting Bush, this commercial was supplemented by other PAC ads featuring relatives of the victims of Horton's crimes, including a man whose wife had been raped by Horton and a woman whose brother had been stabbed by him. More than $2 million was spent on speaking tours for these people who were personally touched by Horton's horrendous acts.[47] The Bush campaign produced ads of its own to reinforce the crime issue.[48]

The cumulative impact of these crime ads was to leave the impression that Michael Dukakis released hardened criminals who then recommitted heinous crimes on innocent victims. By the end of the campaign, 25 percent of the electorate knew who Willie Horton was, what he did, and who furloughed him; 49 percent thought Dukakis was soft on crime.[49] The ads achieved their intended effect.

BOX 7–1 ★

THE WILLIE HORTON AD: "WEEKEND PASSES"

VIDEO	AUDIO
Side-by-side photographs	An announcer says, "Bush and Dukakis on Crime."
Photograph of Bush	"Bush supports the death penalty for first-degree murderers."
Photograph of Dukakis	"Dukakis not only opposes the death penalty, he allowed first-degree murderers to have weekend passes from prison."
Mug shot of Willie Horton	"One was Willie Horton, who murdered a boy in a robbery, stabbing him nineteen times."

Photograph of convict being arrested	"Despite a life sentence, Horton received ten weekend passes from prison. Horton fled, kidnapped a young couple, stabbing the man and repeatedly raping his girlfriend."
Photograph of Dukakis	"Weekend prison passes. Dukakis on crime."

Source: "A 30-Second Ad on Crime," *New York Times,* November 3, 1988, B20.

The amount of negative advertising remained extensive in 1992. L. Patrick Devlin's analysis of candidate advertising in that election found that almost 70 percent of Clinton's ads were negative compared with 56 percent of Bush's. In all, Devlin reports that about half of the presidential ads were negative.[50] In 1996, Devlin found that two out of every three Dole ads was negative. Clinton used only four all negative ads against Dole. One, "Wrong in the Past," went through a litany of popular education and health care programs that Dole ostensibly opposed. The announcer ended the ad by repeating the theme, "Bob Dole, wrong in the past, wrong for our future." According to Professor Devlin, this ad was shown 6,780 times in seventy-five media markets.[51]

Most of Clinton's ads were not totally negative, however. They were ads that compared Dole to Clinton, to Dole's obvious disadvantage. But they were very powerful precisely because they were not perceived as negative.[52] Clinton's media advisers were aware that negative ads had taken their toll on voters.

In the negative ads of 2000, Democrats challenged George W. Bush's record in Texas, accused him of being a captive of special interests, and chided him for proposing policies that would help the rich, bankrupt Social Security, and take away badly needed funds from the public schools for private school vouchers. Republicans, in turn, characterized Al Gore as a proponent of big government, big spending, and big give-away programs. His credibility was sharply challenged at the end of the campaign as were Bush's qualifications for the nation's top job. (See Box 7–2, "The Air Wars of 2000: Excerpts from the Presidential Campaigns.")

On balance, however, the advertisements in 2000 did not seem as negative as in previous campaigns. Until the end of the campaign, most negative commercials were issue-oriented, not character-based. This emphasis on issues muted public criticism. Although people continue to tell pollsters that they dislike negative advertising, political consultants contend that the ads work, and they used them with increasing frequency in the final days before the 2000 vote.

Since 1988 the public has become more leery of the negative ads. Part of their skepticism stems from the legacy of negative advertising, particularly in 1988. Part of it also results from ad watching by major news organizations. Large newspapers, news services, and networks now regularly assign reporters to cover advertising and examine the accuracy of its claims. There has been a steady increase in this type of coverage and a decline in negative advertising.

Impact. People get a lot of information from advertisements, both positive and negative, even *more* than they get from the news. Thomas Patterson and Robert McClure found that voters in 1972 did not learn and retain much information about the substantive issues from television news. They concluded:

1. Most election issues are mentioned so infrequently that viewers could not possibly learn about them.
2. [M]ost issue references are so fleeting that they could not be expected to leave an impression on viewers.
3. [T]he candidates' issue positions generally were reported in ways guaranteed to make them elusive.[53]

BOX 7–2 ★

THE AIR WARS OF 2000:
EXCERPTS FROM THE PRESIDENTIAL CAMPAIGNS

BUSH

Biographical

One of Governor W. Bush's earliest ads presented him in casual clothes sitting alone, talking with common people, and spending time with his wife and family. In the ad, Bush said:

> I think that there's a lot of cynicism today in America because of broken promises. I believe most people expect the best out of elected officials, and when elected officials disappoint them, it creates a cynical environment.
>
> Secondly, I believe oftentimes campaigns resort to mud throwing and name-calling. And Americans are sick and tired of that kind of campaigning. What they want to hear is what's on people's minds and where the candidates' hearts are. I'm going to run a campaign that is hopeful and optimistic and very positive.

Policy/Personal

Run in the final month of the campaign, this sixty-second spot related Bush's issue position to the one personal characteristic that the campaign wished to emphasize in its final days, trust. The ad showed Bush in an open-neck shirt talking to the camera and later interacting with everyday people. Bush narrated the ad.

> I believe we need to encourage personal responsibility so that people are accountable for their actions. And I believe in government that is responsible to the people.
>
> That's the difference in philosophy between my opponent and me. He trusts government. I trust you.
>
> I trust you to invest some of your own Social Security money for higher returns.
>
> I trust local people to run their own schools. In return for federal money, I will insist on performance. And if schools continue to fail, we'll give parents different options.
>
> I trust you with some of the budget surplus. I believe one-fourth of the surplus should go back to the people who pay the bills. My opponent proposes targeted tax cuts only for those he calls the right people. And that means half of all income tax payers get nothing at all.
>
> We should help people live their lives, but not run them. Because when we trust individuals, when we respect local control of schools, when we empower communities, together we can ignite America's spirit and renew our purpose.

Constituency

The Bush campaign played on the governor's multiethnic family and his popularity among Latinos in Texas to appeal to a broad segment of Hispanic voters. In this Spanish-language ad, Bush appeared with his extended family and also with people in the Latino community. The candidate spoke for himself:

Where I come from cultural diversity isn't something you read about. It's something you see everyday. In my core, it's family. I'm proud of the Latino blood that flows in the Bush family. Latinos contribute so much. In return they deserve the full promise of American life. With reforms that say this is your country—this is your home.

Negative

On Halloween, the Bush campaign released an ad entitled "Nonsense" that focused on the misstatements Gore made in support of his programs and misrepresentations of Bush's. The ad pictured Gore in a pharmacy, then froze on a *Washington Times* headline, "Aides Concede Gore Made Up Story" superimposed on the screen; the picture then returned to Gore and the word *nonsense*. The scene shifted to Bush with workers and then back to Gore in his debate with Bill Bradley. At this point an announcer said:

Remember when Al Gore said his mother-in-law's prescription cost more than his dog's? His own aides said the story was made up. Now Al Gore is bending the truth again. The press calls Gore's Social Security attacks "nonsense." Governor Bush sets aside $2.4 trillion to strengthen Social Security and pay all benefits.

Gore: "There has never been a time in this campaign when I have said something untrue."

Announcer: "Really?"

GORE

Biography

Early in the campaign, a commercial titled "Gore's Life as a Principled Fighter" was aired. The story line—Gore fighting for good against evil—presented the candidate's drive, energy, and public-spiritedness as virtues that motivated him to lead a life of service for his country, his causes, and his family. An announcer described his public heroism:

America in turmoil. Al Gore graduates college. His father, a U.S. senator, opposes the Vietnam War. Al Gore has his doubts, but enlists in the Army.

When he comes home from Vietnam, the last thing he thinks he'll ever do is enter politics. He starts a family with Tipper, becomes an investigative reporter.

Then Al Gore decided that to change what was wrong in America, he had to fight for what was right. He ran for Congress. Held some of the first hearings on cleaning up toxic waste . . . made the environment his cause . . . broke with his own party to support the Gulf War. Fought to reform welfare with work requirements and time limits. His fight now is to ensure that prosperity enriches all our families, not just the few. Strengthen Social Security; take on big drug companies to guarantee prescription drugs for seniors; hold schools accountable for results; tax cuts for working families and the middle class.

Al Gore—married thirty years . . . father of four . . . fighting for us.

Policy

Gore sought to stress his support for a Patient's Bill of Rights and contribute to the anti-HMO chorus with a poignant ad that told of the predicament of the Malones of Everett, Washington. Their son, who suffered brain damage as a result of medical misjudgments during his birth, was initially denied private nursing care by the family's HMO even though that care had been prescribed by a doctor as necessary to sustain the child's life. Upon hearing of the Malones' dilemma, Al Gore pitched in to help. Here are excerpts from the ad:

Mrs. Malone: We had gotten to the point of complete desperation.
Announcer: Al Gore heard the story, and fought back.
Mrs. Malone: He [Gore] told the insurance company. "Don't do this. Don't cut this child's coverage."
Announcer: Al Gore got the Malone family the help they needed. But knowing that all families need protection from HMO abuses, he's fighting for a real Patient's Bill of Rights.
Mrs. Malone: Even if he fought half as hard for the people of our country, as he did for my son . . . nobody loses.

Constituency

In the following Spanish-language ad, Gore promised to make college affordable for all and to extend the prosperity to all people in the United States. The ad featured Latinos of all walks of life expressing their accomplishments and hopes for the future:

Woman: We have come far.
Male doctor: But there is more to accomplish.
Student: Things to learn.
Announcer: In the last eight years, record Hispanic employment.
Worker: I am improving every day.
Woman: But I have needs.
Another woman: I want more opportunities.
Announcer: Making college affordable.
Older man: I want to feel secure in life.
Woman: What will the future hold for my children?
Children: I am America.
Young man: I'm on the right track.
Man: But I can do better.
Young woman: That's why I'm voting for Gore.
Announcer: Al Gore will fight for us.

Personality

At the end of September 2000, the Gore campaign began airing a commercial that tied Gore's populism to his experience as a fighter for his beliefs and values. Pictured first in an Army uniform in Vietnam, then with his family, and finally interacting with everyday people, the announcer listed his commitments and achievements:

Vietnam veteran. Father of four. Married thirty years. Al Gore will fight for families.
Tax cuts for middle-class families, including a $10,000-a-year tax deduction for college tuition.
Continued welfare reform with time limits, work requirements.
Force deadbeat parents to take responsibility for their children.
A crime victim's bill of rights to protect victims, not just criminals.

Fight violence and pornography on the Internet, helping parents block out what children shouldn't see.
Al Gore. He'll put his values to work for us.

Negative

Toward the end of the campaign, Gore ran an ad that sharply criticized Bush's Social Security proposal. The point of the ad was to emphasize the impact of draining $1 trillion from the fund's income and allowing people to put that money in private accounts. The audio for the ad follows:

What happens when you promise the same money to two different groups of people? According to the *Wall Street Journal*, George W. Bush is promising young workers a trillion dollars from Social Security to put in private investments. That would cut Social Security benefits for seniors. Bush is also promising seniors that same trillion for their Social Security checks.

So what happens when Bush promises the same to young workers and to seniors?

Answer: One promise gets broken.

Next question: Which one?

Sources: Bush and Gore Campaign Committees, <http://www.georgebush.com>, <http://www.algore2000.com>.

Their findings, which occurred during the era of television journalism when the ABC, CBS, and NBC news organizations dominated the air waves and commanded public attention, have not been refuted by contemporary scholars. Even though there are many other alternative sources of news about the campaign available to the electorate, there is little evidence to suggest these alternative sources of news have produced a more informed public. In fact, recent studies continue to suggest that people learn more from the advertisements about the candidates and their issue positions than they do from the news itself.[54]

THE CUMULATIVE IMPACT OF MEDIA

The time, money, and energy spent on media by the candidates suggest that the mass media have a major impact on campaigns and elections. Why else would so many resources be devoted to them? Yet it is difficult to document the media's precise effect on voting behavior.

Much of the candidates' concern focuses on news coverage. The negativism of the press, the tendency to highlight inconsistencies and misstatements, even the propensity to interpret rather than report events, has led many people, especially candidates, to conclude that this coverage is biased, has adversely affected their campaigns, and unduly influences the results of the election.

Are the media, particularly the news media, really that powerful? Do they affect voter choice? The answer is probably yes, although their impact may depend on the level of public knowledge, strength of partisan attitudes of the electorate, and the initial judgments voters make even before the campaign begins. For knowledgeable partisans, the primary media effect is to reinforce rather than challenge their inclinations to support their party's nominees.

With the decline of strong partisanship in the electorate and the increase in the number of independents, the audience that may be affected during the general election has become larger and is potentially more malleable for a longer period. In 2000, 8 percent of likely voters had not made up their minds for whom to vote by the last week of the campaign according to a survey conducted by the Pew Research Center for the People & the Press.[55] For those without strong partisan identities, an increasing proportion of the electorate, and those who are marginally interested in the election, the news media provide valuable information, according to the Annenberg Public Policy Center and the Shorenstein Center for the Press, Politics, and Public Policy.[56] This information shapes perceptions of the candidates, parties, and issues; and may also motivate people to vote. In general, the media are apt to be more influential during the early part of the election cycle when less is known about the candidates, particularly during the nomination process when partisanship is not a factor.

The bottom line is that voters believe that they have enough information to make a voting decision.[57] When asked if they learned enough from the 2000 campaign to make an informed choice, 83 percent of voters said yes.[58] How much information people *really* need to do so is a question that has been subject to continual debate.[59]

SUMMARY

The mass media have a profound effect on presidential politics: on the organization, strategy, and tactics of the campaign; on the distribution of resources; and directly or indirectly on the electorate's voting decisions. That is why so much of presidential campaign is devoted to media-related activities.

First and foremost, candidates try to affect their news coverage. That coverage is not necessarily favorable. Candidates are often portrayed critically, their statements viewed with suspicion, and their strategies seen as manipulative.

The news media see and report the campaign as a game, fitting statements, events, and activities into various story lines. Their schema highlights drama and gives controversial statements and events the most attention but also downplays deep discussions of policy issues. They also play up personalities and give disproportionate attention to blunders, factual errors, personal exaggerations, and slips of the tongue; they focus on conflict and emphasize the contest.

Candidates naturally try to improve on this coverage. They orchestrate their campaigns for the news media. They choose their words carefully, minimize spontaneity, include sound bites into their speeches, create good visual images, and do all they can to prevent embarrassing situations from occurring. But even with all this preparation and staging, the news of their campaign may not be accurate or complete, and from the candidates' perspective, it is never good enough.

For this reason candidates also try to circumvent the national news media to reach the voters directly. People like to be entertained, so candidates have resorted to various entertainment formats to convey a message, project an image, and energize their supporters. In the past, parades, rallies, and other campaign events were the principal vehicles by which these objectives were achieved. Today, radio and television news interviews, talk-entertainment shows, late-night comedy programs, town meetings, and presidential debates are the most frequently used devices to gain and maintain attention from a sizable segment of the population.

The soft news-entertainment programs have been particularly amenable to a conversational dialogue with the electorate, a dialogue that may itself become a news event. Within this less hostile format, candidates can be more expansive, seemingly more responsive, and better able to display positive personal attributes of themselves. Town meetings are also useful in this respect. They have the additional advantage of allowing candidates to interact directly with the audience, to demonstrate their understanding of their problems and empathy for those who suffer from them, and to present their solutions on a level that the average person can understand and appreciate.

Debates constitute still another entertaining, educational opportunity, particularly for candidates who need to enhance their personal images, convey their policy positions, and demonstrate their communication skills, command of the issues, and commitment to their goals. Not only do debates permit candidates to present their positions on contemporary issues in their own words and often to a large audience, but they facilitate comparisons with their opponents. The news media play a role here as well, covering the debates and often participating in them, reporting the public's reaction as well as their own evaluation, and then integrating the debate into the ongoing campaign story.

Paid advertising is a fourth device, one that candidates and their parties have used extensively to sell themselves and their ideas to the voters. The techniques that they employ, the strategy and tactics they use, even the people who design and target the ads come from the advertising profession, specializing in political commercials.

In recent presidential campaigns, more than half the candidate's budget was spent on media, primarily on the production, airing, and targeting of advertising. Although political commercials tap both positive and negative leadership dimensions, the amount of negativity has produced a backlash within an electorate that has become increasingly leery about the claims of the ads, cynical about the motivations of the candidates, and turned off by the extensive negativism. News organizations have contributed to voters' skepticism by treating ads as campaign news and critically assessing their accuracy.

Most communications analysts believe that media campaigns have an impact. At the very least, they inform the electorate. They may energize supporters. They can affect perceptions of the candidates, parties, and issues, which in turn can influence vote choice. For strong partisans, the cumulative impact of the media is to reinforce predispositions and existing political attitudes; for weaker partisans and independents, however, the impact can also be to alter opinions and help arrive at an informed voting decision. Although one election campaign does not usually change partisan attitudes on a permanent basis, it may cause them to shift, and over a period of time, to change.

The proportion of the electorate whose voting choice is actually influenced by hard and soft news coverage, presidential debates, and candidate advertising is difficult to assess. But campaign managers take no chances. In a close election, influencing even a small number of voters can change the outcome. And from the candidates' and their managers' perspectives, that outcome is what the presidential election is all about.

WHERE ON THE WEB?

In addition to the media outlets previously mentioned in this chapter, here are some others.

- **Alliance for Better Campaigns**
  http://www.bettercampaigns.org
  A public interest group that promotes high standards of media coverage and citizen involvement.
- **Associated Press**
  http://www.ap.org
  The largest news service in the United States. It provides fast-breaking information on its wire service and Web site.
- **Center for Media and Public Affairs**
  http://www.cmpa.com
  Conducts studies on television coverage of the campaign and the "spin" that the candidates and their stands on the issues get.
- **Commission on Presidential Debates**
  http://www.debates.org
  This is the group that plans the debates, selects the cities, decides which candidates can participate, and moderates the discussion on format between the principal candidates. Provides transcripts of presidential debates, past and present.
- **The Freedom Forum**
  http://www.freedomforum.org
  This site provides information on freedom of the press issues, with links to the Newseum, the Media Studies Center, and the First Amendment Center.
- **Newspaperlinks.com**
  http://www.newspaperlinks.com
  Provides links to the on-line editions of local newspapers across the country.
- **The Pew Research Center For The People & The Press**
  http://www.people-press.org
  A nonpartisan research organization sponsored by the Pew Charitable Trusts that surveys public opinion on politics and on media coverage.
- **Politics Online**
  http://www.politicsonline.com
  A good source to access presidential campaigning on the Internet.
- **Washington Post**
  http://www.washingtonpost.com
  A good source of information about the campaign and the mindset of the Washington political establishment.

EXERCISES

1. Contrast the advertisements of the presidential candidates on the basis of their messages, presentations, and target groups. Note also the medium on which the advertisement ran. These ads should be available on the candidates' Web sites.
2. Check the accuracy of the ads you have discussed in question one. Major newspapers such as the *New York Times* and the *Washington Post* and news networks assess some of the campaign advertising.
3. Compare the amount of television coverage given to the horse race and to issues of candidate personality, policy, and issues of strategy and tactics by examining the analysis performed by the Center for the Media and Public Affairs, <http://www.cmpa.com>. Do you feel the coverage was balanced or unbalanced? Did it provide voters with sufficient information to make an intelligent judgement on election day? Did the press display an ideological bias?
4. Take any major event in the 2000 presidential campaign and compare coverage of it by a national newspaper, television broadcast network, a national news magazine, and a major source of information on the Internet. Which coverage was better and why?
5. View one of the presidential debates and note the principal points the candidates wished to make. If elected, did the candidate follow through on the positions he advocated? (These tapes should be available in the C-SPAN archives and at the Commission on Presidential Debates Web site, <http://www.debates.org>.)

SELECTED READING

Ansolabehere, Stephen, and Shanto Iyengar. *Going Negative.* New York: Free Press, 1995.

Buchanan, Bruce. *Renewing Presidential Politics: Campaigns, Media, and the Public Interest.* Lanham, Md.: Rowman & Littlefield, 1996.

Davis, Richard, and Diana Owen. *New Media and American Politics.* New York: Oxford University Press, 1998.

Denton, Robert E. Jr., ed. *The 1992 Presidential Campaign: A Communication Perspective.* Westport, Conn.: Praeger, 1994.

Devlin, L. Patrick. "Contrasts in Presidential Campaign Commercials of 1992." *American Behavioral Scientist* 37 (November 1993): 272–290.

———. "Contrasts in Presidential Campaign Commercials of 1996." *American Behavioral Scientist* (August 1997): 1058–1084.

Diamond, Edwin, and Stephen Bates. *The Spot,* 3rd ed. Cambridge, Mass.: MIT Press, 1992.

Friedenberg, Robert V., ed. *Rhetorical Studies of National Political Debates, 1960–1992,* 2nd ed. Westport, Conn.: Praeger, 1994.

Iyengar, Shanto, and Donald Kinder. *News That Matters: Television and American Opinion.* Chicago: University of Chicago Press, 1987.

Jamieson, Kathleen Hall. *Everything You Think You Know about Politics and Why You're Wrong.* New York: Basic Books, 2000.

———. *Packaging the Presidency: A History and Criticism of Presidential Campaign Advertising.* Oxford: Oxford University Press, 1996.

———. *Dirty Politics: Deception, Distraction, Democracy.* Oxford: Oxford University Press, 1996.

———, and David S. Birdsell. *Presidential Debates.* New York: Oxford University Press, 1988.

Kaid, Lynda Lee and Anne Johnston, "Negative versus Positive Television Advertising in U.S. Presidential Campaigns, 1960–1988." *Journal of Communications* 41 (Summer 1991): 53–64.

Mayer, William G. "In Defense of Negative Campaigning." *Political Science Quarterly* III (Fall 1996): 437–455.

Patterson, Thomas E. *Out of Order.* New York: Knopf, 1993.

Sabato, Larry J., Maria Stencel, and S. Robert Lichter. *Peepshow: Media and Politics in an Age of Scandal.* Lanham, Md.: Rowman & Littlefield, 2000.

West, Darrell M. *Air Wars: Television Advertising in Election Campaigns, 1952–1996,* 2nd ed. Washington, D.C.: Congressional Quarterly, 1997.

NOTES

1. The term *yellow journalism* comes from the comic strip, "The Yellow Kid," which first appeared in Joseph Pulitzer's *New York World* in 1896. The kid, whose nightshirt was colored yellow in the paper, was an instant hit and sparked a bidding war for the comic strip between Pulitzer and William Randolph Hearst. Although the strip's popularity lasted only a few years, the competition between these two media titans continued for decades.

2. David Stebenne, "Media Coverage of American Presidential Elections: A Historical Perspective," in *The Finish Line: Covering the Campaign's Final Days,* ed. Martha FitzSimon (New York: Freedom Forum Media Studies Center, 1993), 83.

3. Center for Media and Public Affairs, "Journalists Monopolize TV Election News," press release, October 30, 2000, <http://www.cmpa.com/pressrel/electpr10.htm>.

4. Thomas E. Patterson, "Television and Election Strategy," in *The Communications Revolution in Politics,* ed. Gerald Benjamin (New York: Academy of Political Science, 1982), 30.

5. Michael J. Robinson and Margaret A. Sheehan, *Over the Wire and on TV: CBS and UPI in Campaign '80* (New York: Russell Sage Foundation, 1983), 148.

6. Ibid., 146.

7. Thomas E. Patterson and Richard Davis, "The Media Campaign: Struggle for the Agenda," in *The Elections of 1984,* ed. Michael Nelson (Washington, D.C.: Congressional Quarterly, 1985), 119.

8. "Clinton's the One," *Media Monitor* (November 1992): 2.

9. "Dole's Summer Doldrums," *Media Monitor* (July/August 1996): 2; "Take This Campaign — Please," *Media Monitor* (September/October 1996): 2–3.

10. Stephen Hess, "Hess Report on Campaign Coverage in Nightly Network News," Brookings Institution, November 11, 2000, <http://www.brookings.edu/GS/Projects/HessReport/week–.htm>.

11. Not only do the news media focus more on the candidates than their policies, but they focus primarily on the major party candidates. When running for their party's nomination, candidates receive coverage roughly in proportion to their popular standing, with the front-runners getting the most. After the conventions are over, it becomes primarily a two-person contest. Minor party and independent candidates tend to receive little, if any, attention, the exceptions being John Anderson in 1980 and Ross Perot in 1992.

12. James Glen Stovall, "Incumbency and News Coverage of the 1980 Presidential Campaign," *Western Political Quarterly* 37 (December 1984): 628.

13. Although partisan sources were equally harsh on the candidates of the other major party, they were not as harsh on Perot, reflecting, perhaps the Republican and Democratic strategies not to criticize him in public. Nonpartisan sources, people who might be considered experts or just plain voters, were more positive about Clinton than Bush. Among both partisan and nonpartisan sources, Perot received the best press. "Clinton's the One," 3–4.

14. Hess, "Hess Report." Another study, this one commissioned by the Project for Excellence in Journalism, found that while the spin was more negative than positive, Bush actually got better coverage than Gore. Jeff Leeds, "Study Finds Negative Media Political Coverage—Especially for Gore." *Los Angeles Times,* November 1, 2000, <http://www.latimes.com/news/politics/elect2000/pres/news2/20001101/t000104484.html>.

15. Kiku Adatto, "The Incredible Shrinking Sound Bite," *New Republic* (May 28, 1990): 22.

16. Quoted in David R. Runkel, ed. *Campaign for President: The Managers Look at '88.* (Dover, Mass.: Auburn House, 1989), 136.

17. Quoted in Adatto, "Sound Bite," 22.

18. "Take This Campaign — Please," 2.

19. Center for Media and Public Affairs, "Journalists Monopolize TV News."

20. Thomas E. Patterson, *Out of Order,* 106.

21. Ibid., 119–120.

22. Ibid., 118–119.

23. Paul Lazarsfeld, Bernard Berelson, and Hazel Goudet, *The People's Choice* (New York: Columbia University Press, 1948); Bernard Berelson, Paul Lazarsfeld, and William McPhee, *Voting: A Study of Opinion Formation in a Presidential Campaign* (Chicago: University of Chicago Press, 1954).

24. Pew Research Center For The People & The Press, poll conducted November 7–10, 1996, Question 15.

25. Michael J. Robinson, "Mass Media and the Margins of Democratic Politics: Non-Transformations in the USA," (unpublished paper, March 1993), 81–83.

26. Lois Romano, "For the Candidates, It's Showtime," *Washington Post,* October 20, 2000, A11.

27. Center for Media and Public Affairs, "Journalists Monopolize TV News."

28. Peter Goldman, Thomas M. DeFrank, Mary Miller, et al., *Quest for the Presidency: 1992* (College Station: Texas A&M Press, 1994), 535.

29. Perot complained bitterly, first appealing to the Federal Communications Commission and then instituting legal action to prevent the debates from being held if he could not participate. Although he failed to stop the debates, he used his exclusion to emphasize one of his campaign themes — the self-serving nature of the two-party system and the need to reform it. The reason that Perot was so agitated was that participating in the debates was part of his campaign strategy. He had boosted his popularity significantly in 1992 by his performance in the presidential debates and hoped to do so again in 1996.

30. Nader protested his exclusion by trying to attend the first debate in Boston, but he was not admitted into the hall.

31. Tony Fabrizio, Dole's pollster, quoted in *Campaign for President '96,* 171.

32. The other networks indicated that they would not carry news shows of their competitors; hence, the debates on regularly scheduled programs would reach a much smaller audience than would the commission's debates.

33. Nixon had closeted himself alone in a hotel before his first debate with Kennedy. He received only a ten-minute briefing. Moreover, he had bumped his knee on a car door

going into the television studio and was in considerable pain. Dukakis had the flu, with a fever of 101 and a sore throat, during his second debate with Bush. Theodore H. White, *The Making of the President, 1960* (New York: Atheneum, 1988), 285; Peter Goldman, et al., *Quest for the Presidency: The 1988 Campaign* (New York: Simon & Schuster, 1989), 387.

34. Quoted in "Campaign '92: Transcript of the First Presidential Debate," *New York Times* (October 12, 1992), A16.

35. In 1996, Jack Kemp foundered on a foreign policy question, allowing Democratic pundits to wonder aloud whether he knew enough about foreign affairs to assume the presidency. Moreover, Kemp was not particularly critical of the vice president or president, something a challenger has to be to make the case for change. His performance so dismayed Republican strategists who were watching it on television that Haley Barbour, the chair of the National Committee was heard to remark, "I told you we should have kept the ball game (the National League playoffs) on one channel!" Haley Barbour, quoted in Evan Thomas, *Back from the Dead* (New York: Atlantic Monthly Press, 1997), 184.

36. James Bennet, "In Spin War after the Debate, Clinton Campaign Takes Lead," *New York Times*, October 8, 1996, A1.

37. Surveys taken at the conclusion of the debate indicated that a majority of people believed Ford had won. After the media played up the Eastern Europe comment and the public had a chance to digest it, the reaction was almost the opposite. By more than two to one, Carter was perceived to be the winner.

38. Gallup Poll, "Bush Gains from Debates as Presidential Campaign Enters Its Final Phase," October 23, 2000, <http://www.gallup.com/poll/releases/pr001023.asp>.

39. Leslie Wayne, "Infamous Political Commercial Is Turned on Gore," *New York Times*, October 27, 2000, A26.

40. In addition to the daisy girl ad which a Republican group ran, there was another controversial Republican advertisement which criticized the vice president's prescription drug policy. During the ad, the work *RATS* flashed across the screen for a split second. The Democrats claimed that the ad was designed to implant a subliminal message, equating bureaucrats to these undesirable rodents. Republicans denied the charge.

41. Nor was he able to purchase the good media times he had four years earlier.

42. Edwin Diamond and Stephen Bates, "The Ads," *Public Opinion* 8 (December 1984/January 1985): 55–57, 64.

43. Dick Morris, *Behind the Oval Office,* (New York: Simon & Schuster, 1996), 139.

44. John Mintz, "Liberals Mobilize against Bush, GOP," *Washington Post*, November 3, 2000, A22.

45. Brennan Center for Justice, press release, October 30, 2000, <http://www.brennancenter.org/tvads2000.html>.

46. Lynda Lee Kaid and Anne Johnston, "Negative versus Positive Television Advertising in U.S. Presidential Campaigns, 1960–1988," *Journal of Communications* 41 (Summer 1991): 54.

47. M. Hailey, "Crime Victims Condemn Dukakis," *Austin-American Statesman*, October 11, 1988, B3.

48. The most potent of these Bush ads, called "Revolving Door," saw inmates walking through a revolving door of a prison with the announcer warning:

> As governor, Michael Dukakis vetoed mandatory sentences for drug dealers. He vetoed the death penalty. His revolving-door policy gave weekend furloughs to first-degree murderers not eligible for parole. While out, many committed other crimes like kidnapping and rape. And many are still at large. Now Michael Dukakis says he

wants to do for America what he's done for Massachusetts. America can't afford that risk!

L. Patrick Devlin, "Contrasts in Presidential Campaign Commercials of 1988," *American Behavioral Scientist* 32 (March/April 1989): 389.

49. Edwin Diamond and Adrian Marin, "Spots," *American Behavioral Scientist* 32 (March/April 1989): 386.
50. Devlin, "Contrasts in Presidential Campaign Commercials of 1992," 288.
51. Ibid., 1064.
52. The public perceived Clinton's 1996 campaign as less negative than his 1992 campaign according to a national survey conducted right after the election by Princeton Survey Research Associates for the Pew Research Center For The People & The Press. Here's the question and the responses:

Compared to past presidential elections, would you say there was more mud slinging or negative campaigning in this campaign or less mud slinging or negative campaigning in this campaign?

	1992	1996	2000
More	68	49	34
Less	16	36	46
Same (volunteered response)	14	12	16
Don't Know	2	3	4

Pew Research Center, "Voters Side with Bush for Now," November 14, 2000, Q24.
53. Thomas E. Patterson and Robert D. McClure, *The Unseeing Eye* (New York: Putnam, 1976), 58.
54. Craig Leonard Brians and Martin P. Wattenberg, "Comparing Issue Knowledge and Salience: Comparing Reception from TV Commercials, TV News, and Newspapers," *American Journal of Political Science* (February 1996): 172–193.
55. Pew Research Center For The People & The Press, "Popular Vote a Toss-up: Final Reelection Poll," November 6, 2000.
56. Annenberg Public Policy Center, "Conventions Increase America's Appetite for News about Presidential Race," University of Pennsylvania, August 13, 2000; "Americans Learned Much about Convention Positions after First Two Debates," October 10, 2000, <http://www.appcpenn.org>. Joan Shorenstein Center on the Press, Politics, and Public Policy, "Conventions Boost Americans' Issue Awareness," Harvard University, August 30, 2000; "News Coverage Propels Election Interest," September 20, 2000; "Debates Boost Issue Awareness Slightly, but Most Americans Are Still Uninformed about Candidates' Policies," October 26, 2000, <http://www.vanishingvoter.org>.
57. In a survey conducted right after the 1996 election by Princeton Survey Research Associates for the Pew Research Center For The People & The Press, 75 percent of the respondents said that they had enough information to make an informed choice; a similar percentage reported the similar conclusion four years earlier. Pew Research Center, "Campaign '96 Gets Lower Grades From Voters," November 15, 1996, 3; see also Morin and Brussard, "Poll Voters Knew Early," A15.
58. Pew Research Center For The People & The Press, "Despite Uncertain Outcome, Campaign 2000 Highly Rated," November 16, 2000.
59. For a very interesting recent article on this subject see Larry M. Bartels, "Uniformed Votes: Information Effects in Presidential Elections," *American Journal of Political Science* 40 (February 1996): 194–230.

PART IV

THE
ELECTION

PREDICTING PRESIDENTIAL ELECTIONS

8

INTRODUCTION

Predicting the results of an election is a favorite American practice. Politicians do it; the news media do it; even the public tries to anticipate the outcome far in advance of the event. It is a form of entertainment — somewhat akin to forecasting the winner of a sporting contest.

Presidential elections are particularly prone to such predictions. National surveys report on the opinions of the American public at frequent intervals during the campaign. On election night, television news commentators project a winner before most of the votes are counted. Election day surveys of voters exiting from the polls assess the mood of the electorate and present the first systematic analysis of the results. Subsequently, more in-depth studies reveal shifts in opinions and attitudes.

Most predictions and analyses of the electorate based on survey data are not conducted solely for their entertainment or news value, although many are. They also provide important information to candidates running for office and to those who have been elected. For the nominees, surveys of public opinion indicate the issues that can be effectively raised and those that should be avoided. They also suggest which audience might be most receptive to specific policy positions. For the successful candidates, analyses of voter preferences, opinions, and attitudes provide an interpretation of the vote, indicate the range and depth of public concern on the key issues, and signal the amount of support newly elected presidents are likely to receive as they begin their administration.

This chapter examines the presidential vote from three perspectives. The first section deals with snapshots of the public at different points during the campaign. It discusses national polls, describes their methodology, and evaluates their effect. The news media's election eve forecasts and analyses are also described.

The next section turns to an examination of the vote itself. After alluding to the election day surveys, it reports on the National Election Studies, which have been conducted since 1952. These studies, which are surveys of the national electorate, provide basic data that scholars have used to analyze elections and understand voting behavior. The principal findings of these analyses are summarized for each presidential election since 1952.

The final section of the chapter discusses the relationship between campaigning and governing, between issue debates and public policy making, between candidate evaluations and presidential style. Do the campaign issues determine the form of agenda building? Does the projected or perceived image of the candidates affect the tone of the presidency or the actions of the one who is elected? Can an electoral coalition be converted into a governing party? Does the selection process help or hinder the president in meeting the expectations it creates? These questions are explored in an effort to determine the impact of the election on the operation of the presidency, the behavior of the president, and the functioning of the political system.

PREDICTING PRESIDENTIAL ELECTIONS

Public Opinion Polls

The most popular question during a campaign is, who is going to win? The public is naturally interested in the answer, and the news media and candidates are obsessed with it, although for different reasons. In focusing on the campaigns, the news media feel compelled to report who is ahead, how the candidates are perceived, and what issues are dividing the voters. In forging a winning coalition, candidates and their organizations need to know how the electorate is reacting to them and their issue positions. Waiting for this information until after the election is obviously too late. That is the reason there are so many public opinion polls.

In recent elections, there have been literally hundreds of polls.[1] Published in newspapers, broadcast by the television networks, and available on-line, they monitor daily shifts in perceptions, opinions, and anticipated voting decisions of the electorate. Polls also provide the major party campaigns with information about how their messages are being received, the type of appeals that seem to resonate most effectively with different groups of voters, and the electoral opportunities which present themselves over the course of the campaign.

Although the number of polls have mushroomed in recent years, polling itself is not a new phenomenon. There have been nationwide assessments of public opinion since 1916. The largest and most comprehensive of the early surveys were the straw polls conducted by the *Literary Digest*, a popular monthly magazine. The *Digest* mailed millions of ballots and questionnaires to people who appeared on lists of automobile owners and in telephone directories. In 1924, 1928, and 1932, the poll correctly predicted the winner of the presidential election. In 1936, it did not: a huge Alfred Landon victory was forecast, and a huge Franklin Roosevelt victory occurred.

What went wrong? The *Digest* mailed 10 million questionnaires over the course of the campaign and received 2 million back. As the ballots were returned, they were tabulated. This procedure, which provided a running count, blurred shifts in public opinion that may have been occurring over the course of the campaign. But that was not its only problem. The principal difficulty with the *Digest's* survey was that the sample of people who responded was not representative of the voting public. Automobile owners and telephone subscribers were simply not typical voters in 1936, since most people did not own cars or have telephones. This distinction mattered more in 1936 than it had in previous years, because of the Great Depression. There was a socioeconomic cleavage within the electorate. The *Literary Digest* sample did not reflect this cleavage; thus its results were inaccurate.

While the *Digest* was tabulating its 2 million responses and predicting that Landon would be the next president, a number of other pollsters were conducting more scientific surveys and correctly forecasting Roosevelt's reelection. The polls of George Gallup, Elmo Roper, and Archibald Crossley differed from the *Digest's* in two principal respects: they were considerably smaller, and their samples approximated the characteristics of the population as a whole, permitting more accurate generalizations of public opinion to be made.

The *Digest* went out of business, but Gallup, Roper, and Crossley continued to poll and to improve their sampling techniques. In 1940, Gallup predicted Roosevelt would receive 52 percent of the vote; he actually received 55 percent. In 1944, Gallup forecast a 51.5 percent Roosevelt vote, very close to his actual 53.2 percent. Other pollsters also made predictions that closely approximated the results. As a consequence, public confidence in election polling began to grow. (See Table 8–1.)

The confidence was short-lived, however. In 1948, all major pollsters forecast a victory by Republican Thomas Dewey. Their errors resulted from poor sampling techniques, from the premature termination of polling before the end of the campaign, and from incorrect assumptions about how the undecided would vote.

In attempting to estimate the population in their samples, the pollsters had resorted to filling quotas. They interviewed a certain number of people with different demographic characteristics until the percentage of these groups in the sample resembled that percentage in the population as a whole. Simply because the percentages were approximately equal, however, did not mean that the sample was representative of the population. For example, interviewers avoided certain areas in cities, and their results were consequently biased.

Moreover, the interviewing stopped several weeks before the election. In mid-October, the polls showed that Dewey was ahead by a substantial margin. Burns Roper, son of Elmo Roper, polling for *Fortune* magazine, saw the lead as sufficiently large to predict a Dewey victory without the need for further surveys. A relatively large number of people, however, were undecided. Three weeks before the election, Gallup concluded that 8 percent of the voters had still not made up their minds. In estimating the final vote, he and other pollsters assumed that the undecided would divide their votes in much the same manner as the electorate as a whole. This assumption turned out to be incorrect. Most of those who were

TABLE 8-1 ★

GALLUP POLL ACCURACY RECORD, 1936–2000

Year	Gallup Final Survey	Election Results	Deviation
2000	46.0% Gore; 48.0% Bush	48.2% Gore, 48.0% Bush	−2.9%
1996	52.0 Clinton	50.1 Clinton	+1.9
1992*	49.0 Clinton	43.2 Clinton	+5.8
1988	56.0 Bush	53.9 Bush	−2.1
1984	59.0 Reagan	59.1 Reagan	−0.1
1980	47.0 Reagan	50.8 Reagan	−3.8
1976	48.0 Carter	50.0 Carter	−2.0
1972	62.0 Nixon	61.8 Nixon	+0.2
1968	43.0 Nixon	43.5 Nixon	−0.5
1964	64.0 Johnson	61.3 Johnson	+2.7
1960	51.0 Kennedy	50.1 Kennedy	+0.9
1956	59.5 Eisenhower	57.8 Eisenhower	+1.7
1952	51.0 Eisenhower	55.4 Eisenhower	−4.4
1948	44.5 Truman	49.9 Truman	−5.4
1944	51.5 Roosevelt	53.3 Roosevelt	−1.8
1940	52.0 Roosevelt	55.0 Roosevelt	−3.0
1936	55.7 Roosevelt	62.5 Roosevelt	−6.8

*The Ross Perot candidacy created an additional source of error in estimating the 1992 presidential vote. There was no historical precedent for Perot, an independent candidate who was accorded equal status to the major party nominees in the presidential debates and had a record advertising budget. Gallup's decision to allocate none of the undecided vote to Perot, based on past performance of third party and independent candidates, resulted in this overestimation of Clinton's vote.

Note: No Congressional poll done in 1986.

Source: Gallup Poll, <http://www.gallup.com/poll/trends/ptaccuracy.asp>, April 4, 1999; updated by Gallup Poll, "Popular Vote in Presidential Race Too Close to Call," November 7, 2000, <http://www.gallup.com/poll/releases/pr00110.asp>.

wavering in the closing days of the campaign were Democrats. In the end, most voted for Truman or did not vote at all.

The results of the 1948 election once again cast doubt on the accuracy of public opinion polls. Truman's victory also reemphasized the fact that surveys reflect opinion at the time they are taken, not necessarily days or weeks later. Opinion and voter preferences may change.

To improve the monitoring of shifts within the electorate, pollsters changed their method of selecting people to be interviewed. They developed more effective means of anticipating who would actually vote. They polled continuously to identify more precisely and quickly any shifts that occurred in public sentiment and reactions to campaign events. They also extended their surveys to the day before the election to get as close to the time people actually voted as they could. Obvi-

TABLE 8–2 ★

ACCURACY OF THE FINAL PREELECTION POLLS, NOVEMBER 6, 2000

Poll*	Bush	Gore	Nader	Buchanan
CBS	44	45	4	1
CNN/*USA Today*/Gallup	48	46	4	1
IBD/CSM/TIPP†	47.9	46	3.7	—
Reuters/MSNBC/Zogby	46	48	5	1
Voter.com	50	45	3.5	—

* All polls include the allocated undecided vote.

† *Investor's Business Daily, Christian Science Monitor,* TIPP poll conducted by TechnoMetrica Market Intelligence.

Source: Polling Report, <http://www.pollingreport.com/election.htm>.

ously, the closer to the vote the more likely the poll should forecast the election results. Public opinion has solidified; more people have made up their minds; and pollsters can usually forecast what that decision will be on election day.

These changes, plus the continued refinement of the questions, have produced better and more accurate polls, particularly in the one hundred days before the election. Between 1936 and 1950, the average error of the final Gallup preelection poll was 3.6 percent; since then it has usually been less than 2 percent.[2] Other polling organizations have also experienced high levels of accuracy. Table 8–2 lists the final preelection polls and results in 2000.

Very close elections in 1960, 1968, and 1976, however, resulted in several pollsters making wrong predictions. In 1980, the size of Reagan's victory was substantially underestimated in some nationwide polls; in 1992 and 1996, Clinton's margin was overestimated, whereas in 2000 Gore's was underestimated by some pollsters. (See Table 8–2.)

Why do pollsters under- or overestimate the results? Although opinions can change after the poll and before the vote, that change should be small since most pollsters now conclude their surveys the day before the election. There are, however, two other variables that pollsters must consider: turnout and undecided voters. Who is likely to vote, whether the undecided will vote, and if so, for whom are factors that can result in a discrepancy between the sample result and the popular vote.

Anticipating likely voters is a tricky business, more so, the further the time from election day. Simply asking people whether they plan to vote is not sufficient because more people will say that they intend to vote than actually do so. People do not want to admit that they may not vote, or that something may interfere with their doing so. Thus, pollsters usually ask a battery of questions to determine the likelihood of the respondent actually voting: Are you currently registered to vote? Did you vote in the last election? By the way, where do people vote around here?

Similarly, it is necessary for pollsters to anticipate who is really undecided, whether they will vote, and if so, for whom. The wording of preference questions can be critical. Researchers at Harvard's Shorenstein Center found that presenting people with a list of choices and asking them for whom they would vote if the election were held today, results in a lower percentage of undecided than if they were given the additional option of choosing an alternative response such as "or haven't you picked a candidate yet?"[3]

As election day approaches, pollsters need to allocate the undecided vote if they are to forecast the results accurately. If their allocation formula proves to be incorrect, then their sample is likely to deviate from the actual vote. This happened in 2000 when some pollsters split the undecided vote between Gore and Bush. As a consequence they failed to capture the extent of the late surge for Gore.[4] Similarly in 1992, pollsters made an incorrect judgment about the Perot vote. Based on the experience of other third-party and independent candidates whose support had declined as election day neared, pollsters underestimated the popular vote that Perot received. Not only did Perot's support not decline, but his campaign succeeded in attracting a large number of first-time voters whose turnout was difficult to predict.

Typically, most voters decide well before the final week. In fact, in a normal election, one-half to two-thirds of the electorate make their decision before or during the national nominating conventions. If most people decide before Labor Day, the polls conducted in September are likely to be close to the final election results. And they have been. In "trial heats" conducted by the Gallup organization, the candidate who was ahead in early September won in eleven of thirteen elections between 1948 and 1996. During this period, the person ahead at the end of September won all but one of these elections, Truman being the only exception.[5]

Television Forecasts

Forecasts continue right to the end, until all the votes are tabulated. The final projections are presented by the major television networks during the night of the election. In broadcasting the results the news media have three objectives: to report the vote, to forecast the winners, and to analyze the returns and do all of this ahead of the other television networks.

Beginning in the 1980s, the major networks and news services established a consortium to pool their resources in reporting the vote count. Known as the News Voter Service (NVS), this consortium assigns thousands of reporters to precincts and county election boards around the country to communicate the presidential, congressional, and gubernatorial vote as soon as it is tallied. The results are telephoned to a center, which feeds them into a central computer. Each of the networks (ABC, CBS, NBC, FOX, and CNN) and the print media that participate in the consortium have terminals indicating how the vote is progressing, but retain their own experts to analyze the data as it is being reported.

If all the news media wished to do were report the results, this type of reporting would suffice. But they wish to do more. They want to analyze the vote and explain its meaning. To do so they depend on a large exit poll in which thousands of people are surveyed after they have voted.

Here's how exit polls work. A large number of precincts across the country are randomly selected. The random selection is made within states in such a way that principal geographic units (cities, suburbs, and rural areas), size of precincts, and their past voting record are taken into account. Approximately 1,200 representatives of the polling organization administer the poll to voters who are chosen in a systematic way (for example, every fourth or fifth person) as they leave the voting booths. Voters are asked to complete a short questionnaire (thirty to forty items) that is designed to elicit information on voting choices, political attitudes, candidate evaluations and feelings, as well as demographic characteristics of those who voted. Several times over the course of the day, the questionnaires are collected, tabulated, and their results telephoned to a central computer bank. After most or all of the election polls in a state have been completed, the findings of the exit poll are broadcast. Over the course of the evening they are adjusted to reflect the actual results as they are tabulated.

The exit poll is usually very accurate. Because it is conducted over the course of the day, there is little bias that would under- or overrepresent certain types of voters who vote at different times of the day. Moreover, only voters are sampled and in large numbers, thereby reducing the error to much less than that of the national surveys conducted by national polling organizations such as the Gallup Poll. In addition, the exit poll provides a sample of sufficient size to enable analysts to discern the attitudes, opinions, and choices of smaller groups and subgroups (such as white southern Protestants, African-American males, and unmarried, college-educated women) within the electorate. In 2000, 13,130 people exiting hundreds of polling places around the country participated in the survey.[6] (See Table 8–3, pages 286–287.)

Early projections of the winner on election night based on exit polling have generated considerable criticism, primarily on the grounds that they discourage turnout and affect voting in states in which the polls are still open. This controversy was heightened in 1980. When the early returns and private polls all indicated a Reagan landslide, the networks projected his victory early in the evening while voting was still occurring in some parts of the country. At 9:30 P.M. eastern standard time (EST), President Jimmy Carter appeared before his supporters and acknowledged defeat. His concession speech was carried live on each of the major networks. Almost immediately Carter's early announcement incurred angry protests, particularly from defeated West Coast Democrats, who alleged that the president's remarks discouraged many Democrats from voting. It is difficult to substantiate their claim, however.[7]

A number of researchers have studied the impact of the 1980 television projections on voting at all levels. They have found a small reduction in turnout in the West, which they associated with the election night predictions.[8] They did not, however, find evidence of vote switching or turnout bias toward or against the projected winner as a result of the early projections.[9]

The minimal effect of the election reporting on the outcome of the election seems to be related to the fact that relatively few people watch the broadcasts and then vote. Most people vote first and watch the returns later in the evening. Perhaps this pattern of voting and then watching or listening to the returns explains why George Bush's projected victory on the networks in 1988 before the polls closed on the West Coast did little to change the results in three out of four Pacific states (Washington, Oregon, and Hawaii) that voted for Michael Dukakis. Nonetheless, sensitivity to the criticism that early returns affect turnout and voting behavior led the networks to agree prior to the 1992 election not to project winners in any election within a state until its polls had closed. Until 2000, they generally adhered to that practice, waiting until the voting in that state had ended before projecting the outcome. In 1996, however, they amended their pledge to make a national prediction even as people were voting on the West Coast. Promptly at 9 P.M., EST, they forecast a Clinton victory. In anticipation of this early forecast, Republicans bitterly criticized the practice of calling the election before the polls had closed and warned of possible legislation to prevent it from happening again. No such legislation has been enacted, however.

Another prediction controversy in which speed and accuracy collided occurred in 2000. Early in the evening of the election (7:50 P.M., EST), the television broadcast networks forecast a victory for Al Gore in Florida on the basis of the exit polls even though Florida Panhandle residents in the central time zone were still voting. The announcement elated Democrats. However, as the evening wore on, a discrepancy was noted between the actual returns and the exit polls in exit poll precincts. On the basis of this discrepancy, CNN retracted its prediction of a Gore victory. The other networks quickly followed suit. At 2:16 A.M. (EST), the Fox News channel declared Bush the winner on the basis of tabulated returns. Again, the other networks followed. Hearing the news, Vice President Gore called Governor George W. Bush to concede the election and was on his way to make a public announcement to his supporters. Before he did so, however, he learned that the election was still too close to call. Gore then telephoned Bush and retracted his concession while the networks retracted their prediction of a Bush victory.[10] In the end, the closeness of the Florida vote combined with the voiding of thousands of improperly punched ballots precluded a valid exit poll prediction.

INTERPRETING THE ELECTION

In addition to predicting the results, the television networks also provide an instant analysis of them on election night. This analysis, based primarily on exit polls, relates voting decisions to the issue positions, ideological perspectives, and partisan preferences of the electorate. Patterns among demographic groups, issue stands, and electoral perceptions and choices are noted and used to explain why people voted for particular candidates.

Although exit polls present a detailed picture of the electorate on election day (see Table 8–3, pages 286–287), they do not provide a longitudinal perspective. To understand changes in public attitudes and opinions, it is necessary to survey people over the course of the campaign, asking the same questions and, if possible, reinterviewing the same people before and after they vote. The nationwide polls conducted by Gallup, Zogby, Pew, and the major news organizations often repeat questions, but they do not do so with the same respondents. The National Election Studies do. They reinterview and repeat some of the same questions they posed to the same people earlier.[11] This interview-reinterview technique has enabled social scientists to discern opinion changes and the factors that have contributed to them over the course of the campaign. The wealth of data that these studies have produced has served as a basis for political scientists to construct theories of why people vote as they do.

Models of Voting Behavior

There are two basic models of voting behavior: the *prospective*, which emphasizes the issues and looks to the future; and the *retrospective*, which emphasizes the candidates and their parties and looks to the past.[12]

In the prospective voting model, voters compare their beliefs and policy preferences with those of the parties and their nominees. They make a determination of which party and which candidate espouse positions that are closer to their own and thus would more likely pursue those positions if elected. In other words, voters make a judgment on the prospects of obtaining future policy they desire based on the current positions of the candidates and the parties and the policies they promise to pursue.

In the retrospective voting model, voters also make a judgment about the future but do so primarily on the basis of the parties and their candidates' performance in the past. How they evaluate that performance is critical to the voting choice they will make on election day. In other words, history serves as a prologue for the future in the retrospective voting model.

Although a variety of factors are considered in performance evaluations, external conditions — how good or bad things seem to be — are almost always a major part of that analysis. If the economy is strong, society harmonious, and the nation perceived as secure, people assume that their leaders, particularly the president, must be doing a good job. If conditions are not good, then the president gets much of the blame.[13] Thus, the key question that voters ask themselves when making a retrospective evaluation is: Am I and my country better off now than before the party now in power and its candidates won control of the White House?

If an incumbent president or even vice president is running, then this retrospective judgment should be closely related to the voting decision. If, however, there is no incumbent seeking reelection (such as in 1952 for example), then the retrospective judgment is less relevant for individuals seeking election but their partisan affiliation remains relevant.

Another component to a retrospective voting decision involves a comparison between the principal contenders. Which of them is more likely to do well in the future?[14] It is not sufficient to assess only the current administration, even if the president is seeking reelection, if the candidate for the opposition is thought to be markedly better or worse. Thus, in any one voting decision, voters weigh the parties and candidates' past performance as well as the promise offered by the challengers and their party for the future.

In both models, partisanship is apt to be an important influence on the evaluations people make to arrive at their voting decision. As noted in Chapter 3, a partisan orientation provides voters with a lens through which the campaign is filtered, the candidates and issues are evaluated, and electoral judgments are made.

In the retrospective model, partisanship itself is the consequence of evaluations of the past performance of parties. It therefore functions as a summary judgment of how the parties and the candidates have performed, and as a basis for anticipating how they will perform in the future. Partisans who make a retrospective evaluation are more apt to rate presidents of their party more favorably and those of the other party less favorably. Similarly, partisans tend to be closer to their candidate's positions on the issues than to their opponent's, although most people do not necessarily arrive at their position by virtue of their partisanship alone.

Since the identification people have with political parties is the most stable and resilient factor affecting the voting decision, it is considered to be the single most important long-term influence on voting. Orientations voters have toward the candidates and issues are short-term factors that fluctuate from election to election. If strong enough, they can, of course, cause people to vote against their partisan inclinations or, over time, change those inclinations as the continuing dealignment of partisan allegiances suggest. For those who resist these changes, who adhere to their partisan identities, these identities serve as an inducement and a rationalization for supporting the party and its candidates.

Since a majority of the electorate continues to identify with a political party or leans in a partisan direction, the candidate of the dominant party should have the advantage — all things being equal. But all things are never equal. Candidates change, issues change, the public mood changes, and even the partisan identity of voters can shift over time. Thus, it is important to understand how the electorate evaluates these changes, how they feel about the candidates, how they perceive and evaluate them and their issue stands, and how their perceptions and evaluations affect their voting decisions and the election outcomes.[15] The next sections discuss the interplay of these components in presidential elections since 1952.

1952–1956: The Impact of Personality

In 1952, the Democrats were the dominant party, but the Republicans won the presidential election and gained a majority in both houses of Congress. The issues of that election — the fear of communism at home and abroad, the presence of corruption in high levels of government, and United States involvement in the Korean War — benefited the GOP, as did the popularity of its presidential candidate, former General Dwight D. Eisenhower. These short-term factors offset the Democrats' longer-term, partisan advantage and enabled the Republicans to win.[16] The electorate saw the Republicans as better able to deal with the problems of fighting communism, promoting efficiency in government, and ending the war. Eisenhower was also perceived in a more favorable light than his opponent, Adlai Stevenson. Although the public still regarded Democrats as more capable of handling domestic problems, the appeal of Eisenhower, combined with the more favorable attitude toward the Republican Party in the areas of foreign affairs and government management, resulted in the victory of the minority party's candidate.

President Eisenhower's reelection four year later was also a consequence of his personal popularity, not his party's. Eisenhower was positively evaluated by voters. His opponent, Adlai Stevenson, was not. The Republicans did not win control of Congress, however, as they had in 1952. Their failure to do so in 1956 testified to the continuing partisan advantage that the Democrats enjoyed among the American electorate during this period.

1960–1972: The Increasing Importance of Issues

Beginning in 1960, the issues of the campaign seemed to play a more important role in the election's outcome than they had since the New Deal realignment. Noneconomic policy issues undercut the impact of a partisanship forged since the 1930s on economic ties. In general, these issues contributed to the defection of Democrats from their party's presidential candidates in 1960, 1968, and 1972 and to defections by Republicans (and southern Democrats) in 1964.

John Kennedy's Catholicism was a primary concern to many voters in 1960 and helps explain the closeness of that election. Despite the Democrats' dominance within the electorate, Kennedy received only 115,000 more votes than Richard Nixon, 0.3 percent more of the total vote. Kennedy's Catholicism cost him votes. He lost about 2.2 percent of the popular vote, or approximately 1.5 million votes, because he was a Catholic.[17] The decline in Democratic voting was particularly evident in the heavily Protestant South. Outside the South, however, Kennedy picked up Democratic votes because of the massive support he received from Catholics. Almost 80 percent of the Catholic vote, 17 percent more than the Democrats normally obtained, went to Kennedy. In fact, the concentration of Catholics in the large industrial states may have contributed to the size of his Electoral College majority.[18]

Although Kennedy barely won in 1960, Lyndon Johnson won by a landslide four years later. Short-term factors also explain the magnitude of the Johnson victory.[19] Barry Goldwater was perceived as a minority candidate within a minority party, ideologically to the right of most Republicans. Moreover, he did not enjoy a favorable public image, as Johnson did. Policy attitudes also favored the Democrats, even in foreign affairs. Goldwater's militant anticommunism scared many voters. They saw Johnson as the peace candidate.

Goldwater's strong ideological convictions, coupled with his attempt to differentiate his policy positions from Johnson's, undoubtedly contributed to a greater issue awareness. Although most policy-conscious voters had their views on the issues reinforced by their partisan attitudes, two groups within the electorate did not. White southern Democrats, fearful of their party's civil rights initiatives, cast a majority of their votes for Goldwater, and northern Republicans, who disagreed with their candidate's policy positions, voted for Johnson. For the first time since the New Deal realignment, five states in the solid Democratic South (plus Goldwater's home state of Arizona) went Republican, auguring the major regional realignment that was to occur.

The impact of a new set of foreign policy and social issues that divided the Democrats began to be evident in 1968. With the Vietnam War, urban riots, campus unrest, and civil rights dividing the nation and splitting the Democratic party, partisan desertions increased. The Democratic share of the vote declined 19 percent, while the Republican proportion increased 4 percent. The third-party candidacy of George Wallace accounted for much of the difference.

Wallace's support was much more issue based than was support for Democrat Hubert Humphrey or Republican Richard Nixon. The Alabama governor did not have as much personal appeal for those who voted for him as did his policy positions.[20] Unhappy with the Democratic Party's handling of a wide range of social issues, white Democratic partisans, particularly in the South but to a limited degree in the urban North as well, turned from their party's presidential candidate, Hubert Humphrey, to vote for Wallace, who received 13.5 percent of the vote. Had Wallace not run, the Republican presidential vote undoubtedly would have been larger, since Nixon was the second choice of most Wallace voters.

The results of the 1968 presidential election thus deviated from the partisan alignment of the electorate. The voters made a retrospective judgment. A significant number of them had grievances against the Democratic Party and against Lyndon Johnson's conduct of the presidency. This included many Democrats who voted for Wallace and, to a much lesser extent, for Nixon. A decline in the intensity of partisanship and a growth in the number of independents contributed to the amount of issue voting that occurred in 1968. Had it not been for the Democrats' large partisan advantage and the overwhelming African-American vote that Humphrey received, the presidential election would not have been nearly so close.[21]

The trend away from partisan presidential voting for the Democratic candidate continued in 1972. With a nominee who was ideologically and personally unpopular, the Democrats suffered their worst presidential defeat since 1920. Richard Nixon enjoyed a better public image than George McGovern. He was seen as the stronger presidential candidate. The electorate reacted to him personally in a positive manner, although less so than in 1960.[22] McGovern, on the other hand, was viewed negatively by non-Democrats and neutrally by Democrats. These perceptions, positive for Nixon and negative for McGovern, contributed to Nixon's large victory, as did his stands on most of the issues. Most of the electorate saw the Republican standard-bearer as closer to their own positions than the Democratic candidate. McGovern was perceived as liberal on all issues and ideologically to the left of his own party. Thus, Democrats defected in considerable numbers, but Republicans did not.[23]

1976–1996: The Evaluation of Performance

1976. Issue differences narrowed in 1976. Neither Gerald Ford nor Jimmy Carter emphasized the social and cultural concerns that played a large role in the previous presidential contest. Both focused their attention on trust in government and on domestic economic matters. In the wake of Watergate and a recession that occurred during the Ford presidency, it is not surprising that these issues worked to the Democrats' advantage.

Carter was also helped by a slightly more favorable personal assessment than that given to Ford.[24] The latter's association with the Nixon administration, highlighted in the public mind by his pardon of the former president, his difficult struggle to win his own party's nomination, and his seeming inability to find a solution to the country's economic woes adversely affected his image as president.

Nonetheless, Ford was probably helped more than hurt by being the incumbent. He gained in recognition, reputation, and stature. He benefited from having a podium with a presidential seal on it. His style and manner in the office contrasted sharply with his predecessor's — much to Ford's advantage. As the campaign progressed, his presidential image improved.[25] It just did not improve quickly enough to allow him to hold on to the office.

With sociocultural issues muted and the Vietnam War over, economic matters divided the electorate along partisan lines. This shift put the candidate of the dominant party back into the driver's seat. Democrats had more faith in their party's ability to improve the economy. Carter won primarily because he was a Democrat and secondarily because his personal evaluation was more favorable than Ford's. Carter was also helped by being a southerner. He received the electoral votes of every southern state except Virginia. In an otherwise divided Electoral College, this southern support proved to be decisive.

1980. When Carter sought reelection in 1980, being a Democrat, an incumbent, and a southerner was not sufficient. Poor performance ratings overcame the advantage partisanship and incumbency normally bring to a president of the dominant party. In 1976, Carter was judged on the basis of his potential *for* office. In 1980, he was judged on the basis of his performance *in* office. As the results of the election indicate, that judgment was very harsh. Carter's vote fell behind his 1976 percentages in every single state, and in approximately half the states it dropped at least 10 percent. Why did he lose so badly?

Personal evaluations of Carter and assessments of his policies were not nearly so favorable as they had been four years earlier. Starting the campaign with the lowest approval rating of any president since the ratings began in 1952, Carter saw his performance in office approved by only 21 percent of the adult population in July 1980. Personal assessments of Ronald Reagan were also low, although, in contrast to Carter's ratings, they became more favorable as the campaign unfolded.

Economic conditions also seemed to benefit Reagan. Concerns about the economy, persistently high inflation, large-scale unemployment, and the decreasing competitiveness and productivity of American industry all worked to the advantage of the party out of power. For the first time in many years, the Republicans were seen as the party better able to invigorate the economy, return prosperity, and lower inflation. The Democrats, and particularly Carter, were blamed for the problems.

Dissatisfaction with the conduct of foreign affairs, culminating in frustration over the Soviet Union's invasion of Afghanistan and especially the failure of the United States to obtain the release of American hostages held in Iran contributed to Carter's negative evaluation and to changing public attitudes toward defense spending and foreign affairs. In 1980, most Americans supported increased military expenditures, a position with which Reagan was closely identified, combined with a less conciliatory approach and a tougher, more militant posture in dealing with problems abroad.

These issues, together with the negative assessment of Carter as president, explain why he lost. Twenty-seven percent of the Democrats who had supported Carter in 1976 deserted him four years later. Approximately 80 percent of these deserters voted for Reagan. They represented all ideological groups, not just conservatives. And Carter's share of the independent vote declined substantially.

John Anderson, a former Republican member of Congress, also ran in 1980 as an independent. He was a protest candidate who drew equally from Democrats and Republicans. Anderson was unable, however, to attract a solid core of supporters. Nor was he able to differentiate his policy positions sufficiently from Carter's and Reagan's to generate an issue-oriented vote. In the end, his failure to win any electoral votes and only 6.5 percent of the popular vote demonstrated the resiliency of the major parties and the legitimacy that their labels provided candidates for office.

In summary, Carter was repudiated by the voters because of how they retrospectively evaluated his presidency. In 1980, it was Reagan who appeared to offer greater potential. He won primarily because he was the option that had become acceptable. He did not win because of his ideology or his specific policy positions. Although there was a desire for change, there was little direct ideological or issue voting.[26] Nor did Reagan's personal appeal in 1980 contribute significantly to his victory.[27]

1984. Four years later, Reagan's personal appeal did contribute to his victory. In 1984, voters rewarded President Reagan for what they considered to be a job well done with a huge victory. What factors contributed to Reagan's impressive victory? Was his landslide primarily a product of his ideology, his issue stands, or his performance in office?

Ideology did not work to Reagan's advantage in 1984 any more than it did in the previous election. In 1984, the average voter considered himself or herself to be a moderate, holding issue positions slightly closer to the liberal Mondale than to the conservative Reagan.[28] This moderate perspective, however, did not easily translate into presidential voting. As a consequence, it did not adversely affect Reagan; nor did it help Mondale.

There was a potential for issue voting in 1984. The electorate did perceive a choice between the two candidates on a range of domestic matters. But it was conditions more than positions that seemed to influence the electorate's judgment. A resurgent economy, strengthened military, and renewed feelings of national pride brought the president broad support. Although voters agreed with Mondale more than with Reagan on many of the specific problems confronting the nation, they viewed Reagan as the person better able to deal with them.

Leadership was a dominant concern. Voters evaluated Reagan much more highly than Mondale in this regard. Reagan was seen as the stronger and more independent of the two candidates, less beholden to special and parochial interests. When leadership was combined with the ability to deal with the most pressing problems and a very favorable personal evaluation of Reagan, the president won hands down. It was a retrospective vote. The electorate supported Reagan primarily for his performance in office. In other words, they voted *for* him in 1984 just as they had voted *against* Carter four years earlier.

1988. The trend of retrospective voting continued in 1988. George Bush won because the electorate evaluated the Reagan administration positively, associated Bush with that administration, and concluded that he, not Michael Dukakis, would be better able and more likely to maintain the good times and the policies that produced them.[29] That Bush was not as favorably evaluated as Reagan had been four years earlier partially accounts for his narrower victory.[30] Bush received 53 percent of the popular vote and 426 electoral votes, compared with Reagan's 59 percent and 535 electoral votes.

Partisanship affected voting behavior more in 1988 than it had in any election since 1960.[31] In the past, a high correlation between partisan identities and voting behavior had worked to the Democrats' advantage. In 1988, it did not. An increase in Republican allegiances and a decline in Democratic ones produced an almost evenly divided electorate. There were slightly more Democrats but greater turnout and less defection among Republicans. In the end neither candidate was appreciably advantaged by partisan voting. Among independents, Bush enjoyed a solid lead of 12 percent. (See Table 8–3.)

Ideological orientations worked to reinforce partisan voting patterns in 1988, with Republican candidate Bush winning overwhelmingly among Republicans and conservatives and Democratic candidate Dukakis doing almost as well among Democrats and liberals. The problem for Dukakis, however, and any liberal for that matter, is that the proportion of the electorate that considers itself liberal has declined substantially. In 1988, almost twice as many people who voted considered themselves conservative rather than liberal.

In addition to ideology and party, issues affected voting behavior in 1988; however, they did not work primarily to benefit either candidate. With neither partisanship nor issues producing a clear advantage for either candidate, the retrospective evaluation of the Reagan presidency seems to have been the deciding factor, the one that best explains the election outcome.[32] Sixty percent of the electorate approved of how Reagan had handled his job, and of them, almost 80 percent voted for Bush.[33]

1992. Four years later, however, Bush was judged on his own performance in office, and that judgment was negative. Bush received only 37.4 percent of the popular vote in a three-person contest and 168 electoral votes (only 31 percent of the total). His 1992 vote declined among every population group.

With the economy in recession, budget and trade deficits rising, and layoffs of white-collar managers and blue-collar workers dominating the news, people were fearful about their economic future. Blaming the president for these unsatisfactory economic conditions, voters turned to the challengers and their promises for change.

Clinton was clearly helped by his partisan affiliation. With slightly more Democrats in the electorate than Republicans, Clinton received the vote of three out of four Democrats. For the first time since 1964, Republican defections actually exceeded those of Democrats and turnout, which traditionally benefits Republicans, was neutralized in 1992. Democratic turnout was up and Republican turnout was down.[34]

TABLE 8-3 ★

PORTRAIT OF THE AMERICAN ELECTORATE, 1992–2000 (IN PERCENTAGES)

Percentage of 2000 Total		1992			1996			2000*		
		Clinton	Bush	Perot	Clinton	Dole	Perot	Bush	Gore	Nader
	Total vote	43%	38%	19%	49%	41%	8%	48%	48%	3%
48	Men	41	38	21	43	44	10	53	42	3
52	Women	46	37	17	54	38	7	43	54	2
81	Whites	39	41	20	43	46	9	54	42	3
10	Blacks	82	11	7	84	12	4	9	90	1
7	Hispanics	62	25	14	72	21	6	35	62	2
2	Asians	29	55	16	43	48	8	41	55	3
65	Married	40	40	20	44	46	9	53	44	2
35	Unmarried	49	33	18	57	31	9	38	57	4
17	18–29 years old	44	34	22	53	34	10	46	48	5
33	30–44 years old	42	38	20	48	41	9	49	48	2
28	45–59 years old	41	40	19	48	41	9	49	48	2
22	60 and older	50	38	12	48	44	7	47	51	2
5	Not high school graduate	55	28	17	59	28	11	38	59	1
21	High school graduate	43	36	20	51	35	13	49	48	1
32	Some college education	42	37	21	48	40	10	51	45	3
24	College graduate	40	41	19	44	46	8	51	45	3
18	Postgraduate education	49	36	15	52	40	5	44	52	3
54	White Protestant†	33	46	21	36	53	10	56	42	2
26	Catholic	44	36	20	53	37	9	47	50	2
4	Jewish	78	12	10	78	16	3	19	79	1
14	White born-again Christian‡	23	61	15	26	65	8	80	18	1
26	Union household	55	24	21	59	30	9	37	59	3
7	Family income under $15,000	59	23	18	59	28	11	37	57	4
16	$15,000–$29,999	45	35	20	53	36	9	41	54	3

$30,000–$49,999	24	41	38	21	48	40	10	48	49	2
over $50,000	25	40	42	18	44	48	7	51	46	2
over $75,000	13	36	48	16	41	51	7	52	45	2
over $100,000	15	—	—	—	38	54	6	54	43	2
Family's financial situation is									
Better today	50	24	62	14	61	35	3	36	61	2
Same today	38	41	41	18	46	45	8	60	35	3
Worse today	11	61	14	25	27	57	13	63	33	4
From the North	23	47	35	18	55	34	9	39	56	3
From the Midwest	26	42	37	21	48	41	10	49	48	2
From the South	31	42	43	16	46	46	7	55	43	1
From the West	21	44	34	22	48	40	8	46	48	4
Republicans	35	10	73	17	13	80	6	91	8	1
Independents	27	38	32	30	43	35	17	47	45	6
Democrats	39	77	10	13	84	10	5	11	86	2
Liberals	20	68	14	18	78	11	7	13	80	6
Moderates	50	48	31	21	57	33	9	44	52	2
Conservatives	29	18	65	17	20	71	8	81	17	1
Employed§	67	42	38	20	48	40	9	48	49	2
Unemployed§	33	56	24	20	49	42	8	48	47	3
First-time voters	9	48	30	22	54	34	11	43	52	4
Approve of Clinton's performance	57							20	77	2
Disapprove of Clinton's performance	41							88	9	2
Continue Clinton's policies	40							11	87	2
Be more conservative	46							85	13	1
Be more liberal	10							35	56	7

* N = 13,130.

† Includes all Protestants in 2000.

‡ Includes all people who identified themselves as part of the religious right in 2000.

§ 1996 question was: Are you employed full time? In 2000: Do you work full-time for pay? Yes answers were categorized as Employed; No, as Unemployed.

Source: Voter News Service.

Still, Clinton's partisan advantage could have been offset by a lopsided vote of independents who constitute more than one-quarter of the electorate. In the 1980s, that vote had strongly favored the Republicans. In 1992, it did not. Independents divided their support among the three candidates, with Clinton the plurality victor at 38 percent and Perot and Bush splitting the rest. (See Table 8–3.) In four years, Bush had lost one-third of the independent vote, thereby dooming his reelection effort.

Nor did ideology work to the president's advantage as it had in previous elections. Although liberals and conservatives continued to support Democratic and Republican candidates respectively, Perot cut into both votes, dropping Bush's support among conservatives 15 percent from his 1988 level. Moreover, Clinton did comparably better among moderates than previous Democratic candidates had done, substantially leading Bush and Perot among this group.

Although Bush was credited with a successful foreign policy, the lower salience of foreign policy issues undercut Bush's achievements in this policy realm and even served to highlight his inattention to domestic matters. The economy was the principal issue and Clinton its principal beneficiary.

Among the traditional support groups Clinton continued to enjoy an advantage among women, Jews, African Americans and Hispanics, and lower-income, less-educated voters. The generational cleavages evident in past presidential elections were muted in 1992 with the youngest cohort of voters, those eighteen to twenty-nine years old, voting for Clinton at about the national average. Clinton also received a plurality of the male vote, the first time a Democratic candidate had done so since 1976. The only demographic groups that continued to vote for Bush were the wealthy; white Protestants, especially born-again Christians; and those voters who identified themselves as homemakers. Perot's numbers were fairly steady among demographic groups. He did comparably better among men than women, among the young than the old, and among independents than partisans. Clinton won a solid victory. Even though he received only 43 percent of the vote, his popular vote margin over the president was 5.6 percent. In the Electoral College, he won thirty-two states and the District of Columbia for a total of 370 votes, demonstrating once again how the Electoral College tends to enlarge the margin of victory for the winning candidate.

Had Perot not run, it is unlikely that the results of the election would have been any different. Exit polls of Perot voters indicate that they would have divided their votes fairly evenly between Clinton and Bush although the number voting would undoubtedly have declined. Among nonvoters surveyed, Clinton received at least as much support as he did among voters. In a two-person contest, however, Clinton would have received a larger mandate for governing.

1996. By 1996, domestic concerns were still dominant, but the economy was stronger, crime had decreased, and the nation remained at peace — all conditions that favor incumbents. Voters responded accordingly, reelecting the Democratic president and the Republican congressional majority. Clinton's popular and electoral vote exceeded his 1992 totals, although the regional composition of his vote remained essentially the same as it was four years earlier.

Despite misgivings about some aspects of the president's character, notably his personal integrity, honesty, and willingness to stand up for his beliefs, voters saw Clinton as more caring, more in touch with the times, and more visionary than his Republican opponent. But it was the nation's economy, not the president's character, that proved to be the critical factor in determining the outcome of the election. Those who perceived themselves to be better off (about one-third of the electorate) supported the president; those who saw themselves as worse off (about 20 percent) supported his opponents.

Democrats stayed with the president and Republicans with their candidate. Clinton, however, did better than either of his opponents among independent voters. Similarly, he won a majority of the votes of people who identified themselves as moderates; as expected, liberals voted disproportionately for Clinton and conservatives for Dole. It is interesting to note that strictly on the issues, the public was slightly closer to Dole's position on the key issues than to Clinton's. But Clinton's performance evaluation and his leadership potential easily overcame these issue positions in the minds of the voters much as they had twelve years earlier when an electorate, closer to Mondale on the issues, voted overwhelmingly for Reagan.[35]

The demographic groups that shifted most in their support of the president were women and younger voters. The gender gap of 17 percent was the largest in the nation's history. For the first time, a majority of women voted for one candidate and a plurality of men for another. And despite the Democrats' appeal to the elderly on the basis of the Medicare issue, it was the youth who gave the president greater support than any other age cohort.

Hispanic voters contributed significantly to Clinton's victory. Alarmed by Republican attempts to limit immigration, deny government benefits to legal aliens, and oppose bilingual education, Hispanics voted in record numbers and overwhelmingly for Clinton. African Americans remained as strongly Democratic as they had in previous elections.

Cleavages were also evident among secular and sectarian voters. Regular churchgoers, particularly religious fundamentalists, voted Republican. Mainstream Protestant groups were less supportive of the Republicans. Those who did not profess a religion or practice it on a regular basis were much more Democratic and likely to vote for Clinton.

In short, the 1996 election was a referendum on the Clinton presidency, and Clinton won. Not only did the electorate evaluate his first term favorably, but they saw the president as more capable of understanding and handling the challenges of the 1990s and building the bridge to the twenty-first century than either Dole or Perot.

2000: The Anticipation of Future Performance

Although the 2000 election could have been another referendum on the Clinton presidency, it was not for many voters. Vice President Al Gore's decision to emphasize the differences between himself and Governor George W. Bush rather than contrast the economic, social, and international conditions at the end of 2000 with those of 1992, the last time the Republicans controlled the White House, focused the attention of the electorate on the future not the past. Encouraging voters to make more of a prospective choice than a retrospective judgment turned out to be a poor strategic decision for the vice president.

Nonetheless, many of the same voting patterns emerged in 2000 as were evident in previous presidential elections, particularly those of the 1990s. (See Table 8–3.) The electorate was clearly and evenly divided. Parity between the major parties contributed to this division. Partisans overwhelmingly supported their party's nominee while independents were almost evenly split between Bush and Gore. A large, persistent gender gap even increased in size from 17 percent in 1996 to 22 percent in 2000, with a majority of women supporting Gore and Lieberman and a majority of men backing Bush and Cheney. Core groups within the parties' traditional electoral coalitions also voted in record proportions along party lines: African Americans, Latinos, and organized labor for the Democratic candidates and the Christian Coalition for the Republicans.

There was also a regional divide, with Gore doing well in the East and Bush in the South. The vote in the other regions of the country was more evenly split between the two candidates.

Religious voting trends continued as well. Jews voted heavily for Gore and his Jewish running-mate, Joseph Lieberman; Catholics gave Gore slightly more support than Bush, but Protestants preferred Bush, particularly those who considered themselves members of the religious right. As in other recent elections, there was also a sectarian-secular divide; moreover, the more regular the voters' attendance at religious services, the greater the likelihood of their voting Republican.

The division within the electorate was also evident in the issue and ideological preferences of Bush and Gore voters. Those who wanted more conservative policies than those of the Clinton administration, particularly those who thought tax cuts should be the number one priority, supported Bush. Most Gore voters favored a continuation of Clinton's policies and saw Social Security solvency as the primary issue. Bush's vote varied directly and Gore's indirectly with income and education levels, with the exception of those with a postgraduate education who leaned toward Gore. Contributing to the size of Bush's vote was the proportion of upper-income voters (with family incomes of $50,000 or more) who cast ballots in 2000 — 53 percent versus 39 percent in 1996.

As expected, the way a person evaluated the Clinton administration and President Clinton personally carried over to their 2000 presidential vote. Those who had supported Clinton in 1996 and those who approved his performance in office cast ballots for Gore; those who did not vote for him in the previous election, including two out of three Perot voters, and those who disapproved of his job performance went for Bush. In short, the nation's bitter political divisions during the Clinton presidency were also evident in the vote for his successor. These partisan divisions fueled the political controversy over the Florida vote that followed the election. Were it not for the strong economy, the general contentment of the society, and people's optimism about the future, these divisions might have generated the same level of intensity within the population as they had among the political elites. Fortunately however, they did not.

CONVERTING ELECTORAL CHOICE INTO PUBLIC POLICY

The President's Imprecise Mandate

It is not unusual for the meaning of the election to be ambiguous. The reasons that people vote for presidents vary. Some do so because of their party affiliation, some because of issue stands, some because of their assessment of the candidates' potential or their past performance. For most, a combination of factors contributes to their voting decision. This combination makes it difficult to discern exactly what the electorate means, desires, or envisions by its electoral choice.

The president is rarely given a clear mandate for governing. For a mandate to exist the party's candidates must take discernible and compatible policy positions, and the electorate must vote for them because of those positions. Moreover, the results of the election must be consistent. If there is a discrepancy between the popular and the electoral vote or if one party wins the White House and another wins the Congress — the rule not the exception since 1968 — it is difficult for a president to claim a mandate for governing.

Few elections meet these criteria for a mandate. Presidential candidates usually take a range of policy positions, often waffle on a few highly divisive and emotionally charged issues, may differ from their party and its other candidates for national office in their priorities and their stands, and rarely have coattails long enough to sweep others in with them. In fact, they may run behind their congressional candidates, as most recently elected presidents have.

Mandates may not exist, but that has not prevented presidents from claiming them. They believe that they need to do so. They need to be sensitive to public desires and needs when fashioning their policy programs, and they need to obtain public support to get others in government, including members of Congress and federal executives, to back their initiatives.

For these reasons the interpretation of the elections is important.[36] However an administration chooses to interpret the results, that interpretation helps to it to define a president's initial goals. The longer the time that elapses after the election, the less that election is a guide to priorities and policy decisions.

Presidents must adjust to changing times. Their refusal to do so can result in an embarrassing defeat that weakens them politically. A case in point was the Clinton administration's resistance in 1993 to dropping its principal campaign promise to stimulate the economy even though the economy was improving. Similarly, Clinton clung to his comprehensive program to reform the health care system even though public support for it was waning. In both cases, he was out of touch with the public mood that had changed since the election.

Assuming that party is an influence on voting behavior, what cues can presidents cull from their partisan connection in defining their programmatic mandate? As described in Chapter 5, party platforms normally contain a large number of positions and proposals, but there are problems in using the platform as a guide for a new administration. First and foremost, presidential candidates may not have exercised a major influence on the platform's formulation. Or, second, they may have had to accept certain compromises in the interests of party unity. It is not unusual for a nominee to disagree with one or several of the platform's positions or priorities. Carter personally opposed his party's abortion stand in 1980 and had major reservations about a $12 billion jobs program that the Democratic platform endorsed. Dole made little mention of the Republican Party's abortion plank once his 1996 campaign began, nor did Bush in 2000.

In addition to containing items the president-elect may oppose, the platform may omit some that the new president favors, particularly if they are controversial. There was no mention of granting amnesty to Vietnam draft dodgers and war resisters in the 1976 Democratic platform, although Carter had publicly stated his intention to do so if he was elected.[37]

On the other hand, presidential nominees usually do exercise influence over the contents of the platform, as did Gore in 2000, Clinton in 1992 and 1996, and Bush and Dukakis in 1988. Surprisingly, Bush did not put as much of his imprint on the 1992 Republican platform even though his delegates controlled the platform committee; his son George W. Bush did in 2000, however.

There is a correlation between campaign promises, party platforms, and presidential performance. Political scientist Jeff Fishel found that from 1960 to 1984 presidents "submitted legislation or signed executive orders that are broadly consistent with about two-thirds of their campaign pledges." Of these, a substantial percentage were enacted into law, ranging from a high of 89 percent of those proposed during the Johnson administration to a low of 61 percent during the Nixon years.[38] Although these figures do not reveal the importance of the promise, its scope, or its impact, they do suggest that, in general, campaign platforms and candidate pledges are important. They provide a foundation from which an administration's early policy initiatives emanate.[39]

Expectations and Performance

When campaigning, candidates also try to create an aura of leadership, conveying such attributes as assertiveness, decisiveness, compassion, and integrity. Kennedy promised to get the country moving, Johnson to continue the New Frontier-Great Society programs, Nixon to "bring us together," Bush to maintain the Reagan policies that produced peace and prosperity for the eight previous years but to do so in "a kinder and gentler" way. In 1992, Clinton pledged policy change in a moderate direction and an end to gridlock between Congress and the presidency; in 1996, he promised to build a bridge to the twenty-first century. In 2000, George W. Bush promised to defuse the strident partisan political climate in Washington while Gore pledged to extend the economic prosperity to working-class Americans.

These promises created expectations of performance. In the 1976 election, Jimmy Carter heightened these expectations by his constant reference to the strong, decisive leadership he intended to exercise as president. His decline in popularity stemmed in large part from his failure to meet these leadership expectations. In contrast, Reagan's high approval before, during, and after his reelection indicate that most of the public believed that he had provided the strong leadership he had promised in his 1980 and 1984 campaigns. Clinton's personal ratings in 1996 and thereafter also indicate public approval for his job performance although not necessarily for some of his personal attributes.

All new administrations, and to some extent most reelected ones, face diverse and often contradictory desires. By their ambiguity, candidates encourage voters to see what they want to see and to believe what they want to believe. Disillusionment naturally sets in once a new president begins to make decisions. Some supporters feel deceived, while others may be satisfied.

One political scientist, John E. Mueller, has referred to the disappointment groups may experience with an administration as "the coalitions of minorities variable." In explaining declines in popularity, Mueller notes that presidents' decisions inevitably alienate parts of the coalition that elected them. This alienation, greatest among independents and supporters who identify with the other party, can produce a drop in popularity over time, although as the Reagan and Clinton presidencies demonstrate, such a drop is not inevitable, particularly if good times prevail.[40]

The campaign's emphasis on personal and institutional leadership also inflates expectations. By creating the aura of assertiveness, decisiveness, and potency, candidates help shape public expectations of their performance in office. Most presidents contribute to the decline in their own popularity by promising more than they can deliver. The question is, can the promise of leadership be conveyed during the campaign without creating unrealistic and unattainable expectations of the candidate's performance as president? For most candidates, especially the challenger, the answer seems to be "no" more often than "yes."

The Electoral Coalition and Governing

Not only does the selection process inflate performance expectations and create a set of diverse policy goals, it may decrease the president's power to achieve them. The political muscle of the White House has been weakened by the decline in the power of party leaders, the growth of autonomous state and congressional electoral systems, and the decentralization and compartmentalization of power within the government.

Today, presidential candidates are largely on their own. They essentially designate themselves to run. They create their own organizations, choose the top people to run them, mount their own campaigns, win their own delegates, and set their own convention plans. They pay a price for this independence, however. By winning their party's nomination, candidates gain a label and some organizational support. But in the general election, they must supplement that support with their own campaign organization as well as expand their prenomination electoral coalition. If elected, they must broaden their appeal and expand the coalition still further. One of Clinton's worst political mistakes in his first term in office was the emphasis he placed on homosexual rights on the second day of his administration, thereby fulfilling a campaign promise but alienating a portion of his electoral constituency in the process. With only 43 percent of the electorate voting for him in 1992, Clinton could ill afford to antagonize some of his supporters.

The personalization of the presidential electoral process has serious implications for governing. To put it simply, it makes coalition building more difficult. The electoral process provides newly elected presidents with fewer political allies in the states and in Congress. It makes their partisan appeal less effective. It fractionalizes the bases of their support.

Personality politics has created a fertile environment for interest group pressures. Without strong party leaders to act as brokers and referees, groups vie for the nominee's attention and favor during the campaign and for the president's after the election is over. This group struggle, a cause and consequence of the decentralization and compartmentalization of power in government, provides a natural source of opposition and support for almost any presidential action or proposal. It enlarges the arena of policy making and contributes to the multiplicity of forces that converge on most presidential decisions.

Finally, the democratization of the selection process has widened the separation between state, congressional, and presidential elections. Moreover, the anti-Washington, antigovernment mood of the electorate, evident since the mid-1970s, has given outsiders, who are less experienced in national politics and may as a result be less able to meet the demands of the office when they first assume it, an electoral advantage. Carter in 1976 and Clinton in 1992 made much of the fact that they did not owe their nomination to the power brokers within their own party nor did they owe their election to members of Congress. Their electoral advantage, however, became an initial governing disadvantage. Almost as soon as they took office, they had difficulty getting Congress to follow their lead.

Personality Politics and Presidential Leadership

What are presidents to do under these circumstances? How can they lead, achieve their goals, and satisfy pluralistic interests at the same time? Obviously, there is no set formula for success. Forces beyond the president's control may affect the course of events. Nonetheless, presidents would be wise to follow certain maxims in their struggle to convert promises into performance and perhaps also to get reelected.

1. They must identify and limit their own priorities rather than have the priorities forced on them by others. Their priorities should be consistent, well focused, and achievable within the current political environment.
2. They must build and rebuild their own issue coalitions rather than depend solely or even mostly on existing partisan or ideological divisions to support their goals. In an age of parity between the major parties and divided partisanship in government, they cannot hew to a partisan line all or even most of the time. Accommodation, moderation, and bipartisanship are the name of the game.
3. They must be flexible enough to adjust to changing conditions and public moods yet consistent enough to provide direction and stability in their policy orientation. People want to know the direction in which their president is heading.
4. They must take an assertive posture rather than let words and actions speak for themselves, being sensitive to public opinion but trying to mold it at the same time. Leadership often requires interpreting public opinion

and making policy decisions that are consistent with it, although the president must not be perceived as a captive of the polls.

5. Finally, they must grow in office utilizing the status of their position to enhance their personal esteem in the eyes of the public. To counter the increasingly negative media coverage, the White House must be a source of good news, good pictures, and important events.

Priority setting is a necessary presidential task. Without it, an administration appears to lack direction and leadership. People question what presidents are doing and have difficulty remembering what they have done. The absence of clear, achievable priorities at the beginning of the Carter administration, combined with the president's perceived inconsistency in some of his economic and foreign policy decisions, affected Carter's approval ratings in the public opinion polls and contributed to his defeat four years later.

The Reagan administration understood the lessons of the Carter experience, but the Clinton administration did not, at least not initially. Reagan limited the issues, controlled the agenda, and, most importantly, focused the media on his principal policy objectives during his first term in office. Clinton did not. He had too many goals, too little public support, and took too much on himself. All of these factors adversely affected his leadership image and his opportunities to achieve his policy objectives during his first two years in office. But he learned from this experience and became more focused in his words, decisions, and actions after that.

Presidents have discretion in deciding on their priorities. Reagan used this discretion at the beginning of his first term when he jettisoned his conservative social agenda in favor of major economic reforms. Bush chose to emphasize foreign policy and deemphasize domestic issues in the first three years of his administration, despite his campaign's emphasis on domestic concerns. Clinton stuck with his principal priority of stimulating the economy (even though the economy was recovering) but added a host of other policies from deficit reduction to child immunization to ending discrimination against homosexuals in the military to comprehensive health care and welfare reform. By doing so, he overwhelmed Congress and dissipated much of his energy and public support.

Beyond establishing priorities and positions, presidents have to get them adopted. Their electoral coalition does not remain a cohesive entity within the governing system. The inevitable shifting of that coalition forces them to build and rebuild their own alliances around their policy objectives. Constructing these alliances requires organizing skills different from those used in winning an election.

Public appeals are often necessary to maintain a high level of support on potentially divisive national issues and to use that support to influence those in power to back the president's initiatives. The Reagan administration effectively marshaled public support in 1981 and 1982. The president took to the airwaves to explain his program to the American people and rally them behind it, particularly his budget and tax proposals. The White House then orchestrated the public's favorable response, directing it toward members of Congress. Bush and Clinton initially were much less successful in convincing the public to support controversial domestic policies, but Clinton was able to gain support for his trade policies

(NAFTA and GATT) and mobilize opposition to Republican budget proposals in 1995 and 1996.

In addition to building an external coalition, presidents need to employ other inducements and tactics to convince public officials, who have their own constituencies and must be responsive to them, to back presidential policy. This effort requires time, energy, and help. The president cannot do it alone.

As campaign organizations are necessary to win elections, so, too, are governing organizations necessary to gain support for presidential policies. Several offices within the White House have been established to provide liaison and backing for the president on Capitol Hill, in the bureaucracy, and with interest groups and the public. By building and mending bridges, presidents can improve their chances for success. They can commit, convince, cajole, and otherwise gain cooperation despite the constitutional and political separation of institutions and powers.

Unlike winning the general election, making and implementing public policy are not all-or-nothing propositions. Assessments of performance are based on expectations, somewhat as they were in the elections. Part of the image problem all presidents face is the contrast between an idealized public conception of the institution's powers with the president's actual ability to get things done. The gap between expectations and performance explains why presidents need a public relations staff and why constant campaigning seems inevitable today.

If presidents cannot achieve their goals, they can at least look good trying, and perhaps they can even claim partial success. And finally, they can always change their public priorities to improve their batting average. Public appeals may or may not generate support within the governing coalition, but they can boost support outside it, and create political capital which they can use later on.

SUMMARY

Americans are fascinated by presidential elections. They want to know who will win, why the successful candidate has won, and what the election augurs for the next four years. Their fascination stems from four interrelated factors: elections are dramatic; they are decisive; they are participatory; and they affect future policy and leadership.

These factors suggest why so much attention has been devoted to predicting and analyzing presidential elections. Public opinion polls constantly monitor the attitudes and views of the electorate. They reflect and, to some extent, contribute to public interest through the hypothetical elections they continuously conduct and the news media report. Private surveys also record shifts in popular sentiment, helping the candidates who pay for them know what to say, to whom to say it, when and even how to say it, and whether their words and actions have achieved their desired effect.

Polls have become fairly accurate measures of opinion at the time they are taken. They provide data that can be employed to help explain the meaning of an election: the issues that were most salient, the positions that were most popular, and the hopes and expectations that are initially directed toward the elected leaders of government.

The personality of the candidates, the issues of the campaign, and the evaluation of the administration and the party that have controlled it have dominated recent elections and the voting decisions of the electorate. Singularly and together, these factors, along with partisanship, explain the outcome of the vote. In 1960, it was Kennedy's Catholic religion that seemed to account for the closeness of the popular vote despite the large Democratic majority in the electorate. In 1964, it was Goldwater's uncompromising ideological and issue positions that helped provide Johnson with an overwhelming victory in all areas but the deep South. In 1968, it was the accumulation of grievances against the Democrats that spurred the Wallace candidacy and resulted in Nixon's triumph. In 1972, ideology, issues, and the perception of McGovern as incompetent split the Democratic party and culminated in Nixon's landslide. In 1976, however, partisanship was reinforced by issue, ideological, and personal evaluations to the benefit of the dominant party's nominee. But in the next two elections, it was not. Dissatisfaction with Carter's performance in 1980 and satisfaction with Reagan's in 1984 overcame the Democrats' decreasing numerical advantage within the electorate, leading voters to cast their ballots for Reagan as the person they thought would be best qualified to lead. By 1988, the Democrats had appeared to lose their partisan advantage. The issues in that election, although important, did not favor one candidate at the expense of the other. This left the retrospective evaluation of the Reagan years as the critical factor. A majority of voters evaluated these years favorably and believed that Bush, not Dukakis, would be better able and more likely to continue them.

In a certain sense, the 1992 election was a rerun of 1980. The incumbent was rejected on the grounds that his performance in dealing with the nation's most pressing issue, the economy, was unsatisfactory. Almost two-thirds of the electorate voted against the incumbent president. Of the other two candidates, Clinton was elected primarily because of his partisan affiliation and public perception of him as a moderate. That he came from the South, chose Gore as his running mate, and ran an excellent, highly focused campaign all contributed to his victory. Perot ran a strong race for an independent candidate in that election, but independent candidates are disadvantaged within the electorate because they lack a solid base of support and within the Electoral College because of the winner-take-all system used by most of the states to cast their electoral votes. These disadvantages, combined with Perot's early withdrawal and later reentry and his lack of experience in the public sector, were just too great to overcome.

If the 1992 election was a rejection of Bush, the 1996 election marked an approval of Clinton. The president won reelection easily. His share of the popular vote increased by 6 percent; he received slightly more electoral votes as well with the geographic bases of his coalition remaining largely the same. Helped by a stronger economy, a skilled campaign, and effective use of the presidential office, Clinton augmented his partisan support from Democrats with a successful appeal to moderates and to independent voters. Women in particular were attracted to his candidacy whereas men slightly favored his Republican opponent. Younger voters also supported the president. In general, Clinton was seen as the more caring, more energetic, more visionary candidate, the one who was more likely to understand contemporary challenges and future needs.

Partisan divisions, issue differences, and mixed performance evaluations of the Clinton presidency carried over into the 2000 election, although the focus tended to be more on future policies and leadership than on past performance. The electorate was evenly divided about the candidates, the direction in which they wanted to move the country, and the priorities and policies they wished to pursue. Disputes over the vote count and the apparent discrepancy between the popular and electoral vote heightened these divisions, clouded the election mandate, and undercut the good will that the victor normally enjoys after the results are in and the new administration begins to take shape.

The public has a diverse and inflated set of expectations after the election. That they may be conflicting, unrealistic, or in other ways unattainable matters little for a new president. They are expected to lead, to achieve, and to satisfy the interests of a heterogeneous coalition. Their failure or success will depend in large part on their ability to fulfill these expectations.

The election provides them with an open-ended mandate that means different things to different people, including the presidents themselves but does not provide them with the political clout to get things done. In the past, the electoral and governing coalitions were more closely connected by partisan ties than they seem to be today.

This situation has presented serious governing problems for recent presidents, none more serious than in 2001. To overcome these problems, presidents must establish their own priorities, construct their own governing alliances, provide a sense of direction while flexibly moving among policy options, mold but be sensitive to public opinion, and use their office to enhance their image and their programs' chances for being enacted into law. It is not an easy task but one that may be necessary for reelection.

WHERE ON THE WEB?

Public Opinion

Access the latest polls about the election from the following sites:

- **Gallup Organization**
  http://www.gallup.com
- **CBS News Poll**
  http://www.CBSNews.com
- **The Pew Research Center For The People & The Press**
  http://www.people-press.org
- **Roper Center For Public Opinion Research at the University of Connecticut**
  http://www.lib.uconn.edu/Roper Center
- **Zogby International**
  http://www.zogby.com

Election Results

The Web sites of most major news organizations will have the unofficial results as collected by the Associated Press just as soon as the election is over and the results have been tabulated. These results may not include absentee ballots which are counted later or the results of any vote challenges. The official results are available from the Federal Election Commission <http://www.fec.gov> later in the year.

Election Analysis

Most major news organizations carry the final election exit poll on their Web sites. In addition, data from the National Election Studies conducted by the Center for Political Studies at the University of Michigan <http://www.umich.edu/nes> are made available to faculty and students at universities and colleges that are members of the Inter-University Consortium for Political and Social Research about six months after the election is completed.

EXERCISES

1. Look at polls over the course of the election and try to explain opinion shifts on the basis of events in the campaign or in the country as a whole. You can obtain a graph of Gallup polling over the course of the 2000 election at that organization's Web site.
2. Compare the results of several national polls at different points in the last election cycle to determine how the results contrast and compare to one another. If the polls show different results for the same period, try to ascertain who the respondents were (the general public, the electorate, registered voters, or most likely voters), whether they were asked the same questions, how many people were surveyed, and whether the results were within the margin of error of the polls.
3. After the election has concluded, access the large exit poll of the Voter News Service. Analyze the election results on the basis of this poll. In your analysis, note how major demographic groups voted, what the major issues were, how important partisanship and ideology seemed to be, and the feelings voters had toward the candidates and their parties.
4. On the basis of the results of the last presidential election, write a memo for the person who was elected about the meaning (mandate) of the election for governance. What do the people expect the new president to do? Given the vote controversy, what would you advise the president to do? What is the order in which his priorities should be tackled?

SELECTED READING

Abramson, Paul R., John H. Aldrich, and David W. Rohde. *Change and Continuity in the 1996 and 1998 Elections.* Washington, Congressional Quarterly, 1999.

Dahl, Robert A. "Myth of the Presidential Mandate." *Political Science Quarterly* 105 (Fall 1990): 355–372.

Fiorina, Morris. *Retrospective Voting in American National Elections.* New Haven, Conn.: Yale University Press, 1981.

Fishel, Jeff. *Presidents and Promises.* Washington, D.C.: Congressional Quarterly, 1985.

Kelley, Stanley. *Interpreting Elections.* Princeton, N.J.: Princeton University Press, 1983.

Ladd, Everett Carll. "The 1992 Vote for President Clinton: Another Brittle Mandate?" *Political Science Quarterly* 108 (Spring 1993): 1–28.

———. "1996 Vote: The 'No Majority' Realignment Continues." *Political Science Quarterly* 112 (Spring 1997): 1–28.

Miller, Arthur H. and Martin P. Wattenberg. "Throwing the Rascals Out: Policy and Performance Evaluations of Presidential Candidates, 1952–1980." *American Political Science Review* 79 (1985): 359–372.

Pomper, Gerald M., F. Christopher Arterton, Ross K. Baker, et al. *The Election of 1996.* Chatham, N.J.: Chatham House, 1997.

Popkin, Samuel L. *The Reasoning Voter.* Chicago: University of Chicago Press, 1991.

Shanks, J. Merrill, and Warren E. Miller. "Partisanship, Policy and Performance: The Reagan Legacy in the 1988 Election." *British Journal of Political Science* 21 (1991): 129–197.

Wattenberg, Martin P. *The Rise of Candidate-Centered Politics.* Cambridge, Mass.: Harvard University Press, 1991.

NOTES

1. Robert S. Erikson and Christopher Wlezien, "The Timeline of Political Campaigns" (paper presented at the annual meeting of the American Political Science Association, Boston, September 3–6, 1998), Table 1.

2. Professors Erikson and Wlezien analyzed election polls from 1944 to 1996. They found less variation among the polls in the last one hundred days before the election. They attribute this consistency to the "polarization of underlying preferences [of the electorate] during the campaign." Erikson and Wlezien, "The Timeline of Political Campaigns," 10.

3. Joan Shorenstein Center on the Press, Politics, and Public Policy, "One in Seven Likely Voters Still Undecided on a Presidential Candidate," Harvard University, October 18, 2000 <http://www.vanishingvoter.org>.

4. The results of Gallup's final unallocated poll was 47 percent for Bush, 45 percent for Gore, 4 percent for Nader, less than 1 percent for Buchanan, and 4 percent undecided. Anticipating that half of the undecided would not vote, Gallup split the remaining 2 percent between Bush and Gore. Either because more than half the undecided voted and/or voted more heavily for Gore, the final Gallup Poll underestimated Gore's vote by more than 2.5 percent.

5. James E. Campbell and Kenneth A. Wink, "Trial-Heat Forecasts of the Presidential Vote," *American Politics Quarterly* 18 (July 1990): 257. Updated by author.

6. In the midterm election of 1994 two exit polls were conducted: one focusing on demographic data and voting patterns for members of Congress and the other on issue positions of the electorate, including an evaluation of government performance.

7. In general, turnout declined more in the East and Midwest than it did in the far West in 1980. Even if there was a decline after Carter's concession, there is little evidence to suggest that Democrats behaved any differently from Republicans and Independents. Hawaii, the last state to close its polls, voted for Carter.

8. Raymond Wolfinger and Peter Linquiti, "Tuning In and Turning Out," *Public Opinion* 4 (February/March 1981): 57–59.

9. Harold Mendelsohn and Irving Crespi, *Polls, Television, and the New Politics* (Scranton, Penn.: Chandler, 1970), 234–236.

10. Sandra Sobieraj, "The Story Behind the Near-Concession." Associated Press, November 8, 2000<http://www.ap.org>.

11. Normally, respondents are interviewed two months before and two months after the election.

12. Morris P. Fiorina, *Retrospective Voting in American National Elections* (New Haven, Conn.: Yale University Press, 1981).

13. Presidents will not be blamed for natural disasters or even acts of terrorism over which they have no control, but they will be evaluated on how quickly and effectively they react to the problem, empathize with the victims, and provide federal assistance.

14. This view of retrospective voting was advanced by Anthony Downs, *An Economic Theory of Democracy* (New York: Harper & Row, 1957). Downs suggests that people evaluate the past performance of parties and elected officials in order to anticipate how they will perform in the future compared with their opponents.

15. For a very interesting, albeit sophisticated, article on the impact of emotions on learning, perceptions, and voting see George E. Marcus and Michael B. Mackuen, "Anxiety, Enthusiasm, and the Vote: The Emotional Underpinnings of Learning and Involvement During Presidential Campaigns," *American Political Science Review* 87 (September 1993): 672–685.

16. For an analysis of the components of the 1952 presidential election, see Angus Campbell, Philip E. Converse, Warren E. Miller, and Donald Stokes, *The American Voter* (New York: Wiley, 1960), 524–527.

17. Philip E. Converse, Angus Campbell, Warren E. Miller, and Donald E. Stokes, "Stability and Change in 1960: A Reinstating Election," in *Elections and the Political Order*, ed. Angus Campbell, Philip E. Converse, Warren E. Miller, and Donald E. Stokes (New York: Wiley, 1966), 92.

18. Kennedy's Catholicism may have enlarged his Electoral College total by 22 votes. See Ithiel de Sola Pool, Robert P. Abelson, and Samuel Popkin, *Candidates, Issues, and Strategies* (Cambridge, Mass.: MIT Press, 1965), 115–118.

19. For a discussion of the 1964 presidential election, see Philip E. Converse, Aage R. Clausen, and Warren E. Miller, "Election Myth and Reality: The 1964 Election," *American Political Science Review* 59 (June 1965): 321–336.

20. Philip E. Converse, Warren E. Miller, Jerrold G. Rusk, and Arthur C. Wolfe, "Continuity and Change in American Politics: Parties and Issues in the 1968 Election," *American Political Science Review* 63 (December 1969): 1097. Wallace claimed that there was not "a dime's worth of difference" between the Republican and Democratic candidates and their parties. He took great care in making his own positions distinctive. The clarity with which he presented his views undoubtedly contributed to the issue orientation of his vote. People knew where Wallace stood.

21. Converse, et al., "Continuity and Change," 1085.

22. Warren E. Miller and Teresa E. Levitin, *Leadership and Change* (Cambridge, Mass.: Winthrop, 1976), 164.

23. Arthur H. Miller, Warren E. Miller, Alden S. Raine, and Thad A. Brown, "A Majority Party in Disarray: Policy Polarization in the 1972 Election," *American Political Science Review* 70 (1976): 753–778.

24. Arthur H. Miller and Warren E. Miller, "Partisanship and Performance: Rational Choice in the 1976 Presidential Elections," (paper presented at the annual meeting of the American Political Science Association, Washington, D.C., September 1–4, 1977).

25. Ibid., 99.
26. Ibid., 7; Warren E. Miller, "Policy Directions and Presidential Leadership: Alternative Interpretations of the 1980 Presidential Election," (paper presented at the annual meeting of the American Political Science Association, New York: September 3–6, 1981).
27. According to Arthur H. Miller and Martin P. Wattenberg, "Reagan was the least positively evaluated candidate elected to the presidency in the history of the National Election Studies, which date back to 1952." "Policy and Performance Voting in the 1980 Election," (paper presented at the annual meeting of the American Political Science Association, New York, September 3–6, 1981), 15.
28. Paul R. Abramson, John H. Aldrich, and David W. Rohde, *Change and Continuity in the 1984 Elections* (Washington, D.C.: Congressional Quarterly, 1986), 171–180.
29. J. Merrill Shanks and Warren E. Miller, "Alternative Interpretations of the 1988 Election," (paper presented at the annual meeting of the American Political Science Association, Atlanta, Georgia, August 31–September 3, 1989), 58.
30. Paul R. Abramson, John H. Aldrich, and David W. Rohde, *Change and Continuity in the 1988 Elections* (Washington, D.C.: Congressional Quarterly, 1990), 195.
31. Ibid., 212.
32. J. Merrill Shanks and Warren E. Miller, "Partisanship, Policy, and Performance: The Reagan Legacy in the 1988 Election," *British Journal of Political Science* 21 (April 1991): 129–197.
33. Abramson, et al., *Change and Continuity in the 1988 Elections*, 193, 195, and 198.
34. This pattern reversed itself in the midterm elections of 1994 when Republican turnout was up and that of Democrats was down.
35. Abramson, Aldrich, and Rohde, *Change and Continuity in the 1996 Elections*, 190.
36. For a discussion of election interpretation, see Marjorie Randon Hershey, "The Constructed Explanation: Interpreting Election Results in the 1984 Presidential Race," *Journal of Politics* 54 (1992): 943–976; Dan B. Thomas and Larry R. Baas, "The Postelection Campaign: Competing Construction of the Clinton Victory in 1992," *Journal of Politics* 58 (1996): 309–331.
37. Another limitation to using a platform as a guide to the partisan attitudes and opinions of the public is that many people, including party rank and file, are unfamiliar with most of its contents. The platform per se is not the reason people vote for their party's candidates on election day.
38. Jeff Fishel, *Presidents and Promises* (Washington, D.C.: Congressional Quarterly, 1994), 38, 42–43.
39. One reason campaign promises are important is that they are part of the public record; candidates and parties can be held accountable for them. Another is that they represent the interests of a significant portion of the population. To gain public approval, presidents must respond to these interests. In addition, organized groups, to whom promises have been made, have clout in Congress and in the bureaucracy. Presidents can either mobilize these groups to help them achieve their campaign promises or be thwarted by them if they fail to do so. George Bush ran into this problem in 1990 when he recanted on his pledge not to raise taxes. Conservative Republican members of Congress, who opposed tax increases in their own campaigns for office, voted against the budget compromise that contained a tax increase, a compromise that the president supported.
40. John E. Mueller, *War, Presidents, and Public Opinion* (New York: Wiley, 1973), 205–208; 247–249.

REFORMING THE ELECTORAL SYSTEM

9

INTRODUCTION

The American political system evolved significantly in the second half of the twentieth century. Party rules, finance laws, and media coverage are very different from what they were before the 1960s. The composition of the electorate has changed as well, with the expansion of suffrage to all citizens eighteen years of age or older and the reduction of legal obstacles to voting. In addition, the Electoral College certainly does not function in the manner in which it was originally designed to do so. Have these changes been beneficial? Has the system been improved? Are further structural or operational adjustments desirable? These questions have elicited a continuing, and sometimes spirited, debate.

Critics have alleged that the electoral process is too long, too costly, and too burdensome, that it wears down candidates and numbs voters, resulting in too many personal accusations and too little substantive discussion of the issues, too much name-calling and "sound bite" rhetoric, and too little real debate. They have said that many qualified people are discouraged from running for office and much of the electorate is uninformed, uninterested, and uninvolved. Other criticisms are that the system benefits special interests, encourages factionalism, weakens parties, overemphasizes personality and underemphasizes policy, and that it is unduly influenced by the news media. It has also been contended that voters do not receive the information they need to make an intelligent, informed decision on election day.

In contrast, proponents argue that the political system is more democratic than ever. More, not fewer, people are involved, especially at the nomination stage. Candidates, even lesser-known ones, now have an opportunity to demonstrate

303

their competence, endurance, motivation, and leadership capabilities. Parties remain important as vehicles through which the system operates and by which governing is accomplished. Those who defend the process believe voters do receive as much information as they desire and that most people can and do make informed and rational judgments.

The old adage "where you stand influences what you see" is applicable to the debate about electoral reform. No political process is completely neutral. There are always winners and losers. To a large extent the advantages that some enjoy are made possible by the disadvantages that others encounter. Rationalizations aside, much of the debate about the system, about equity, representation, and responsiveness, revolves around a very practical, political question: Who gains and who loses?

Proposals to change the system need to be assessed in the light of this question. They should also be judged on the basis of how such changes would affect the operation of the political system and influence governance. This chapter discusses some of these proposals and the effect they could have on the road to the White House. The chapter is organized into two sections: one dealing with the more recent developments and proposals in party rules, campaign finance, and media coverage; and the other examining the long-term, democratic issues of participation and voting.

MODIFYING RECENT CHANGES

Party Rules

Of all the changes that have recently occurred in the nomination process, the reforms governing the selection of delegates continue to engender controversy and constant fine-tuning. Designed to encourage grassroots participation and broaden the base of representation, these reforms have also lengthened the nominating period, made the campaign more expensive, generated candidate-based organizations, weakened the influence of state and local party leaders, converted conventions into coronations, and loosened the ties between the parties and their nominees. All of these consequences have made governing more difficult.

Since 1968, when the Democrats began to rewrite their rules for delegate selection, the parties have suffered from these unintended repercussions. Each succeeding presidential election has seen reforms to the reforms, modifications that have attempted to reconcile expanded participation and representation with the traditional need to unify the party and have it play a consequential role in the national campaign. Although less reform conscious than the Democrats, the Republicans have also tried to steer a middle course between greater rank-and-file involvement and more equitable representation on the one hand and the maintenance of successful electoral and governing coalitions on the other.

How to balance these often competing goals has been a critical concern. Those who desire greater public participation have lauded the trend toward having more primaries and a larger percentage of delegates selected in them. Believing that the reforms have opened up the process and made it more democratic, they favor the continued selection of pledged delegates based on the proportion of the popular vote their candidate receives. In contrast, those who believe that greater control by state and national party leaders is desirable argue that the reforms have gone too far. They would prefer fewer primaries, a smaller percentage of delegates selected in them, more unpledged delegates participating in the nominating conventions, and a larger role for state and national party organizations in the entire presidential campaign. Giving all federal funds to the national party committees, and not to the candidates, has been proposed as one way to achieve the latter objective; continuing to have the national parties solicit, distribute, and coordinate the spending of soft money is another that effectively achieves a similar objective.

Stronger party advocates appear to be in the ascendancy. Democratic Party rules have consistently sought to limit participation in its primary elections to registered or self-declared Democrats, although such restrictions are difficult to enforce in states that allow voters to request the ballot of either party (open primaries). Crossover voting by the partisans of one party in the other's primary became a particularly contentious issue in the 2000 nominations when John McCain and Bill Bradley directed their appeals to independent and independent-minded partisan voters.

From the party's perspective, the issue of crossover voting is critical to control of its own nominations. To allow nonpartisans to participate dilutes the influence of party regulars and creates the possibility of a nominee who does not best reflect the interests, needs, or ideological views of most of the rank and file. A particular fear is that adherents of the other party will cross over to vote for the weaker candidate in order to enhance their own nominee's chances in the general election. There is little empirical data to support this fear, however.

From the perspective of the citizenry, on the other hand, a primary closed to all but registered partisans precludes much of the population from participating and reduces the incentive for these voters to become informed and get involved. Moreover, parties can benefit from an open primary system if it leads to its recruitment of more active supporters or makes their nominees more electable. John McCain pointed to the votes he received from Democrats and independents as evidence that he would be a stronger candidate than George W. Bush in the presidential election.

Another rules issue concerns the allocation of votes in primaries. Since 1992, the Democrats have used a straight proportional voting system that allocates pledged delegates according to the proportion of the popular vote a candidate receives. The Republicans permit the states to decide on the method of allocation which could be proportional or winner-take-all within districts or on an at-large basis.

Proportional voting more closely reflects the view of a state's primary electorate, but it also could have the effect of extending the nomination and delaying a consensus on the eventual nominee. The more disunified the party is going into its nominating convention, the weaker its candidates are likely to be in the general election, or so the thinking has been within the party's national leadership.

Although Democrats Michael Dukakis in 1988 and Bill Clinton in 1992 had amassed large leads early and seemed headed toward easy nominations, opponents Jesse Jackson and Jerry Brown were able to contest primaries and caucuses through June. In the process they garnered headlines, criticized the front runners, and appealed to their constituencies. Although they eventually agreed to support the national ticket, their extended campaign had the effect of weakening their party's nominees, effectively undercutting the impact of their own endorsements, and in the case of African Americans who supported Jackson in 1988, reducing turnout in the general election. Robert Dole also had to endure a costly and divisive nomination process in contrast to Clinton's clear sailing to renomination — a disadvantage that started Dole far behind his Democratic opponent in the 1996 general election.

There has been widespread public support for shortening the nomination campaign, which Professor Thomas E. Patterson has argued ". . . disrupts the policy process, discourages the candidacies of responsible officeholders, and wears out the voters."[1] It also diverts public attention from issues of government to campaign-related controversies. Moreover, Patterson notes that the long campaign generates more negative news about the candidates as it progresses, thereby souring voters on the choices they have on primary day.[2]

Several proposals have been made for addressing this issue. Some have even been introduced in the form of legislation in Congress. One would limit the period during which primaries or caucuses could be held; a second would cluster primaries and caucuses, forcing states in designated regions or as groups to hold their elections on the same day; a third would create a national primary.

Having an official period during the spring of the election year for primaries and caucuses has been suggested as a way to reduce the impact the early contests have had on the nomination. A second but equally important objective has been to reduce the news media's influence on public opinion during these initial stages of the process.

The Democratic Party has attempted to achieve these goals since 1984 by imposing its own window period during which primaries and caucuses could be held. Opposition from several states, however, including Iowa and New Hampshire, has forced the party to grant them exceptions to the imposed time frame. The exceptions, in turn, continue to produce the problem that generated the proposal in the first place — the holding of early contests that receive extensive media coverage and for that reason are disproportionally important to the candidates. This problem, in turn, has encouraged other states to move their primaries toward the beginning of the window period, thereby compressing the nomination process and starting the campaign earlier in the election cycle.

The Republicans have faced this problem as well. With no specified time frame imposed on their state parties, the GOP has encountered even more front-loading than the Democrats in recent elections. In 2000, 17 percent of the Republican delegates were selected before March, an additional 28 percent on the first Tuesday of that month (46 percent accumulated), and 21 percent during the following week. A total of 67 percent of all Republican delegates had been selected by March 14.

Front-loading creates inequities. It gives greater influence to those states that hold their contests earlier and less to those that hold them later. To the extent that partisans in the early states are not representative of the party's rank and file, they can skew the results of the election. The winning candidate may not be the first or most acceptable choice for the party as a whole.

Front-loading helps well-known and well-financed candidates. Conversely, it hurts long shots who now must raise more money more quickly and must also enter more contests before they have had amble opportunity to demonstrate their electability. The stepping-stones to the nomination have become more concentrated as a result, lessening the prospects that a non-front-runner can win the nomination.

Front-loading moves the campaign forward, well into the year before the general election. Not only does it lengthen the nomination process, it also shortens its competitive phase. In 2000, the competitive period lasted only six weeks. Thus candidates have to begin their quest for the nomination earlier, and if successful, continue it longer.

From a democratic perspective, perhaps the most serious consequence of front-loaded campaigns is that the decisive stage of the nomination process occurs before most people are paying attention to it. By the time the party's electorate tunes in, many of the candidates may have dropped out. This happened to the Republicans in 2000 when six of the twelve serious candidates withdrew before the first state selected its delegates; three additional candidates dropped out shortly thereafter. Moreover, there is little incentive for the public to stay attentive or even turn out to vote in later primaries after the nomination has been effectively determined.

Inequitable state representation and declining participation were two of the reasons that both major parties established commissions to examine the impact of their nomination procedures on the party, its candidates, and its partisan electorate. After a series of public forums, the Republican Advisory Commission proposed scheduling changes that would have reversed the adverse impact of front-loading. The commission recommended the adoption of a plan submitted by the state party chair in Delaware, a population-based nominating system. The Delaware plan grouped states into four categories according to their size. Over a period of four months, each of the groups would hold their primaries or caucuses on the same day, beginning with the first Tuesday in March. The smallest states would go first and the largest last.

Opposition immediately developed to the proposal. The large states feared that they would lose influence going last, that the nominee would already have been determined. Some party officials and campaign managers saw the plan as raising the money stakes and increasing dependence on the mass media, thereby giving nationally known candidates an even greater advantage than they currently have. Moreover, the controversy over scheduling threatened to divide states at the 2000 Republican convention, upsetting the plans of George W. Bush to have a unified, upbeat, and harmonious gathering from which to launch his presidential campaign. Bush urged delegates on the rules committee to vote against the proposed reforms, and they did, thereby killing the proposal for at least four years.

An alternative to the Delaware plan, which the Republican Advisory Commission considered and judged second best, was regional primaries, a proposal put forth by the National Association of Secretaries of States. The idea was to hold rotating regional contests over a four-month period.

The concept of regional primaries had been taking shape since 1988 when southern Democrats, unhappy over the national party's liberal tilt, convinced their state legislatures to hold their nominating contests on the second Tuesday in March. Most of them have continued to do so. Meanwhile states in the Northeast, with the exception of New Hampshire, have moved their contests to the first Tuesday for the last two presidential nomination cycles and several of the midwestern states now schedule theirs on the third Tuesday of that month. Despite this movement toward regional primaries, the front-loading of the system, particularly in 2000, has worked to undercut the benefits of a regionalized process.

The case for regional primaries is based on the assumption that such a system would be more equitable for the states and provide more focus for the candidates. As long as the regions adopted some plan to rotate their nomination dates, which they do not do at present, each area, over a period of time, would be able to exercise approximately equal influence over the selection of a party's nominees. Moreover, candidates would be forced to address regional concerns and appeal to regional interests. A nomination that extended to the four regional primaries would probably ensure that the winning candidate had broad-based geographic support, the kind of support that is necessary to win in the Electoral College.

But regionalization is not without its critics who fear that it would exacerbate sectional rivalries, encourage local or area candidates, and produce more organizations to rival those of the state and national parties. Moreover, like straight proportional voting, a regional primary system could impede the emergence of a consensus candidate, thereby extending the process to the convention and increasing, not decreasing, costs, time, and media attention.

In addition, regional primaries help the best-organized and best-financed candidates, such as Bill Clinton and George Bush in 1992, Bob Dole in 1996, Al Gore and George W. Bush in 2000. They make it more difficult for candidates who lack a national reputation and a huge war chest to compete in regions outside their own.

Another option, and the one that represents the most sweeping change, would be to institute a national primary. Given the increasing number of delegates selected on the first Tuesday in March, such a proposal may be evolving on its own. Although party leaders, including members of the reform commissions, have opposed this idea and Congress has been cool to it, the general public seems to be more favorably disposed. Gallup polls taken over the last two decades indicate that about two-thirds of the electorate prefers such an election to the present system.[3]

Most proposals for a national primary call for it to be held in the late spring or early summer, followed by party conventions. Candidates who wished to enter their party's primary would be required to obtain a certain number of signatures. Any aspirant who won a majority would automatically receive the nomination. In some plans a plurality would be sufficient, provided it was at least 40 percent. In the event that no one received 40 percent, a runoff election would be held several weeks later between the top two finishers. Nominating conventions would continue to select the vice presidential candidates and to decide on the platforms.

A national primary would be consistent with the "one person, one vote" principle that guides most aspects of the U.S. electoral system. All participants would have an equal voice in the selection. No longer would those in the early, small primary and caucus states exercise disproportionate influence.

It is also likely that a national primary would stimulate turnout. The attention given to such an election would provide greater incentives for voting than currently exists, particularly in those states that hold their nomination contests after the apparent winner has emerged. A national primary would probably result in nomination by a more representative electorate than is currently the case.

A single primary election for each party would accelerate a nationalizing trend. Issues that affect the entire country would be the primary focus of attention. Thus, candidates for the nation's highest office would be forced to discuss the problems they would most likely address during the general election campaign and would most likely confront as president.

Moreover, the results of the election would be clear-cut. The media could no longer interpret primaries and caucus returns as they saw fit. An incumbent's ability to garner support through the timely release of grants, contracts, and other spoils of government might be more limited in a national contest, but it would not be eliminated entirely. On the other hand, such an election would undoubtedly discourage challengers who lacked national reputations. No longer would an early victory catapult a relatively unknown aspirant into the position of serious contender and jeopardize a president's chances for renomination. In fact, lesser-known candidates, such as George McGovern, Jimmy Carter, Michael Dukakis, and even Bill Clinton in 1992, might find it extremely difficult to raise money, build an organization, and mount a national campaign. John McCain would have had more difficulty challenging George W. Bush if he had had to campaign in all fifty states.

From the standpoint of the major parties, a national primary would further weaken the ability of their leaders to influence the selection of the nominee. Successful candidates would probably not owe their victory to party officials. Moreover, a postprimary convention could not be expected to tie the nominee to the party, although it might tie the party to the nominee, at least through the election. The trend toward personalizing politics would probably continue.

Such nominees, if elected, might also find governing much more difficult. They could not count on the support of party leaders if those leaders played little or no role in the candidate's nomination. Party leaders and members of Congress who have no stake in the election of the president would be hard to mobilize and quick to jump ship should the president get into political difficulty.

Whether a national primary winner would be the party's strongest candidate is also open to question. With a large field of contenders, those with the most devoted or ideological supporters might do best. On the other hand, candidates who do not arouse the passions of the diehards but who are more acceptable to the party's mainstream might not do as well. Everybody's second choice might not even finish second, unless a system of approval voting or cumulative voting were used.[4] Approval or cumulative voting systems, however, complicate the election, confuse the result, undercut its legitimacy, and perhaps add to its costs.

In addition to weakening the party, a national primary could lessen the ability of states to determine when and how their citizens would participate in the presidential nomination process, thereby undercutting the federal system of nominations. The ability of state party leaders and elected officials to affect the process and influence the outcome would suffer. These likely consequences have made it difficult to mobilize wide political support for such a plan despite the general appeal of the idea to the public.

Finance Laws

Closely related to the delegate selection process are the laws governing campaign finance. Enacted in the 1970s in reaction to secret and sometimes large, illegal bequests to candidates, to the disparity in contributions and spending among the candidates, and to the spiraling costs of modern campaigns, particularly television advertising, these laws were designed to improve accountability, reduce spending, subsidize nominations, and fund the general election. Some of these objectives have been achieved, but in the process other problems have been created.

The laws have taken campaign finance out of the back rooms and put much of it into the public spotlight. They have also, however, created a nightmare of compliance procedures and reporting requirements. Detailed records of practically all contributions and expenditures of the presidential campaign organizations must now be kept and periodically reported to the Federal Election Commission.[5] Good accountants and attorneys, specializing in election law, are now as necessary as pollsters, image makers, and grassroots organizers.

But there are loopholes in the laws which party and nonparty groups, such as the Christian Coalition, the National Rifle Association, and pro- and antiabortion groups, have exploited to their political advantage. The latest loophole, section 527 of the U.S. tax code, permitted nonprofit organizations which were active in elections to raise and spend unlimited and unreported amounts of money so long as they did not advocate the election of a particular candidate. After one such group, Republicans for Clean Air, spent $2.5 million in advertisements critical of John McCain's environmental record, Congress acted to close this loophole. Beginning on June 30, 2000, such organizations that raise over $25,000 are required to report to the Internal Revenue Service any donations of $200 or more and expenditures of $500 or more. The law does not inhibit their campaign activity, however.

The amount wealthy individuals can donate to the candidates for their party's nomination is limited by law, but not the amount they can contribute to their party's soft-money account, PACs' soft-money accounts, or the amount they can spend independently (or on themselves were they to run and not accept federal funds). This situation still contains incentives for candidates to obtain broad-based public support for their campaign, but it has not decreased their need for frequent appeals for funds as they seek the nomination and even after they effectively wrap it up.

The law also places severe budget constraints on candidates who accept federal matching grants. The Federal Election Campaign Act (FECA) sets individual state and overall spending limits on candidates who get federal funds, thereby putting them at a disadvantage compared to opponents who have the resources to campaign without government matching funds. Had John McCain continued his campaign after the first Tuesday in March, he would have quickly reached his overall spending ceiling for the entire nomination period, whereas George W. Bush would not have faced such a limit. State spending limits, especially, have encouraged candidates for their party's nomination to circumvent the law as a matter of prudent campaign practice.

Not only has federal funding not equalized the financial status of serious aspirants for the Republican and Democratic Party nominations, it has also encouraged fringe candidates like Lyndon LaRouche, Alan Keyes, and Gary Bauer who want to use the election to espouse their views or pursue their political ambitions, partially at public expense.

One way to deal with the dual problems of inequity and what some regard as the imprudent use of taxpayers' funds is to stiffen the eligibility requirements by increasing the amount that many candidates must raise to obtain government support but also increasing the size of the federal grant if they do meet the new and tougher requirements. Such a change would still permit those with some recognition and support to enter the race but would make more money available to them as they obtained private donations. The problem, of course, is that increasing matching funds would drain the elections fund more rapidly, creating the potential for even greater shortfalls than the ones that occurred in 1996 and 2000 and pressuring Congress to increase the tax checkoff amount still further.

And a financial discrepancy between the major party candidates still exists in the general election. The Republicans have enjoyed an advantage over the years by virtue of their party's superior organizational and financial base at the national, state, and local levels. But the Democrats have also raised huge amounts of money in recent elections, helped by their party's control of the White House and their liberal use of its facilities as inducements and "thank yous" for the largest contributors.

The law has also not reduced or controlled candidate spending. On the contrary, the need to supplement increasing expenditures for fund-raising, media, polling, and other important campaign activities has actually increased the amount of money that the campaign organizations believe that they must raise and spend to compete effectively. This need combined with the failure to raise the contribution limits set in 1974 for individuals and groups has forced candidates to spend more time fund-raising and has encouraged them to shift as many of their campaign costs as possible to the national and state parties in the general election.

The soft-money loophole is particularly egregious. Soft-money expenditures are now expected to supplement the presidential campaign. Unofficial liaisons with nonparty groups have also extended the campaign resources through issue advocacy and grassroots activity. Although such collusion with nonparty groups ostensibly violates the FECA, enforcement is nearly impossible given the partisan composition of the commission — three Republicans and three Democrats.

All of these unintended consequences of the campaign law have worked to undermine public support for the electoral process and its public financing system. One illustration of this trend is the declining percentage of taxpayers who allocate their taxes to the campaign election fund. Another is the persistence of campaign finance reform on the congressional agenda. A third is the salience which that issue received during the 2000 presidential primaries and general election campaign. Democrat Al Gore promised that the first proposal he would introduce to Congress, if elected, would be the McCain-Feingold bill that would ban soft money in presidential campaigns.

Many changes have been suggested to fix the finance problem. Contributions and expenditures from noncitizens could be prohibited. Both parties have solicited and accepted legal contributions from individuals who were permanent residents in the United States and from American subsidiaries of foreign businesses. But in the 1995–1996 cycle, they also accepted money from foreign citizens and corporations who were not entitled to give under U.S. law. In fact, there even was an allegation that the Democratic Party accepted a large donation from a Chinese businessman, funnelled to him from the Chinese military. Although the Clinton administration vehemently denied that any of its policy decisions were affected by these contributions, the perception that they might have been has raised anew concerns about foreign money and the influence it may have over American politics and policy.

But foreign contributions pale by comparison to the amount of soft money raised and spent by the parties. Soft money contributions, some of them running as high as $1 million, have given rise to the age-old debate about the influence that big contributors exert over the parties, their candidates, and public policy decisions.

One proposal to deal with this very serious concern is to simply rescind the 1979 amendment that permitted soft-money contributions, thereby eliminating them entirely; another is to tighten the rules on how this money can be spent or limit the amount of it that can be contributed. However, if the soft-money loophole were tightened or closed as the McCain-Feingold bill proposes, the parties would have to find other sources of revenue or their party-building efforts would be damaged, their candidates would get much less issue-oriented advertising, and turnout, the reason for the amendment in the first place, could be adversely affected.

How could other campaign revenues be increased? One way would be to increase the amount of individual or group contributions to parties and congressional candidates and to presidential candidates during the nomination phase of their campaign. The purchasing power of contributions has declined by about two-thirds since the individual and group limits were initially established. The problem with increasing the limits is that the wealthy would gain greater influence, as they have with soft money, and candidates and parties could become more dependent on them.

Another option would be to increase the amount of individual contributions that could be matched by federal grants. Such a provision would shift the burden of costs from those who were more willing and able to pay to the American taxpayers. Not only might such a shift be seen as politically undesirable, but it might also be unfeasible given the limited amount of money generated by the current income tax check-off provision.

There are other things that Congress could do. It could enact legislation requiring television stations which operate over the public airways to allow candidates free time to respond to political advertising, debate, or simply state their policy positions. Candidates might also get reduced rates for mailing campaign literature to the voters. But these proposals are opposed by profit-making media and would require a federal subsidy if they applied to the U.S. Postal Service.

Moreover, a law that forced the media to provide free time might even be counterproductive, reducing rather than increasing the amount of public communications during the campaign. Television and radio stations would undoubtedly be discouraged from selling time to nonparty groups and individuals if they were under obligation to provide it free to the person or party who was the object of the commercial. A decrease in media advertising would reduce the information available to the public and increase the electorate's dependence on the candidates and the news media.

Besides, the appearance of candidates on talk-entertainment shows beginning in 1992 and the proliferation of all-news cable channels has in point of fact given major candidates more "free" time to respond to questions about their policy positions and personal character. But it has also given the producers, hosts, and commentators on these shows subtle ways of influencing the electorate through the wording and sequencing of their questions to the candidates and even by their choice of who to interview and when to do so.

On the other hand, there are those who contend that soft money is not a problem and should not be reduced or eliminated. They argue that the parties and their candidates need more money, not less, and that contrary to popular belief, Americans do not spend all that much on elections. If the size of the population is taken into consideration, about $30 per voter was spent in the federal elections in 2000.

Independent spending by individuals and groups is cited as still another campaign finance problem. Particularly troublesome have been efforts by both national parties to "suggest" to PACs (Democrats to organized labor; Republicans to business groups and allegedly also to the Christian Coalition) and to individuals of both political persuasions how to spend their money most effectively, going so far as to suggest which commercials to buy, from whom, and when to air them.

PAC contributions and PAC spending on electoral activities constitute another very contentious issue, at least from the perception of the general public. One way to decrease the influence of PACs is to prohibit or reduce the amount of money that they could contribute to federal elections. But limiting their independent spending is not an option so long as the Supreme Court's *Buckley v. Valeo* decision stands. That decision equates campaign spending with freedom of speech which is protected by the First Amendment. If individual and group spending were seen as the use of personal property in political campaigns, restrictions might not encounter the same constitutional proscriptions that they do with free speech.

Although many lawmakers see problems with the finance laws and how they are being enforced, they have had difficulty agreeing whether legal reforms are necessary and if so, what they should be. One of the principal difficulties in reforming the campaign finance is that the people who need to design the solutions are the very ones who have benefited the most from the existing laws, members of Congress and the president. The Democrats and Republicans not only wish to gain advantage with each other, but they also wish to preserve their advantage over third parties and independent candidacies. Is it any wonder that even though the public supports changing the campaign finance system, Congress has taken little action?

And there is another, perhaps more basic problem. In addition to the question of political equity, there is also the issue of individual political liberty. Competing needs within the society have created contradictory goals. Freedom of speech implies the right to advance beliefs by contributing to the candidates and party of one's choice and spending independently on their behalf. In a democratic political system, however, a system in which the vote and presumably the voice of all citizens should be equal, the wealthy should not have an advantage. Yet appeals to a large segment of the electorate are very expensive. The difficulty of ensuring that the candidates have sufficient funds, protecting freedom of speech, and promoting political equality — all without partisan advantage — generated considerable debate in the halls of Congress in the 1990s but no policy solutions.

News Media Coverage

A third significant change in the electoral process concerns the way in which information about the campaign is communicated to the voters. Beginning in the 1950s, television became the principal medium through which candidates made their appeals and by which voters obtained information. Since then, television's emphasis on the contest, the drama, and the style of candidates has affected every nook and cranny of the campaign from public perceptions of the candidates and the parties to the judgment of the electorate on election day.

Changes in party rules and finance laws have also contributed to the media's impact. The increasing number of primaries and caucuses have provided the news media with greater inducements to cover these events and interpret their results. The desire of the party to obtain maximum exposure for its nominating convention has resulted in two simultaneous conventions, the "official" one at the podium, carefully orchestrated by the party to benefit its nominees in the eyes of the public, and the unofficial one, mediated by the news media, designed to interest and entertain viewers and readers with behind-the-scenes reporting and analysis. The limited money available to presidential candidates who accept federal funding has also increased the importance of news about their campaign and may have contributed to the news media's impact on the voters. Today candidates do not leave their coverage to chance. They attempt to influence it by carefully releasing favorable information and "spinning" the news to their advantage, by staging events and designing speeches in sound-bite formats, and by paying for many commercial messages.

Is the coverage adequate? Do voters receive sufficient information from the news media to make an intelligent decision? Many believe they do not. Academicians, especially, have urged that greater attention be paid to policy issues and less to the game format of who is ahead, most likely to win, and why. One proposal would have the networks and wire services assign special correspondents to cover the issues of the campaign, much as they assign people to report on its color, drama, and personal aspects. Another would be to place greater emphasis on campaign coverage itself and assess the accuracy of the statements and advertising claims of the candidates as some newspapers, such as the *Washington Post* and the *New York Times*, and major television networks have begun to do on a regular basis.

In addition to criticizing the news media's treatment of the issues and its watchdog function in the campaign, academicians and others have frequently called into question the amount and accuracy of election reporting. The law states that if the networks provide free time to some candidates, they must provide equal time to all running for the same position, including those of fringe parties. This "equal time" provision has in fact resulted in little or no free time, although coverage of debates between candidates for their party's nomination, and later between candidates of the major parties in the general election, is permitted. In 1996, for the first time the major networks gave the candidates limited time to use as they wished before the election. Networks are also required to be impartial in their coverage. Station licenses can be challenged and even revoked if biases are consistently evident in the presentation of the news.

Other than requiring fairness, preventing obscenity, and ensuring that public service commitments are met, there is little the government can do to ensure adequate coverage without impinging on the constitutional protections of freedom of the press. The news media are free to choose which elections and candidates to emphasize, what kind and how much coverage to provide, how to interpret the results of primaries and caucuses, and even to predict who will win before the election is concluded. And these freedoms tend to be exercised with public programming desires in mind. Not only do corporations that own media affiliates engage in constant polling to discern the interest of the viewing, listening, and reading public, but people "vote" everyday when they turn on a particular program on radio or television or buy a particular newspaper or magazine.

There is much that candidates can do, however, to affect the coverage they receive. If their words are unreported or not reported correctly, or if their ideas are misinterpreted or their motives suspected by the national news, they can seek other mass media formats for reaching the general public as they did in 1992 and 1996 by using the entertainment and talk shows. They can also employ satellite technology to reach local and regional audiences directly and thereby circumvent the national press. And they can agree to other "competitive" formats that will get national coverage because they fit into the game motif that the news media use.

Another media-related issue is the election night projections based on exit polling data that the networks air before all voting has been completed. Since 1964, when a Lyndon Johnson landslide was predicted before the polls on the West Coast had closed, proposals have been advanced to limit or prohibit these glimpses into the immediate future. Beginning in 1984, the networks promised not to forecast the outcome in any state until a majority of its polls had closed.

This voluntary restriction does not rectify the problem of having different time zones nor preclude a national prediction from being made before voting is completed in the continental United States.

Proposals to deal with the election night projection issue include one that would establish a uniform hour at which voting ends in the continental United States or another to terminate the current process entirely and replace it with a national system of mail ballots or eventually voting on the Internet. These proposals have also encountered criticism. Could the networks be expected to wait until voting ended across the nation, given the competitive character of news reporting? Even if there was a uniform closing hour for the entire country, there still would be no guarantee that early forecasts, based on exit polls, could be eliminated. Moreover, a law, such as the one the House of Representatives passed in 1989 that would have forced thirty-nine states to change their voting hours, reduces their constitutional prerogative to conduct elections for federal officials. Eight states, including California, would have had to reduce the hours during which people could vote, conceivably contributing to lower turnout while others would have increased hours and correspondingly increased costs. A mail ballot, such as the one used in Oregon, might be possible in the nation as a whole although it might also be potentially more subject to fraud than the system that currently exists.

In addition to the obvious First Amendment problems that would be generated by restricting what and when the news could report about the election, there is another more general media-related issue. People enjoy the election night broadcasts. After a lengthy campaign, workers and sympathizers are eager to learn the results and to celebrate or commiserate, whereas the public desires the ritualistic conclusion that the reporting and analysis of the results on election night provide. Moreover, exit polls have considerable value in the information they provide about the beliefs, attitudes, and motivations of the voters. In a democracy, it is essential to get as clear a reading of the pulse of the electorate as possible.

ENHANCING ELECTORAL CHOICE

Turnout

Although suffrage has expanded, a gap remains between those eligible to vote and those who actually do so. This gap, which will always exist in a system that does not compel voting, widened during the last forty years. In 1996, more than half those eligible chose *not* to vote; it remained low in 2000, around 51 percent.

The decline in the intensity of partisan allegiances, the shift from party-centered to candidate-centered campaigns, the growing levels of mistrust and lower confidence in public officials, and the weakening sense of efficacy on the part of many people have all contributed to lower turnout and produced a "disconnect" between American citizens and their political system. That disconnect threatens to undermine the legitimacy of American electoral institutions and reduces the ability of elected officials to build and maintain a cohesive governing majority.

Low turnout in a free and open electoral system has been a source of embarrassment to the United States and of concern to its political leaders. How can a president legitimately claim a public mandate with the electoral support of so few of those who are eligible to vote? In the last four presidential elections, the winning candidate has received the votes of only about one-quarter of those members of the voting-age population. Can a government still claim to be representative and democratic, if almost half the population chooses not to participate in elections for public officials?

A variety of legal, institutional, and political obstacles must be overcome if turnout is to increase. Congress addressed one of the problem areas in 1993 when it enacted legislation to ease registration procedures. Other proposals to make registration automatic, as it is in many European countries, or extending it to election day itself, as is already permitted in a few states, have also been advanced. Countries or states, which have facilitated registration in these ways, have considerably higher levels of turnout than those that do not.

Another proposal to enhance turnout would make election day a national holiday or move election day to Veterans Day, which comes later in the month. Presumably either change would prevent work-related activities from interfering with voting for the bulk of the population. Many countries follow the practice of holding their elections on a holiday or Sunday. The problem here is that an additional national holiday would cost employers millions of dollars in lost revenue and productivity, with no guarantee that turnout would increase, and veterans would probably oppose having politics obscure the meaning that the holiday was intended to have for the end of hostilities in the two World Wars. For workers in certain service sectors, the holiday might be a workday anyway.

Some states have extended the period for voting up to twenty-one days prior to the election to increase the number of voters. Others have enacted a "no fault" absentee ballot system for those who find it difficult or inconvenient to get to the polls on election day. Under a liberalized absentee voting procedure, any eligible voter can obtain an absentee ballot, no questions asked. Twenty states currently provide one or both of these options, and voting turnout in them has increased.[6]

Oregon has gone so far as to institute a mail ballot. After experimenting with voting by mail in a special election for Senate and later in the presidential primaries of 1996, Oregonians voted in favor of a ballot initiative that permanently institutes this method of voting beginning in 2000. Turnout in Oregon has exceeded the national average in those elections in which mail balloting has been used.[7]

But extending the voting period and balloting by mail are not without their costs. Fear of fraud, if the ballots get into the wrong hands, is one concern. Voting without all pertinent information is another. People who vote early do so without knowing what may be revealed at the end of the campaign. And for the candidates themselves, there is the added cost of mailing thousands of ballots to voters and appealing to them to use them when voting. Nonetheless, the benefit of increasing turnout has motivated more states to modify their single day, geographically based voting tradition.

Perhaps the most radical proposal for the United States would be to compel people to vote: to force them to go to the polls or cast an absentee ballot. Penalties would be imposed on those who refused to do so. Australia, Belgium, and Chile require voting and their turnout is very high. One obvious problem with forcing people to vote is the compulsion itself. Some may be physically or mentally incapable of voting. Others may not care, have little interest, and have very limited information. They might not even know the names of the candidates. Would the selection of the best-qualified person be enhanced by the participation of these uninformed, uninterested, uncaring voters? Might demagogy be encouraged, or even slicker and more simplistic advertising designed? Would government be more responsive and more popular, or would it be more prone to what British philosopher John Stuart Mill referred to as "the tyranny of the majority"? Finally, is it democratic to force people to vote? If the right to vote is an essential component of a democratic society, then what about the right *not* to vote? Should it be protected as well?

In addition to easing or removing legal obstacles or creating a legal requirement to vote, there have been other kinds of suggestions for encouraging more people to participate. One is to change the electoral system itself to provide more incentives for those in the minority by increasing the likelihood that their vote would produce tangible results. Instituting proportional representation for Congress or in the apportionment of electoral votes could produce this effect; directly electing the president might also do so. In these cases those in the minority would have greater incentive to vote than they do under the current system. Winner-take-all voting, which occurs in single-member legislative districts and in most states in the Electoral College, discourages turnout in noncompetitive areas.

Systemic changes, however, are difficult to accomplish. They upset the established political order and are likely to generate opposition from those who fear change, resistance from those who are used to the current arrangement, or support from those who believe that they will benefit more if the system is changed in a certain way. Moreover, reforming the electoral system in this manner would require a constitutional amendment, which is always more difficult than enacting legislation. As a consequence, these proposals are not likely to be implemented in the short run nor in the absence of other changes.

Creating a more hospitable and engaging electoral climate is another way to increase turnout. If parties were strengthened, if their organizations were more broad-based, if they encouraged more participatory politics by providing more information to voters and more grassroots activities, turnout would likely be enhanced. But revitalizing the parties has proven to be extremely difficult, particularly in the current era in which so many people are turned off by partisan politics. Moreover, changes in the nomination process have weakened, not strengthened party structures, although organizational control over money and other campaign resources has begun to reverse that effect.

We have already referred to another potential arena of change — the communications industry. If candidates had greater access to the media, if they were given free time in addition to the time they purchased, if advertising were less expensive, if there were more debates during prime time, if candidates appeared on more interactive programs and more general entertainment formats, then more of the public might become engaged in the campaign and thus would turn out to vote rather than tune out, which unfortunately has been the case for far too many people today.[8] Greater exposure, however, might also numb the electorate; entertainment formats often emphasize style over substance and might trivialize the campaign. More television exposure might result in the election of more media celebrities and fewer civic-minded political leaders.

Educating the people on the merits of participating and the responsibilities of citizenry might also generate greater involvement. If the public better understood what difference it makes who wins, if they had greater confidence that elected officials would keep their promises and that government would address salient issues, then voter turnout would likely be enhanced. But invigorating the electoral environment and encouraging more people to participate is not an easy task. If it were, it would have already occurred. It is difficult to convince nonvoters to spend the time and effort it takes to educate themselves about the candidates and the issues, to get involved in the campaign, and to vote unless people can see what is in it for them and what might happen if they do not do so.

If, however, more people did vote, the parties and candidates would have to broaden their appeal. They would have to address the needs and desires of all the people and not concentrate on those who were most likely to vote. Those who have not participated as frequently in the current voluntary system of voting — the poorer, less educated, less fortunate, and younger — would receive more attention not only from candidates for office but from elected officials in office. More equitable policies might result, but also more socioeconomic divisions within the political structure might be evident. At the worst, these divisions could lead to a more volatile political system and more extreme variations in public policies.

The Electoral College

In addition to the problem of who votes, another source of contention is how the votes should be aggregated. Theoretically, the Constitution allows electors chosen by the states to vote as they please. In practice, all votes are cast for the popular vote winner. The reason for this outcome is simple. The vote for president and vice president is actually a vote for competing slates of electors selected in all but two states on a statewide basis. The slate that wins is the slate proposed by the winning candidate's party. Naturally the electors are expected to vote for their party's nominees.

This de facto system has been criticized as undemocratic, as unrepresentative of minority views within states, and as potentially unreflective of the nation's popular choice. Over the years, there have been numerous proposals to alter it. The first was introduced in Congress in 1797. Since then, there have been more than five hundred others. In urging changes, critics have pointed to the Electoral College's archaic design, its electoral biases, and the undemocratic results it can produce. (See Chapter 1.) Four major plans — automatic, proportional, district, and direct election — have been proposed as constitutional amendments to alleviate some or all of these problems. The following sections will examine these proposals and the impact they could have on the way in which the president is selected.

The Automatic Plan. The electors in the Electoral College have been an anachronism since the development of the party system. Their role as partisan agents is not and has not been consistent with their exercising an independent judgment. In fact, sixteen states plus the District of Columbia prohibit such a judgment by requiring electors to cast their ballots for the winner of the state's popular vote. Although probably unenforceable because they seem to clash with the Constitution, these laws strongly indicate how electors should vote.

The so-called automatic plan would do away with the danger that electors may exercise their personal preferences. First proposed in 1826, it has received substantial support since that time, including the backing of Presidents John Kennedy and Lyndon Johnson. The plan simply keeps the Electoral College intact but eliminates the electors. Electoral votes are automatically given to the candidate who has received the most popular votes within the state.

Other than removing the potential problem of faithless or unpledged electors, the plan would do little to change the system as it currently operates. It has not been enacted because Congress has not felt this particular problem to be of sufficient magnitude to justify a constitutional amendment to fix it. There have in fact been only eight faithless electors, who failed to vote for their party's nominees — six since 1948.[9] Additionally, one Democratic West Virginia elector in 1988 reversed the order of the nominees, voting for Lloyd Bentsen for president and Michael Dukakis for vice president.

The Proportional Plan. Electing the entire slate of presidential electors has also been the focus of considerable attention. If the winner of the state's popular vote takes all the electoral votes, the impact of the dominant party is increased within that state and the larger, more competitive states, where voters tend to be more evenly divided, are benefited.

From the perspective of the other major party and minor parties within the state as well as third-party candidates, this winner-take-all system is not desirable. In effect, it disenfranchises people who do not vote for the winning candidate. And it does more than that: it discourages a strong campaign effort by a party that has little chance of winning the presidential election in that state, such as Democrats in Utah or Nebraska or Republicans in Hawaii or West Virginia. Naturally the success of other candidates of that party is affected as well. The winner-take-all system also works to reduce voter turnout.

One way to rectify this problem would be to have proportional voting. Such a plan has been introduced on a number of occasions. Under a proportional system, the electors would be abolished, the winner-take-all principle would be eliminated, and a state's electoral vote would be divided in proportion to the popular vote the candidates received within the state. A majority of electoral votes would still be required for election. If no candidate obtained a majority in the Electoral College, most proportional plans call for a joint session of Congress to choose the president from among the top two or three candidates.

The proportional proposal would have a number of major consequences. It would decrease the influence of the most competitive states and increase the importance of the least competitive ones, where voters are likely to be more homogeneous. Under such a system, it would be the *size* of the victory that counted.

By rewarding large victories in relatively homogeneous states, the system would seem to encourage competition within those states. Having the electoral vote proportional to the popular vote provides an incentive to all the parties, not simply the dominant one, to mount a more vigorous campaign and to establish a more effective organization. This incentive could strengthen the other major party within the state, but it might also help third parties as well, thereby weakening the two-party system. Ross Perot, who received no electoral votes under the present winner-take-all system, would have received approximately 102 under the proportional plan in 1992 and 49 in 1996. More important, Bill Clinton would not have received a majority in 1992 or 1996 (he would have been about 6 electoral votes short) if electoral votes were distributed according to the proportion of the vote candidates received in individual states. Under these circumstances, third-party candidates, such as Perot, might have the power to influence the election between the major party candidates by instructing their delegates to support one of them.

If no candidate received a majority of the electoral votes, the House of Representatives would choose the president. Selection by the House, however, weakens a president's national mandate, might make the president more dependent on the House or might require promises or favors to legislators whose support was critical for victory, and in general, could decrease presidential influence in the initial period of an administration. And what happens if the leading candidate is of one party and the House is controlled by the other party? Would legitimacy be enhanced under that arrangement?

Operating under a proportional plan would in all likelihood make the Electoral College vote much closer, thereby reducing the claim most presidents wish to make that they have received broad public backing for themselves, their new administration, and the policy proposals they have advocated during their campaign. George Bush would have defeated Michael Dukakis by only 43.1 electoral votes in 1988, Jimmy Carter would have defeated Gerald Ford by only 11.7 in 1976, and Richard Nixon would have won by only 6.1 in 1968. (See Table 9–1.) And in at least one recent instance, a proportional electoral vote in the states might have changed the election results. Had this plan been in effect in 1960, Richard Nixon would probably have defeated John Kennedy by 266.1 to 265.6.[10]

The District Plan. The district electoral system is another proposal aimed at reducing the effect of winner-take-all voting. This plan has had several variations, but its basic thrust would be to keep the Electoral College but to change the manner in which the electoral votes within the states are determined. Instead of selecting the entire slate on the basis of the statewide vote for president, only two electoral votes would be decided in this manner. The remaining votes would be allocated on the basis of the popular vote within individual districts (probably congressional districts). Maine and Nebraska currently employ such a system. A majority of the electoral votes would still be necessary for election. If the vote in the Electoral College were not decisive, then most district plans call for a joint session of Congress to make the final selection.

TABLE 9–1 ★

VOTING FOR PRESIDENT, 1956–2000: FOUR METHODS FOR AGGREGATING THE VOTES

Year	Electoral College	Proportional Plan	District Plan	Direct Election (percentage of total votes)
1956				
Eisenhower	457	296.7	411	57.4
Stevenson	73	227.2	120	42.0
Others	1	7.1	0	0.6
1960				
Nixon	219	266.1	278	49.5
Kennedy	303	265.6	245	49.8
Others (Byrd)	15	5.3	14	0.7
1964				
Goldwater	52	213.6	72	38.5
Johnson	486	320.0	466	61.0
Others	0	3.9	0	0.5
1968				
Nixon	301	231.5	289	43.2
Humphrey	191	225.4	192	42.7
Wallace	46	78.8	57	13.5
Others	0	2.3	0	0.6
1972				
Nixon	520	330.3	474	60.7
McGovern	17	197.5	64	37.5
Others	1	10.0	0	1.8
1976				
Ford	240	258.0	269	48.0
Carter	297	269.7	269	50.1
Others	1	10.2	0	1.9
1980				
Reagan	489	272.9	396	50.7
Carter	49	220.9	142	41.0
Anderson	0	35.3	0	6.6
Others	0	8.9	0	1.7
1984				
Reagan	525	317.6	468	58.8
Mondale	13	216.6	70	40.6
Others	0	3.8	0	0

TABLE 9–1 ★ *(continued)*

VOTING FOR PRESIDENT, 1956–2000:
FOUR METHODS FOR AGGREGATING THE VOTES

Year	Electoral College	Proportional Plan	District Plan	Direct Election (percentage of total votes)
1988				
Bush	426	287.8	379	53.4
Dukakis	111	244.7	159	45.6
Others	1	5.5	0	1.0
1992				
Bush	168	203.3	214	37.5
Clinton	370	231.6	324	43.0
Perot	0	101.8	0	18.9
Others	0	1.3	0	0.6
1996				
Clinton	379	262.0	345	49.2
Dole	159	219.9	193	40.7
Perot	0	48.8	0	8.4
Others	0	7.3	0	1.7
2000				
Gore	266*	258.4	267	48.2
Bush	271	260.2	271	48.0
Others	0	19.4	—	3.8

*One Democratic elector in the District of Columbia cast a blank electoral vote to protest the District's absence of voting representation in Congress.

Sources: Figures on proportional and district vote for 1952–1980 were supplied to the author by Joseph B. Gorman of the Congressional Research Service, Library of Congress. Calculations for 1984–1992 were made on the basis of data reported in the *Almanac of American Politics* (Washington, D.C.: National Journal, annual) and Federal Election Commission. Calculations for 1996 were made on the basis of official returns as reported by the FEC. For 2000, they are based on the unofficial returns as reported by <CNN.com/ALLPOLITICS>, November 26, 2000; 2000 District Plan figures are based on Tom Squitieri, "Bush Would Still Win with Electoral Reforms," *USA Today,* <http://www.usatoday.com/news/vote2000/bush25>.

For the very smallest states, those with three electoral votes, all three electors would have to be chosen by the state as a whole. For others, however, the combination of district and at-large selection would probably result in a split electoral vote. On a national level, this change would make the Electoral College more reflective of the partisan division of the newly elected Congress rather than of the popular division of the national electorate.

The losers under such an arrangement would be the large, competitive states and, most particularly, the cohesive, geographically concentrated groups within those states. The winners would include small states. Third parties, especially those that are regionally based, might also be aided to the extent that they were capable of winning specific legislative districts.

It is difficult to project whether Republicans or Democrats would benefit more from such an arrangement, since much would depend on how the legislative districts within the states were apportioned and how they tended to vote. If the 1960 presidential vote were aggregated on the basis of one electoral vote to the popular vote winner of each congressional district and two to the popular vote winner of each state, Nixon would have defeated Kennedy 278 to 245, with 14 unpledged electors. In 1976, the district system would have produced a tie, with Carter and Ford each receiving 269 votes. In 1992, Clinton would have beat Bush 324 to 214; in 1996, he would have won 345 to Dole's 193. (See Table 9–1.)

The Direct Election Plan. Of all the plans to alter or replace the Electoral College, the direct popular vote has received the most attention and support. Designed to eliminate the college entirely and count the votes on a nationwide basis, it would elect the popular vote winner provided the winning candidate received a certain percentage of the total vote. In most plans, 40 percent of the total vote would be necessary. In some, 50 percent would be required.[11] In the event that no one got the required percentage, a runoff between the top two candidates would be held to determine the winner.[12]

A direct popular vote would, of course, remedy a major problem of the present system — the possibility of electing a nonplurality president. It would better equalize voting power both among and within the states. The large, competitive states would lose some of their electoral clout by the elimination of the winner-take-all system. Party competition within the states and perhaps even nationwide would be increased. Turnout should also improve. Every vote would count in a direct election.

A direct election, however, might also encourage minor parties to enter and compete more vigorously, which could weaken the two-party system. The possibility of denying a major party candidate 40 percent of the popular vote might be sufficient to entice a proliferation of candidates and produce a series of bargains and deals in which support was traded for favors with a new administration. The new administration might even look more like a coalition government in a multiparty system than one that existed in a two-party system. Moreover, it is possible that the plurality winner might not be geographically representative of the entire country. A very large sectional vote might elect a candidate who trailed in other areas of the country. This result would upset the representational balance that has been achieved between the president's and Congress's electoral constituencies.

The organized groups that are geographically concentrated in the large industrial states would have their votes diluted by a direct election. Take Jewish voters, for example. Highly supportive of the Democratic Party since World War II, they constitute about 2.5 percent of the total population but 14 percent in New York, one of the largest states. Thus, the impact of the New York Jewish vote is magnified under the present Electoral College arrangement as is that of Hispanic voters in Florida, Texas, and California and the Christian Coalition in the South.[13]

The Republican Party has also been reluctant to lend its support to direct election. Republicans perceive that they benefit from the current arrangement, which provides more safe Republican states than Democratic ones. Although Republican Benjamin Harrison was the last nonplurality president to be elected, Gerald Ford came remarkably close in 1976. On the other hand, Richard Nixon's Electoral College victory in 1968 could conceivably have been upset by a stronger Wallace campaign in the southern border states.

A very close popular vote could also cause problems in a direct election. The winner might not be evident for days, even months. Voter fraud could have national consequences. Under such circumstances, large-scale challenges by the losing candidate would be more likely and would necessitate national recounts rather than confining such recounts to individual states, as the current Electoral College system does.

The provision for the situation in which no one received the required percentage of the popular vote has its drawbacks as well. A runoff election would extend the length of the campaign and add to its cost. Considering that some aspirants begin their quest for the presidency a year or two before the election, a further protraction of the process might unduly tax the patience of the voters and produce an even greater numbing effect than currently exists. Moreover, it would also cut an already short transition period for a newly elected president and would further drain the time and energy of an incumbent seeking reelection.

There is still another difficulty with a contingency election. It could reverse the order in which the candidates originally finished. This result might undermine the ability of the eventual winner to govern successfully. It might also encourage spoiler candidacies. Third parties and independents seeking the presidency could exercise considerable power in the event of a close contest between the major parties. Imagine what Perot's influence would have been in a runoff between Clinton and Bush in 1992.

Nonetheless, the direct election plan is supported by public opinion and has been ritualistically praised by contemporary presidents. Gallup polls conducted over the last three decades have consistently found the public favoring a direct election over the present electoral system by substantial margins.[14] Former presidents Carter and Ford have both urged the abolition of the Electoral College and its replacement by a popular vote.

In 1969, the House of Representatives actually voted for a constitutional amendment to establish direct election for president and vice president, but the Senate refused to go along. Despite public opinion, it seems unlikely that sufficient impetus for a change that requires a constitutional amendment will occur until the issue becomes salient to more people. It may take the election of a nonplurality president or some other electoral crisis to produce the outcry and generate the momentum needed to change the Electoral College system.

Despite the complaints that are ritualistically voiced during the election period that the candidates are no good, that there is very little difference between them, and that the campaigns are negative, superficial, and irrelevant, the electorate has not demanded that its congressional representatives change the system beyond extending suffrage to all citizens. Although as noted earlier in this chapter, there is increasing public concern that the campaign finance part of the system is broken and needs fixing. The electoral system may not be perfect, but it has functioned with public support for over two hundred years, a significant achievement in itself. This achievement is cited by those who oppose changing it. If it works, if it is open and accessible, if it encourages participation, if it has for the most part resulted in the election of capable leaders, then why change it, they ask.

SUMMARY

There have been changes and continuities in the way we select a president. In general, the changes have made the system more democratic. The continuities link the system to its constitutional roots and its republican past.

The nomination process has been affected more than the general election. Significant modifications have occurred in the rules for choosing delegates, in the laws regulating contributions and expenditures, and in the news media through which appeals are made and voters obtain most of their information about the campaign. The composition of the electorate has been altered as well. In contrast, the Electoral College has continued to function in much the same way for the last century and a half, although certainly not as the Framers intended.

Have these changes been beneficial or harmful? Have they functioned to make the system more efficient, more responsive, and more likely to result in the choice of a well-qualified candidate? Politicians, journalists, and political scientists disagree in their answers.

Some of the current controversy over campaign reform has focused on party rules. Designed to encourage greater rank-and-file participation in the selection of delegates, the new rules have helped democratize presidential nominations. In the process, however, they have also fractionalized and personalized the parties, weakened the position of their leadership, and disadvantaged presidential candidates, who had to undergo vigorous preconvention struggles and then face unopposed or weakly opposed incumbent presidents or vice presidents in the general election. These unintended consequences have stimulated a debate over the merits of the reforms.

A consensus seems to be emerging that some of them have gone too far and that stronger party control over the nomination process is needed. The Democrats have tried to move in this direction, modifying some of their rules. Their imposition of straight proportional voting in 1992, however, has the potential of producing the opposite effect, factionalizing the party still further and thereby preventing or delaying agreement on the nominee until later in the process. The Republicans continue to allow their state parties to determine the rules by which their caucuses and primaries are conducted. Although they have approved an incentive system to encourage states to hold their contests later in the nomination process, their plan did not prevent even greater front-loading in 2000 than in previous elections. The rules committee at the 2000 Democratic convention voted *not* to accept the recommendations of its advisory commission to restructure its primary process.

Despite the inclinations of some party leaders to eliminate the undesirable effects of the nomination process by changing the rules once again, much of the electorate would go even further — but perhaps in the other direction. They would have more participatory democracy, not less. They would abolish the present patchwork of state caucuses and primaries and replace them with regional primaries or a single, national primary.

The most contentious recent issue has been campaign finance and the alleged violation in fund-raising and expenditures that occurred during the 1996 presidential election. Campaign finance legislation was designed to improve accountability, equalize contributions, control spending, and provide public disclosure. This legislation has enhanced public information, but it has done so only by increasing the burden on candidate organizations to keep detailed records and submit frequent reports. The law has reduced the *direct* influence of large donors on the presidential candidates but not eliminated their *indirect* influence through the soft money contributions and independent expenditures on the parties and nonparty groups. It has also contributed to the factionalizing of parties, encouraging multiple candidacies for the nomination. By giving the bulk of federal funds directly to the candidates, it has encouraged the development of separate candidate organizations and provided incentives for political action committees. The legislation has not lessened the advantage of wealth and effectively opened the process to a much larger group of aspirants. There is a consensus that the law has broken down but much less agreement on how to fix it.

News media coverage has also been the subject of controversy, perhaps reflecting some of the antimedia feeling on the part of the general public. Television has made more people aware of presidential candidates than in the past, but that awareness has also tended to be indirect, more passive, and less issue oriented. The reporting of information about personalities and campaign events exceeds that of substantive policy issues. Television news, in particular, is often blamed for the average voter's low level of interest and knowledge. Conversely, the media have also been accused of exercising undue influence on the electorate.

Despite the grousing, few changes in media coverage are likely. There does not seem to be a groundswell of support for forcing changes on the media; nor are they likely to do it on their own so long as their audiences remain sizable. Moreover, any nonvoluntary attempt to change coverage is apt to run up against the protections of the First Amendment.

Who votes and how the votes should be aggregated continue to prompt debate and elicit concern. The expansion of suffrage has made the election process more democratic in theory, but low rates of participation have called this theoretical improvement into question. Although the failure of about one-half of the electorate to exercise the franchise has been a source of embarrassment and dismay, there is also little agreement on how to deal with this problem in a federal system that values individual initiative, civic responsibility, and states' rights.

Finally, the equity of the Electoral College has also been challenged, but none of the proposals to alter or abolish it, except by the direct election of the president, has received much public backing. With no outcry for change, Congress has been reluctant to alter the system by initiating an amendment to the Constitution and seems unlikely to do so until an electoral crisis or unpopular result forces its hand.

Does the electoral process work? Yes. Can it be improved? Of course. Will it be changed? Probably, but if the past is any indication, there is no guarantee that legally imposed changes will produce only, or even, their desired effect. If politics is the art of the possible, then success is achieved by those who can adjust most quickly to the legal and political environment and turn it to their advantage.

WHERE ON THE WEB?

Public Interest Groups

At one time or another, all of these groups have expressed concern for electoral reform.

- **Center for Responsive Politics**
  http://www.crp.org
- **Common Cause**
  http://www.commoncause.org
- **Destination Democracy**
  http://www.destinationdemocracy.org
- **Public Citizen**
  http://www.citizen.org

Think Tanks

- **The American Enterprise Institute for Public Policy**
  http://www.aei.org
  A moderate, Republican-leaning institute interested in public policy.
- **The Brookings Institution**
  http://www.brookings.org
  Washington's oldest think tank, it has a moderate, centrist orientation.
- **Cato Institute**
  http://www.cato.org
  A Libertarian-oriented institute that examines contemporary public policy issues.
- **Democratic Leadership Council**
  http://www.dlcppi.org
  A moderate, policy-oriented group within the Democratic party.
- **Heritage Foundation**
  http://www.heritage.org
  A conservative group concerned with salient public policy issues.
- **Joint Center for Political and Economic Studies**
  http://www.jointctr.org
  A liberal-oriented think thank specializing in issues of particular concern to minority groups.
- **Urban Institute**
  http://www.urban.org
  A nonpartisan institute for the study of domestic public policy.

Government

- **Congress**
  http://thomas.loc.gov
- **Presidency**
  http://www.whitehouse.gov

EXERCISES

1. From the perspective of American democracy, explain what you consider to be the major problem facing the presidential electoral system today and why you think so. Then describe whether (and if so, how) liberal, moderate, and conservative groups as well as the Democratic, Republican, and Reform Parties see the problem and indicate any solutions they propose to fix it. Which of their solutions do you think is best and why? If you do not think any of their solutions will be effective, then propose one of your own.

2. Examine the legislative proposals currently before Congress <http://thomas.loc.gov> that concern the presidential electoral process. Which of these proposals do you feel are merited and which are ill-conceived? Do you think any of them will be enacted into law?

3. From the perspective of the presidential candidates, what is the most odious feature of the current presidential electoral system? Under the existing law, advise the candidates how to deal with this problem and/or propose reforms to reduce or eliminate it.

SELECTED READING

Alexander, Herbert E. and Anthony Corrado, *Financing the 1992 Election.* Armonk, N.Y.: Sharpe, 1995.

Best, Judith. *The Case against Direct Election of the President: A Defense of the Electoral College.* Ithaca, N.Y.: Cornell University Press, 1975.

Caeser, James W., and Andrew Busch. *Upside Down and Inside Out: The 1992 Elections and American Politics.* Lanham, Md.: Rowman and Littlefield, 1993.

Heard, Alexander. *Made in America: The Nomination and Election of Presidents.* New York: HarperCollins, 1991.

Longley, Lawrence D., and Alan G. Braun. *The Politics of Electoral College Reform.* New Haven, Conn.: Yale University Press, 1975.

Peirce, Neal R., and Lawrence D. Longley. *The People's President.* New Haven, Conn.: Yale University Press, 1981.

Polsby, Nelson W. *Consequences of Party Reform.* New York: Oxford University Press, 1983.

Sundquist, James L. *Constitutional Reform.* Washington, D.C.: Brookings Institution, 1986.

Wayne, Stephen J. *Is This Any Way to Run a Democratic Election?* Boston: Houghton Mifflin, 2001.

NOTES

1. Thomas E. Patterson, *Out of Order* (New York: Knopf, 1993), 210.
2. Ibid.
3. *Gallup Poll,* No. 226 (July 1984): 23.
4. Approval voting allows the electorate to vote to approve or disapprove each candidate who is running. The candidate with the most approval votes is elected. In a system of cumulative voting, candidates are rank ordered, and the ranks may be averaged to determine the winner.

5. It normally takes the Federal Election Commission more than two years to complete an audit of the expenses and determine which of them may not have been in compliance with the law.

6. Eleven states currently allow early voting; sixteen have liberal absentee voting systems. Lois Romano, "Growing Use of Mail Voting Puts Its Stamp on Campaigns," *Washington Post*, November 29, 1998, A1, 6, and 7.

7. Romano, "Growing Use of Mail Voting," A6.

8. A bipartisan presidential commission recommended that broadcasters voluntarily provide at least five minutes of free air time to candidates for public office in the last thirty days of the election campaign. Half of the commission would have gone further and required them to do so. Lawrie Mifflin, "Voluntary Political TV Advertising Urged," *New York Times*, December 18, 1998, A16.

9. There is some controversy whether three other electors in 1796 might also have gone against their party when voting for president. They supported John Adams although they were selected in states controlled by the Democratic Republicans. However, the fluidity of the party system in those days, combined with the weakness of party identification, makes their affiliation (if any) hard to establish.

10. It is difficult to calculate the 1960 vote precisely because the names of the Democratic presidential and vice presidential candidates were not on the ballot in Alabama and because an unpledged slate of electors was chosen in Mississippi.

11. Abraham Lincoln was the only plurality president who failed to attain the 40 percent figure. He received 39.82 percent in 1860, although he probably would have received more had his name been on the ballot in nine southern states.

12. Other direct election proposals have recommended that a joint session of Congress decide the winner. The runoff provision was contained in the resolution that passed the House of Representatives in 1969. A direct election plan with a runoff provision failed to win the two-thirds Senate vote required to initiate a constitutional amendment in 1979.

13. John Kennedy carried New York by approximately 384,000 votes. He received a plurality of more than 800,000 from precincts that were primarily Jewish. Similarly, in Illinois, a state he carried by less than 9,000, Kennedy had a plurality of 55,000 from the so-called Jewish precincts. Mark R. Levy and Michael S. Kramer, *The Ethnic Factor* (New York: Simon & Schuster, 1972), 104.

14. George H. Gallup, *The Gallup Poll* (Wilmington, Del.: Scholarly Resources, 1981), 258–260.

PART V

APPENDIXES

APPENDIX A ★

RESULTS OF PRESIDENTIAL ELECTIONS, 1900–2000

Year	Candidates		Electoral Vote		Popular Vote	
	Democrat	Republican	Democrat	Republican	Democrat	Republican
1900	William J. Bryan	William McKinley	155 35%	292 65%	6,358,345 45.5%	7,218,039 51.7%
	Adlai E. Stevenson	Theodore Roosevelt				
1904	Alton B. Parker	Theodore Roosevelt	140 29%	336 71%	5,028,898 37.6%	7,626,593 56.4%
	Henry G. Davis	Charles W. Fairbanks				
1908	William J. Bryan	William H. Taft	162 34%	321 66%	6,406,801 43.0%	7,676,258 51.6%
	John W. Kern	James S. Sherman				
1912	Woodrow Wilson	William H. Taft	435 82%	8 2%	6,293,152 41.8%	3,486,333 23.2%
	Thomas R. Marshall	James S. Sherman				
1916	Woodrow Wilson	Charles E. Hughes	227 52%	254 48%	9,126,300 49.2%	8,546,789 46.1%
	Thomas R. Marshall	Charles W. Fairbanks				
1920	James M. Cox	Warren G. Harding	127 24%	404 76%	9,140,884 34.2%	16,133,314 60.3%
	Franklin D. Roosevelt	Calvin Coolidge				
1924	John W. Davis	Calvin Coolidge	136 26%	382 72%	8,386,169 28.8%	15,717,553 54.1%
	Charles W. Bryant	Charles G. Dawes				
1928	Alfred E. Smith	Herbert C. Hoover	87 16%	444 84%	15,000,185 40.8%	21,411,991 58.2%
	Joseph T. Robinson	Charles Curtis				
1932	Franklin D. Roosevelt	Herbert C. Hoover	472 89%	59 11%	22,825,016 57.4%	15,758,397 39.6%
	John N. Garner	Charles Curtis				
1936	Franklin D. Roosevelt	Alfred M. Landon	523 98%	8 2%	27,747,636 60.8%	16,679,543 36.5%
	John N. Garner	Frank Knox				
1940	Franklin D. Roosevelt	Wendell L. Willkie	449 85%	82 15%	27,263,448 54.7%	22,336,260 44.8%
	Henry A. Wallace	Charles L. McNary				

Year	Presidential Candidate	Vice Presidential Candidate	Electoral	%	Popular Vote	%
1944	Franklin D. Roosevelt	Harry S Truman	432	81%	25,611,936	53.4%
	Thomas E. Dewey	John W. Bricker	99	19%	22,013,372	45.9%
1948	Harry S Truman	Alben W. Barkley	303	57%	24,105,587	49.5%
	Thomas E. Dewey	Earl Warren	189	36%	21,970,017	45.1%
1952	Adlai E. Stevenson	John J. Sparkman	89	17%	27,314,649	44.4%
	Dwight D. Eisenhower	Richard M. Nixon	442	83%	33,936,137	55.1%
1956	Adlai E. Stevenson	Estes Kefauver	73	14%	26,030,172	42.0%
	Dwight D. Eisenhower	Richard M. Nixon	457	86%	35,585,245	57.4%
1960	John F. Kennedy	Lyndon B. Johnson	303	56%	34,221,344	49.8%
	Richard M. Nixon	Henry Cabot Lodge	219	41%	34,106,671	49.5%
1964	Lyndon B. Johnson	Hubert H. Humphrey	486	90%	43,126,584	61.0%
	Barry Goldwater	William E. Miller	52	10%	27,177,838	38.5%
1968	Hubert H. Humphrey	Edmund S. Muskie	191	36%	31,274,503	42.7%
	Richard M. Nixon	Spiro T. Agnew	301	56%	31,785,148	43.2%
1972	George McGovern	Sargent Shriver	17	3%	29,171,791	37.5%
	Richard M. Nixon	Spiro T. Agnew	520	97%	47,170,179	60.7%
1976	Jimmy Carter	Walter F. Mondale	297	55%	40,828,657	50.1%
	Gerald R. Ford	Robert Dole	240	45%	39,145,520	48.0%
1980	Jimmy Carter	Walter F. Mondale	49	10%	35,483,820	41.0%
	Ronald Reagan	George Bush	489	90%	43,901,812	50.7%
1984	Walter F. Mondale	Geraldine Ferraro	13	2%	37,577,137	40.6%
	Ronald Reagan	George Bush	525	98%	54,455,074	58.8%
1988	Michael S. Dukakis	Lloyd Bentsen	111	21%	41,809,074	45.6%
	George Bush	Dan Quayle	426	79%	48,886,097	53.4%
1992	Bill Clinton	Al Gore	370	69%	44,909,889	43.0%
	George Bush	Dan Quayle	168	31%	39,104,545	37.5%
1996	Bill Clinton	Al Gore	379	70%	45,628,667	49.2%
	Robert Dole	Jack Kemp	159	30%	37,869,435	40.7%
2000*	Al Gore	Joseph Lieberman	267	49.6%	50,156,783	48.2%
	George W. Bush	Dick Cheney	271	50.4%	49,819,600	48.0%

*Unofficial returns as reported by <CNN.com/ALLPOLITICS>, November 26, 2000.

APPENDIX B ★

2000 ELECTORAL AND POPULAR VOTE SUMMARY

	Electoral Vote		Popular Vote			
State	Bush	Gore	Bush	Gore	Nader	Other
AL	9		943,799 (57)	696,741 (42)	18,055 (1)	13,849 (—)
AK	3		136,068 (59)	64,252 (28)	22,789 (10)	7,558 (3)
AZ	8		715,122 (51)	635,730 (45)	41,937 (3)	12,532 (1)
AR	6		472,120 (51)	420,424 (45)	13,275 (2)	21,119 (2)
CA		54	4,370,933 (42)	5,584,137 (53)	397,285 (4)	112,713 (1)
CO	8		884,047 (51)	738,470 (42)	91,482 (5)	26,843 (2)
CT		8	545,954 (39)	795,861 (56)	60,644 (4)	17,282 (1)
DE		3	137,081 (42)	180,638 (55)	8,288 (3)	1,863 (—)
DC		2*	17,020 (9)	162,004 (86)	9,925 (5)	641 (—)
FL	25		2,910,618 (49)	2,910,266 (49)	97,419 (2)	37,226 (—)
GA	13		1,415,999 (55)	1,110,737 (43)	—	47,389 (2)
HI		4	137,785 (38)	205,207 (56)	21,609 (6)	3,196 (—)
ID	4		336,299 (69)	138,354 (28)	—	13,819 (3)
IL		22	2,019,256 (43)	2,588,884 (55)	103,754 (2)	29,854 (—)
IN	12		1,242,372 (57)	899,836 (41)	—	34,154 (2)
IA		7	634,225 (48)	638,355 (49)	29,352 (2)	11,967 (1)
KS	6		616,829 (48)	392,867 (37)	35,706 (3)	14,327 (2)
KY	8		869,946 (57)	637,518 (41)	23,125 (2)	10,078 (—)
LA	9		924,670 (53)	789,837 (45)	20,817 (1)	24,485 (1)
ME		4	284,724 (44)	316,109 (49)	37,842 (6)	8,108 (1)
MD		10	770,911 (40)	1,093,344 (57)	51,078 (3)	9,923 (—)
MA		12	876,906 (33)	1,610,175 (60)	173,758 (6)	30,268 (1)
MI		18	1,947,100 (47)	2,141,721 (51)	83,838 (2)	19,716 (—)
MN		10	1,110,290 (46)	1,168,190 (48)	126,586 (5)	33,231 (1)
MS	7		549,426 (57)	400,845 (42)	7,899 (1)	7,877 (—)
MO	11		1,189,521 (51)	1,110,826 (47)	38,488 (2)	20,307 (1)

APPENDIX B ★ *(continued)*

2000 ELECTORAL AND POPULAR VOTE SUMMARY

State	Electoral Vote Bush	Gore	Popular Vote Bush	Gore	Nader	Other
MT	3		239,755 (58)	137,264 (34)	24,487 (6)	9,292 (2)
NE	5		408,719 (63)	215,616 (33)	22,975 (3)	6,422 (1)
NV	4		301,539 (49)	279,949 (46)	15,004 (2)	12,407 (2)
NH	4		273,135 (49)	265,853 (47)	22,156 (4)	5,652 (1)
NJ		15	1,252,843 (41)	1,742,426 (56)	92,213 (3)	17,305 (—)
NM		5	285,933 (48)	286,112 (48)	21,227 (4)	4,171 (—)
NY		33	2,235,776 (35)	3,767,609 (60)	223,547 (4)	74,269 (1)
NC	14		1,607,238 (56)	1,236,721 (43)	—	21,225 (1)
ND	3		175,572 (61)	96,098 (33)	9,530 (3)	8,675 (3)
OH	21		2,294,167 (50)	2,117,741 (46)	114,482 (3)	43,571 (1)
OK	8		744,335 (60)	474,326 (38)	—	15,616 (2)
OR		7	718,291 (47)	711,533 (47)	77,094 (5)	19,198 (1)
PA		23	2,264,309 (47)	2,465,412 (51)	102,453 (2)	43,795 (—)
RI		4	132,535 (32)	254,500 (61)	24,194 (6)	3,333 (1)
SC	8		804,826 (57)	578,143 (41)	21,008 (2)	11,453 (1)
SD	3		190,515 (60)	118,750 (38)	—	6,758 (2)
TN	11		1,056,480 (51)	977,789 (48)	19,694 (1)	10,172 (—)
TX	32		3,796,850 (59)	2,429,329 (38)	137,716 (2)	35,592 (1)
UT	5		512,168 (67)	201,734 (26)	35,661 (5)	16,282 (2)
VT		3	119,273 (41)	148,166 (51)	19,812 (7)	3,310 (1)
VA	13		1,431,654 (52)	1,221,094 (45)	59,270 (2)	22,500 (1)
WA		11	1,047,693 (45)	1,165,074 (50)	94,543 (4)	23,571 (1)
WV	5		329,708 (52)	291,088 (46)	10,440 (2)	5,381 (—)
WI		11	1,235,035 (48)	1,240,431 (48)	93,553 (4)	20,862 (—)
WY	3		147,674 (69)	60,421 (28)	—	5,331 (3)
Total:	271	266*	49,819,600 (48.0)	50,156,783 (48.2)	2,756,010 (2.7)	1,079,584 (1)

*One Democratic elector in the District of Columbia cast a blank electoral vote to protest the District's absence of voting representation in Congress.

Note: Percentages of popular vote appear in parentheses.

Source: CNN.com/ALLPOLITICS, unofficial returns as of November 26, 2000.

APPENDIX C ★ 2000 ELECTORAL VOTE DISTRIBUTION

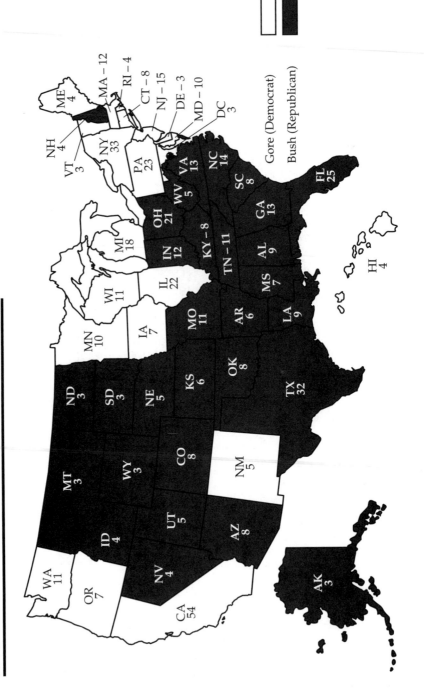

Gore (Democrat)

Bush (Republican)

APPENDIX D ★

STATE-BY-STATE PRIMARY RESULTS, 2000

Democrats

| Date | State | Total Vote | Percentage of Vote | | | Winner |
			Gore	Bradley	Others	
February 1	New Hampshire	154,639	49.7	45.6	4.7	Gore
February 5	Delaware	11,141	57.2	40.2	2.6	Gore
February 22	Michigan	44,850			100.0	Uncommitted
February 29	Washington	297,001	68.2	31.4	0.4	Gore
March 7	California	2,654,114	81.2	18.2	0.6	Gore
	Connecticut	177,301	55.4	41.5	3.0	Gore
	Georgia	284,431	83.8	16.2		Gore
	Maine	64,279	54.0	41.3	4.7	Gore
	Maryland	507,462	67.3	28.5	4.2	Gore
	Massachusetts	570,074	59.9	37.3	2.8	Gore
	Missouri	265,489	64.6	33.6	1.8	Gore
	New York	974,463	65.6	33.5	0.9	Gore
	Ohio	978,512	73.6	24.7	1.7	Gore
	Rhode Island	46,844	57.2	40.6	2.2	Gore
	Vermont	49,283	54.3	43.9	1.8	Gore
March 10	Colorado	88,735	71.4	23.3	5.3	Gore
	Utah	15,687	79.9	20.1		Gore
March 11	Arizona	86,762	77.9	18.9	3.2	Gore
March 14	Florida	551,916	81.8	18.2		Gore
	Louisiana	157,551	73.0	19.9	7.1	Gore
	Mississippi	88,602	89.6	8.6	1.8	Gore
	Oklahoma	134,850	68.7	25.4	5.8	Gore
	Tennessee	215,203	92.1	5.3	2.6	Gore
	Texas	786,890	80.2	16.3	3.4	Gore
March 21	Illinois	809,648	84.4	14.2	1.4	Gore
April 4	Pennsylvania	704,150	74.6	20.8	4.6	Gore
	Wisconsin	371,196	88.5	8.8	2.7	Gore
May 2	District of Columbia	19,417	95.9		4.1	Gore
	Indiana	293,172	74.9	21.9	3.1	Gore
	North Carolina	544,922	70.4	18.3	11.3	Gore
May 9	Nebraska	105,271	70.0	26.5	3.6	Gore
	West Virginia	253,310	72.0	18.4	9.6	Gore
May 16	Oregon	354,594	84.9		15.1	Gore

APPENDIX D ★ (continued)

STATE-BY-STATE PRIMARY RESULTS

Democrats

Date	State	Total Vote	Percentage of Vote			Winner
			Gore	Bradley	Others	
May 23	Arkansas	246,900	78.5		21.5	Gore
	Idaho	35,688	75.7		24.3	Gore
	Kentucky	220,279	71.3	14.7	14.1	Gore
June 6	Alabama	278,527	77.0		23.0	Gore
	Montana	87,867	77.9		22.1	Gore
	New Jersey	378,272	94.9		5.1	Gore
	New Mexico	132,280	74.6	20.6	4.8	Gore
Total		14,659,481	75.7	20.0	4.4	Gore

Note: Bill Bradley quit the Democratic race after the round of primaries on March 7. Results are based on official returns for all states except Arkansas, where nearly complete but unofficial returns are used, and Pennsylvania, where the tally of write-in votes is not included. There was no statewide Democratic vote tallied in New York or Ohio; the vote is an aggregate of district-by-district returns. No Democratic primary was held in South Dakota, where Al Gore ran unopposed.

Source: The *Rhodes Cook Letter,* July 2000.

Republicans

Date	State	Total Vote	Percentage of Vote				Winner
			Bush	McCain	Keyes	Others	
February 1	New Hampshire	238,206	30.4	48.5	6.4	14.7	McCain
February 8	Delaware	30,060	50.7	25.4	3.8	20.0	Bush
February 19	South Carolina	573,101	53.4	41.9	4.5	0.2	Bush
February 22	Arizona	322,669	35.7	60.0	3.6	0.7	McCain
	Michigan	1,276,770	43.1	51.0	4.6	1.4	McCain
February 27	Puerto Rico	92,749	94.2	5.3	0.1	0.4	Bush
February 29	Virginia	664,093	52.8	43.9	3.1	0.3	Bush
	Washington	491,148	57.8	38.9	2.4	0.9	Bush
March 7	California	2,847,921	60.6	34.7	4.0	0.7	Bush
	Connecticut	178,985	46.3	48.7	3.3	1.7	McCain
	Georgia	643,188	66.9	27.8	4.6	0.6	Bush
	Maine	96,624	51.0	44.0	3.1	1.9	Bush
	Maryland	376,034	56.2	36.2	6.7	1.0	Bush
	Massachusetts	501,951	31.8	64.7	2.5	1.0	McCain
	Missouri	475,363	57.9	35.3	5.7	1.0	Bush

APPENDIX D ★ *(continued)*

STATE-BY-STATE PRIMARY RESULTS

Republicans

Date	State	Total Vote	Percentage of Vote				Winner
			Bush	McCain	Keyes	Others	
	New York*	2,161,518	51.0	43.4	3.3	2.3	Bush
	Ohio	1,397,528	58.0	37.0	4.0	1.1	Bush
	Rhode Island	36,120	36.5	60.2	2.6	0.8	McCain
	Vermont	81,355	35.3	60.3	2.7	1.7	McCain
March 10	Colorado	180,655	64.7	27.1	6.6	1.6	Bush
	Utah	91,053	63.3	14.0	21.3	1.4	Bush
March 14	Florida	699,317	73.8	19.9	4.6	1.6	Bush
	Louisiana	102,912	83.6	8.9	5.7	1.8	Bush
	Mississippi	114,979	87.9	5.4	5.6	1.0	Bush
	Oklahoma	124,809	79.1	10.4	9.3	1.2	Bush
	Tennessee	250,791	77.0	14.5	6.7	1.7	Bush
	Texas	1,126,757	87.5	7.1	3.9	1.5	Bush
March 21	Illinois	736,857	67.4	21.5	9.0	2.1	Bush
April 4	Pennsylvania	643,085	73.5	22.7		3.9	Bush
	Wisconsin	495,769	69.2	18.1	9.9	2.8	Bush
May 2	District of Columbia	2,433	72.8	24.4		2.8	Bush
	Indiana	406,664	81.2	18.8			Bush
	North Carolina	322,517	78.6	10.9	7.9	2.7	Bush
May 9	Nebraska	185,758	78.2	15.1	6.5	0.2	Bush
	West Virginia	109,404	79.6	12.9	4.8	2.8	Bush
May 16	Oregon	349,831	83.6		13.4	3.0	Bush
May 23	Arkansas	44,573	80.2		19.8		Bush
	Idaho	158,446	73.5		19.1	7.4	Bush
	Kentucky	91,323	83.0	6.3	4.8	5.9	Bush
June 6	Alabama	203,079	84.2		11.5	4.2	Bush
	Montana	113,671	77.6		18.3	4.1	Bush
	New Jersey	240,810	83.6		16.4		Bush
	New Mexico	75,230	82.6	10.1	6.4	0.8	Bush
	South Dakota	45,279	78.2	13.8	7.7	0.3	Bush
Total		20,707,157	63.2	29.8	5.3	1.6	Bush

Note: John McCain quit the Republican race after the round of primaries on March 7. Results are based on official returns. An asterisk (*) indicates there was no direct vote for Republican candidates in New York; percentages are based on the aggregate district-by-district vote for delegates.

Source: Federal Election Commission.

APPENDIX E ★

DELEGATE ACCUMULATION IN 2000

Republicans

Date	State	Method	Number of Delegates	Cumulative Number of Delegates	Cumulative Percent of Delegates
1/24	Alaska	C	23		
1/24	Iowa	C	25	48	2
2/1	New Hampshire	P	17		
2/8	Delaware	C	12		
2/7–2/13	Hawaii	C	14		
2/9	South Carolina	P	37		
2/22	Arizona	P	30		
2/22	Michigan	P	58		
2/23	Nevada	C	17		
2/26	American Samoa	C	4		
2/26	Guam	C	4		
2/26	Virgin Islands	C	4		
2/27	Puerto Rico	P	14		
2/29	North Dakota	C	19		
2/29	Virginia	P	56		
2/29	Washington*	P	12	346	17
3/7	California	P	162		
3/7	Connecticut	P	25		
3/7	Georgia	P	54		
3/7	Maine	P	14		
3/7	Maryland	P	31		
3/7	Massachusetts	P	37		
3/7	Minnesota	C	34		
3/7	Missouri	P	35		
3/7	New York	P	101		
3/7	Ohio	P	69		
3/7	Rhode Island	P	14		
3/7	Vermont	P	12		
3/7	Washington*	C	25	959	46
3/10	Colorado	P	40		
3/10	Utah	P	29		
3/10	Wyoming	C	22	1,050	51
3/14	Florida	P	80		
3/14	Louisiana	P	29		
3/14	Mississippi	P	33		

APPENDIX E ★ *(continued)*

DELEGATE ACCUMULATION IN 2000

Republicans

Date	State	Method	Number of Delegates	Cumulative Number of Delegates	Cumulative Percent of Delegates
3/14	Oklahoma	P	38		
3/14	Tennessee	P	37		
3/14	Texas	P	124	1,391	67
3/21	Illinois	P	74	1,465	71
4/4	Kansas	P	35		
4/4	Wisconsin	P	37		
4/25	Pennsylvania	P	78	1,615	78
5/2	D.C.	P	15		
5/2	Indiana	P	55		
5/2	North Carolina	P	62		
5/9	Nebraska	P	30		
5/9	West Virginia	P	18		
5/16	Oregon	P	24		
5/23	Arkansas	P	24		
5/23	Idaho	P	28		
5/23	Kentucky	P	31	1,902	92
6/6	Alabama	P	44		
6/6	Montana	P	23		
6/6	New Jersey	P	54		
6/6	New Mexico	P	21		
6/6	South Dakota	P	22	2,066	100

*Washington state has a split system for allocating delegates.

Democrats

Date	State	Method	Number of Delegates	Cumulative Number of Delegates	Cumulative Percent of Delegates
1/24	Iowa	C	57	57	1
2/1	New Hampshire	P	29	86	2
3/7	American Samoa	C	12		
3/7	California	P	435		
3/7	Connecticut	P	67		
3/7	Georgia	P	92		
3/7	Hawaii	C	33		
3/7	Idaho	C	23		

APPENDIX E ★ *(continued)*

DELEGATE ACCUMULATION IN 2000

Democrats

Date	State	Method	Number of Delegates	Cumulative Number of Delegates	Cumulative Percent of Delegates
3/7	Maine	P	33		
3/7	Maryland	P	95		
3/7	Massachusetts	P	118		
3/7	Minnesota	C	91		
3/7	Missouri	P	92		
3/7	New York	P	294		
3/7	North Dakota	C	22		
3/7	Ohio	P	169		
3/7	Rhode Island	P	33		
3/7	Vermont	P	22		
3/7	Washington	C	94	1,811	41
3/9	South Carolina	P	52		
3/10	Colorado	P	61		
3/10	Utah	P	29		
3/10	Wyoming	C	18		
3/11	Arizona	P	55		
3/11	Michigan	P	157		
3/12	Nevada	C	29		
3/10–14	Democrats Abroad	C	9	2,221	51
3/14	Florida	P	186		
3/14	Louisiana	P	73		
3/14	Mississippi	P	48		
3/14	Oklahoma	P	52		
3/14	Tennessee	P	81		
3/14	Texas	P	231	2,892	66
3/21	Illinois	P	190	3,082	71
3/25	Alaska	C	19		
3/26	Puerto Rico	P	61		
3/27	Delaware	C	22	3,184	73
4/1	Virgin Islands	C	12		
4/4	Kansas	P	42		
4/4	Wisconsin	P	92		
4/15–17	Virginia	C	95		
4/25	Pennsylvania	P	191	3,616	83
5/2	D.C.	P	33		

APPENDIX E ★ *(continued)*

DELEGATE ACCUMULATION IN 2000

Democrats

Date	State	Method	Number of Delegates	Cumulative Number of Delegates	Cumulative Percent of Delegates
5/2	Indiana	P	88		
5/2	North Carolina	P	103		
5/6	Guam	C	12		
5/9	Nebraska	P	32		
5/9	West Virginia	P	42		
5/16	Oregon	P	58		
5/23	Arkansas	P	47		
5/23	Kentucky	P	58	4,089	94
6/6	Alabama	P	63		
6/6	Montana	P	24		
6/6	New Jersey	P	124		
6/6	New Mexico	P	35		
6/6	South Dakota	P	22	4,357	100

*Remainder of Delegates are unassigned superdelegates.

Source: Republican and Democratic National Committees, updated by author.

APPENDIX F ★

REPUBLICAN PARTY CONVENTIONS AND NOMINEES, 1900–2000

Year	City	Dates	Presidential Nominee	Vice Presidential Nominee	Number of Presidential Ballots
1900	Philadelphia	June 19–21	William McKinley	Theodore Roosevelt	1
1904	Chicago	June 21–23	Theodore Roosevelt	Charles Fairbanks	1
1908	Chicago	June 16–19	William Taft	James Sherman	1
1912	Chicago	June 18–22	William Taft	James Sherman, Nicholas Butler*	1
1916	Chicago	June 7–10	Charles Evans Hughes	Charles Fairbanks	3
1920	Chicago	June 8–12	Warren Harding	Calvin Coolidge	10
1924	Cleveland	June 10–12	Calvin Coolidge	Charles Dawes	1
1928	Kansas City	June 12–15	Herbert Hoover	Charles Curtis	1
1932	Chicago	June 14–16	Herbert Hoover	Charles Curtis	1
1936	Cleveland	June 9–12	Alfred Landon	Frank Knox	1
1940	Philadelphia	June 24–28	Wendell Willkie	Charles McNary	6
1944	Chicago	June 26–28	Thomas Dewey	John Bricker	1
1948	Philadelphia	June 21–25	Thomas Dewey	Earl Warren	3
1952	Chicago	July 7–11	Dwight Eisenhower	Richard Nixon	1
1956	San Francisco	August 20–23	Dwight Eisenhower	Richard Nixon	1
1960	Chicago	July 25–28	Richard Nixon	Henry Cabot Lodge, Jr.	1
1964	San Francisco	July 13–16	Barry Goldwater	William Miller	1
1968	Miami Beach	August 5–8	Richard Nixon	Spiro Agnew	1
1972	Miami Beach	August 21–23	Richard Nixon	Spiro Agnew	1
1976	Kansas City	August 16–19	Gerald Ford	Robert Dole	1
1980	Detroit	July 14–18	Ronald Reagan	George Bush	1
1984	Dallas	August 20–23	Ronald Reagan	George Bush	1
1988	New Orleans	August 15–18	George Bush	Dan Quayle	1
1992	Houston	August 17–21	George Bush	Dan Quayle	1
1996	San Diego	August 11–16	Robert Dole	Jack Kemp	1
2000	Philadelphia	July 29–Aug. 4	George W. Bush	Dick Cheney	1

*The 1912 Republican convention nominated James Sherman, who died on October 30. The Republican National Committee subsequently selected Nicholas Butler to receive the Republican electoral votes for vice president.

Source: Updated from *National Party Conventions, 1831–1972* (Washington, D.C.: *Congressional Quarterly,* 1976), 8–9. Copyrighted materials reprinted with permission of Congressional Quarterly, Inc. Updated by author.

APPENDIX F ★ *(continued)*

DEMOCRATIC PARTY CONVENTIONS AND NOMINEES, 1900–2000

Year	City	Dates	Presidential Nominee	Vice Presidential Nominee	Number of Presidential Ballots
1900	Kansas City	July 4–6	William Jennings Bryan	Adlai Stevenson	1
1904	St. Louis	July 6–9	Alton Parker	Henry Davis	1
1908	Denver	July 7–10	William Jennings Bryan	John Kern	46
1912	Baltimore	June 25–July 2	Woodrow Wilson	Thomas Marshall	1
1916	St. Louis	June 14–16	Woodrow Wilson	Thomas Marshall	43
1920	San Francisco	June 28–July 6	James Cox	Franklin Roosevelt	103
1924	New York	June 24–July 9	John Davis	Charles Bryan	1
1928	Houston	June 26–29	Alfred Smith	Joseph T. Robinson	4
1932	Chicago	June 27–July 2	Franklin Roosevelt	John Garner	Acclamation
1936	Philadelphia	June 23–27	Franklin Roosevelt	John Garner	1
1940	Chicago	July 15–18	Franklin Roosevelt	Henry Wallace	1
1944	Chicago	July 19–21	Franklin Roosevelt	Harry Truman	1
1948	Philadelphia	July 12–14	Harry Truman	Alben Barkley	1
1952	Chicago	July 21–26	Adlai Stevenson, Jr.	John Sparkman	3
1956	Chicago	August 13–17	Adlai Stevenson, Jr.	Estes Kefauver	1
1960	Los Angeles	July 11–15	John Kennedy	Lyndon Johnson	1
1964	Atlantic City	August 24–27	Lyndon Johnson	Hubert Humphrey	Acclamation
1968	Chicago	August 26–29	Hubert Humphrey	Edmund Muskie	1
1972	Miami Beach	July 10–13	George McGovern	Thomas Eagleton, Sargent Shriver*	1
1976	New York	July 12–15	Jimmy Carter	Walter Mondale	1
1980	New York	August 11–14	Jimmy Carter	Walter Mondale	1
1984	San Francisco	July 16–19	Walter Mondale	Geraldine Ferraro	1
1988	Altanta	July 18–21	Michael Dukakis	Lloyd Bentsen	1
1992	New York	July 13–16	Bill Clinton	Al Gore	1
1996	Chicago	August 26–29	Bill Clinton	Al Gore	1
2000	Los Angeles	August 14–17	Al Gore	Joseph Lieberman	1

* The 1972 Democratic convention nominated Thomas Eagleton, who withdrew from the ticket on July 31. On August 8, the Democratic National Committee selected Sargent Shriver as the party's candidate for vice president.

Source: Updated from *National Party Conventions, 1831–1972* (Washington, D.C.: *Congressional Quarterly,* 1976), 8–9. Copyrighted materials reprinted with permission of Congressional Quarterly, Inc. Updated by author.

APPENDIX G ★

WHY POLLS TEND TO BE ACCURATE AND HOW THEY ARE CONDUCTED

The main reason polls have become increasingly accurate is the improvement in sampling procedures. Because the objective of surveying is to generalize from a small number, it is essential that the people interviewed be representative of the population. The odds of the sample being representative can be estimated when that sample is randomly selected.

Random selection does not mean haphazard choice. Rather, it means that every element in the population (in this case, the eligible electorate) has a known and usually equal chance of being included in the sample, and the choice of any one element is independent of the choice of any other. The *Literary Digest* sample of 1936 and the quota sample of 1948 were not random. There was no way to determine whether the people interviewed were typical. As it turned out, they were not — at least not of those who voted on election day.

Random selection is thus the key to sampling. One way to conduct a random sample is to divide the population into geographic units and then group them on the basis of the size of communities. Within each stratum, smaller and smaller units are then randomly selected until a block in a city or part of a township is isolated. Then, a number of interviews are conducted according to a carefully prescribed procedure at each of these sampling points. Interviewers have no choice whom they interview or where they conduct the interviews. The Gallup organization randomly selects 350 sampling points and conducts about five interviews at each.

Since sampling is based on probability theory, the likelihood of being right or wrong can be calculated mathematically. In a random sample the odds of being right are determined primarily by the size of the sample. The larger the sample, the more likely it is to be accurate, and the more confidence can be placed in the results. For national surveys, a sample of approximately eleven hundred yields an error of plus or minus 3 percent in 95 percent of the polls conducted. In other words, the population as a whole will not differ by more than 3 percent in either direction from the results of the sample, 95 percent of the time. The way to improve the accuracy of a sample is to enlarge it.

The typical media poll is conducted on the telephone. Numbers are randomly selected; random selection is also used to determine the voter in the household to be interviewed. The average length of such an interview is fifteen to twenty minutes, during which voters are asked to evaluate the candidates, the issues, the parties, and frequently, the campaign itself. Information on the demography of the voter (race, age, sex, religion, education, and income) is also solicited. These demographic data can be weighted to reflect the population in the country as a whole.

Interviews are conducted over a one- to three-day period. The number of respondents vary. The total surveyed range anywhere from 600 to 2,400. The larger the sample, the more accurate it tends to be. Larger samples have the added benefit of allowing analysts to break down the sample into smaller demographic groupings for the purpose of analyzing the vote. However, enlarging the sample adds to its cost. At some point a law of diminishing returns sets in. For example, to increase the accuracy of a nationwide sample to plus or minus 2 percent, a total of approximately 2,400 randomly selected respondents is needed, as opposed to about 9,600 for plus or minus 1 percent and 600 for plus or minus 4 percent.

The accuracy of a poll in measuring public opinion is also affected by the order and wording of the questionnaire and the relationship between the interviewer and the respondent. A survey is only as good as its questions. If they suggest a particular answer, then they force opinion, rather than reflect it.

The focus of the questions is normally dictated by the objectives of the study. Public polls, such as those conducted by independent research organizations like Gallup and Harris and syndicated to newspapers and magazines, usually focus on who is ahead and how different groups of people feel about the candidate. "If the election were held today, for whom would you vote?" is the key question.

In addition to random selection and sample size, the likelihood of those interviewed actually voting must also be considered. Pollsters regularly ask respondents a series of questions to differentiate potential voters from nonvoters. Those whose answers suggest that they probably will not vote are eliminated or separated from the others when analyzing the results.

Finally, pollsters and candidates alike are interested in the currency of their polls. A survey measures opinion only during the time in which interviews are conducted. To monitor changes over time, a technique known as tracking is used. Instead of simply interviewing the entire sample in one or two days and then analyzing the results, interviews are conducted continuously. As new responses are added, old ones are dropped. This procedure produces a rolling sample. Continuous analyses of this sample can identify emerging issues, monitor a candidate's strength among various constituencies, and evaluate the impact of the candidate's media advertising.

Table: "Public Opinion on the Florida Vote Controversy." From the Gallup Organization, Gallup Poll, "Public Opinion on Key Issues in the Florida Recount Situation," December 2000 (Web site). Reprinted by permission.

Table 1–1: "Number of Presidential Primaries and Percentage of Convention Delegates from Primary States, by Party, 1912–2000." 1912–1964, F. Christopher Arterton. Reprinted with the permissions of the American Enterprise Institute for Public Policy Research, Washington, D.C. 1980, Austin Ranney, from materials distributed by the Democratic and Republican National Committees; 1980–2000, the author from data supplied by the Democratic and Republican National Committees.

Figure 1–1: "State Size According to Population: The 2000 Electoral Vote." The *New York Times,* December 28, 1990, A9. Copyright © 1990 by the New York Times Company. Reprinted by permission.

Table 2–1: "Costs of Presidential General Elections, Major Party Candidates, 1860–1972." Data based on *Financing Politics: Money, Elections, and Political Reform,* 3e, by Herbert E. Alexander. Copyright © 1984 by Congressional Quarterly, Inc. Reprinted with permission.

Table 2–2: "Costs of Presidential Nominations, 1964–2000." 1964–1972 based on data from *Financing Politics: Money, Elections, and Political Reform,* 3e, by Herbert E. Alexander, 45–47. Copyright © 1984 by Congressional Quarterly, Inc. 1992 data based on Tables 2–1 and 2–4 in *Financing the 1992 Election* by Herbert E. Alexander and Anthony Corrado. Copyright © 1995 by M. E. Sharpe, Inc. Reprinted with permission of the publishers.

Box 2–3: "Al Gore's Profitable Trip to the Big Apple." From "The $55 Million Man," *Washington Post Magazine,* April 4, 1999. Copyright © 1999, the Washington Post. Reprinted with permission.

Table 3–1: "Suffrage and Turnout." Population figures for 1824–1920 based on estimates and early census figures that appear in Neal R. Peirce, *The People's President.* Copyright © 1979 by Neal R. Peirce. Reprinted by permission of Yale University Press.

Table 3–5: "Vote by Groups in Presidential Elections, 1968–2000." From the Gallup Organization, "Vote by Groups," November 6, 2000, and "Final Preelection Poll," November 7, 2000 (Web site). Reprinted by permission.

Table 3–6: "Republican and Democratic Party Profiles, 2000." From the Gallup Organization, Gallup Poll July 30–August 11, 2000 (Web site). Reprinted by permission.

Table 4–3: "The Ideology of National Convention Delegates, 1976-1996." CBS News Delegate Surveys, 1968–1980. Warren J. Mitofsky and Martin Plissner, "The Making of the Delegates, 1968–1980," *Public Opinion* December–January, 1980: 43. Reprinted with the permission of American Enterprise Institute. 1984, 1988 data supplied by CBS News from its delegate surveys and printed with the permission of CBS News. 1992 data published in the *New York Times,* July 13, 1992, B6 and the *Washington Post,* August 16, 1992, A19. Copyright © 1992 by The New York Times. Washington Post/ABC News Surveys as appear in the *Washington Post,* August 10, 1996, M8, and August 25, 1996, M4. Copyright © 1992, 1996 by The Washington Post. Reprinted by permission.

Herblock Cartoon: From the *Washington Post,* November 1, 1988, A18. Copyright © 1998 by Herblock. Reprinted by permission.

Figure 4–1: "News Coverage of the Presidential Nominations, 1988–2000." From "The Parties Pick Their Candidates," *Media Monitor* VI (March 1992): 2, and "The Bad News Campaign," *Media Monitor* X (April 1996): 1–3, and from "Campaign 2000 — The Primaries," *Media Monitor* XIV (March/April 2000): 1–3. *Media Monitor* is published by the Center for Media and Public Affairs, a nonpartisan and nonprofit research organization. Reprinted with permission of the Center for Media and Public Affairs.

Figure 4–2: "Television Coverage of the Candidates in the 2000 Campaign." From "Campaign 2000 — The Primaries," *Media Monitor* XIV (March/April 2000): 2. *Media Monitor* is published by the Center for Media and Public Affairs, a nonpartisan and nonprofit research organization. Reprinted with permission of the Center for Media and Public Affairs.

Table 5–1: "Candidate Qualities and Issue Positions." From the Gallup Organization, "Poll Finds Bush and Gore Closely Matched on Image Ratings," March 20, 2000 (Web site). Reprinted by permission.

Table 5–2: "Delegate Votes at Nominating Conventions, 1940–2000." Adapted from Appendix C in *Convention Decisions and Voting Records,* 2e, by Richard C. Bain and Judith H. Parris. Copyright © Brookings Institution, 1973. Reprinted with the permission of Brookings Publications.

Table 5–5: "Tolerance in Voting for Women and Minorities for President." From "Americans Today Much More Accepting of a Woman, Black, Catholic, or Jew as President," Gallup Organization (Web site), April 1, 1999. Reprinted by permission.

Figure 7–1: "Focus of Campaign Coverage, 1992–2000." From Stephen Hess, "Hess Report on Campaign Coverage in Nightly Network News," Brookings Institution (Web site). Copyright © Brookings Institution. Reprinted with the permission of Brookings Publications.

Figure 7–2: "Good News versus Bad News in Campaign 2000." From Stephen Hess, "Hess Report on Campaign Coverage in Nightly Network News," Brookings Institution (Web site). Copyright © Brookings Institution. Reprinted with the permission of Brookings Publications.

Table 7–1: "Presidential Debates, 1960–2000." Estimates of audience size from 1960–1992 from "How Many Watched" in the *New York Times,* October 6, 1996, A25. Copyright © 1996 by The New York Times. Reprinted by permission. Estimates for 1996 from "Debate Ratings Beat Baseball," Associated Press, October 17, 1996. Copyright © 1996 by The Associated Press. Reprinted by permission. Estimates for 2000 based on ratings by Nielsen Media Research as reported in the *New York Times,* October 19, 2000, A22. Copyright © 2000 The New York Times. Reprinted by permission.

Box 7–1: "The Willie Horton Ad: 'Weekend Passes.'" Photo courtesy of the Lawrence Police Department, Lawrence, Mass.

Table 8–1: "Gallup Poll Accuracy Record, 1936–2000." 1936–1996 data from Gallup Poll (Web site), April 4, 1999. 2000 data from Gallup Poll (Web site), "Popular Vote in Presidential Race Too Close to Call," November 7, 2000. Reprinted by permission.

Table 8–3: "Portrait of the American Electorate, 1992–2000." 1992–1996 data from the *New York Times,* November 10, 1996, 28. Copyright © 1996 by The New York Times. Reprinted by permission. 2000 data supplied by the author.

Table 9–1: "Voting for President, 1956–2000: Four Methods for Aggregating the Votes." Calculations for 1996 based on unofficial returns for the three major candidates as reported by the *Associated Press,* November 7, 1996. 2000 data based on the unofficial returns as reported by the *Associated Press,* November 8, 2000; 2000 District Plan data are from Tom Squitieri, "Bush Would Still Win with Electoral Reforms," *USA Today* (Web site).

INDEX